ANIMATION: A WORLD HISTORY, VOLUME I

A continuation of 1994's groundbreaking *Cartoons*, Giannalberto Bendazzi's *Animation: A World History* is the largest, deepest, most comprehensive text of its kind, based on the idea that animation is an art form that deserves its own place in scholarship. Bendazzi delves beyond just Disney, offering readers glimpses into the animation of Russia, Africa, Latin America, and other often-neglected areas and introducing over fifty previously undiscovered artists. Full of firsthand, never-before-investigated, and elsewhere unavailable information, *Animation: A World History* encompasses the history of animation production on every continent over the span of three centuries.

Features include:

- Over 200 high-quality head shots and film stills to add visual reference to your research
- Detailed information on hundreds of never-before-researched animators and films
- Coverage of animation from more than ninety countries and every major region of the world
- Chronological and geographical organization for quick access to the information you're looking for

Volume I traces the roots and predecessors of modern animation, the history behind Émile Cohl's *Fantasmagorie*, and twenty years of silent animated films. Encompassing the formative years of the art form through its Golden Age, this book accounts for animation history through 1950 and covers everything from well-known classics like *Steamboat Willie* to animation in Egypt and Nazi Germany. With a wealth of new research, hundreds of photographs and film stills, and an easy-to-navigate organization, this book is essential reading for all serious students of animation history.

A former professor at the Nanyang Technological University of Singapore and the Università degli Studi of Milan, Italian-born **Giannalberto Bendazzi** has been thoroughly investigating the history of animation for more than forty years. A founding member of the Society for Animation Studies, he authored or edited various classics in a number of languages, and has lectured extensively on every continent.

'Giannalberto Bendazzi is a highly gifted historian, scholar, observer, teacher, and most of all, lover of animation in all of its many forms. His painstaking and detailed research, as well as his social and cultural observations about the various times during which many animated pieces were produced, give his writing an authenticity rarely seen in other books on the subject. I cannot think of anything better than to curl up with one of his books and have him tell me the world history of the animation medium I love.'

**Eric Goldberg, Animator and Director,
Walt Disney Animation Studios**

'Giannalberto Bendazzi's book gives us the complete overview of how the art of animation developed around the world in the last one hundred years. It is a book global in scope for an art form now global in appeal and being created around the world. This work is an essential addition to the library of any serious scholar of cinema.'

**Tom Sito, Chair of Animation,
University of Southern California**

'A staple of any animation library, this encyclopedic book covers the far reaches of production worldwide, throughout history. It is an incredible resource from one of the animation world's leading scholars.'

**Maureen Furniss, Director of the Program in
Experimental Animation at CalArts**

'Giannalberto Bendazzi is one of the world's finest historians and scholars of the art of animation. We are indeed fortunate that his thorough research, cogent perceptions, and eloquent writing is now in this . . . acclaimed masterly tome on world animation.'

**John Canemaker, Oscar winning independent Animator,
Animation Historian, Author, and Professor**

'I feel that one looks into Giannalberto Bendazzi's exhaustive book as one does into a mirror – it is the whole history of the animated film and all its creators . . . In taking up such a grand endeavor, Bendazzi has shown a determination, a predisposition, and above all, a talent comparable to that of the finest filmmakers . . . With this talent Giannalberto Bendazzi gives meaning to our work. To our creativity and volition, to both the ability to withstand hard work and the temperamental nature of a creative spirit, to study, to our artistic caprices, to accuracy, and to our eccentricities, creative perfection and human imperfection, expectations and improvisations, passions and doubts, successes and failures . . . This is a book that has long been anticipated by professionals and enthusiasts of animation from all over the world.'

Jerzy Kucia, Director, Poland

'Giannalberto Bendazzi is the greatest animation historian I have ever met.'

Priit Pärn, Director, Estonia

'I am extremely proud that Giannalberto Bendazzi, at the beginning of my career, was my first official biographer. And I like to believe that I was the flame that led him to become one of the world's top experts in the field of animation.'

Bruno Bozzetto, Director, Italy

'I don't know any historian of animation more reliable than Giannalberto Bendazzi.'

Yamamura Koji, Director, Japan

'I have been anxiously waiting for this sum total on animation . . . Giannalberto Bendazzi monitored, saw, and noted everything and met everyone in the world of my beloved profession – and for so long, way before it was fashionable. Wherever I went – to both festivals and meetings throughout continents – he was there. Welcome to the monumental book that takes into account a great art and the whole planet.'

Michel Ocelot, Director, France

ANIMATION: A WORLD HISTORY

Volume I: Foundations— The Golden Age

Giannalberto Bendazzi

A Focal Press Book

First published in paperback 2017
by Routledge
711 Third Avenue, New York, NY 10017

First published in 2016
CRC Press
Taylor & Francis Group
6000 Broken Sound Parkway NW, Suite 300
Boca Raton, FL 33487-2742

CRC Press is an imprint of the Taylor & Francis Group, an informa business

© 2016, 2017 Giannalberto Bendazzi

This book contains information obtained from authentic and highly regarded sources. Reasonable efforts have been made to publish reliable data and information, but the author and publisher cannot assume responsibility for the validity of all materials or the consequences of their use. The authors and publishers have attempted to trace the copyright holders of all material reproduced in this publication and apologize to copyright holders if permission to publish in this form has not been obtained. If any copyright material has not been acknowledged please write and let us know so we may rectify in any future reprint.

Except as permitted under U.S. Copyright Law, no part of this book may be reprinted, reproduced, transmitted, or utilized in any form by any electronic, mechanical, or other means, now known or hereafter invented, including photocopying, microfilming, and recording, or in any information storage or retrieval system, without written permission from the publishers.

For permission to photocopy or use material electronically from this work, please access www.copyright.com (http://www.copyright.com/) or contact the Copyright Clearance Center, Inc. (CCC), 222 Rosewood Drive, Danvers, MA 01923, 978-750-8400. CCC is a not-for-profit organization that provides licenses and registration for a variety of users. For organizations that have been granted a photocopy license by the CCC, a separate system of payment has been arranged.

Trademark notice: Product or corporate names may be trademarks or registered trademarks, and are used only for identification and explanation without intent to infringe.

Library of Congress Cataloging-in-Publication Data
A calalog record for this title has been requested.

ISBN: 978-1-138-85452-9 (hbk)
ISBN: 978-1-138-03531-7 (pbk)
ISBN: 978-1-315-72105-7 (ebk)
ISBN: 978-1-138-94307-0 (hbk pack)
ISBN: 978-1-138-03534-8 (pbk pack)

Typeset in Baskerville and Optima
by Apex CoVantage, LLC

Visit the Taylor & Francis Web site at http://www.taylorandfrancis.com
and the CRC Press Web site at http://www.crcpress.com

Printed and bound in the United States of America by Sheridan

THIS BOOK IS DEDICATED TO GENTLEMEN
FRIENDS MANUEL CRISTÓBAL, OLIVIER COTTE,
FERENC MIKULÁS, AND MIDHAT AJANOVIĆ AND
TO THE SMILE OF ILARIA, 23 YEARS OLD.

Contents

Contributors and Collaborators — xi
Acknowledgements — xii

1 Foundations — 1

What It Is — 1
Mapping Chaos — 1
Turning Points — 1
Periods — 1
Guilty, but with an Explanation — 2
Traces — 2
You Won't Find… — 3
A Hybrid — 3

The First Period — 5

The First Period spans the years before the screening of Émile Cohl's film *Fantasmagorie* in Paris, France. There is no 'animation' as such there, but the film still incorporates many features that look like what nowadays we would consider to be animation. We will call this period 'Before *Fantasmagorie* (0–1908)'.

2 Before *Fantasmagorie* (0–1908) — 7

Archaeology — 7
  Phidias' Animating Chisel — 8
    Representation — 8
    The Motion Analysis — 8
    Music — 9
    The Meaning of the Implicit Movement — 11
    An Object of Philosophy — 11
Pre-History I — 12
  Science, Science, Science — 12
  Writing with Light — 13
Pre-History II — 14
  A Static Mirror? — 14
  The Flipbook — 15
  Émile Reynaud — 15
    Birth of the *Théâtre Optique* — 16
  The *Théâtre Optique* and How It Worked — 18
  On with the Lantern Show — 19
  Colour Music — 19
Cinema of Attractions — 21
  Frame by Frame — 21
  Arthur Melbourne-Cooper — 22
  Walter Robert Booth — 23
  Edwin Stanton Porter — 24
  James Stuart Blackton — 25

The Second Period — 27

The Second Period embraces the entire silent film era and ends with a specific date: 18 November 1928, the day of the public screening of Walt Disney's first 'talkie', the short film *Steamboat Willie*. We will call this period 'The Silent Pioneers (1908–1928)'.

3 The Silent Pioneers (1908–1928) — 29

The Cradle — 29
  Days of Heaven and Hell — 29
  Culture — 29
  Cinema — 30
  Narrative and Non-Narrative — 30
  Fantasmagorie — 31
The Fathers — 32
  Émile Cohl — 32
  Georges Méliès — 33
  The First Abstract Cinema — 34
  Arnaldo Ginna — 34

Léopold Survage	35
Winsor McCay	35
Colour	37

4 Silent America I 38

The Fathers' Sons	38
Comics, Animation, and Cinema	38
Birth of the Industry	38
Raoul Barré	38
Cut, Insert, Replace	39
John Randolph Bray	39
The International Film Service	40
Other American Artists	41
Willis O'Brien	41
Instruments and Language	42

5 Silent America II 44

The Fleischer Brothers	44
Felix, Pat, and Otto Messmer	45
Terry and the Fables	46
Bowers Unbound	47
Lantz's Debut	48
Bray, Hurd, and Mintz	48
Sarg and Dawley	48
The Young Walt Disney	50

6 Silent Europe 52

The Individualists	52
Great Britain	52
Ireland	53
France	54
Lortac	54
Advertisers and Illustrators	54
Germany: Animation in the Weimar Republic	55
The Matrix	56
Walther Ruttmann	56
Viking Eggeling	57
Hans Richter	58
Lotte Reiniger	59
Austria	63
Switzerland	64
Denmark	65
Storm P.	65
Sweden	67
Grogg the Sailor Man	67
Other Swedish Animators	68
Norway	69
Finland	70
Hungary	70
Spain	70
Portugal	71
The Rest of Europe	72
Russia/Soviet Union	72
Ladislas Starewich	72
After the Revolution	75
Ukraine	81

7 Silent Asia 82

Japan	82
The Narrator	84

8 Silent Latin America 85

Mexico	85
Colombia	85
Brazil	86
Chile	86
Argentina: The World's First Animated Feature Film	86
Quirino Cristiani	86

9 Silent Africa 88

Union of South Africa	88

10 Silent Oceania 90

Australia	90
More About It	90

The Third Period 93

The Third Period includes the years when Walt Disney dominated the industry and the development of film animation as a primary form of entertainment, acclaimed by critics and beloved by audiences throughout the world. An appropriate denomination of this period is 'The Golden Age (1928–1951)'.

11 The Golden Age (1928–1951) 95

Steamboat Willie	95
Sync or Sink	95
The Non-Concurrence Factor	96
Sound	97

12 America Laughs!	**98**
Walt Disney the Tycoon	98
The Fixed Star	99
Human or Animal?	100
Years of Expansion	101
The Ones Who Made the Magic	101
Another Disney Folly	102
The Pillar Brother	103
Disney's Animation Declines	105
The Twelve Rules of the Nine Men	107
Animation Heads West	109
The Masters' Master	111
Lantz from the Rabbit to the Woodpecker	111
Ub Iwerks	113
Mintz, Krazy, and Columbia	113
Van Beuren	114
Terrytoons and Mighty Mouse	114
The Fleischers: Betty Boop, Popeye, and Two Feature Films	115
Warner Bros.	118
Tex Avery	119
Bob Clampett	123
Carl W. Stalling, Musical Animator	125
Metro-Goldwyn-Mayer: Cat, Mouse, and Tex	126
Tashlin the Wanderer	127
The American Avant-Garde	128
Canada	129
13 Europe	**131**
Great Britain	131
Len Lye	132
France	135
Anthony Gross	137
Berthold Bartosch	138
Alexandre Alexeïeff	140
Belgium	147
The Netherlands	147
Germany in Nazi Time	148
Hans Fischerkoesen	150
The Brothers Diehl	151
Heinz Tischmeyer	151
Hans Held	151
Wolfgang Kaskeline	152
Avant-Garde	152
Oskar Fischinger	153
Austria	157
Switzerland	159
Denmark	160
Sweden	162
Norway	162
Poland	163
Stefan and Franciszka Themerson	164
Czechoslovakia	165
Hungary	166
George Pal	166
Yugoslavia	167
Greece	167
Italy	167
Spain	169
Catalan Vibrancy	169
The *Edad Dorada*	170
Barcelona's Entrepreneurs	170
Barcelonese Feature-Length Films	171
Madrid	172
Valencia	172
Portugal	173
14 Soviet Union	**174**
Russia	174
Lithuania	177
Ukraine	177
Georgia	177
Armenia	178
Azerbaijan	179
15 Asia	**180**
Japan	180
Ofuji Noburo	181
Masaoka Kenzo	182
Kimura Hakuzan	184
A Brave New World	184
Mochinaga Tadahito and His Legacy	184
Ichikawa Kon	186
China	187

16 Latin America — 189

- Mexico — 189
- Colombia — 190
- Venezuela — 190
- Brazil — 191
- Argentina — 191

17 Africa — 194

- Egypt — 194
- Union of South Africa — 194

Index — 197

Contributors and Collaborators

Supervising Collaborators

Cinzia Bottini and Paolo Parmiggiani

Contributors

Fabia Abati, Midhat Ajanović, Ricardo Arce, Rolf Bächler, Laura Buono, Stefania Carini, Alessandro Cavaleri, Joe Chang, Camilo Cogua, Olivier Cotte, Rolando José Rodríguez De León, Janeann Dill, David Ehrlich, Raúl Rivera Escobar, Dizseri Eszter, Shoyista Ganikhanova, Mohamed Ghazala, Silvano Ghiringhelli, George Griffin, Francesca Guatteri, Mikhail Gurevich, Orosz Anna Ida, Marcel Jean, Corinne Jenart, Heikki Jokinen, Mariam Kandelaki, Annemette Karpen, Antonina Karpilova, Elena Kasavina, John Lent, Marcos Magalhães, Lisa Maya Quaianni Manuzzato, Philippe Moins, Hassan Muthalib, Ebele Okoye, Tsvika Oren, Irena Paulus, Marco Pellitteri, Valentina Pezzi, Francesca Pirotta, Igor Prassel, Liliana de la Quintana, Maddalena Ramolini, Thomas Renoldner, Alberto Rigoni, Emilio de la Rosa, Federico Rossin, Giovanni Russo, Jaan Ruus, Shanaz Shapurjee Hampson, Elena Shupik, Charles Solomon, Vibeke Sorensen, Gunnar Strøm, Enis Tahsin Özgür, Ieva Viese, Hans Walther, Ulrich Wegenast, Jumana Al-Yasiri, and Ran Zhang.

Columnists

Gianluca Aicardi, Anna Antonini, Marianna Aslanyan, Marianna Busacca, Adam De Beer, Nobuaki Doi, Sara Fumagalli, Maureen Furniss, Dina Goder, Tommaso Iannini, George Khoury, Clare Kitson, Jónas Knútsson, Mihai Mitrică, Michela Morselli, Tsvetomira Nikolova, C. Jay Shih, Georges Sifianos, Gulbara Tolomushova, and Paul Wells.

Editors

Ray Kosarin and Andrew Osmond

Acknowledgements

First and foremost, my gratitude goes to my contributors, especially to the memory of Francesca Pirotta, who didn't live long enough to see the book published.

Second, no endeavour would have been successful without the help of the filmmakers themselves, whom I will not list in a page that doesn't deal with their art.

With warmth and generosity, the following people made it possible to create this book. (The list is voluntarily and freely chaotic.):

John Canemaker, Heitor Capuzzo, Michael Barrier, Leonard Maltin, Rastko Ćirić, Adam Abraham, Ron Diamond, Amid Amidi, Chris Robinson, Marcin Gizycki, Don Crafton, Lara Ermacora, Michal Husák, Anna Catella, Clarissa Filippini, Michel Roudévitch, Alice Dugoni, Andrew Osmond, Ricardo Desplats, Hilmar Sigurdsson, Jiří Kubiček, Luigi Scarpa, Kathryn Weir, Mark Langer, Bob Kurtz, Mette Peters, Ton Crone, Luke McKernan, Paolo Bottaro, Lali Gorgaslidze, Giorgia Bianchi, Ingo Petzke, Andrijana Ružić, Orosz Márton, Ivanyi-Bitter Brigitta, Nina Kazakova, Anna Larina, Oscar Sierra Quintero, Paulo Cambraia, Abi Feijó, Lloyd Michaels, Noriko T. Reider, Léona Béatrice Martin, François Martin, Dennis Tupicoff, George Komrower, Magdalena Šebestová, Yokota Masao, Koide Masashi, Michaela Mertova, Bruce Burness, Nelson Shin, Pierre Courtet-Cohl, Cristina Lima, Timo Linsenmaier, Pavel Horáček, Jakub Hora, Jaromir Hník, Artan Dauti, Artur Muharremi, Artan Maku, Bertrand Shijaku, Delia Xhovalin, Ilir Butka, Shaquir Veseli, Alexis Komnakos, Angeliki Salamaliki, Effie Pappa, Georges Sifianos, Kostantinos Pardalis, Myrmigi Design House (Myriam Levis, Michael Toumazou, and Yiannis Bartzis), Stelios Plychronakis, Yannis Vassiliadis, Guerino Morselli, Stathis Melistas, Dáša Váňová, Kim Joon-yang, Han Yoon-jung, Ms. Nourghiz Chekilova and Dr Birgit Beumers, Lizzie Dunn, Euan Frizzell, Janette Goodey, Eve Gordon, Miriam Harris, Gray Hodgkinson, Roger Horrocks, Dan Inglis, Tom Reilly, Martin Rumsby, Robert Stenhouse, Raewyn Turner, Rowan Wernham, Juan Manuel Pedraza Medina, Oscar Andrade, Anatoly Petrov, Irina Margolina, Noureddin Zarrinkelk, Leila Ranjbar, Nasrine Médard de Chardon, Yusif Sheykhov, Benjamin Ettinger, Stefano Gariglio, Kamei Rieko (Madhouse Studio), Kon Satoshi, Morimoto Koji, Ilan Nguyên, Oyama Kei, Yokosuka Reiko, Yonesho Maya, Jeffrey A. Dym, Gianluca Di Fratta, Cristian Giorgi, Pedro J. Rocca Petitjean, Elmer Junior Zambrano, Jean-Charles L'Ami, Centro CNAC, Alain Nasnas, Juan Manuel Pedraza, Oscar Andrade, Alessandra Maggi, Ülo Pikkov, Adrian Lopez, Agnieszka Zając, Alejandro R. González, Juan Camilo González, Alex and Paddy Stitt, André Eckardt, Bob and Cima Balser, Breana, Caroline Pintoff, Julie Roy, Hélène Tanguay, Dan Torre, Andi Spark, Françoise Bettiol, Pier Giorgio Giraudo, Adam Snyder, Anne Denman, Arthur Cantrill, Corinne Cantrill, Barbara Mones, Cecile Starr, Eric Goldberg, Firdoze Bulbulia, Gregor Zootzky, Harvey Deneroff, Heather Kenyon, Hrvoje Turković, Joseph Janeti, Johannes Wolters, Katarina Minichova, Kenneth D. Graham, Leslie Bishko, Natalia Lukinykh, Olga Belyayeva, Otto Alder, Pat Raine Webb, Robin Allan, Russell Merritt, Stanislav Ulver, Fiorella Arrobbio Piras, Namiki Takashi, Tee Bosustow, Hana Cannon, Tjitte de Vries, Ati Mul, Vivien Halas, Tereza Brdečková, Isabelle Vanini, Jean-Luc Slock, Jo-Anne Blouin, Laurent Million, Marcel Jean, Marco de Blois, Michèle Reverdy, Monique Gailhard, Serge Bromberg, Thierry Steff, Carles Grangel, Daniel Divinsky, Antonio Delgado, Isabel Herguera, Emilio de la Rosa, Maria Pilar Yébenes Cortés, Manuel Cristóbal, Natalia Montoya, Jordi Artigas, Jesús Robles, Ambra Senatore, Cinzia Angelini, Guido Fink, Patrizia Raveggi, Donata Pesenti Campagnoni, Massimo Rabboni, Sandro del Rosario, Marisa Ghilardi, Andrea Martignoni, Paola Bristot, Muhammad Javad Khajavi, Paolo Polesello, Nancy Denney-Phelps, Birgit Beumers, Kunyi Chen, Kathrin Albers, Melanie Hani, Maria Roberta Novielli, Howard Green, Dave Bossert, Eric Goldberg, Adele Hutchinson, and Davide Freda, plus many more that my memory can't recall – but to whom my gratitude goes. Finally, a smile to my agent, Stefania Fietta, and my editor, Haley Swan: two great young ladies who ran along with me on the longest yard of this marathon – the last one.

1
FOUNDATIONS

What It Is

This history is a linear narrative, chronologically structured in ages and, furthermore, divided up into nations and authors – a traditional approach.

There were other, newer options.

Worth taking into consideration were, for instance: a history of the cross-pollination between animation and society or a history of transnational market networks – namely, the American 1910s until today, the 1945–1991 in Russia, and the Japanese 1960s until today. Counterfactual history could have been a promising option, too: For instance, what would have happened to the art, craft, and industry if no theatre had decided to screen Walt Disney's *Steamboat Willie* in 1928?

Those unbeaten tracks, based on already known (or easy to get) information, would have been exciting intellectual exercises, both for the writer and for the readers.

However, animation studies – as a whole – are still in their infancy. In history, many facts, pure and simple, still need to be unearthed. No less important is the need to honour quality. Too many good films and filmmakers, be they mainstream or independent, were (are) risking oblivion and are missing from the current showcase.

On this ground, investigating, exploring and, eventually, reporting were considered the writer's primary duties – and goals as well.

Mapping Chaos

Mapping is one of the strongest tools the human mind can use to achieve knowledge. It is unsophisticated and possibly elementary, but certainly it is needed when a journey has to start in a *terra incognita*, an unknown land, like, in our case, the facts and feats of animation as they developed globally.

Mapping is the principal ambition of this book: finding paths; setting landmarks; entering names, titles and dates into the sector's general knowledge as a result of the aforementioned exploration. To younger scholars, the pleasure to examine everything closely. . .

Turning Points

One more avowal. Periodization is one of the most difficult tasks a historian has to face. It's mandatory to identify coherent periods of mapped facts, basically through the 'discovery' of clear turning points.

A turning point is an event that's so important as to characterize what happened *before* and *after* it as two separate chapters – although linked by elements of continuity.

A historical period shows an affinity between certain events and a component that stabilizes them all around a core.

In such a context, we *narrate* – i.e. we *explain* the facts.

In this writer's opinion, a good historian seeks to narrate/explain the facts, not list them. In order to narrate them, he or she must go back to the origins and decipher the causes and effects, since a fact, to be historical, must be significant.[1]

Periods

Let's then identify, within the history of animation, periods and turning points.

---

[1] This is the basic difference (not always clear even to highbrow people) between chronology and history. Chronologically, there is no doubt that the Europeans (Vikings) landed on the American continent 500 years before Christopher Columbus – but with no lasting effects. Historically, the event that produced a world revolution was the 'discovery of America' on 12 October 1492. Again, a fact, to be historical, must be significant.

The First Period spans the years before the screening of Émile Cohl's film *Fantasmagorie* in Paris, France. There is no 'animation' as such there, but the film still incorporates many features that look like what nowadays we would consider to be animation. We will call this period 'Before *Fantasmagorie* (0–1908)'.

The Second Period embraces the entire silent film era and ends with a specific date: 18 November 1928, the day of the public screening of Walt Disney's first 'talkie', the short film *Steamboat Willie*. We will call this period 'The Silent Pioneers (1908–1928)'.

The Third Period includes the years when Walt Disney dominated the industry and the development of film animation as a primary form of entertainment, acclaimed by critics and beloved by audiences throughout the world. An appropriate denomination of this period is 'The Golden Age (1928–1951)'.

The Fourth Period, covered in Volume II of this series, is short and runs from 1951 (the date of projection of the UPA short *Gerald McBoing Boing*) to 1960, the date of the first international animation film festival (Annecy, France). It is characterized by indecision. Disney and his imitators lost momentum, the UPA proposed a new style, the television age began and an original animation output was born in Europe. We'll christen it 'The Birth of a Style (1951–1960)'.

The Fifth Period (Volume II) begins with the blooming of the television series and *auteur* animation and ends with the conclusion of the Cold War. Although it is varied and subjected to strong changes within the market (in the field of television or advertising) and within technology (e.g. computers), it is substantially uniform, as it obeys the political and economic division of the world into two major areas: one influenced by the liberal United States and one influenced by the communist Soviet Union. This period is called 'The Three Markets (1960–1991)'.

The Sixth Period (Volume III of this series) begins in 1991 and features economic globalization; the expansion of television series; the progress of countries like Japan, Korea, China, and India; and the consolidation of elitist *auteur* animation. But it is impossible to write history while it is still being made. We'll leave this period uncharacterized until the day we witness its ending: These are then 'Contemporary Times (1991–2015)'.

Guilty, but with an Explanation

No written history is but a subjective history. Sincerity, respect and honesty may be guaranteed; objectivity, never. No narrator is the same.[2]

This writer is acutely aware of his personal limitations. We must be even more aware of the project's limitations. Could a better mind, or the best possible mind, write a completely satisfactory history of a phenomenon that spans over three centuries and the whole globe?

Obviously not.

Nevertheless, the phenomenon called animation is – perversely – as important as it is underestimated and underinvestigated. This book will try to answer a few questions (perhaps too few) but will hopefully raise many.

In other words, this is a step upwards – and just this. Both the book and the step will have achieved their goal as soon as they simultaneously become useless.[3]

Traces

Sources about animation are scanty. Film copies, drawings, puppets, sketches, accounting books, and letters are perishable. Most of them have perished. Almost always, they were disbanded or thrown away once a company or a single filmmaker died. Very scarce media coverage and very scarce opportunities for screening have always been given to *auteur* animated films. Sometimes people who control some sources deny access to them, for reasons known to them only. And so on and so on.

So, beware. 'Historical study', G. R. Elton stated,

---

[2] This writer is a European, born during the Cold War, with an education based on classical studies, influenced by the cultural, political, social, philosophical, and religious beliefs and disbeliefs of his times. The reader will either agree or disagree with the approach. An example? This historian praises quality over quantity. He might believe that a film, famous and extremely successful at the box office, was artistically poor: You will be reading in these pages that that film was a poor film. This historian cares about freedom. Any blessed-by-money film has enough power to stand up and make itself known. A film of humble origins has much less power and hence much less freedom. To rectify the situation, more room will be devoted in these pages to the less powerful films – value being the same, of course.

[3] Links, names, and chapters will almost certainly be missing from the following pages. In addition, other pages (filled with names, titles, and dates) may be boring to the reader but were necessary because it was imperative to do some 'pre-emptive archaeology' (pardon the oxymoron) and leave at least a trace that could be later used by younger and better-equipped scholars.

is not the study of the past, but the study of present traces of the past; if men have said, thought, done or suffered anything of which nothing any longer exists, those things are as though they had never been. . . . The past is over and done with: it cannot be relived. It can be reconstructed – seen and understood again – only if it has left present matter behind.[4]

You Won't Find. . .

For more than forty years, Henry Jamison Handy (1886–1983) operated one of the leading industrial film studios in the United States: the Jam Handy Organization. Based in Detroit, Handy's studio was conveniently located in America's industrial heartland and produced hundreds of advertising, training, and informational films for General Motors, RCA, the National Cash Register, and a number of growing industries looking to take advantage of business opportunities afforded by the new media. Until the firm dissolved in 1970, its clients included local governments, the military, and educational and religious organizations.

There have been thousands of Henry Jamison Handys in the world. Future historians will acknowledge their merits and relate their accomplishments.

This book, instead, focuses on entertainment and art. To satisfactorily deal with advertising and training and educational films, too, would have required many more years of research. As the old saying goes, 'Perfect is the enemy of good'.

A Hybrid

For many reasons, a book that started with one author became a hybrid between an authored and an edited book. This writer read, edited, in most cases interpolated and eventually approved every single line of the contributors' texts in order for the final result to be consistent. (Obviously, no *concept* by any contributor was modified or censored.) This is a claim for shared responsibility, not for shared authorship on my part. In other words: If readers enjoy the texts by the contributors, let these authors be praised; if not, let this writer be blamed.

---

[4] G. R. Elton, *The Practice of History*, Fontana Press, London, 1987.

THE FIRST PERIOD

The First Period spans the years before the screening of Émile Cohl's film *Fantasmagorie* in Paris, France. There is no 'animation' as such there, but the film still incorporates many features that look like what nowadays we would consider to be animation. We will call this period 'Before *Fantasmagorie* (0–1908)'.

2
BEFORE *FANTASMAGORIE* (0–1908)

Archaeology

A forerunner is just a runner. He doesn't – nor does he care to – predict what posterity, with hindsight, will call him.

Most of the actions, productions, and inventions that took place before the nineteenth century and look like something we now call animation were produced by forerunners. To what we now call animation, they have no cause-and-effect connection. They are purely anecdotic and thus useless to our historical discourse.

For the sake of completeness, we will look for a few examples from history.

On 30 December 2004, an article called 'First Animation of the World Found in Burnt City, Iran' was published.

This is the text:

> An animated piece on an earthen goblet that belongs to 5000 years ago[1] was found in Burnt City in Sistan-Baluchistan province, south-eastern Iran.
>
> On this ancient piece that can be called the first animation of the world, the artist has portrayed a goat that jumps toward a tree and eats its leaves. . . . On this goblet, with a diameter of 8 cm and height of 10 cm, the images show movement in an intricate way that is an unprecedented discovery. Some earthenware found in Burnt City show repetitive images, but none of them implicate any movements.[2]

Trajan's Column is still standing in downtown Rome. It was erected in 106 to 113 AD to commemorate Emperor Trajan's victories in Dacia (now Romania) between 101 and 102 AD and 105 and 106 AD.

A helicoidal band of beautifully carved reliefs winds around its height of 42 m (138 ft). The band is more than 180 m (600 ft) long. Its width varies from 60 cm (2 ft) at the bottom to 120 cm (4 ft) at the top. There are more than 2,000 carved figures depicting the story of the expeditions. These start with soldiers preparing for the war, and then we see the bridges Trajan built, the forts he attacked, the camps he destroyed, and the enemy he forced to retreat. The reliefs were not always in plain white: Originally, they were gilded and, like many Roman monuments, brightly coloured. This was a story told with figures – perhaps like an animated puppet film, a comic book, or a documentary.

In 1952, French animation scholar Marie-Thérèse Poncet published a book to state that Middle Age illustrations had a lot in common with animated cartoons;[3] even better, they already were animated films. She wrote:

Figure 2.1 Earthen goblet of Burnt City, 3000 BC Tehran, National Museum of Iran.

---

[1] More precisely, to 2,600–2,700 BC.
[2] A serious filmed reconstruction of the action is available at http://cela.etant.free.fr/stories/wp-content/burnt_city_old_animation.mov.
[3] A. G. Nizet, 'Étude comparative des illustrations du moyen âge et des dessins animés', Paris, 1952.

We won't be listing all the possible films; we will choose some typical examples. . . . In the XI century, the historical film of the Tapestry of Bayeux.[4] In the XII century, the evangelical films, narrative and didactic, of the frieze of St. Gilles du Gard and of St. Trophime d'Arles. In the XIII century, the jubé of the church in Bourget du Lac, around Chambéry in Savoy. . .

Like animated cartoons, these Middle Age images took their subjects from flora and fauna, and were designed, inked, painted, and put in the order that spectators watched them. The ancient chromatism is not different from that of Walt Disney – the education and entertainment of common people, via simple but attractive drawings, are the goals of both forms of art.

In 1999, animation director and fine intellectual Takahata Isao published a book on the art of *emaki*, picture scrolls, in relation to the 1999 exhibition at the Chiba City Art Museum. The exhibition showcased Ghibli's animation art and *emaki* scrolls side by side. *Emaki* is a horizontal, illustrated narrative form that was created during the eleventh to sixteenth centuries in Japan. It combines both text and pictures and is drawn, painted, or stamped on a hand scroll. Topics include battles, romance (the best known are *emaki* based on *The Tale of Genji*), religion, folk stories, and tales of the supernatural world. The reading of *emaki* alone, done so that the right hand opens the upcoming pictures while the left hand closes the scroll, resembles a film turning on the projector. The same characters appear from scene to scene, with their story continuing. *Emaki* show human poses and expressions, depicting their energy and movement; 'movement lines' represent quick actions; sometimes, within the same scene, a character is drawn in different stages in succession according to its displacement.

Phidias' Animating Chisel[5]

1. In the Parthenon frieze, there is an intentional analysis of movement and a conscious use of this analysis.
2. The representation of the phases of the movements is a structuring element of the composition.
3. The frieze is designed like a musical symphony. The motion analysis provides support for rhythmic and melodic organization and also the use of counterpoint.
4. It is possible to decode the frieze as a musical score and for an orchestra to interpret the music.
5. The movement that between the lines connects several figures has a specific philosophical meaning.

Representation

The Parthenon was built in Athens between 447 and 432 BC. Phidias sculpted on it a frieze in low relief, about 160 m (525 ft) long and 1.05 m (3.45 ft) tall. Experts see it as a representation of the great Panathenaic procession, a celebration in honour of the goddess Athena.

The action begins at the rear of the Parthenon in the western section; it continues along the northern and southern friezes and ends at the eastern frieze. Scenes of the preparations on the western wall are followed by impressive rows of knights on the northern and southern walls. Further, we see the representation of the *apobatein*, during which a young soldier jumps from a running carriage, runs by its side, and then jumps back on it. Bearers of offerings, musicians, and animals for sacrifice come before the carriages. In the eastern section, action converges towards the centre, where the scene of the offering of the peplos to the goddess takes place. The gods of Olympus are seated to the left and right of this scene, followed by two groups of men and framed by the arrival of young women, the *Ergastines*, who have woven the peplos.

The Motion Analysis

Looking closely at the frieze, we see a deep knowledge of both anatomy and movement analysis. The first example is the cattle in the southern frieze. Although parts of the frieze are missing, we see

---

[4] The tapestry (made, preserved, and displayed in Bayeux, Normandy, France) has more or less the same meaning as the Trajan's Column. It was probably commissioned in the 1070s by Bishop Odo of Bayeux and is in fact an embroidery, 50 cm by 70 m (20 in. by 230 ft) long. It shows the events leading up to the Norman conquest of England under the aegis of William the Conqueror.

[5] By Georges Sifianos. Images digitally processed from pictures of Sokratis Mavrommatis.

that every animal is a stage – a 'key frame' – of the movement of an animal that resists being tamed.

If we superimpose the animals, we get a beautiful animation that shows the strength of the struggling beast. Another example is in the eastern frieze in the representation of the gods Athena, Hephaestus, Poseidon, Apollo, Artemis, Aphrodite, and Eros. Individually, the gods have positions that reflect their identities: Poseidon holds a trident (drawn and now deleted); Artemis adjusts her clothes in a gesture reminiscent of an archer, etc. Looking at the same figures as a whole, we find that their arms are organized in a sequence through the key phases of an action that points to the right. From Athena's relaxed position, we go to Poseidon's anticipation, and gradually we reach the outstretched arms of Aphrodite. Moreover, if we shoot these figures frame by frame, we obtain coherent animation. The movement implicit in this sequence has an important meaning, since the arms point to the arrival of the procession, which is the subject of the frieze.

We see another example in the northern frieze. There, we see a structured use of the analysis of movement in the *apobatein* exercise.[6] The action is implicitly represented through distinct figures, although it is more spread out this time.

There are other places where motion analysis is used, each time for a precise reason. In the cavalry, for instance, horses do not follow the entire movement (as in the case of the cattle) but deploy a variety of postures in a succession according to a musical logic.

Elsewhere, as in the scene of the handover of the peplos, motion analysis provides fairly remote phases, so accurate in their attitude and perspective, though, that we can deduce the exact timing of the action.

In other places, there is movement that operates in two directions, following two actions that overlap but are carried out by the same figures.

Overlapping actions, anticipation, decomposition of movement, follow-up of harmonious action lines: All these things are common both to film animation and to the frieze.

Figure 2.2 Phidias' Parthenon frieze.

Music

What we have just discussed – the dual representation of both individual postures and implicit action – is a general principle of the dramaturgy of the frieze.

Another principle is the musical organization. Glancing at the frieze, intuitively, we look for the similarities. From the Gestalt psychology until cognitive science today, we know that the human brain seeks to establish correlations by examining the similarities. In the frieze, there is no movement in the sense of filmic trompe-l'oeil, but it is possible to identify the similarity of forms and establish associations. Via the similarities we create sequences between the lines, readable by a knowledgeable or simply attentive person.

---

[6] The analysis of the action is detectable despite the missing parts, and utilizing those known only from Jacques Carrey's drawings, made before the bombardment of the Parthenon in 1687.

Analogy is the basis of music, too. The harmonic resonance of the octave is based on this very principle of proportional similarity of the frequencies of sounds. In the frieze, by resemblance, we bounce from one figure to another, and we do so in a rhythmic and melodic way, hence creating a harmony.

Just look at the frieze systematically: You will see that the development of the actions follows harmonic curves. Marey's chronophotography demonstrates that human or animal locomotion traces harmonic trajectories. This balance, in nature, is produced by a complex dynamism that is equivalent to the polyphony and to the counterpoint complementarity.

If we analyze the part of the eastern frieze with the gods (Figure 2.2), we realize that our glance is guided by a form, organized on several layers.

Large masses of bodies alternate profiles to three fourths; stools are rationally put in place; heads evolve in pairs responding one another; legs alternate a crossed position and a separated position; the abundant clothes drapery and the arms develop the main theme, responding in counterpoint to each other to form that significant gesture of indicating, suggested as an implicit meaning.

These groups are organized as 'sound', from the most bass (large bodies) to the highest one (the drapery of clothing). It is a polyphonic composition that commands the complementarity of counterpoint. The most surprising thing is that, according to most historians of music, the practice of counterpoint was developed from the ninth to the twelfth centuries, and that ancient music, in general, is considered to have been monophonic.

The mastery of a polyphonic composition with the use of counterpoint is also apparent in the overall composition which, furthermore, develops in space and not on a surface.

The procession begins in the western frieze in a random dissonance of preparations. It propels itself simultaneously in the northern and southern friezes, with the massive hammering of a cavalry divided into two unequal parades. The knights are a group, the carriages are individual subjects, but the procession always shows energy. Then, it softens in the serene and melodic representation of musicians and bearers of offerings, momentarily disturbed by the agitation of the animal sacrifice. Parallel and similar actions in

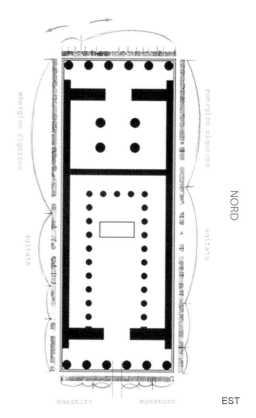

Figure 2.3 Phidias' Parthenon frieze.

the northern and in the southern wall respond to one another.

The procession synchronizes at the corners of the eastern frieze – and there and then it becomes solemn.

In the few notes that Aristotle wrote about music, he observed that nothing is more charming to the ear than 'the unity succeeding the diversity' (τό ἐκ διαφόρων τό κοινὸν ἥδιστον). That synchronization of the overall composition around the eastern frieze corresponds to the form considered by Aristotle as pleasant. If we compare the organization of different segments, we find that they could be qualified as *energico con rigore, agitato, andante cantabile, maestoso,* etc.

Clearly the frieze is designed as a symphonic score as a whole and in detail. Georges Sifianos himself began the deciphering of this partition, and composer Ivan Boumans transcribed a fragment of the western frieze in music.

Figure 2.4 Phidias' Parthenon frieze.

The Meaning of the Implicit Movement

At the time of the Parthenon, the debate of ideas was in an unprecedented blossoming. Philosophers such as Zeno, Anaxagoras, Protagoras, Gorgias, and Socrates were contemporaries to this construction; Parmenides, Heraclitus, Pythagoras, and/or Thales preceded it. Plato, Aristotle, and Epicurus were born later, but the foundations of their ideas were already taking shape. The dominant conception sees the cosmos as a perfectly harmonious entity. Hence, one's ethical duty was to seize this harmony and become one with it. The greatest evil, *hybris*, was excess: the rupture of the cosmic harmony.

The dialectical process of reasoning, which seeks the truth by comparing opposing views, was initiated at that time by Zeno of Elea. The synthesis of opposites comes from several philosophers, from the Pythagoreans ('music is a harmonious combination of opposites') to Heraclitus, and from Socrates' maieutics to the oxymoric proverb 'σπεύδε βραδέως' (more haste, less speed). In such a context, the analysis of motion in the frieze, and the representation of implicit actions, does not simply reflect a thorough knowledge of the movement in nature. It represents the thought of a society, a thought that works dialectically – i.e. by synthesis after a debate.

An Object of Philosophy

The frieze shows a procession that every Athenian of the time witnessed or participated in. Set very high, it was hardly visible. But we know that the principle of our current society of communication 'only the visible exists' was not valid at the time. The statues of the pediments were carefully completed on their backs, too, though the sculptor knew full well that the back would never be visible. To an ancient Greek, harmony was to be sought as a value in itself – regardless of its visibility or not. Rather than appearance (to look), truth mattered (to be). In the frieze, we see the dialectical functioning of Athenian society, not its image.

The frieze is a 'model' or a 'paradigm' that mimics such functioning. Rather than a metaphorical form, we have a metaphorical structure. The frieze is dialectic – thus necessarily polyphonic – and the audience is necessarily involved; it's a representation of the Athenian democracy and of its conception of the cosmos.

A structure developed on several levels – anecdotal, musical/plastic, philosophical – is made possible thanks to the analysis of the movement.

The rhetoric of the frieze, like the maieutics of Socrates, leads the viewer to draw his or her own conclusions. Phidias provides a beautiful score; it's up to the viewer to interpret the music and catch the meaning.

> Phidias's wink at animation is not about a technique or an illusion but about a way of being. The frieze is a reference object, designed to be looked at mentally rather than visually. In this sense, the composition transcends the mere plastic drama. It becomes an object of philosophy, an object of art in its full right. In short, great art.

Whether the image was drawn (animated cartoons' alleged lineage) or photographed (live-action films' alleged lineage), it didn't matter.

In other words, the pre-history of animation and the pre-history of cinema are the very same thing.

The actual physiognomy – or, better, the actual body – of the twin moving image arts would take shape by the first decade of the twentieth century only, as we will discuss later on.

Pre-History I

Most decades of the nineteenth century and the first decade of the twentieth century were a culture media that eventually gave birth to what we now call animation and at the same time to what we now call cinema.

Hindsight is a tricky work tool. Many of the mistakes made by film historians in the course of the decades were produced by their idea of 'cinema', an idea that matched the actual cinema they were currently witnessing – and that had nothing to do (for instance) with the cinema of the last decade of the nineteenth century. To really understand facts, a recommended approach is to reconstruct what things meant to the people who produced them and to their contemporaries.

The visual world of people, in the early nineteenth century, was poor – certainly richer than the world of the sixteenth century, when sight was considered only the third most important sense, far behind hearing and touch,[7] but still limited to paintings, frescoes, drawings, statues, popular prints, magic lantern shows, and perspective view shows (when available).

Furthermore, people knew that man-made images were motionless. Painters and sculptors often suggested figures' motion and often unbalanced the structure of their works in order to achieve general dynamism, but the works stood still.

The facts that took place, from the 1820s onward, were aiming at the pursuit of a moving image. Scientists, inventors, toy makers, showmen and, above all, the paying audience were interested in one single thing: motion.

Science, Science, Science

In the nineteenth century, the world (a scarcely populated world) was ruled by England and France in the beginning and by Europe and the United States at the end. It was the century of industrial expansion. Of the middle class, its values and its aspirations. Of capitalism. Of explorations. Of positivism. Of indestructible faith in progress. Of modernity, whatever the meaning of this word. Of science.

In physics, and particularly in optics, the scholars, academicians, and simple practitioners who determined the course of technological progress in that era found time to study the persistence of images on the retina. In 1824, Peter Mark Roget (1779–1869), who was then examiner of physiology at the University of London, published *Persistence of Vision with Regard to Moving Objects*. As Roget explained, images were retained by the retina of the human eye for fractions of a second before being replaced by the succeeding ones. If the succession was sufficiently rapid, the viewer had the impression of movement even when looking at still pictures. This phenomenon led to further exploration over the next fifty years.[8]

During some centuries, the word 'philosophy' had meant 'science' and 'knowledge', too. In the language of the eighteenth and early nineteenth centuries, a microscope was a philosophical instrument.

Not surprisingly, many apparatuses that were invented or adapted in order to explore vision and/or the human eye's reactions – but at the same time served a function of popular or children's amusement – were originally called 'philosophical toys'. The best known of them all, and the

---

[7] Lucien Febvre and Robert Mandrou, quoted in Gian Piero Brunetta, Il viaggio dell'icononauta, Marsilio, Venice, 1997.

[8] This is very important. The perception of fluid motion (also known as persistence of vision or, better, as perception of continuity of motion) is due to the assembly of still images made by the human brain. This phenomenon happens provided that an image persists for at least one eighth of a second on the eye. Anything that moves more slowly than one eighth of a second is perceived by the human mind as 'motionless' (the blossoming of a flower, for example). The German psychologist Max Wertheimer (the founder of Gestalt) showed in 1912 in the essay 'Experimentelle Studien über das Sehen der Bewegung' that the assembly of still images is made by the human brain, and he called this process the 'phi phenomenon'.

most enduring one, was the kaleidoscope invented by David Brewster in 1816. Instead of a toy maker, Scottish Dr. David Brewster (1781–1868) was a physicist and physiologist who first described the pathology known as colour blindness and in 1816 was experimenting with mirrors and symmetry.

In 1825,[9] a well-known English physician, John A. Paris (1785–1856), created the prototype of the aiming-at-motion philosophical toys, the thaumatrope: a disc with a complementary image on each side and strings attached at each end of its horizontal axis. When the disc is spun on the strings, the two complementary images appear to merge. In 1832, the Belgian physicist and mathematician Joseph Plateau (1801–1883) invented the phenakistiscope. Plateau always called his device a 'phenatisticope', without the central 's'.

This was a device made of a pivot and a cardboard disc, along the edge of which successive images of an object in motion had been drawn. By focusing on one drawing while viewing the rotating disk through a slit, one had the illusion that the drawing moved.

More or less at the same time, and independently from Plateau, Austrian mathematician Simon von Stampfer (1792–1864) presented his stunningly similar stroboscope or stroboscopic disc.

About one year more, and here is the improvement: a cylinder mounted on a vertical axis, with slits at regular intervals, and a sequence of drawings on the opposite inside surface of the cylinder. It was invented in 1834 by Bristol-born mathematician William Horner (1789–1837). He called it the daedaleum, but it became world-famous as the zoetrope.

Writing with Light

In the meantime, chemistry was hitting its stride. A petroleum derivative called bitumen of Judea hardens with

Figure 2.5 Joseph Plateau's phenakistiscope.

---

[9] The date, as well as the paternity, is debated. Some scholars attribute the actual invention to geologist William Henry Fitton, others to Charles Babbage.

Figure 2.6 Simon von Stampfer, jumping boy disc.

exposure to light; on this ground, a French inventor, Nicéphore Niépce (1765–1833) smeared some bitumen of Judea on a metal surface and exposed it for hours to sunlight. Then he washed away the unhardened material and polished the metal plate, rendering a negative image that then he coated with ink and impressed upon paper, producing a print. In 1826, Niépce made the first successful photograph ever – a view of his courtyard, seen from his house. Although bad, blurred, retouched, and retouched again, we still have it.

Niépce's business partner was Louis-Jacques-Mandé Daguerre (1787–1851), a painter and printmaker who took over from him after his death in 1833.

Daguerre found that the iodide of silver, formed by exposing silver to the vapour of iodine, was sensitive to light. If an iodized silver plate hold within a camera was exposed, faint images of bright objects were impressed upon it. By accident (!), Daguerre also discovered that by treating the exposed plate to the vapour proceeding from liquid mercury, he could greatly reduce the time of exposure necessary to produce a satisfactory picture. Eventually, a fixing agent was needed. This was just a solution of common salt in which the plate was soaked and that dissolved the iodide of silver that had not been acted on by light.[10]

On 7 January 1839, members of the French Académie des Sciences were shown products of an invention that would forever change the nature of visual representation: photography.[11]

In other words, the gadget was a daguerreotype: a one-of-a-kind image on a highly polished, silver-plated sheet of copper. A daguerreotype could not be copied because it was a positive-only process allowing no reproduction of the picture. Its high definition is still impressive nowadays.

When the news got to England, William Henry Fox Talbot (1800–1877) was impressed. A graduate of Trinity College, Cambridge; a member of Parliament; and a specialist of mathematics, chemistry, astronomy, botany, philosophy, philology, Egyptology, classic literature, and art history, Talbot had been too versatile to go thoroughly into an approach he had invented years before to better study vegetation.

The scientist rushed to the Royal Society and presented his art of photogenic drawing.[12] In 1840, he made a leap forward. He coated paper sheets with silver chloride to create an intermediate negative image. This negative could be used to reproduce many positive prints. Talbot patented this process and called it the calotype.

The popularity of photography was huge and immediate, and its technical improvements were many, quick, and never-ending until the digital era. Above all, it was an intellectual revolution.

This 'mirror with a memory', as Oliver Wendell Holmes, Sr., would call it,[13] suddenly changed the rules of visual arts (painting first), improved historical research (the Civil War between the states was the first military event to get vast pictorial coverage and consequently vast pictorial evidence), changed the behaviour of scientists, writers, politicians, and common people. It gave birth to the iconocentric society we are still experiencing in this millennium.

Pre-History II
A Static Mirror?

In 1851, the Londoner Frederick Scott Archer (1813–1857) invented the collodion process; in 1887, the American Episcopal priest Hannibal W. Goodwin (1822–1900)

---

[10] Soon to be substituted, upon astronomer Sir John Herschel's suggestion, by hyposulfite of soda (also known as hypo or sodium thiosulfate).

[11] The word was coined by Sir John Herschel and is based on the ancient Greek words 'photos' (light) plus 'graphein' (writing or drawing).

[12] At that stage, the art of photogenic drawing was better suited for recording the shadows of plant specimens, lace, or similar flat objects by direct contact than for camera images.

[13] 'The Stereoscope and the Stereograph', *The Atlantic Monthly*, No. 3, June 1859.

patented the use of celluloid as support for film; in 1888, the American inventor George Eastman (1854–1932) designed the Kodak,[14] an easy-to-carry simple camera that eliminated focusing and lighting.

Photography – this 'objective' instrument – would be extensively used to dissect reality.

French astronomer Pierre Jules César Janssen (1824–1907) invented the photographic revolver to record a solar eclipse in 1874; Briton Eadweard Muybridge (real name: Edward Muggeridge, 1830–1904) used a series of cameras in sequence in order to study the human and the animal figure in motion (1878–1881, 1884–1885, in the United States); French physiologist Étienne Jules Marey (1830–1904) introduced his *fusil photographique* (photographic rifle) to study birds' flight in 1882; German photographer Ottomar Anschütz (1846–1907) devised in 1886 his *Schnellseher* (or electrical tachyscope) to reproduce the movements captured by chronophotographs; French physiologist Georges Demeny (1850–1917), long-time collaborator of Marey, devised the 'beater' movement for precisely advancing celluloid film and in 1892 patented the phonoscope with glass discs for projection and paper discs for direct viewing.

But as far as the production of moving images was concerned, photography never became easier to handle, more available, and cheaper than drawing – until the 1890s.

The Flipbook

Philosophical toys were good business, as they appealed to children and grown-ups alike. The most successful one, the stereoscope,[15] was sold by the millions all over the world; the London Stereoscopic Company alone sold more than half a million viewers in 1856–1858 and more than a million viewers in 1862.

Although the Frenchman Pierre-Hubert Desvignes is generally credited with being the inventor of the flipbook, John Barnes Linnett from Britain, a lithograph printer based in Birmingham, was the first to patent the invention. The patent dates back to September 1868, when it was called the kineograph.[16]

Early flipbooks consisted of drawings stacked in sequential stages of movement with a single staple binding. When the pages were flipped, they would create the optical illusion of motion.

Flipbooks were then popularized in the early twentieth century by various manufacturers who gave them away as free in-pack prizes. Without ever becoming star material, this tiny object is still produced today.

Oddly enough, good filmmakers and good artists have seldom devoted interest to the flipbook, a promising medium that lets the creator narrate a three- to four-second optical illusion.[17]

Furthermore, the simple technology of the flipbook has nothing to do with the camera–film–projector–theatre system that we summarize with the locution 'cinema', thus demonstrating that even before the digital era, the universe of the moving image had always been larger than that of cinema in the strict sense of the word.[18]

Émile Reynaud

Émile Reynaud was born in Montreuil-Sous-Bois (a few kilometres from Paris) on 8 December 1844.

---

[14] The word has no actual meaning and was invented by Eastman himself.

[15] It was invented in 1830–1835 by Gloucester physicist Charles Wheatstone (1802–1875), who described the properties of binocular/stereoscopic vision as early as 1838, one year before the invention of photography. Stereoscopes present to a user two slightly differing figures, one to each eye. If the figures have appropriate horizontal disparities, the effect of depth is produced.

[16] In the United States, it was patented on 16 May 1882 by Henry Van Hovenbergh of Elizabeth, New Jersey.

[17] In 2005, under the curatorship of Christoph Schulz and Daniel Gethmann, the Kunsthalle Düsseldorf (Germany) hosted an exhibition and a show called Daumenkino ('thumb cinema'). Retrospectives were devoted to American animators Ruth Hayes and George Griffin, and among the exhibited authors were Pedro Almodóvar, Guillaume Apollinaire, Darren Aronofsky, Robert Breer, John Canemaker, Émile Cohl, Douglass Crockwell, Shamus Culhane, Gene Deitch, Paul Driessen, Peter Földes, Taku Furukawa, Keith Haring, William Kentridge, Miroslaw Kijowicz, Yoji Kuri, Karl Lagerfeld, Vladimir Lehky, Jan Lenica, Sol LeWitt, Baz Luhrmann, Otto Messmer, Zdenek Miler, Moebius, Marv Newland, Yoko Ono, Kaj Pindal, Joanna Priestley, Kathy Rose, Daniel Szczechura, Stan Van der Beek, and Andy Warhol.

[18] The mutoscope, a peep-show device patented by Herman Casler in 1894, which was quite successful for about twenty years, was sort of a perfected flipbook.

As a boy, he apprenticed in a precision mechanics shop and worked for Antoine Adam-Salomon, the French photographer who imported Franz Hanfstaengl's method of negative retouching from Bavaria to France. This knowledge of optics and mechanics enriched Reynaud's artistic skills, which he had learned from his mother (who had been a student of the painter Pierre-Joseph Redouté, the 'Raphael of the Flowers', 1759–1840).

In 1872, Reynaud came upon an issue of *La Nature* magazine that illustrated the latest findings on the optical reproduction of movement. Combining experience and ingenuity, he built a device of his own: the praxinoscope. It consisted of a cylindrical box attached to a pivot. A coloured strip of paper on the inside face of the cylinder showed the consecutive stages of a movement. When the cylinder rotated, these stages were reflected in rapid succession on a mirrored prism mounted on the pivot, and the viewer who looked at the prism would see the drawn image move freely. It was actually a mere – although brilliant – improvement of the already-existing zoetrope, but Reynaud patented the praxinoscope in 1877, and the following year he received honourable mention at the Paris World Exposition. He later opened a small workshop and began manufacturing the instrument in large quantities, selling it throughout Europe as a children's toy.

Birth of the Théâtre Optique

Unwilling to return to anonymity, Reynaud modified the praxinoscope, hoping to transform this family amusement into an entertainment device for large audiences. After several metamorphoses (all of them patented), in 1888, the praxinoscope became what the inventor had wished. In October, Reynaud invited some friends to an experimental projection in his home and showed one film, *Un bon bock* (A Good Beer), his very first work of the kind.[19] Pleased with the response, in December he applied for a patent at the Prefecture of Seine.

The patent, numbered 194482, was granted on 14 January 1889. Although the new device was a modification of the praxinoscope, Reynaud gave it a new name, *théâtre optique* (optical theatre). By means of a projector and more mirrors, the images that the viewer of the praxinoscope had once seen directly on the prism were now brought to a screen. Images were no longer arranged on a short, self-terminating strip placed within the cylinder but were painted on a long ribbon, which reproduced 'a considerable series of actions, thus reconstructing, through optical synthesis, a full scene'[20] of fifteen to twenty minutes.

This rather complex and fragile instrument had one fundamental defect: It had to be turned manually by a skilled operator. The projection included stops and rewinds at pre-established times, acoustical effects, and so on. In other words, the operator had to be a cinematic puppeteer – animated cinema and animated theatre were walking hand in hand. Reynaud planned to sell his device to entrepreneurs at home and abroad. He hoped to establish a profitable business supplying new films for his clients, who would want a variety of programmes. This proved to be an illusion. Excessive costs, the fragility of the instrument, and the difficult operations it involved discouraged any potential buyers.

Reynaud himself had to be the projectionist if he wanted his *théâtre optique* to be shown. On 11 October 1892, four years after his first experimental performance, he signed a contract with the Grévin Museum, the well-known wax museum that also offered variety programmes. The contract required daily performances, which Reynaud had to run in person, and an entirely new repertory every year.

---

[19] This is the plot: A man enters a country inn and calls the maid. She doesn't come; he beats on the table with his walking stick until he gets attention. The girl brings a beer, and lo! she's very attractive. So the man forgets his thirst, falls on his knees, winces with fondness to no success – not realizing that in the meantime the scullion has drank his beer. Astonished in front of the empty glass, he requests one more. While the beauty leaves to fetch a new drink, a traveller with a suitcase enters and teases the would-be lover. The two customers quarrel, and during the quarrel the scullion empties the second glass, too. The traveller leaves; the protagonist, lonely and ridiculed, pays and disappears. The scullion tells the waitress what happened. Both greet the fool's departure with mocking gestures.

[20] Gaston Tissandier, 'Le théâtre optique', *La Nature*, No. 999, Paris, 23 July 1992.

A clause prohibited the sale or rental of similar instruments and films in France and abroad. Reynaud was also tied hand and foot, having to spend all his free time creating new films. He complied, however, and showed his first *pantomimes lumineuses* (Lit Pantomimes) on 28 October 1892. The billboards read *Le clown et ses chiens* (The Clown and His Dogs), *Pauvre Pierrot* (Poor Pierrot), and *Un bon bock* (A Good Beer).

As the years went by, Reynaud made some improvements on his device (by pushing a lever, he was able to simulate the sound of Pierrot's thrashings). He also painted new films. There was always an audience for the *pantomimes lumineuses*; for when they ended screenings in 1900, it was estimated that over half a million people had seen them. In 1895, however, after the Lumières' historical projection only a few hundred yards from the Grévin Museum, the audience began to wane. Reynaud tried new techniques to speed up the manual work. He saved some time by using photographic instruments while drawing, but did not want to make films 'Lumière style'. Whenever he used photographs, he reworked them by hand until they were transformed into drawings. Because of his craftsman way of working, he was left behind the times, which were becoming ever more fast paced. The Grévin Museum offered the *théâtre optique* until 1 March 1900, when English marionettes and a Gypsy orchestra replaced the *pantomimes lumineuses*.

At fifty-six, Reynaud did not want to retire and kept experimenting with new machinery, such as the stereoscopic viewer. But cinema was opening its door to the industrialists, not to the craftsmen who could not compete. In a moment of vexation, a depressed Reynaud smashed the three *théâtres optiques* he owned. Then, day after day, he threw the painted films into the Seine. He died on 9 January 1917.

> The device is designed to create the illusion of movement, no longer limited to the repetition of the same poses each time the instrument is turned, as happens with all of the current devices; on the contrary, its indefinite length and variety produce true animated scenes with unlimited length.

In this awkward prose (from the report accompanying the patent application for the *théâtre optique*), Reynaud summarized the meaning of his work. He was aware of his unique contribution that expanded the time dimension and theoretically opened unlimited possibilities to images in rapid succession. From that time on, images would no longer be repeated at each turn of the crank, but would flow, telling a story, forming a narrative movement. Before, the available devices were visual music boxes which displayed a few images over and over again. After Reynaud's invention, the core of the performance was no longer the simple 'wonder' originated by a drawing (or a picture) that moved, but 'entertainment' itself.

Two films by Reynaud remain[21]: *Pauvre Pierrot* and *Autour d'une cabine* (Around a Bathing Hut), true little comedies performed by drawn actors in the spirit of the times. The exquisitely delicate *Autour d'une cabine* displays an amiable turn-of-the-century taste, a narrative enriched by details (a flight of seagulls, a group of comic bathers) and a feeling for colour. While the drawing itself is nothing more than an example of good graphics, the movement is impressive even to the present-day viewer. (This is even truer if we take the praxinoscope bands into consideration.) Indeed, animation is not the art of drawing that moves, but the art of movement which is drawn, as Norman McLaren remarked fifty years later. Reynaud's drawing becomes beautiful when it moves, because the inventor of animation sensed that drawings had to be functional to their dynamics.

Reynaud did not want to use photography for his pantomimes, despite the advantages that this might have brought him. A one-time photographer, he did not like the exact reproduction of physical reality. On the contrary, he was a graphic artist in the tradition of Salomon, who had brought the art of retouching to virtuoso levels, working by hand on the negatives and obtaining images that had little to do with the original but were graphic and pictorial creations. When Reynaud agreed to use photographic equipment

---

[21] In Reynaud's case, 'to remain' is an improper verb. To make a long restoration story short, let's say that we can currently view the films that Julien Pappé and Andrzej Dyja have made from the original bands.

in the last years of the century, he did so in order to lighten his workload as a draftsman. He called upon two comics, Footit and Chocolat, and filmed their routines. He asked the actor Galipaux to perform the piece that had made him famous, *Le premier cigare* (The First Cigar), in front of the camera. Then he chose the photographs one by one and retouched them. What counted was human intervention; craftsmanship, to Reynaud, was the mother of art.

Historically speaking, this man's adventure is an island of time before time. He wrote, designed, drew, directed animated motion pictures, and even had them set to music (by Gaston Paulin, 1839–1903). He successfully projected them onto a screen to paying audiences. If we decide we believe in records and primacies, the actual history of animation starts with him.

But his experience was sterile.

Ironically enough, this inventor who believed in rational science and mechanics failed because he put his faith in machinery that was too tortuous to function well. Also too tortuous, in the era of the masses, to be mass produced, mass handled, and to satisfy mass production and mass entertainment.

The *Théâtre Optique* and How It Worked

The celluloid band upon which the images are painted is represented in (A); the operator can rotate it both ways by means of two levers.

The images go past a lantern (B). Thanks to a lens (C), they are projected onto an inclined mirror (M); the latter projects them onto a transparent screen (E). A further projection lantern (D) casts the fixed scenery on the screen (*La Nature*, No. 999, Paris, 23 July 1892).

By using two large spools to feed and take up the extended picture band, sequences were no longer limited to short cyclic movements. The images were originally painted on a celluloid band, with holes between the pictures engaging in pins on the revolving wheel, so that each picture was aligned with a facet of the mirror drum. After a few weeks of Musée Grévin shows, the band proved to be too easily subject to wear, so Reynaud painted his stories again on gelatine squares that he fastened between leather bands, with holes in metal strips between the pictures. The mirror drum had thirty-six facets (instead of the twelve of the praxinoscope), and its rotation was perfectly synchronized with the picture band.

Figure 2.7 Émile Reynaud, *Théâtre optique*.

The *théâtre optique* was presented at the 1889 Universal Exhibition in Paris, which both Thomas A. Edison and the Lumière brothers attended. It is possible that either one or both parties were impressed by Reynaud's idea to use the perforation on the band to drag the series of images and stole it. Edison would use four perforations, Louis and Auguste Lumière two.

On with the Lantern Show

'The magic lantern is a small optical machine that in the darkness, on a white wall, shows various spectres and monsters, so dreadful that people who don't know its secret believe that everything is done out of magic', wrote Antoine Furetière in his *Dictionnaire Universel*, way back in 1690.[22]

It is unclear when and by whom this machine was invented, but we have evidence that by the second half of the seventeenth century it already existed. It was

> the most enduring, the most inventive, and the most artistic out of all the mother-ideas that would pay with their life for the birth of cinema. During its reign, which spread out along three centuries, it offered still and animated artificial images to more and more admiring and demanding audiences, and travelled round the world at an unbelievable speed.[23]

In the nineteenth century, it was at the height of its glory. By the end of it, this invention had disappeared.

In a way, one could even maintain that cinema and animation started to exist along with the magic lantern shows. In fact, these projections often told stories, were often enriched with optical and sound effects, and often used double exposures and movable glass slides (instead of still ones) to give the feeling of action.[24] However, the history of the magic lantern ran parallel to the pre-history of cinema and animation, almost without mutual influences.

The older brother bequeathed moving images – the fundamental element of projection – to a public audience; without it, moving images wouldn't have made the leap from optical curiosity to mass entertainment. Furthermore, it is also true that the projectors and the film reels that we have known during the whole twentieth century were neither more nor less than modified and perfected magic lanterns and magic lantern slides.[25]

Like old soldiers, the tool didn't die, it only faded away. Slowly it became a toy to be used domestically. Lantern slides lasted until the 1950s of the twentieth century, when their popularity declined with the introduction of transparencies. Finally, the Kodachrome 35-mm slides proved less expensive to produce than lantern slides.

Colour Music

Since the seventeenth century, some Western men of learning meditated on synaesthesia, an idea that means either appreciating the same thing with various senses (which is a normal case: We all savour, smell, touch with the tongue our food/drink),

---

[22] Quoted in Laurent Mannoni, Le grand art de la lumière et de l'ombre, Nathan, Paris, 1994.
[23] Laurent Mannoni, Le grand art de la lumière et de l'ombre, Nathan, Paris, 1994.
[24] On the other hand, they entirely depended on the action, skill, and inspiration of the projectionist showman, so to our intellect they seem to be more 'theatre' – the way puppeteering is 'theatre'.
[25] Some more information, good to stir even more up the querelle on the birth of animation, is provided by the French scholar Yves Rifaux. In his booklet 'A propos de l'invention du cinéma d'animation' (Jica Diffusion, Annecy, France, 1990), Rifaux writes:

> As soon as 1897, some manufacturers of magic lanterns for children launched on the toy market projection devices for animated views. These manufacturers were . . . Lapierre in France, Bing, Carette, Karl Bub and Ernst Planck in Germany. All these devices . . . were equipped with a Maltese cross or a cam to project films in loops. [The latter] were what we can consider as the first cartoons.
>
> British historian David Robinson also deals with this matter in his 'Incunabula of Animation' (*Griffithiana*, No. 38–39, October 1990, Pordenone, Italy).

or feeling the same experience through different senses.[26]

Creators especially looked for colour music. In other words, they looked for a work of art that could be exactly the same to the eye and to the ear. They were inspired by Isaac Newton's statement that in his opinion each one of the seven notes of the Western scale corresponds to a colour in the rainbow. The question was then raised: Since we have a musical scale, can we have a chromatic scale? Is it music perfectly translatable into vision? Or is possible to reach just a combination, a marriage of two parallel experiences, like music plus physical movement (= dancing)?

The search for colour music was like a Karstic river, which flows, falls into the subsoil, resurfaces, falls again. Most of the inventors/artists who devoted themselves to the project were actually convinced than nobody else had previously tried his hand at it.

The French Jesuit monk Louis-Bertrand Castel (1688–1757) published in 1725 an essay proposing an 'eye harpsichord' (*clavecin oculaire*) and reportedly built two prototypes in 1734 and 1754, to no success. In England, in 1789, Erasmus Darwin suggested producing visual music by projecting light from oil lamps through coloured glass. In 1844, his compatriot D. D. Jameson published a pamphlet, *Colour-Music*, in which he described a system of notation for the new art form and an instrument that filtered light through liquids of various colours and reflected it off of metal plates onto a wall. The Swiss Frédéric Kastner proposed a pyrophone around 1870 (it used coloured gas flames to produce light and sound at the same time, obtaining the physical effect of so-called singing flames); the New Yorker Bainbridge Bishop (1837–1905) patented a colour organ in 1876; the Briton Alexander Wallace Rimington (1854–1918) patented a different device by the same name in 1894 and wrote the stimulating book *Colour-Music – The Art of Mobile Colour*[27]; James M. Loring from Saint Louis, Missouri, applied for his musical chromoscope (a piano with coloured light bulbs) in 1900.

French poets Charles Baudelaire (1821–1867) and Arthur Rimbaud (1854–1891), French novelist Joris-Karl Huysmans (1848–1907), Russian composer Aleksandr Skriabin (1872–1915), and more artists later maintained that they were synaesthetes – not in the medical sense of the word, but metaphorically. Baudelaire wrote that 'Perfumes, colours and sound reply to one another' (*Correspondances*), while Rimbaud even invented letters' colours in his *Vowels Sonnet* ('A black, E white, I red, U green, O blue / Someday I'll crack your nascent origins . . . '). In the same second half of the nineteenth century, German opera composer Richard Wagner was looking for the Total Work of Art (*Gesamtkunstwerk*).

That was the era of symbolism, an intricate artistic and spiritualistic movement where occultism and esoteric wisdom let people cherish parallel universes and cosmic fusion according to Pythagoras's (570–490 BC) ancient speculations.

Even science was influenced by the spirit of the age: The chart of published papers on synaesthesia from the 1850s to the 1990s has its peaks in the 1880s and in the 1890s.

What does this have to do with the subject matter of this book?

Without this Karstic river, we wouldn't have had abstract animation, which was not originally born out of trivial transposition from the suddenly successful abstract painting. The two things of course combined. It would be a mistake, for instance, to consider Walther Ruttmann a colour-music filmmaker, while his contemporary Oskar Fischinger certainly was.[28]

---

[26] Scientifically speaking, synaesthesia is also a serious (although rare) psychiatric condition. The patient senses tastes while touching a surface, sees colours while hearing sounds, and so on.
[27] Hutchinson & Co., London, 1912.
[28] The fireworks shows, documented in China as early as the seventh century, were chronologically the first example of abstract animation. Every firework is made of motion, light, colour, sound, and time. Furthermore, it is endlessly repeatable: a skyrocket does not produce a different result every time (= performing arts) but a consistent one (= fine arts). Pyrotechnics evolved on its own without influencing other arts, and about its history and aesthetics very little (too little) has been written.

Cinema of Attractions

We all know by heart the date of the birth of cinema: Paris, 28 December 1895. That night, the brothers Louis and Auguste Lumière 1) projected 2) photographic moving pictures 3) on a screen 4) in front of a paying audience.

Of course, it's pure convention. That Parisian winter night only witnessed something that looked very much like what people would consider 'cinema' twenty-five years later.

Cinema – and animation – had many fathers, inventors, creators, and improvers. They also had many good-intentioned patriotic scholars who claimed for their country the glory that France had already boasted. This writer is convinced that such a problem shouldn't even be raised and thus will certainly not attempt to propose a solution.

On the other hand, both in the United States and in Europe, from about 1894 to about 1908, the moving image shows didn't actually look very much like *Gone with the Wind* or *Spirited Away*.

Screenings seldom took place in specialized places. They rather did so in fairs, markets, country festivals, churches, schools, and vaudeville theatres. Programmes consisted of separate views: The earlier ones shocked spectators just because of the old surprise, the reproduction of 'true life' on a screen (for instance, *Rough Sea at Dover*, Birt Acres, 1895); the latter ones carried them away because of the exhibition of any sort of sensational thrills.

In vaudeville theatres, the film was an act within the variety format, and the performer often interacted with the artificial images. Emcees, no less than serious lecturers and teachers inheriting the lantern tradition, made the most of the new entry. Unlike the posterior narrative cinema, which imitated theatre acting and was based on a 'willing suspension of disbelief',[29] much of early cinema showed a magician or exhibitor acknowledging the audience, looking towards the camera, and sometimes soliciting the viewers' attention.

In Europe, the exploitation and exhibition was often done by itinerant fairground showmen, while the first American nickelodeon[30] (cheap, plebe, but permanent theatre) was opened as late as 1905 by Pittsburgh impresario John P. Harris.

Three nations led the market of the era: the United States, Great Britain, and France. By 1910, British inventiveness and industry suffered greatly at the hands of aggressive American competition; World War I and its economic aftermath put them once and for all in a secondary world position.

Historians Tom Gunning and André Gaudreault called this phase the 'cinema of attractions', to be followed by a period, whose beginning and end are difficult to exactly identify, in which films increasingly organized themselves around the tasks of narrative.

Frame by Frame

Technology was simple. A camera recorded actions on a celluloid negative photographic strip: 'film' par excellence. This happened because the operator, with his manual crank, exposed the strip to the actions through the camera objective, at a certain speed (normally sixteen frames per second). From the negative, some positive copies were printed, and eventually a projector equipped with a lamp screened the copies – at the same sixteen-frame-per-second speed.

Did that technology have secrets? It did. A good cameraman had to know or invent many 'tricks': reverse projection, slow motion, fast motion, substitution of actors with objects, use of reduced scale models, mask and counter-mask, double exposure, etc.

One of these matters a great deal: the frame-by-frame technique.

Assuming that the projection speed is sixteen frames per second, what will happen if we shoot those frames one by one, instead of consecutively?

A still object, click, a picture. The same – slightly displaced – a picture. The same – slightly displaced again – a third picture. And so on, thirteen more times. Eventually we will project the film and we'll see . . . one second of a self-moving object. Self-motion of a motionless entity.

This 'trick' was special. It was bound to become a language, and to give birth, as such, to the twin of live-action cinema, animation.

In the following paragraphs, we'll examine the deeds of some pioneers who made good use of the frame-by-frame technique.

---

[29] Samuel T. Coleridge coined the phrase in his *Biographia Literaria* (1817).
[30] Admittance cost: a nickel (equal to five cents of a dollar). Nickelodeons are often mistaken for pre-existing penny arcades, places that provided a variety of inexpensive amusement, including, for instance, Edison's kinetoscopes (individual peep-show machines).

Arthur Melbourne-Cooper

The son of a photographer, Arthur Melbourne-Cooper was born on 15 April 1874 in Saint Albans, Hertfordshire, UK, and died on 24 November 1961 in Coton, near Cambridge.[31]

In 1892, when he applied at Birt Acres[32] for a job, he was an eighteen-year-old professional who had learned the rudiments of photography in his father's workshop. A weak entrepreneur, Acres couldn't provide his assistant with a bright future, so Melbourne-Cooper became a freelance cameraman. He would either make sponsored films or sell his own productions to exhibitors. The leading Empire Theatre, Leicester Square, London, customarily showed his pictures as part of its variety programmes.

During the Boer War (1899–1902), there was a shortage of matches with the troops at the African fronts, and Bryant and May, one of England's important brands of matches, launched a marketing campaign to appeal to customers. On the request of a women's welfare committee to support the troops, Melbourne-Cooper made a film called *Matches' Appeal*, which premiered at the Empire Theatre in 1899. It's the oldest frame-by-frame film ever made.[33]

We see some matches forming themselves into two matchstick figures and a ladder. One figure holds the ladder steady and the other one climbs it so that he can write something on a black wall: 'An appeal. For one guinea,[34] Messrs Bryant and May will forward a case, containing enough matches to give a box to each man in a battalion with name of the sender inside N.B. Our soldiers need them.'

The film was made in the cellars of Garrick Mansions, 12 Charing Cross Road, London, where at the time Cooper had his trading offices under the name of Cine Syndicate and a small studio and showroom.[35]

Out of the thirty-six pictures of the animated filmography established by Tjitte de Vries and Ati Mul, more were based on matchstick figures. Only two still exist: *Matches' Handball* (or *Animated Matches: Playing Volleyball*, 1899; the existing print has no original title) and *Animated Matches: Cricket: Vestas V. Pine* (1899). In 1908, Cooper made another memorable animated film, *Dream of Toyland*, in which toys, given as presents to a child one afternoon, come alive in the child's dream. The puppets are animated with precision and delicacy, despite quickly rotating shadows that give rise to a somewhat bizarre atmosphere (instead of artificial illumination, the animator still used sunlight, and the frame-by-frame work was affected by the Earth's rotation).

Figure 2.8 Arthur Melbourne-Cooper, *Matches' Appeal*, 1899.

---

[31] All we know about Arthur Melbourne-Cooper was dug out by historians Tjitte de Vries and Ati Mul, whom this writer owes gratitude to. The evidence that *Matches' Appeal* was made in 1899 was challenged by some scholars and is not 100 per cent final, but this writer's choice is to accept such a dating until this is proven otherwise.

[32] Birt Acres (1852–1918) was a photographic technician who became a leading film pioneer. Independently, he invented a cinematographic (Kinetic) camera by early 1895. His first public screenings date just a few days after the Lumière brothers' ones.

[33] Also known as *Matches: An Appeal*. It may not be the first animated work of this filmmaker, but information is too scarce about his former films.

[34] A guinea was worth twenty-one shillings (a little more than a pound) and was used to pay for honourable causes.

[35] By the mid-1890s, Cooper had his own frame-by-frame device. From an old photographic camera he took the shutter with a spring button and put this behind the lens. Inside the camera, at the side of the sprocket, he placed a pin with a spring. He bore a hole in the side of the sprocket in which the sprung pin fitted. The pin would prevent the sprocket going further than one frame at a time and keep the film steady and the image registered. After the picture was taken, the pin would be released and the film could be wound forward until the pin would get stuck into the hole again to hold it for the next shot. Cooper refused to patent his animation camera, on the grounds that 'patents didn't do any good to [my master] Birt Acres'.

It would be a mistake to consider Arthur Melbourne-Cooper an animator only. As most pioneers in those days, he was an all-round filmmaker. In 1901, back in his hometown of Saint Albans, he formed his own Alpha Cinematograph Company. Under this aegis, he produced a large number of live-action commercials, documentaries, comedies, dramas, plus some animated films. In 1908, he opened the elegant Alpha Picture Palace in Saint Albans; a second film theatre would follow in 1909 in Letchworth.

One year later, the theatre in Letchworth suffered two fires, while the American film import was eroding national production. Cooper was forced to sell his properties and leave Saint Albans. He went with his family to Manor Park in Lee (then Kent, now Lewisham) where he continued filmmaking. His Alpha Trading Company was bought out by a new company, Kinema Industries Ltd., with offices in London. A year later, he established with Andrew Heron a second company, Heron Films Ltd., for the production of feature films. But in 1914 World War I put an end to this, as Andrew Heron joined the army, and Cooper (rejected for being short of stature and already forty years old) became a munitions inspector in Luton.

After the war, he was for a time a season photographer in South End, but a couple of years later he had his own department, Animads, with Langford Advertising Agency in Blackpool. Here, he produced, next to advertisement slides for the national cinemas, a series of sponsored animation pictures. He lived in retirement for the last twenty years of his life.

Walter Robert Booth

By the turn of the century, Walter Robert Booth (Worcester, 1869–Birmingham, 1938), a former china painter, cartoonist, and conjurer, had entered into a collaboration with cinema pioneer, inventor, producer, and showman Robert William Paul (1869–1943).

They started, writes Denis Gifford,[36]

with *The Miser's Doom* and *Upside Down; or, the Human Flies* (1899) in which, by turning the camera upside down, he made his actors perform on the ceiling. Many of his early films were based on conjuring tricks (*Hindoo Jugglers*, *Chinese Magic*, both 1900), and with *The Devil in the Studio* (1901) he began to introduce effects involving cartoon type artwork. Later that year his *Artistic Creation* featured rudimentary animation, while his *Political Favourites* (1903) featured Booth in person rapidly drawing caricatures of Lord Rosebery, Joseph Chamberlain and other current politicians.

Charles Urban (1867–1942), an American who was born in Cincinnati, Ohio, and had moved to London in 1897, swiftly became the most significant figure in the British film industry at that time. In 1903, he formed the Charles Urban Trading Company, specializing in documentary and news films but not neglecting the works of Walter R. Booth. The latter was the protagonist in 1906 of a Paul-Urban co-production, which resulted in a typical lightning sketch animated film, *The Hand of the Artist*. The hand sketches a man and a woman who embrace and dance. More subjects follow, and after each of them the hand crumples up the paper and dispenses it in the form of confetti.

Booth constructed his own outdoor studio in the back garden of Neville Lodge, Woodlands, Isleworth, London W, and here, with F. Harold Bastick as his cameraman, he directed many more pictures for Urban.

He specialized in action adventure trick films, some of which have attracted the praise of science fiction current specialists and fans.

The Airship Destroyer (1909) plays on the ever-recurring fear of aerial invasion. A dirigible fleet attacks the country, and only a missile created by a young inventor saves the day – and his love story. Although it betrays its sparse budget, *The Airship Destroyer* is fairly good. It was projected again in 1915, during World War I, when German Zeppelin

---

[36] www.victorian.cinema.net/walterbooth.htm, retrieved 10 August 2009.

air raids were an actual threat. (By the end of the war, about 1,500 British civilians were killed.)

In 1910, *The Aerial Submarine* followed. A boy and his sister detect submarine pirates from a cliff, but they are made prisoners. They witness the torpedoing and looting of a liner, the flight into the sky of the wonder vehicle, an accident to the engines. The submarine drops to Earth and the pirates swarm out, but to their death. The kidnapped children escape, leaving the aerial submarine a total wreck.

One year more, and Booth depicted what anarchists (the terrorists of 1911) could do if equipped with the most advanced technology. *The Aerial Anarchists* shows the bombing raid of some flying political extremists who destroy a fort, a railway bridge, London's St. Paul Cathedral, a church, and a just-married couple until they are defeated in an air battle, have to land, reach their hideout, and finally are exterminated by the explosion of one of their own bombs.

Walter R. Booth stopped in 1915, when he entered the publicity film market, making advertising shorts for Cadbury's cocoa and chocolate, including *A Cure for Cross Words*. He also invented an advertising method called Flashing Film Ads: 'Unique colour effects in light and movement'.

Edwin Stanton Porter

The name of Edwin Stanton Porter (Connellsville, Pennsylvania, 21 April 1870–New York, 30 April 1941) is famous among the specialists of early cinema and unknown elsewhere.

'Basically a mechanic-inventor rather than an artist-director', wrote scriptwriter Budd Schulberg,[37] 'Ed Porter happened to see one of the supernatural films that the French magician Georges Méliès had made in Paris. . . . With his mechanical mind . . . he examined these innovative movies frame by frame'. Then he experimented with trick photography, puppet animation, and split-screen shots.

In 1902, he turned out for Thomas A. Edison a five-minute subject titled *Life of an American Fireman*, the first American motion picture in which editing was utilized to create a dramatic continuity from several otherwise unrelated scenes. Then in 1903 came his masterpiece, *The Great Train Robbery*, the father of all Western movies and the fledgling industry's first box office hit. Oddly enough, they were both very realistic live-action films and are considered the groundbreaking examples of narrative cinema.

At the same time, feeling no contradiction, Porter directed many trick films (for instance, the excellent *Jack and the Beanstalk*, 1902).

In 1907, he directed along with his collaborator Wallace McCutcheon *The 'Teddy' Bears*, 'part charming fairy tale, part violent political satire, and part accomplished puppet animation'.[38] In short, the script takes the Goldilocks children's story, combines it with the (true) anecdote of hunting President Theodore 'Teddy' Roosevelt, who had declined to shoot a bear cub after killing its mother, and seasons the whole thing with those furry stuffed toys called teddy bears that had become a nationwide fad. The film was meant, according to its advertisements, to be a satire on that craze.

The relevant (to us) element is the frame-by-frame animated sequence showing a group of toy teddy bears of various sizes putting on an acrobatic ballet. Their behaviour is rather mechanical, more 'motion' than 'animation', but technically impeccable for the times.

Porter left Edison in 1909 to produce films on his own; then, little by little, he retired from the business, aware that he was only fit for first-decade motion pictures, with nickelodeons, illiterate audiences, popular entertainment – but not for the sophisticated middle-class dream machine that cinema was becoming. As an epitaph, Budd Schulberg comments:

---

[37] *Moving Pictures – Memories of a Hollywood Prince*, Stein and Day, Briarcliff Manor, New York, 1981. Budd Schulberg, the 1954 Academy Award winner for his screenplay for *On the Waterfront*, is the son of writer and manager B. P. Schulberg. He had a nephew-uncle relationship with Edwin S. Porter, whom his father was writing screenplays for. Born on 27 March 1914 in New York City, Budd Schulberg died on 5 August 2009 in Westhampton Beach, Long Island, New York.

[38] Scott Simmon, *More Treasures from American Film Archives 1894–1931*, National Film Preservation Foundation, San Francisco 2004 (booklet included in the three-DVD case).

> Fifty years later I happened to mention Porter's name to one of this country's most famous directors. 'Edwin S. Porter?' he said. 'I never heard of him'. 'Pal', I said, 'if there hadn't been an Edwin S. Porter, there might never have been a you'.

James Stuart Blackton

As for what he actually put up on the screen, a short list of credits that could arguably be ascribed to [James Stuart] Blackton include: the first combination actor-director-producer; the first national exhibitor-distributor; the first star maker; the first film propagandist; the first motion-picture-studio chief; a pioneer in single-frame animation; an experimentalist in colour; an originator of special effects; the first to adapt theatrical classics to films of any significant length; the first to shoot films for use in plays; the editor and publisher of the first important star magazine; a developer of backlighting and the close shot; organizer of the forerunner to the Association of Motion Picture Producers and Distributors of America; the first to make a series of comic shorts featuring the same character; the first exhibitor to open an upscale movie theatre; and the inventor of the newsreel.[39]

James Stuart Blackton was an Englishman, born (as far as can be ascertained) in Sheffield on 4 January 1875. Ten years later, his family settled in Morrisania, now the southwestern Bronx; he developed most of his career in and around New York City. Although he made war propaganda films for the United States,[40] he always boasted his British patriotism and didn't apply for American citizenship until 1915; the founder of American Vitagraph Company, he died in Los Angeles on 13 August 1941.

This pioneer was an outstanding and multifaceted motion picture tycoon. The biography written by his daughter[41] never even mentions his involvement in animation. Although an immodest and accustomed public relations man, he never claimed any paternity to the art.[42]

James Stuart Blackton started his show business career as a stage entertainer along with his friend and long-lasting associate Albert E. Smith (1875–1958).

> [In 1896] the duo . . . travelled the Lyceum circuit of churches and YMCA's, putting on an evening's entertainment made up of a variety of acts: sleight of hand, chapeaugraphy, ventriloquism, Blackton's lightning sketches and a magic lantern show which customarily closed the evening. Blackton apparently painted many of the slides which were projected onto a screen accompanied by his monologue.[43]

This is why and how Blackton entered moviemaking: He needed films of himself at work in order to screen them during his act and a library of self-produced films in order to match up to the seething, competitive, and often illegal New York market of copies. For various years, he was in an endless collaboration/lawsuit relationship with Thomas A. Edison.[44]

The lightning sketches (or 'chalk talks') were vaudeville acts during which an artist drew quick caricatures of viewers or modified a drawing while doing his monologue. (Many English and American animated proto-films were no more than lightning sketches that had been transposed to the screen.) *The Enchanted Drawing* (1900) is among the few remaining ones. It's a trick film in the Méliès

---

[39] Don Dewey, 'Man of a Thousand Firsts', *American Film*, Vol. XV, No. 14, November 1990.
[40] The most famous being *Tearing Down the Spanish Flag* (1898) and *The Battle Cry of Peace* (1915).
[41] Marian Blackton Trimble (with the help of Anthony Slide), *J. Stuart Blackton – A Personal Biography by His Daughter*, The Scarecrow Press, Metuchen, New Jersey, 1985.
[42] There are rumours of a frame-by-frame film of 1898, *The Humpty Dumpty Circus*, made with toys, but the copy is lost and the date is uncertain – to put it mildly.
[43] Charles Musser, 'American Vitagraph: 1897–1900', *Cinema Journal*, Vol. XXII, No. 3, Spring 1983.
[44] It is a made-up (by Blackton) legend that he met the Edison as a young journalist, sketched him from life, and was hired by him out of pure artistic admiration.

style that shows the artist (Blackton) drawing on a large sheet of paper, transforming a drawn bottle into an actual one and then having more drawings undergo 'magic' changes. His most famous production, *Humorous Phases of Funny Faces* (1906), featured comic portraits of a man rolling his eyes and puffing smoke, a long-nosed character and a dog jumping through a ring. It still is a lightning sketch, although the drawings displayed an exceptional autonomy, while the artist-designer's presence was suggested by the appearance of his hand on the screen.

In 1907, Blackton released *The Haunted Hotel*, a live-action film in which the frame-by-frame technique enlivened the supernatural effects of the haunted hotel. Donald Crafton writes:

> The impact of *The Haunted Hotel* was much greater in Europe than at home. . . . It was showcased and heavily advertised when the [Vitagraph] company opened its Paris office in February 1907. There is evidence that an aura of secrecy surrounding the technique of animation was created deliberately.[45]

Then, the animator that was in Blackton vanished. Years later, in a note, he would carelessly dismiss his early camera tricks. In spite of that, notes Donald Crafton again:

> [His] interest in animation, from the time he began experimenting with it around the turn of the century through 1909, was more than just a diversion. He created and modified techniques for perfecting the illusion of 'real' motion that is at the heart of animation. In his films that incorporated the Hand of the Artist motif, he articulated the theme of self-figuration, representing the artist as the mythic bringer of life to his inanimate art.[46]

The Haunted Hotel was amply imitated, and it spurred a search for the trick behind that uncanny movement that most filmgoers were seeing for the first time. It also triggered many people's interest in cinema, including Émile Cohl's.

For their animated works, Blackton and his contemporaries used the frame-by-frame technique as a way to 'stupefy' people by creating 'magical' effects. After Blackton's contribution, only one more step was needed before film animation became such in the full sense of the word. That step would be taken by Émile Cohl in Paris.

---

[45] Donald Crafton, 'J. Stuart Blackton's Animated Films', in Charles Solomon (ed.) *The Art of the Animated Image*, The American Film Institute, Los Angeles, 1987.

[46] Donald Crafton, 'J. Stuart Blackton's Animated Films', in Charles Solomon (ed.) *The Art of the Animated Image*, The American Film Institute, Los Angeles, 1987.

THE SECOND PERIOD

The Second Period embraces the entire silent film era and ends with a specific date: 18 November 1928, the day of the public screening of Walt Disney's first 'talkie', the short film *Steamboat Willie*. We will call this period 'The Silent Pioneers (1908–1928)'.

3

THE SILENT PIONEERS (1908–1928)

The Cradle

Days of Heaven and Hell

Politically, economically, and militarily, the first fourteen years of the twentieth century were the continuance of the century before. The only novelty was the dawning of Japan as a modern power after the Meiji Restoration of 1868, the annexation of Formosa (which later became Taiwan) in 1896, the victorious war against Tsarist Russia in 1904–1905, and the conquest and colonization of Korea in 1910.

The global map was only slightly and peripherally retouched according to new colonized areas or because of changes of influence (since 1898, for instance, after having defeated Spain, the United States has exercised a de facto protectorate on Cuba, Puerto Rico, Guam, and the Philippines). In 1901, Australia became independent; in 1910, Mexico was the scene of the first revolution of the century, with many social and political implications; and in 1911, the Chinese Empire became the Chinese Republic.

In the developed countries, the middle class was in such full bloom that the era was called the Belle Époque.

On 28 June 1914, in Sarajevo (Bosnia), a student by the name of Gavrilo Prinčip assassinated Archduke Franz Ferdinand of Habsburg, heir to the throne of the Austro-Hungarian Empire. The Viennese Chancellery regarded the government of Serbia, Prinčip's country, as responsible. A month later, the chancellery declared a war that would become the largest slaughter in history up to that point in time.

Six or seven years later, after the end of World War I and the signature of various peace treaties, the map of Europe was almost intact on the western side but was completely new on the eastern one. Austria had become a small country; Poland was independent again after more than 120 years; independent again, although territorially mutilated, were Hungary and Ireland; a new republic combined the Czech and the Slovak peoples; a new kingdom tried to glue together, under the name of Yugoslavia, Serbs, Croats, Slovenes, Bosnians, Macedonians, Montenegrins, and various minorities; and Albania, Lithuania, Latvia, Estonia, and Finland made their debut on the international stage.

Germany and Austria-Hungary had lost the war, but everybody in Europe lost peace.

Economies were out of breath. Great Britain started to realize that her gigantic empire was more expensive than profitable; France suffered from a chronic political instability; and Italy fell into a fascist dictatorship. After the Bolshevik coup d'état and a civil war (1917–1920), Russia had become everybody's bugbear. Her new name was the Union of the Socialist[1] Soviet Republics, and until the late 1920s her project was to expand the proletarian revolution to the whole planet. The threat was real: In many states, communist parties were active and had well-organized groups of devotees.

The United States, whose intervention in 1917 had tipped the scale in favour of England and her allies, eventually disagreed with European politics and chose isolationism. She enjoyed a good economic situation and experienced exciting times that were called the Roaring 1920s, the Jazz Age, or the Lawless Decade – depending on the standpoint.

Culture

Intellect ran a different course. Most revolutions took place before World War I. In 1900, Sigmund Freud

---

[1] Why 'socialist' instead of 'communist'? According to Marxist principles, 'socialist' is the temporary system that eventually leads to a 'communist' society. Of course, democratic socialist parties such as the British Labour Party gave the word a very different meaning.

published *The Interpretation of Dreams* and Max Planck developed quantum theory; in 1903, Ivan P. Pavlov discovered conditioned reflexes; in 1905, Albert Einstein introduced the theory of relativity, while Fauvism (Matisse, Derain, and Vlaminck) was marking French painting and the artistic movement Die Brücke was founded in Dresden. In 1907, Pablo Picasso painted *Les demoiselles d'Avignon*, starting cubism, and Georges Braque enthusiastically seconded him; in 1908, Wilhelm Worringer published *Abstraktion und Einfühlung – Ein Beitrag zur Stilpsychologie* (*Abstraction and Empathy: Essays in the Psychology of Style*, one of the most widely read books on the theory of art); in 1908, Arnold Schönberg started atonal music, the first phase of dodecaphony (and in 1908, Émile Cohl created *Fantasmagorie*). In 1909, Filippo Tommaso Marinetti published the 'Futurist Manifesto'[2]; in 1913, Marcel Proust published *Swann's Way*, the first tome of his *In Search of Lost Time*. In the same year, Igor Stravinsky wrote *The Rite of Spring*, Ferdinand de Saussure wrote the *Course in General Linguistics*, and Bengali poet Rabindranath Tagore was given the Nobel Prize.

The rush would slow down but not stop. During the war, James Joyce, Luigi Pirandello, Franz Kafka, and Vladimir Mayakovsky published their works; various artists founded the Dada movement; and Piet Mondrian and Theo Van Doesburg founded De Stijl. After the war, Walter Gropius founded the Bauhaus in Weimar and American writers such as Gertrude Stein, Ernest Hemingway, Sherwood Anderson, Eugene O'Neill, and later Francis Scott Fitzgerald (the 'lost generation') gathered in Paris. In 1922, poet Thomas S. Eliot published the verses of *The Waste Land* and philosopher Ludwig Wittgenstein published his *Tractatus logico-filosoficus*; one year later, another German philosopher, Martin Heidegger, published *Being and Time*. In 1923, Lu Hsun published his collected short stories with the title of *A Call to Arms*. Surrealism was born in 1924, the same year as George Gershwin's *Rhapsody in Blue* and the first jazz orchestra conducted by Duke Ellington. German physicist Werner Heisenberg developed the uncertainty principle in 1927.

Cinema

The world of film expanded vigorously, too. Production companies stopped aiming at an illiterate and proletarian audience, as middle-class customers proved that they considered cinema as entertaining as legitimate theatre. Movie houses began to replace itinerant shows more and more, distribution became a well-organized profession, and the star system gained a footing.

By 1915 (the year of David W. Griffith's *The Birth of a Nation*), the cinema of attractions had given way to classical cinema (or the cinema of institutions). By the end of the 1920s, cinema was already considered the Seventh Art,[3] and some masterpieces had already made their mark, including Charlie Chaplin's shorts and features *The Kid* (1921) and *The Gold Rush* (1925); Robert J. Flaherty's *Nanook of the North* (1921); Friedrich Wilhelm Murnau's *Nosferatu* (1922), *The Last Laugh* (1925), and *Sunrise* (1927); Sergei M. Eisenstein's *Battleship Potemkin* (1925); Buster Keaton's *The General* (1927); Carl Th. Dreyer's *The Passion of Joan of Arc* (1928); and King Vidor's *The Crowd* (1928).

Within this general outline, silent animation matters for the specialists only. Although some good animated films were made, the phenomenon as a whole was little more than a curiosity.

Narrative and Non-Narrative

Handbooks tell us that the cinema of attractions was based on non-fiction films, while the classical cinema was based on narrative and narrative language. The shift took more a decade, but little by little audiences were driven to agree that consecutive scenes meant various moments of the same action; that a close-up didn't imply that the actor had been beheaded; that an iris in/iris out signified the passing of time or a change of place; and so on. In other words, via trial and error, an alliance of audiences and filmmakers created the special visual (later audiovisual) language of cinema.

---

[2] Futurism was unique in that it existed entirely on paper some time before any actual works were produced. It was, in fact, not only an artistic but also a cultural, political, and ethic movement, and the Manifesto was basically a harangue. Its aim became the representation, by distorting and disarranging images, of the ceaseless activity and confusion of modern urban life. It was an age in which intoxicating new forms of transport and communication – bicycles, motorcycles, cars, express trains, planes, ocean liners, the telegraph, the telephone – seemed to be transforming the globe and even the human race. The initial futurist exhibition opened in Paris in February 1912, eliciting outraged criticism, and then went on a tour of northern European capitals, taking in London, Berlin, Amsterdam, and Brussels, from which news of the movement rapidly spread, soon reaching the United States, Russia, and Japan.

[3] Italian-French critic Ricciotto Canudo created the definition in 1911.

It would be an international language. It would also be the first example in history of global cultural colonization, as the rest of the world, without exception, accepted what had been decided in Europe and in the United States.[4]

Handbooks, however, don't clearly tell us what narrative is. Is it just a duplicate of a novel on the screen? Or is it the linking together of various expressions in time, according to a rule?

Actually, non-narrative films do tell a 'story' – for instance, the story of the evolution of a feeling – via analogy or metaphor, and in this writer's opinion, in order to avoid misunderstandings, the appropriate term could be fourth-dimensional art.[5]

Terminological fussiness? Maybe – but for a reason that will be clarified in the next paragraph.

Fantasmagorie

A hand draws a little white clown on black scenery. The character disappears behind a man who drops from above and who we then see sitting in a movie house, disturbed by the enormous hat of the lady before him. He takes all the hat feathers away one by one. The clown comes out again from the lady's *lorgnette* spectacles; engulfs the man; plays jokes; meets a soldier, sees a bottle, and meets an elephant; enters a house, goes to the first floor, falls down, and loses his head after falling on the sidewalk. The hand glues the body together again; the clown swells like a balloon, mounts a horse, and eventually rides away with it.

Figure 3.1 Émile Cohl, *Fantasmagorie*, 1908.

Running time: about two minutes, with about seven hundred drawings.

Fantasmagorie was made by Frenchman Émile Cohl, whose career we'll discuss later, and screened at the Théâtre du Gymnase on 17 August 1908.

Do these two minutes start the history of our art?

First remark: The public welcomed this new type of show. The people of 1908 recognized that an animated film was different from a *film à trucs* (a film with special effects) or a *féerie* (a fairy tale or magic story) and wanted as much as possible of it. The producers entrusted Cohl with the creation of more new films. Before the year 1908 had ended, Cohl had made eight animated pictures.[6] In the future, people would ask for animation; other people would go in for the newborn profession of animation filmmaker. In history, a process 'begins' when it gives rise to a new productive stage.

Second remark: Worried about verisimilitude, James Stuart Blackton and the other lightning sketch specialists were always careful to *justify* the presence of a cartooned world next to a real world. On the contrary, the Frenchman jumped into a graphic universe filled with graphic characters. The hand was not a conjurer's hand, and the drawn figures were not moving out of magic; they were living a life of their own, thus establishing that a separate artistic universe existed.

Third remark: There is a concatenation, a flow of incoherent images there; in other words, no narration but fourth-dimensional art. It was an uncommon thing, yet nobody cared about this. It was accepted into the moving image arena the same way that limericks or nursery rhymes had been accepted in literature.

Fourth and most important: The frame-by-frame system, alone, successfully portrays those events that develop in time. And what events do we see? An elephant becoming a house, people becoming somebody else, a thin character inflating like a balloon. Metamorphoses. The metamorphosis[7] is an inborn possibility of frame-by-frame shooting, and of frame-by-frame shooting only.

Hence, a conclusion: The first stage of a new language was born. Since 17 August 1908, live action and animation would live parallel but distinct lives.

---

[4] The writer remembers a late twentieth-century conversation with some Arab live-action filmmakers who confessed that pan shots and travellings from left to right still make them feel uneasy. (Arabs write from right to left.)

[5] Neither musical symphonies nor abstract films tell the tale of somebody's adventures (narration); instead, these develop in time according to a precise artistic project (fourth-dimensional art).

[6] *Fantasmagorie, L'Hotel du silence, Le Cauchemar du Fantoche, Un Drame chez le Fantoches, Les Allumettes animées, Le Cerceau magique, Les Frères Boutdebois*, and *Le Petit soldat qui devient Dieu*.

[7] Nowadays we would call this 'morphing'.

The Fathers

Émile Cohl

Émile Cohl was born Émile Courtet on 4 January 1857 in Paris. He was proud of his surname, as Parisian as the Seine. His family, he wrote, had lived for centuries in the neighbourhood where the Bourse is situated, and his most distant ancestor was mentioned in the civil annals of 1292. Courtet worked as an apprentice to a jeweller and an assistant to a magician. He developed his congenital talent for drawing while serving in the military when he sketched portraits of the entire regiment, including his colonel. Having returned to civilian life, he studied with artist André Gill. Just as he was about to become famous, he changed his name to the Alsatian-sounding Cohl, thinking that a pinch of the exotic might be helpful. ('Cohl' sounded a bit Jewish, too, and this would ingratiate him with the Parisian press, whose ruling class was mostly Jewish.)

Cohl was a chameleon of many colours. He worked as a caricaturist for several magazines, such as *Les hommes d'aujourd'hui*, to which he supplied caricatures of Verlaine and Toulouse-Lautrec. (In 1894, that same magazine confirmed Cohl's vast notoriety by dedicating to him a cover caricature signed by Uzès.[8]) It must be noted that *Les hommes d'aujourd'hui* was a four-page magazine, each issue being monographic on the person whose caricature was published on the cover. In the 1880s, Cohl turned successfully to photography. His light comedies were performed in the theatres of the boulevards and, last but not least of his numerous hobbies, he was interested in puzzles, riddles, and toy making.

Cohl did not enter into cinema until 1907, when he and a friend, Robert Péguy (later a film director, scriptwriter, and actor), tried their luck on the travelling show business with a projector and a tent. They quickly went bankrupt. Just a few weeks later, Cohl entered Gaumont's offices; he had noted that Gaumont had plagiarized one of his vignettes and was now demanding compensation. Not only did Gaumont make no objections, but he also invited Cohl to join his 'brain trust' in the department of film tricks. Cohl accepted. At this point, history and legend overlap. According to the latter, at the same time that Cohl entered the world of cinema, Blackton's *The Haunted Hotel* arrived on French screens. Filmmakers racked their brains to understand how it was done. The legend goes that the only one to solve the problem, discovering the basic laws of what was to become his own art form, was Émile Cohl.

Indeed, the American film caused much commotion. As for Cohl, he did come to understand the technical process, and after a few months of work he completed *Fantasmagorie*.[9]

Production continued frantically until 1923. By then, Cohl remembered having made over 300 shorts, but he certainly forgot some – the actual number was much larger – adding animated films to special effects comedies, live-action shorts, and so on. By the end of 1909, he had made more than forty films. In 1910, he left Léon Gaumont and signed a contract with Pathé. In 1912, after joining the Éclair Company, he was transferred to the American branch office in Fort Lee, where he animated The Newlyweds, comic strip characters that were created by George McManus (1884–1954).[10]

The possibility that American colleagues had stolen some secrets from him was regularly suggested, but tangible evidence was never found; in any case, studying and copying other people's techniques was common. A passage from a letter he wrote from Fort Lee shows Cohl's high spirits and admiration for the teamwork and for the producers' generous compensation to the artists. His mood changed in the following years when he saw that the rationalization of labour and the economic-managerial machine enabled the Americans to produce films for the European market in such a way as to defeat competition by individual filmmakers.

In March 1914, three months before the outbreak of World War I, Cohl returned to Paris. During the war, he worked on a series similar to the ones he had produced in the United States, this time featuring characters by the cartoonist Benjamin Rabier (1864–1939). The series was entitled Flambeau. He also made war propaganda films. The inspiration of his earlier years weakened as he limited his productions to series. Even the famous *Les Aventures des Pieds Nickelés* (Lacking Agreement), with drawings by Louis

---

[8] The pen name of Achille Lemot (1846–1909).
[9] Isabelle Marinone (*Émile Cohl et la bohème*, '1895', No. 53, December 2007, Paris) suggests that the title came to Émile Cohl's mind after a homonymous 1866 illustration of his master André Gill. Phantasmagorias had been in the eighteenth and nineteenth centuries' well-attended lantern/horror/necromancy shows, whose master had been the Belgian Etienne Gaspard Robert, also known as Robertson (1763–1837). The only visible connection with this is the 'skeleton' look of the thin white figures on black scenery.
[10] Only *He Poses for His Portrait* is available today. Almost all films made by Émile Cohl in America were destroyed in a fire of the Fort Lee Éclair warehouse in 1914.

Forton (1879–1934), no longer had the stamp of Cohl's personality. Later he concerned himself primarily with scientific and advertising films for other studios before his death on 20 January 1938 at the age of eighty-one.

The most interesting period of Émile Cohl's cinematographic career was certainly the first, which ended in approximately 1911. In an age when cinema was swamped by conceited theatrical costumes, he gave lessons in stylization, visual metaphors, and before-the-fact surrealism.[11] His characters create and destroy themselves, are run through by umbrellas without losing a drop of blood, and fall victim to monsters with humanoid faces and eyeballs on the tips of their tails. Nor did Cohl content himself strictly with drawing. He animated puppets, cut-outs, and objects (a famous film of his featured animated matches); studied new tricks; and hand-painted colours on film, as in *L'éventail animé* (The Animated Fan).

Such a fertile imagination commands interest even today when other films of the same period may appear tiresome. The episodes featuring Fantoche are little comedies of intrigue, based on the contrast between characters, the intervention of foils (such as a policeman), and misunderstandings. Cohl's drawings emphasize lines over volume, and his comedies favour gags over psychology, but his films display one exceptional element: the dazzling twist that spurts without explanation or logical connection like a rabbit from a magician's top hat. This joyousness reverberates in the drawings, which are naïve, despite Cohl's fine craftsmanship. Cohl's stylization depended on his need to reduce the number of lines to be animated, but perhaps never before had an artist known how to make a virtue of necessity.

The years directly following 1911 marked a slow decline, although Cohl still released a few good works. His last entertainment film was *Fantoche cherche un logement* (The Puppet Looks for Lodging, 1921). The sixty-four-year-old artist resuscitated a character that had been dear to him in younger times from *Drame chez les fantoches* (Drama Amongst the Puppets) or *Le cauchemar du fantoche* (The Nightmare of the Puppet).

Georges Méliès

The language of animation is less realistic than the language of live-action cinema; in the beginning, it was totally unrealistic. An imaginary world was needed. Somebody had already provided it.

Georges Méliès (Paris, 8 December 1861–21 January 1938) was an illusionist who bought the Robert-Houdin Theatre and became an artist impresario of magic and variety shows. As a prospective client of the Lumières, he was invited to the historical projection of 28 December 1895. That event had a dramatic impact on him: He turned to directing and producing (he projected his first film on 4 April 1896) and was a leader in his field for the next ten years. In a world of 'newsreel' filmmakers, Méliès was the first to view cinema as the realm of the imagination. He was also a pioneer in studying the effects obtainable with the camera, anticipating breakthroughs that have transformed into today's cinematic language. He abandoned cinema in 1913 after having made more than 500 films, about 150 of which still survive. Having explored every kind of trick and special effect – féerie, fantasy, science fiction, horror – Méliès probably shot some scenes frame by frame during his career.[12] But this is not what really matters.

Screening Méliès' films today is like viewing an animated film . . . without animation. The story unravels against unnaturally painted backgrounds; the actors themselves seem purely figurative elements, covered by masks, costumes, or camouflages. In addition to this, the movie camera is stationary (Méliès filmed according to the principle that the movie camera should be like a gentleman in his armchair); therefore, all the action occurs as if in an animated puppet theatre. This is where Méliès' cinema contains the seeds of its own negation; for, if there is a stylistic clash in his films, it lies in the contrast between the two-dimensional scenery and the clumsy movement of the three-dimensional actors. Still, Méliès paved the way for a similarly rooted cinema in which this contradiction would be overcome by improved technology. Characters

---

[11] The artistic group of the Incohérents (1882–1887), which Cohl belonged to, promoted the absurd, the surprising, the vilification of good manners, and the derision of institutions: many things that would characterize surrealism forty years later.

[12] According to Alexander Sesonske ('Sight and Sound', *The Origins of Animation*, Vol. 49, No. 3, Summer 1980):

> Méliès produced in 1898 the first sequences of photographed animation in a series of little commercial films made to be projected on an open-air screen on the Boulevard des Italiens. In some of these 'films de publicité' a comic scene would end with a shot of scrambled letters arranging themselves to form the name of the product, e.g. Bornibus Mustard. Méliès achieved this effect, which delighted the pedestrians on the boulevard, by arranging white letters on a black table-top and then rearranging them between the moments when the crank of the camera was given an eighth or quarter turn to expose one or two frames.

and scenery (drawn or modelled) were to be stylistically homogeneous, and movement would no longer be left to the actors but would be created by the directors.

The First Abstract Cinema

Cinema was a new phenomenon and the filmmakers a new breed: Only rarely did artists from other disciplines, intellectuals, or philosophers embrace and praise this new medium. They considered cinema a poor copy of theatre and a place that the artistically gifted should avoid. With few exceptions, a similar attitude greeted the avant-garde movements that were subverting the formal and ideological order of the traditional arts. Facing ostracism by the bourgeois intelligentsia, cinema and avant-garde movements led a somewhat parallel life, and each caused a division in the humanist culture of the century.

Contact between the two, however, was sporadic. While futurists, Dadaists, and Surrealists loved filmed shows, there was no corresponding interest from film producers in the fine arts, and even less in the avant-garde. With a few exceptions, cinema was the industry of the masses.

The avant-garde, restrained by technical and economic obstacles, produced only a few marginally successful films. These include: *Vita futurista* (Futuristic Life) by Ginna; the Dada films by Man Ray, Fernand Léger, and Clair-Picabia; and *Un chien andalou* (An Andalusian Dog) and *L'âge d'or* (The Golden Age) by Buñuel-Dalí. Why were these artists interested in film? Because cinema offered movement. The search for movement, which had constantly marked the history of art, had become pressing after impressionism, when paintings strove ever more to capture life itself, leaving static representations to photography. Seurat succeeded in painting the vibrations of air, while the futurists, who believed in 'dynamism' as an ideological and aesthetic principle, forgot the figure and painted the action. Balla painted the scurrying of a Basset hound in *Dog on a Leash* (1912) and hands moving rapidly on an instrument in *The Violinist's Hands* (1912). Bragaglia actuated 'photodynamics', synthesizing the development of a gesture in a single image; during the same years, Marcel Duchamp created the *Nude Descending a Staircase*, and the list of examples continues.

These artistic currents were all based on a 'plastic' concept of movement: The new mode of painting and taking photographs tried to express optical effects or psychological concepts of action. From here to film was a short step. Capable of moving – or, in futurist terminology, rendering any object mobile – animation was the medium closest to the purposes of designers, sculptors, and painters. The history of animation is marked by contact with painters as well as the equally fertile attention of animators to the innovative currents in graphics and plastic arts (Picasso himself was on the brink of entrusting some of his drawings to animator Giulio Gianini). Curiously, the Spanish master had another bout with animation: Animated experiments featuring his drawings appear in *Le mystère Picasso* (1956), a documentary by Henri-Georges Clouzot.[13] In the 1950s, the birth of 'kinetic' art supplied the missing link in the evolutionary chain that tied the traditional plastic arts to animation. Europe, a cultural centre for the first forty years of this century, was also host to experiments, debate, and a large number of talented animators. In America, experimental art films began in the late 1930s.

Arnaldo Ginna

'Since 1907 I understood the kinetic-pictorial potential of cinema', Arnaldo Ginna recalled. 'In 1908–09, a movie camera which could film one frame at a time did not exist. I thought of painting directly on the film.'[13] A writer, futurist theoretician, painter of some of the first abstract paintings in the history of Western art (*Neurasthenia*, 1908), and director of the only official futuristic film, *Vita futurista* (Futuristic Life, 1916, filmed in Florence with the participation of the movement's major exponents), Ginna created a radically new technique for film animation – a technique that Len Lye and Norman McLaren would skillfully develop 25 years later.

Ginna, whose real name was Arnaldo Ginanni Corradini, was born in Ravenna, Italy, on 7 May 1890. With his brother Bruno (Ravenna, 9 June 1892–Varese, 20 November 1976), who used the pen name Bruno Corra, he developed an original theory of the arts. According to the two brothers, a mutual relationship exists among the arts: A *musical motif* is formed by sounds changing within a time sequence; likewise, in painting, a *chromatic motif* can be obtained by cinematographic techniques that offer colours changing within a time sequence. Just as the musical chord is a fixed sound in space like that emitted by

---

[13] Mario Verdone, *Cinema e letteratura del Futurismo* (Edizioni di Bianco e Nero), Rome, 1968.

an organ when one presses a key, the 'chromatic chord', in Ginna's terms, defines what would later be called an 'abstract painting'. Ginna wrote:

> Pointillism was the starting point for the studies on the chromatic chord, the chromatic symphony and so on, because the different dots or segments of painting paralleled the succession of different musical notes. This allowed us to approach certain areas of colour in the paintings of Segantini. For example: a particular colour area in a field by Segantini was a chromatic chord taken precisely from the nature of those mountain meadows.[14]

Ginna painted four works directly on film: *A Chord of Colour* from Segantini, *Study of the Effects of Four Colours* and *Song of Spring* from Mendelssohn, and *Flowers* from Mallarmé. While the first film was the development of a colour chord, the second studied the effects among complementary colours (red-green, blue-yellow), and the last two were chromatic renderings of music and poetry.

> I have not seen frames of the experiments done in 1910 for many years. Perhaps someone has them? Are they lost? Or destroyed? You will understand, it was so many years ago, with so many events and moves from one city to another! Besides, no one gave them much importance. Those experiments, especially the sequence regarding Segantini's work, were made in order to produce chromatic music, chromatic motifs and symphonies. Even small black and white animations were made. The very earliest consisted of a little book whose many pages, when flipped quickly, yielded the impression of movement. These were then transcribed by hand on to the celluloid film, but without pigment sensitive to silver nitrate. This film was sent to us by our optician Magini, in Ravenna. That's all: very distant recollections, almost a dream. I noticed later that these little books with animated drawings were being sold to entertain small children.[15]

It must be clear that these experiments did not belong to futurism. The two artists joined Marinetti's movement about one year after having abandoned them, and only vaguely, later, some mention was made in futurist manifestos of abstract cinema. The experiments still had a definite symbolist aura, aimed at inner life, spiritualism, and intra-sensorial and extra-sensorial correspondence.[16] As William Moritz sharply put it, the late ones 'relied . . . on the sort of symbolic color drama dear to the Theosophists'.[17]

Ginna continued his unpublicized artistic activity, but he never ventured into cinema again. He died in Rome on 24 September 1982.

Léopold Survage

Around 1914, the Cubist painter Léopold Survage, of Scandinavian, Russian, and French descent, wanted to make a film based on the rhythm of colours, filming image by image according to traditional principles. 'Coloured rhythm is not at all an illustration or interpretation of a musical work. It is an autonomous art form, even if it is based on the same psychological data as music', Survage wrote on the pages of Apollinaire's magazine, *Soirées de Paris*. Survage's long but ideologically weak manifesto, however, explored the same field as Ginna and arrived at somewhat similar conclusions. The war put an end to Survage's cinematographic ambitions, and the film never came to be. As a result, only a few preparatory paintings remain.

Winsor McCay

> Animation should be an art, that is how I conceived it. But as I see, what you fellows have done with it is make it into a trade . . . not an art, but a trade . . . bad luck.

Winsor McCay did not mince words when closing the dinner party his fellow New York animators had given in his honour one night during the fall of 1927.[18]

---

[14] Letter by Arnaldo Ginna to Giannalberto Bendazzi, 1 March 1972.
[15] Letter by Arnaldo Ginna to Giannalberto Bendazzi, 18 February 1972.
[16] In those times, occultism was largely practised in aristocratic circles of the Ravenna area. After having left futurism, Ginna would paint 'animistic' portraits for many years, aiming at depicting the 'soul' in addition to the body of the subject.
[17] William Moritz, *Abstract Film and Color Music*, in Maurice Tuchman (ed.) *The Spiritual in Art: Abstract Painting 1890–1985*, Abbeville, New York, 1986.
[18] Isadore Klein, 'How I Came to Know the Fabulous Winsor McCay', *Cartoonists Profiles*, No. 30, June 1977.

What Émile Cohl was to Europe, Winsor McCay was to America: the beginner. A wonderful cartoonist (his comic strip *Little Nemo in Slumberland*, published from 15 October 1905 in the *New York Herald*, is still one of the best in the field), Winsor Zenis McCay can be considered the first 'classical' artist of American animation. McCay was born in Canada in 1867[19] and, like many of his colleagues and contemporaries, basically was a self-taught artist who started by drawing billboards, vaudeville stage settings, and newspaper comic strips. After fifteen years in Cincinnati, he was invited to New York by James Gordon Bennett, a legendary figure in American journalism, publisher of the *New York Herald* and the *New York Evening Telegram*. There, McCay made a name for himself. Admired and respected by his colleagues, he was an amiable artist who managed to combine high-quality work with mass success, topped with a keen intuition for public relations.

'In mid-April 1906', writes McCay's biographer John Canemaker, 'a representative of F.F. Proctor, famous vaudeville producer and theatre owner, approached Winsor McCay with an offer to appear at Proctor's 23d Street Theatre, a top vaudeville house, twice a day for two weeks in June'.[20] For eleven years, the artist toured with his successful show, never neglecting his comic strips and illustrations.

It was for his vaudeville act that McCay prepared his first animated movie.

In early 1911, under the supervision of [James Stuart] Blackton, both the drawings and a live-action prologue and epilogue for the film called *Little Nemo* were shot at the Vitagraph studio on Avenue M. . . . Vitagraph released the short in movie theatres on April 8, and McCay used it in his vaudeville act. . . beginning on April 12 at New York's Colonial Theatre.[21]

The excuse (as told in the live-action segments of the short) was a bet with some of his fellow cartoonists, who challenged him to film the thousands of drawings he tirelessly created. In January 1912, McCay created *The Story of a Mosquito* (or *How a Mosquito Operates*). This time, however, he requested that the movie not be distributed while he was exhibiting it in the theatre. *Little Nemo* is truly a 'first movie'; without plot or background, it is little more than a sequence of images,

Figure 3.2 Winsor McCay, *Gertie the Dinosaur*, 1914.

materializing and then vanishing as if to prove their ability to exist on screen. This experimentalism is overcome in *The Story of a Mosquito*, the funny, ironic tale of a huge mosquito wearing a top hat that is insatiably hungry for the blood of a drunkard. The gluttonous bug ends up exploding.

The first part of McCay's production is characterized by extraordinarily sharp drawings and animation. The rich, elegant art nouveau style of his comic strips is simplified but not impoverished. Movements are slow, fluid, perfectly suited to such personal graphics, with a display of elegance that is nearly unmatched in the history of animation. Since McCay produced his own movies, he could afford expensive workmanship, using thousands of drawings on paper and careful control over the fluidity of animation (he used an old mutoscope roll to flip through the drawings before filming them).

On 8 February 1914, at the Palace Theatre in Chicago, McCay showed his masterpiece, *Gertie the Dinosaur*.

The film features the unlikely act of an animal tamer and his dinosaur. The large animal peeks from behind some rocks, eats an apple, drinks a lake, plays with a mammoth, and dances at McCay's command. Sometimes she is reluctant and, when scolded, she cries. The animation and drawings are not only admirable but also surprising for the personality they give to this puppy-like brontosaurus. Certainly the animal's performance, well endowed with

---

[19] The date is uncertain.

[20] John Canemaker, *Winsor McCay – His Life and Art*, Abbeville, New York, 1987.

[21] John Canemaker, *Winsor McCay – His Life and Art*, Abbeville, New York, 1987.

timing and mimicry, reduced McCay's stage role to that of a straight man. A unique chronicler, Émile Cohl, wrote in a letter from the United States:

> The main actor, or perhaps the sole actor, was a prehistoric animal. . . . McCay stood very elegantly in front of the screen, armed with a whip. He would give a short speech and then, turning toward the screen like an animal trainer, he would call the animal. (Gertie) would come out of the rocks, and at this point, an exhibition of the highest quality would begin.

McCay ended his theatrical career when the newspaper for which he worked claimed the exclusive rights to his performances of *Gertie the Dinosaur*. Because he wished to avoid any battle, McCay first limited his performances to New York and eventually quit. He re-edited *Gertie* by adding a prologue and a few live-action scenes; by the end of 1914, he delivered it to William Fox for distribution in the movie circuits.

Four years were to pass before another movie by McCay could be seen on the screen. This time it was a totally different film, lasting over twenty minutes. Entitled *The Sinking of the Lusitania* (July 1918), it was based on a sad episode of wartime history, the sinking of the British ship *Lusitania* by a German submarine in May 1915. Of the 1,198 passengers who died, 124 were US citizens. American public opinion was indignant, and the accident played a determining role in favour of American participation in the war. An outraged McCay created a dramatic, extremely detailed, gripping movie that maintained the rhythm and style of contemporary documentaries or newsreels. Basically, it was a filmic version of the very popular illustrated re-enactments of accidents, which appeared in American and European newspapers of the time. McCay's characteristic floral style emerged even in the ethical and dramatic undertones of the movie, as can be seen in the beautifully drawn head of the child surfacing in the waves.

Among McCay's remaining movies and fragments, the most relevant are the three *Dreams of a Rarebit Fiend*, filmed by McCay and his son Robert around 1921. The first, *The Pet*, tells the story of a dog that grows to a monstrous size and wanders around the city. The second, *Bug Vaudeville*, features non-anthropomorphic insects performing sleights of hand, dances, and bicycle acts. In the third movie, *The Flying House*, a middle-aged husband and wife equip their house with wings and an engine and fly away through the universe. *Bug Vaudeville* is a serene and elegantly animated film with much originality; undoubtedly, it is the best of the three. Yet, these movies are far from McCay's initial efforts. Having abandoned the technique of drawing on paper, he used the cel process, with sometimes unfortunate results; his inspiration and his rhythmic sense, similarly, seemed less assured.

In the following years until his death in Sheepshead Bay, New York, on 26 July 1934, McCay limited his production to drawings and illustrations. Even so, he always considered himself an animator, declaring in an interview that he was most proud of his movies. For many years, in fact, no animated film showed so great a drawing craftsmanship and so fine a sense of movement. More than anything else, he had marked forever the American approach to animation: characters, personality, and acting. Gertie is tender, naughty, and capricious, like every baby; being a dinosaur, she's at the same time a giant and a child, and the contrast moves us and makes us laugh. In the decades to come, Americans would always look for *personality animation*; this would not be Europeans' strength, causing them to pursue other types of animation.

Colour

Contrary to what many still believe, silent cinema was never solely in black and white. Often the individual positive film copies were subjected to staining procedures such as imbibition, toning, *pochoir*, and various others. (To clarify: The *negative* film was not yet able to reproduce the colours of reality; *every single positive* copy in black and white was coloured by special craftsmen.) In the case of imbibition or toning, an entire sequence was tinted monochrome, and this established conventions. It was intended that such a scene coloured in blue took place at night; in yellow, sunlight; in orange, artificially lighted indoors; in red, near a fire; in green, in the fields. Sometimes the colour had psychological meaning (red for anger). An example of good use of this early colour is the final sequence of F. W. Murnau's live-action film *Nosferatu* (1922). Sinister, the vampire enters the bedroom of the girl and moves towards her (blue, night). When he passes in front of the window, lo: a few pink frames, the first beacon of dawn. Exposed to the sun, he winces and dies while the scene turns to the daylight's yellow.

Despite hundreds of attempts and useless patents, in the 1910s and 1920s, the negative colour film stock made its real debut in the 1930s and began to be the standard only in the early 1960s.

4

SILENT AMERICA I

The Fathers' Sons
Comics, Animation, and Cinema

The link between the two very American forms of art – comic strips and animated cartoons – was clear from the start (although comic strips had fed live-action cinema itself since its early days[1]). Many animators were either creators of comic strips as well or had started in that field. Many characters also moved to the screen directly from the printed page, and for the most part they communicated through the balloons typical of comic strips.

The man in the street – and not only he – for many decades believed that printed comic strips and film cartoons were almost the same thing and often called one the other's name.

The influence of the former on the latter was strong in the formative period of American drawn animation. The films inherited the shape of the characters, their behaviour, some graphic gambits (a big exclamation mark for emphasis, a big question mark for doubt, flashing short lines around the face to represent surprise, movement lines around the body or the limbs to signify quick action, broken lines starting from the eyes to show the trajectory of a look, etc.), and some comedy gambits (pratfalls, takes, double takes – often borrowed from vaudeville acts).

With time, the roads diverged. By the end of the 1920s, it was apparent that a character could maintain more or less the same physiognomy but had to display different psychology and behaviour to succeed in both media. By the late 1930s, everybody in the business was aware that filmic gag-linked Popeye, Donald Duck, and Mickey Mouse were just distant relations to their narration-linked likes of the printed page. At the same time, Walt Disney and Don Graham together had made a clean sweep of any graphic gambits.

The most successful comics of the 1930s – Alex Raymond's Flash Gordon, Harold Foster's Prince Valiant, Roy Crane's Captain Easy, and Milton Caniff's Terry and the Pirates – did not influence animation. If they had any connection with filmmaking, it was with live action. These comics were influenced by Western, action, noir, horror, and gangster films.

Birth of the Industry

After 1911, pioneers of American animation emerged everywhere, but with little organization. New York City became a major centre, housing the most thriving studios that offered the best opportunities and the most efficient systems of production. It's often difficult to find a way out of the maze of studios that have opened, closed, and been renamed. This is further complicated by those that are working on a subcontract or sub-subcontract or have hired full-time employees and freelancers. We'll try our best to sort it out.

Raoul Barré

Raoul Barré, a French-Canadian painter and cartoonist (born in Montreal on 29 January 1874) moved to New York in 1903 after a few trips to Europe. From 1912 to 1913, he collaborated with William C. Nolan (1894–1956)

---

[1] For instance, Frederick Burr Opper's Happy Hooligan (which first appeared in the *New York Journal* on 11 March 1900) was portrayed in various sketches by James Stuart Blackton in the summer of the same year; Richard F. Outcault's Buster Brown (whose comic strip began in the *New York Herald* on 4 May 1902) was the protagonist of a series produced and directed by Edwin S. Porter in 1904.

to produce and direct animated advertising films. The following year, they set up their own studio for entertainment films. Shortly thereafter, they were joined by some future talents, including Gregory La Cava, Frank Moser,[2] Dick Huemer (1898–1979), and Pat Sullivan (1887–1933).

Barré introduced the use of standard perforations in the drawing paper – thus avoiding jerkiness from one image to the next – and the slash system.

Cut, Insert, Replace

The slash system consisted of drawing the set only once, leaving a blank space for the characters' movements, and inserting sheets of paper cut to fit in the blank space. The character was drawn in progressive phases of movement on these paper cuttings. This was Barré's solution to what had been the animator's problem from the very beginning: how to animate a character that operates in a particular environment without having to draw both the character and the environment each time.

In 1915, Barré produced *The Animated Grouch Chasers* for distribution by Edison. In this series, live-action film clips introduce the animated sections: Whenever an actor reads a caricature album entitled *The Grouch Chaser*, this comes to life. Here, Barré's drawings are sharp and purposely ungraceful.

In 1916, Barré was commissioned by the International Film Service (which will be discussed later) to film seven *Fables* based on a comic strip by T. E. Powers[3] (other episodes of the serial were created by Vernon George Stallings and Frank Moser). That same year, in partnership with Charles Bowers (1889–1945), Barré successfully produced the animated adventures of Mutt and Jeff. Bud Fisher (3 April 1885–7 September 1954) had invented the comic strip 'odd couple' of Mutt (tall, skinny, and smart – the straight man) and Jeff (diminutive, irascible, and clumsy – his funny counterpart) in 1908. The success was instantaneous, and Fisher, money minded as well as creative, copyrighted the strip in his own name. Various live-action Mutt and Jeff comedies were made from 1911 to 1916, and eventually the artist licensed the production of animated Mutt and Jeff comic strips with Raoul Barré and Charles Bowers. The series continued until 1927 with more than 300 episodes.

In 1919, Barré, a victim of a plot allegedly masterminded by Bowers – apparently, Bowers consistently ostracized sensitive Barré, who had a nervous breakdown and left the company – abruptly abandoned his business and took up painting in a Long Island country house. He made a fleeting return in 1926–1927 as the animator of *Felix the Cat* for Pat Sullivan. Then he went back to Montreal, where he devoted himself to painting and political satire until his death on 21 May 1932.

John Randolph Bray

In the first decade of American animation, a dominant personality was John Randolph Bray. Resolute, manipulative, and far sighted, he laid the foundations for the American animation industry and gave it direction. Born on 25 August 1879 in Addison, Michigan (he died at nearly 100 years of age on 10 October 1978 in Bridgeport, Connecticut), he became successful as a cartoonist and an illustrator in New York between 1906 and 1907. He probably moved to cinema in an attempt to emulate Winsor McCay; however, his attitude differed greatly from McCay's creativity. According to Bray, the field of animated drawings was a for-profit enterprise. From the very start, he sought ways to rationalize labour, eliminate unnecessary effort, and speed up production time.

The *Artist's Dreams* (or *The Dachshund and the Sausage*, July 1913) tells the story of a drawing that comes alive as soon as the artist leaves the studio. In this case, the drawing represents a dog hurriedly eating sausages until it explodes, exactly like McCay's mosquito. Here, Bray experimented with the technique of printing background scenes rather than drawing them repeatedly by hand. The film was received with enthusiasm by Charles Pathé, a leader in world cinematography who at the time was visiting New York. Pathé postponed a trip to Paris so that he could sign a six-movie contract with Bray, then a 34-year-old novice.

---

[2] Born in Oketo, Kansas, on 27 May 1886, Moser died in Dobbs Ferry (New York) on 1 October 1964. Parallel to his career in animation, he made a name for himself as a distinguished painter.

[3] Thomas E. Powers (1870–1939) was a political and satirical cartoonist for the Hearst newspapers for nearly forty years.

Bray Studios was founded in December 1914 on the basis of competition, commission, and the subsequent need for constant production. When the United States intervened in World War I, Bray promptly began marketing government-funded instructional and training films, a move that was later echoed by Walt Disney during World War II. Bray's studios were almost contemporary with the founding of Raoul Barré's group, but their structure was very different. In Bray Studios, work was divided and compartmentalized. Having become a businessman, Bray laid down his pencil and employed animators who were responsible for the creation of the movies. In turn, the animators supervised assistants and helpers.

Bray stressed technological development. Within two years, he had filed three patents: in January 1914, the use of printed background scenes; in July 1914, the application of grey shades to drawings; and in July 1915, the use of scenery drawn on transparent celluloid to be applied over the drawings to be animated. These patents made him a leader in the field and ensured that he would have an effective monopoly over his competitors. Bray was equally prompt at averting the danger posed by Earl Hurd (Kansas City, 1880–Hollywood, 1940), who had filed a patent for an alternative technique on 19 December 1914.[4] In fact, Hurd's process was not only alternative, but ultimately more important than Bray's: It consisted of the cel process, involving the drawing of characters on transparent celluloid sheets, which were then applied over painted background scenes. The transparent sheet was called *cel* in English and *cellulo* in French (from celluloid). Most animated movies worldwide were to be produced with this technique. At a time in which the animation industry was still developing, the importance of Hurd's discovery was not immediately apparent. For good measure, Bray hired the inventor/moviemaker in late 1915 and made him a partner in the Bray-Hurd Patent Company, a firm that sold licenses for the patented techniques. Until the patents expired in 1932, the company earned healthy profits from royalties.

The hero of Bray Studios was the comic character Colonel Heeza Liar. A short, bald, nearsighted man, the colonel was a Münchhausen-like character: physically unassuming but exuberantly daring. His first adventure (January 1914), entitled *Colonel Heeza Liar in Africa*, jokingly referred to the big-game hunting experiences of former US president Theodore Roosevelt, whose expeditions were a popular topic in the media. The colonel went through several changes as, in time, different animators were assigned to draw him (a phenomenon typical in American animation until the 1930s), but he always maintained his place in the comic category of aggressive rascals.

Another protagonist of Bray Studios was Bobby Bumps, a creation of Earl Hurd, who brought his character along when he left Bray. Bobby was a little boy who experienced daily life in the inseparable company of his dog Fido. With the exception of McCay, Hurd was probably the best American animator of his time. His well-structured movies display an uncommon visual inventiveness, gentle humour, and attention to drawing and theatre background design.

The International Film Service

In 1916, William Randolph Hearst's media empire of newspapers, news agencies, and movies opened a new branch: the International Film Service (IFS). Hearst is known among cinema devotees as the stubborn promoter of his companion Marion Davies's acting career as well as the model for Orson Welles's character of Charles Foster Kane in *Citizen Kane* (1941). The goal was to use the copyrights of several popular comic strips published in Hearst's newspapers for cinematographic purposes. These strips included *Bringing up Father*, *Krazy Kat*, *Happy Hooligan*, and *The Katzenjammer Kids*.

Gregory La Cava (1892–1952) later pursued a career as a director of live-action movies. His masterpiece was *My Man Godfrey* in 1936. Gregory La Cava was in charge of the service and was able to obtain the participation of old friends such as Bill Nolan and Frank Moser, whom he had met when working with Barré, as well as newcomers such as Alabaman Jack King (1895–1958); Grim Natwick; Burt Gillett; the former comic strip artist Leon A. Searl; the sixteen-year-old Walter Lantz; and, from Georgia, the self-taught Vernon George Stallings (1891–1963). Despite its promising beginnings, the IFS was forced to close after two years on 6 July 1918, a victim of changes in the policies of its mother company. The magnate still wanted his characters animated, so he licensed various studios (Barré's was one of them) to continue the series. Most of the staff got jobs with John Terry's studio for a few months before Terry's studio went out of business as well. The animators were

---

[4] Approved on 15 June 1915.

then hired by Bray Studios. The IFS's productions were not able to surpass those by the competition, and the only relevant achievement of Hearst's foray into animation was to launch talented artists who later emerged on their own.

Other American Artists

Henry 'Hy' Mayer (1868–1953) was born in Germany. Originally a prolific illustrator, he moved on to animation from 1913 to 1926. Among his various (and still understudied) creations are various 'lightning sketch' films; two *Topical War Cartoons* (1914; probably vignettes for newsreels); and the Such Is Life series, with titles such as *Such Is Life at the Zoo* (1920), *Such Is Life in Italy* (1922), and *Tripping the Rhine* (1926). This series combined animation with live-action films taken in exotic locations. Mayer also was the first employer and mentor of Otto Messmer, later to become famous as the 'father' of Felix the Cat.

In 1915, Paul Terry made his debut with the distribution of his *Little Herman*, featuring the caricature of a popular magician. Born in San Mateo, California, on 19 February 1887,[5] Terry studied in San Francisco. In 1911, he moved to New York. After attending a vaudeville performance by McCay, he decided to forget his ambitions as a cartoonist and become an animator. A modestly gifted artist (after many rejections, his *Little Herman* was bought by a minor distributor for little money), Terry was nevertheless a hardheaded, independent spirit.

For the major part of his career, he worked on his own, sometimes accepting commissions from other studios. Despite endless disagreements over the use of animation techniques, Terry did work briefly as a hired animator for John Randolph Bray (in the 1920s, an altercation between Bray and Terry led to a lawsuit). In 1916, he directed eleven Farmer Al Falfa films for Bray and then left, taking the rights to the character with him.

Terry's first important character, Farmer Al Falfa, was a representative of rural America; Al Falfa was a bald old farmer, bearded and good natured. Although the character was never deeply developed, it survived several changes and lasted until the late 1930s.

The work of other New York animators is less well documented. Harry S. Palmer, creator of the series Keeping Up with the Joneses[6] for Gaumont America, had to give up in 1917 when Bray accused him of using patented techniques without a license. Palmer was also the author of animated satirical vignettes, which were inserted in newsreels. Several students of Bray's also became caricaturists. They included painter and illustrator Louis Glackens (1866–1933), F.M. Follet,[7] and Leighton Budd, who worked for Pathé's newsreels between 1916 and 1918 and later focused on comic strips. John Terry (Paul's older brother) and Hugh M. Shields had distinguished themselves with some experimental animation work in 1911 in San Francisco.

In Chicago, Sidney Smith (Bloomington, Illinois, 13 February 1877–Chicago, 20 October 1935) became famous with his comic strip based on the human goat Old Doc Yak, which first appeared in the *Tribune* on Monday, 5 February 1912. Only one year later, Smith produced and directed a series based on this character that was distributed by Selig Polyscope. The first film, called *Old Doc Yak*, was screened on 8 July 1913; nineteen more would follow until 1915. In 1917, Smith introduced a new comic strip starring The Gumps. It was a drawn situation comedy featuring the everyday adventures of a middle-class family, and it enchanted readers. Fellow Chicagoan Wallace A. Carlson (1884–1967), who had worked on animated vignettes and series, created the character Dreamy Dud (1913) for Essanay, founded his Carlson Studios in 1919, and was asked by Paramount to work on an animated version of the strip. In 1920–1921, with writing credited to Smith, Carlson produced and directed more than 50 Gumps shorts.[8]

Howard S. Moss, a specialist with animated puppets, also worked in Chicago. His *Motoy Films*, produced around 1917, were based on caricatures of movie stars such as Charlie Chaplin, Mary Pickford, and Ben Turpin.

Willis O'Brien

In the field of puppet animation, Willis O'Brien (Oakland, 2 March 1886–Hollywood, 8 November 1962) played an important role in the 1910s. After an adventurous youth

---

[5] He died in New York on 25 October 1971.

[6] Cartoonist Arthur R. 'Pop' Momand invented this domestic comedy for Joseph Pulitzer's *New York World* in 1913. Today it survives only as a catchphrase.

[7] Follet is credited with an uncommonly political short called *The Mexican Crisis* (1917). What's more, this short also dealt with foreign affairs.

[8] A good artist of his own, Carlson later teamed with Gumps writer Sol Hess; together, the pair started a successful strip called The Nebbs, which lasted from 1923 to 1946.

(he even led a paleontological expedition in Oregon), O'Brien discovered how to animate clay figurines in the laboratory of a San Francisco marble cutter. Later, he substituted India rubber for clay and made figurines equipped with metal skeletons. In 1915, he completed his first short, *The Dinosaur and the Missing Link*; Edison's company bought the movie (which was distributed one year later) and invited the sculptor-director to continue his work in New York.

In addition to some animated works, such as *R.F.D. 10,000 B.C.* and *Prehistoric Poultry, the Dinornis or Great Roaring Whiffenpoof*, O'Brien made other films mixing live actors and animated figurines. Towards the end of 1917, he left the economically troubled Edison and accepted an offer by Herbert M. Dawley, a wealthy New Jersey sculptor, to work on *The Ghost of Slumber Mountain*.

Dawley had already experimented on his own with the animation of prehistoric monsters. *The Ghost of Slumber Mountain* (1919) is about a man who befriends an old hermit who gives him a special telescope that allows him to see the most remote past. O'Brien made his new dinosaurs quite realistic, although they were still far from being credible. It is still unclear whether the film originally was a feature or a featurette, but Herbert Dawley, unsatisfied with the result, cut it down to sixteen minutes. Furthermore, he took all screen credit, so that for many years to come he was labelled by specialists as the villain against the genius. Puppet animation film historian Stephen Czerkas disagrees:

> Contrary to popular belief, Dawley did a great deal of the animation in *Ghost*. . . . [He] does not deserve the poor reputation that has been created by previous film historians. Dawley treated O'Brien very fairly. It is not true that [he] was untalented or incapable of making his own films. He went on to make *Along the Moonbeam Trail* [1920] completely without O'Brien. . . . Contrary to the suspicion that footage from *The Ghost of Slumber Mountain* was used in this second film, footage from [it] has been discovered recently which conclusively demonstrates that none of it was made using out-takes from *Ghost*. Dawley did all the animation for *Moonbeam*. Also during the following decade, Dawley made many films that were entirely puppet animation. Some of his later films were primarily live-action, but Dawley incorporated puppet animation into some of these as well.[9]

O'Brien's first efforts are excellent for their believable (at the time) animation of prehistoric animals. As works of art, however, they lack substance and display corny, simplistic humour; clumsy rhythm; and uninteresting plots. Essentially, they show that, from the very beginning, O'Brien was above all a master of special effects – a quality that returns in his famous, glorious contribution to later movies, such as *The Lost World* (1925, directed by Larry O. Hoyt), *King Kong* (1933, directed by Ernest B. Schoedsack and Merian C. Cooper), and *The Son of Kong* (1933, directed by Ernest B. Schoedsack).

Instruments and Language

With the exception of Winsor McCay, who can be considered a special case, American animation in 1910 was characterized not so much by valuable productions as by the filmmakers' search for devices, technical processes, and language. In 1913, Bill Nolan used the travelling shot: While the character remained still, the background scene slowly moved under its feet (since the frame-by-frame technique was used, the character would appear to be moving). At the IFS, Nolan introduced the 'rubber hose' animation style – people, animals, minerals, anything was elastic, flexible, ductile, disarticulated. Elsewhere, an assistant of Barré and Bowers forgot to insert the background element and filmed the character walking on air. This episode initiated the immortal generation of characters walking into the void and falling only when they become aware of what they are doing. Another time, Stallings, bothered by the difficult task of drawing on a fixed table, invented the rotating panel, which allowed the artist to work from every side of a sheet of paper. Artists also tried to use many various devices in order to keep the sheets of paper aligned (the most reliable was still Barré's peg system, featuring a standard perforation on the bottom of the paper), although it took years to solve the problem.

The cel was rarely used, and animation was done on paper. Labour was structured in such a way that animators first sketched their drawings with light blue pencils. Since the orthochromatic films then in use were insensitive to a light blue colour, light blue pencils reproduced as white, so lines could be changed and corrected over and over again. The drawings were then passed over to assistants for colouring. The assistants were also responsible for

---

[9] E-mailed letters to the author, 15 July 2009 and 23 July 2009.

adding those details that the animators, concerned with the fluidity of action, did not have time to draw: physiognomic traits, clothing details, etc. Theoretically, the task of the animator involved the creation of stories and gags as well as the animation of characters. Sometimes one individual was responsible for a whole movie or a series, but generally the job was divided, and the people who worked on its fragments did not take care to maintain continuity of action. This resulted in unbalanced movies based on incongruous or even non-existent plots. The underlying principle (which lasted for the next twenty years) was to make the viewers laugh at any cost, even if the movie resulted in an assembly of primitive, expedient methods.

Graphically, none of these movies sparkled. Produced at a frantic pace for distributors who did not understand, or did not care about, the details of workmanship, they were unsophisticated and coarse, featuring rounded, simplified forms that were the easiest to animate. For their part, viewers had low expectations: Animation was a curiosity exactly like the many others offered by that popular, populist form of entertainment that was cinema. On the screen, animation mingled with newsreels, slapstick comedies, endless serials, and low-quality fiction (with the exception of the works of T. H. Ince and D. W. Griffith). Animators themselves lacked ambition. They were usually self-taught graphic artists whose education was limited to comic strips and whose commercial craftsmanship was a far cry from fine art. Significantly, their works were called 'animated cartoons' rather than 'animated drawings'.

The early movies were also influenced by vaudeville, a secondary but still-significant element. The commonly used formula of the drawing that becomes autonomous after a real-life artist has sketched it is derived from the acts of vaudeville artists and magicians. In the following years, popular shows still influenced animated movies, but vaudeville was replaced by live-action cinema.

5
SILENT AMERICA II

During the 1920s, animation grew its deepest roots in the United States, although it would be wrong to think of it as a flourishing industry. With the exception of Disney's small group in California, operations concentrated in New York, where a few dozen people founded and dissolved production companies, moved from one studio to another, and constituted what in the industry was called the 'cartoon racket'. It cannot be said, either, that the public loved the films produced by those groups: As many veterans later recalled, animated films were more or less considered fillers; whether they were shown or not was of no major consequence to the audience.

The three most prosperous enterprises were the Fleischer Group, which underwent a number of organizational changes before ending in a takeover by Paramount; Pat Sullivan's group, which thrived on the extraordinary domestic and European success of *Felix the Cat* and its clever merchandising strategies; and Terry's Aesop's Fables Studio, of which 90 per cent was owned by its distributor, the Keith-Albee Theatre circuit. From time to time, films served to support the more lucrative field of comic strips by reminding the audiences of their favourite characters. The world of New York animators was a closed group, dominated to a certain degree by a 'ghetto' mentality: The artists who did not belong to 'the racket' were outsiders, branded as lacking in humour and incapable of inventing comic situations. Quality artists were both envied and despised, and newcomers were discouraged from attending art schools and pursuing anatomy studies or etching.

The desire for experimentation and discovery also suffered: Forms, actions, and movements became routine, and learning animation basically meant learning the recipes for what were openly called stock actions. Despite a few exceptions, the industry's assembly-line systemization did not inspire competition between the companies, nor did it instigate demanding consumers; consequently, this led to inbreeding. Winsor McCay was correct in reproaching his colleagues for their lack of artistic impulses in the mid-1920s.

The Fleischer Brothers

Max Fleischer (Krakow, Austro-Hungarian Empire,[1] 19 July 1883–Woodland Hills, California, 11 September 1972) was the second son of an Austrian-Jewish family that left Europe in 1887 and moved to New York. Interested in both drawing and small mechanical inventions, Max invented the rotoscope (around 1915), a device that permitted a live-action sequence to be transferred to drawings frame by frame. His collaborators were his brothers Joe and Dave. Before the patent for the rotoscope became active in 1917, Max showed a short film sample to producer John Randolph Bray, whom he had met ten years earlier when they both gravitated around a newspaper, the *Daily Eagle*. Bray hired both Max and Dave.

During the war, Max worked successfully on military training films. Promoted to director of his own group, in 1919 he created a series featuring Koko, a clown emerging from an inkwell in every new episode (the series was entitled Out of the Inkwell). The format was standard for the time: Max, the artist, would create Koko, a character that would live out its own adventures in a drawn world and would play tricks on its creator.

In 1921, the Fleischer brothers left Bray and founded their own studio, which was to be second only to Disney's both in America and worldwide until 1942. The enterprise was largely a family business. Dave (New York, 14

---

[1] The Austro-Hungarian Empire is now Poland.

Figure 5.1 Bray Studios – Max Fleischer, *Out of the Inkwell. Fishing,* 1921.

July 1894–Hollywood, 25 June 1979), always second in command, had a position that could broadly be defined as artistic director. Max's other brothers, Charles, Joe, and Lou; his sister Ethel; and his son-in-law Seymour Kneitel all participated in the enterprise at various times. In 1924, the economic expansion of Out of the Inkwell Films (as the company had been first named; it later became Inkwell Studios) led Max to found the Red Seal Distribution Company, which was to circulate the short films of Koko the Clown, the Song Car-Tunes; documentaries, and live-action series and comedies. The distribution company lasted only one year, after which Alfred Weiss handled the films; Paramount eventually took over in 1927. The production company continued its operations and in 1928, after ups and downs among its shareholders, the company was renamed Fleischer Studios.

The Song Car-Tunes were short films based on the sing-along formula – i.e. a song that was a known classic of American light theatre was sung by the whole audience. In place of a singer on the stage, it was the film that invited the audience to join in the melody. The Fleischers introduced the concept of the 'bouncing ball': Bouncing on the words of the song projected on the screen, the ball directed which word was to be sung. In the finest films, these drawings were much more than a simple ball bouncing on title cards; Koko or another character often appeared on the screen, and the words of the song were visually interpreted by comical drawings. An orchestra or a pianist provided the music, except for the few short films that had been synchronized with Lee de Forest's Phonofilm system. Although not much is known about this system, at least four or five experiments were produced in 1924–1925, the first of which might have been *Come Take a Trip in My Airship*. While the Fleischers did not actually introduce a new age, they preceded all other animators in the rush towards sound.

Among other enterprises of this decade of production, two educational-scientific documentaries made Max Fleischer especially proud: *The Einstein Theory of Relativity* (1923) and *Evolution* (1925, based on Charles Darwin's theory). Only parts of the two documentaries were animated.

Along with the films featuring Felix the Cat by the Sullivan Studio, the films starring Koko (who later became Ko-ko) and his dog Fitz were the most lively, clever American productions of that time. Koko does not have a very distinct personality (his main trait is a hilarious insolence clearly borrowed from clowns in the circus), and his world is rigorously graphic: Every object can become something different at any time because everything is, after all, nothing but drawing. While this principle was more or less shared by American animators of the 1920s, it found its best expression in these films, in which the character always emerged from the artist's inkwell and returned to it at the end of the adventure.

Within the silent production of the Fleischer brothers, some sequences are so wildly nonsensical as to remain unparalleled, worthy of the honour list of twentieth-century comedy. Regrettably, the Fleischers bet everything on gags. There is no doubt that a collection of good gags can make up a good film, but this must be done with restraint: a simple yet very strong character must handle them, such as Charlie Chaplin's Tramp, Buster Keaton's Stoneface, and Harold Lloyd's Optimistic Young Man. Koko the Clown is flimsy and vague, and it is no surprise that his films were never as popular as (for instance) the ones of the well-shaped Felix the Cat.

The Fleischers' style fluctuated constantly, depending on the 'hands' of several animators (the company's organization of labour remained informal, even in the highly departmentalized age of sound cinema). A few elements, however, remained from the beginning as a sort of trademark: the 'rubbery' animation of characters, which moved constantly, and a taste for black humour, perhaps distantly rooted in middle European influences.

Felix, Pat, and Otto Messmer

Until the late 1960s, producer Pat Sullivan was considered the creator of Felix the Cat, the most important character in American animation before Mickey Mouse and the prototype of the 'animal hero' that reigned supreme in the next twenty years. The rules of the studio system, as well as the reserved character of Felix the Cat's actual creator, Otto Messmer, contributed to the longest-lasting case of embezzlement in the history of cinema. Otto Messmer was born in Union City, New Jersey, on 16 August 1892 and died in Teaneck, New Jersey, in October 1983. A lover of drawing and cinema, in 1913 Messmer met the cartoonist-animator Hy Mayer, who taught him the basics of the craft. As an assistant to Mayer, Messmer created comedies and some advertising films. In 1916, Pat Sullivan noticed Messmer's skills and hired him for his small, recently opened studio. Their collaboration was to last the next twenty years.

In 1919, in his own time, Messmer created Felix for Paramount's newsreel *Screen Magazine*. The cat was well received, and Paramount patented its name and rights. In order to continue to have Messmer draw the black cat, Paramount chose the easiest way, asking the Pat Sullivan Studio to produce the episodes. When, in 1922, the Paramount newsreel began having problems, Sullivan cannily acquired the rights to Felix. Thereafter, Messmer directed a long series of animators that included, at different times, Bill Nolan, Vernon George Stallings, Raoul Barré, Burt Gillett, and Al Eugster (1909–1997). For years, films were produced at a pace of one every fifteen days; they were distributed by Educational Films. Messmer also created comic strips with Felix for the Sunday comic page.

A difficult man (he even served some months in prison for the rape of a minor), Patrick Peter Sullivan was born in Paddington (New South Wales, Australia) on 22 February 1885. He moved to London in 1909 to further his cartoonist and music hall ambitions but was unable to make a name for himself. By early 1910, he was in New York, where he boxed for prize money, and in 1911 he eventually created a couple of short-lived comic strips, Willing Waldo and Old Pop Perkins. In October 1914, Sullivan joined the Raoul Barré studio and was laid off after nine months because of unsatisfactory work. He stubbornly managed to open his own factory, and by 1916 his staff was producing films under his name. Winning the approval of the usually very cautious Charlie Chaplin, he created an animated series based on Chaplin's comic character. Even though he was quite occupied with business affairs, he signed every graphic or cinematographic creation produced by his company. He also capitalized on the great success of Felix with one of the first instances of merchandising, a phenomenon that Roy Disney later developed and mastered for the Disney Company. Toys, stuffed animals, and various objects displaying the image of Felix increased Sullivan's profits. The films – and from 1923 the published comic strips – spread to Europe and in 1924, when the producer and his wife toured England, Felix was so famous that entrepreneurs were producing pirated dolls and toys. Sullivan managed to obtain a share of the royalties.

Felix disappeared from screens at the height of his success. Pat Sullivan no longer had the strength or the determination to adapt his studio to the changes that sound cinema required. He suffered from syphilis, and his mental faculties declined; the death of his wife, in 1932, further undermined his health, and on 15 February 1933 he died of pneumonia and alcoholism in Sharman Square Hospital, New York.

The disposition of Sullivan's estate was so intricate that Messmer could not continue with the production of Felix (it was first necessary to determine who owned the rights to the character). Messmer retired from cinema and devoted himself to comics and illustrations.

In the panorama of the decade, Felix was uniquely complex, being at the same time feline, human, and 'magical' (to avoid using 'surreal', an improper term here). His shape cleverly mixed rounded and gracious forms, with corners suggesting the character's shrewdness and naughtiness. Felix was probably the only example of a great animated mime that did not need situations or comic accidents to provoke laughter; his habit of walking in a circle when worried or thoughtful is still famous. Messmer's work on the animated version of Charlie Chaplin probably helped him to understand how a movement or a typical gesture, used with the appropriate timing, could become by itself a powerful, humorous technique. The smooth use of every element in Felix's graphic world contributed to the character's magic. His tail transformed itself into all kinds of useful objects; exclamation and question marks that the animator superimposed on the character could become baseball bats or fishhooks – even the door of a faraway house could be used, regardless of perspective, as a hatch in a blank wall.

As the creation of a great scriptwriter, artist, and filmmaker who was assisted by a staff of professionals that provided a unique style, Felix was an isolated case in the panorama of American animation of the times. Messmer's animation, sober yet elegant, did not result from an imitation of other animators. It is ironic that Felix's originality cost its creator years of dispossession.

Terry and the Fables

Back home after having served in World War I, Paul Terry formed the Fables Studio in 1920 along with Amadée J. Van Beuren (1879–1938), introducing to audiences a new series entitled Aesop's Fables. Actually, the only common link his fables shared with Aesop's stories was the fact that they both were populated by animals of all kinds and that they had a more or less appropriate moral ('Three thousand years ago, Aesop said . . . ') concluding the story. Terry's character, the old farmer Al Falfa, as previously mentioned, was inserted in this new thespian group. The films, which were produced at the suffocating pace of one every week, could not compete in terms of quality among the other films of the time. They were, however, influential for the then-debuting Walt Disney, for they were filled with all kinds of animals and mice – some characters even resembled the early Mickey Mouse of 1927. There is actually tangible evidence that the young Disney and his staff imitated Terry's output and that even after the success of *Steamboat Willie*, Walt considered him an example to match.

Financially, the Keith-Albee Theatre Company,[2] which took care of film distribution, held the majority of shares until 1928, when the group sold its shares to Amadée J. Van Beuren. The friction between the two partners grew intolerable and ended only when Terry and the majority of the animators left and opened the Terrytoons Studio in 1929. (At the same time, his former partner created Van Beuren Studios.) One of the reasons for the disagreement between Terry and Van Beuren was the advent of sound, which Terry, reluctant to undertake additional expense and innovation, opposed. Ironically, it was one of Terry's productions (*Dinner Time*) that preceded *Steamboat Willie* by a few weeks in becoming the first really popular animated sound short. By the end of this first decade, Terry demonstrated a tendency that was to characterize his career: stylistic and organizational conservatisms striving towards maximum savings, regularity, and punctuality in delivery to distributors. Overall, his films were of average quality, with occasional instances of comic creativity.

Bowers Unbound

Born in 1889 in Cresco, Iowa, Charles R. Bowers lived a gypsy-like childhood and youth, moving from place to place and from job to job. Fascinated by animation, Bowers collaborated briefly with Raoul Barré, as previously mentioned. In 1916, he began working independently on the production of the Mutt and Jeff series. Filled with energy and ideas – and with no scruples – he plotted against Barré but in turn was expelled by Bud Fisher, who had remained the company's sole owner. The rich, resolute Fisher owned all rights to the characters he had created and made successful for comic strips years before. Fisher also claimed all credit for himself, demanding the rights to every film made in the studio, when in fact he appeared there only sporadically. It did not take long for Bowers to re-enter Fisher's good graces, and he returned to work again on the production and design of the series, albeit as a subcontractor, for five or six more years after 1919.

Bowers' most ambitious project (which he planned with unique precision for such an explosive personality) concerned live-action cinema. From 1926 to 1928, he produced, wrote, acted in, and directed about fifteen comedy shorts in which animated objects and puppets were his co-stars. As Louise Beaudet wrote:

The dichotomy between the animated films of the Mutt & Jeff series and the comic films called 'novelty type' of Bowers is startling. Setting aside the surrealist aspect of the two kinds of films, the construction and orchestration, the manner of expression, the spirit and the letter of the two styles do not come together in any way.[3]

Judging from the few that remain, Bowers' films were extremely fascinating, characterized by a striking originality. According to Beaudet:

He succeeded in bringing about an almost unique kind of marriage of slapstick with frame-by-frame animation. Moreover, he had a mind and spirit too bizarre to fail to delight today's lovers of the fantastic.

Bowers disappeared from public life after 1928 to occasionally resurface by the mid-1930s when he was briefly hired by the New York Universal branch in competition with Walter Lantz (already based in California) on the claim that he could provide better work at a lower price. He died in New Jersey on 25 November 1945.

---

[2] The Keith-Albee Group, later Keith-Orpheum, the largest vaudeville circuit in North America, was the foundation on which RKO, one of Hollywood's major production companies, was later built. RKO stands for Radio-Keith-Orpheum and is the result of the merger of Radio Pictures with Keith-Orpheum.
[3] Louise Beaudet et Raymond Borde, *Charles R. Bowers ou le mariage du slapstick et de l'animation* (The Marriage of Slapstick and Animation), Cinémathèque de Toulouse: La cinémathèque québécoise, 1980, p. 13.

Lantz's Debut

Walter Lantz made his directorial debut in the 1920s. Born on 27 April 1900 in New Rochelle, New York[4] (he died on 22 March 1994 in Los Angeles), to a family of Italian origins (the Lanzas), at the age of fifteen he moved to New York. While working at Hearst's *New York American*, he took a correspondence course in drawing and practiced tirelessly. Impressed by the boy's enthusiasm, the newspaper director, Morrel Goddard,[5] sent him to Hearst's newly founded International Film Service, where Lantz, then sixteen years old, learned animation from the twenty-four-year-old Gregory La Cava. When Hearst's venture ended two years later, Lantz moved to Charles Bowers' group at Mutt & Jeff Cartoons. In 1921, he was hired by Bray. He advanced quickly and in 1923 became responsible for all of the animated production as well as for his own series entitled Dinky Doodle. Dinky Doodle was a boy with a cap and a dog called Weakheart – like Wallace Carlson's Dreamy Dud and Earl Hurd's Bobby Bumps, the character was unappealing. Lantz himself appeared regularly in the films, continuing the formula of 'live action plus animation'.

During the four years in which Lantz worked in Bray's studio, he was the artistic driving force. When the studio closed in 1927, there were few opportunities in New York, and Lantz decided to start over in Hollywood.

Bray, Hurd, and Mintz

In the 1920s, John Randolph Bray (now associated with Samuel Goldwyn and strongly influenced by him) continued to diversify his company. Busy with newsreels, live-action comedies, and educational films, he left more and more of his artistic responsibilities to others (Max Fleischer first; Walter Lantz later). His enterprises in the field of animation ranged from the temporary resurrection of Colonel Heeza Liar in 1922 through Lantz's Dinky Doodles to the series Unnatural History, which had been initiated autonomously by Earl Hurd. A risky project (a documentary on the Colorado River that endangered the life of the crew during filming and later led to legal troubles due to a delay in delivery to the distributor) accelerated the pioneering tycoon's growing dissatisfaction. In 1927, he closed the entertainment department of his company and concentrated on more modest, but safer, educational works.

After a stint at Paul Terry's, Earl Hurd began his own business in 1920, continuing his Bobby Bumps series and producing more aesthetically good but unsuccessful films. After the aforementioned Unnatural History series, Hurd created the Pen and Ink Vaudeville Sketches, a series of unrelated episodes set in a true puppet theatre, complete with rising curtains. After he resumed working for Bray, he disappeared from the scene until the 1930s, when he joined Charles Mintz's studio. In 1934, he moved to Disney, where he worked on films such as *Snow White* and *Fantasia*, where he remained until his death in 1940.

Charles Mintz (1889–1940), along with his brother-in-law George Winkler, founded Winkler Pictures in 1925 to produce a Krazy Kat[6] series.[7] The new version, originally handled by Bill Nolan, was subcontracted to Emanuel 'Manny' Gould (1904–1975) and his associate Ben Harrison and, although it was hopelessly bad, lasted until the relocation of the studio to Los Angeles in 1930.

Sarg and Dawley

Anthony Frederick 'Tony' Sarg was born in Cobán, Guatemala, on 21 April 1880, to a German father (Charles Francis Sarg) and an English mother (Mary Elizabeth Parker). In 1887, the Sarg family returned to Germany, and at the age of fourteen, Tony embarked on a military career, though he was more interested in painting and drawing than he was in weapons. In 1905, he resigned and moved to the United Kingdom, where he married the American Bertha Eleanor McGowan. He began to enjoy some success as an illustrator and then as a puppeteer.

To avoid World War I, he moved with his wife and child to the United States – first to Cincinnati and then to New York. From 1917, his passion for puppets became a means of earning a living; he was naturalized in 1920 and set up his own company. Obviously endowed with a flair for publicity and commerce and unbelievable energy, he became

---

[4] In the last couple years of his life, Lantz maintained that he had discovered that he was actually born in 1899.
[5] In the history of journalism, Goddard deserves credit for having created the Sunday colour insert.
[6] George Herriman (1880–1944) first published the Kat's strip in 1913 in the *New York Evening Journal*. The daily's publisher, William Randolph Hearst, and a horde of intellectuals loved it enormously, although it never really became popular with readers.
[7] The character had appeared in its first cinematographic performance in 1916 under the care of Frank Moser at Hearst's International Film Service; in 1920–1921, it was taken care of by Bray Studios.

the most famous string puppeteer in America. He went on to become a millionaire, but finally his company was dissolved in 1939, leaving him bankrupt. He died in New York on 9 March 1942 of appendectomy complications.

Born in Chillicothe, Ohio, on 15 March 1880, Herbert M. Dawley[8] was actually a jack of all trades. On the stage, he would direct 115 musicals, comedies, and dramas over a fifty-two-year period. From 1912 to 1917, he was the head of the art department and a designer of special cars for the Pierce-Arrow Company and was credited with having originated the placing of automobile headlights on fenders. He directed quite a few live-action films, often including some animation in them. In the 1930s and 1940s, he appeared as an actor in such radio serials as *Gang Busters* (started in 1935 as *G-Men*) and *Hilltop House* (started in 1937). Herbert M. Dawley died in New Providence, New Jersey, on 15 August 1970.

On 13 May 1921, a front-page article in *Variety* announced the creation of Sarg-Dawley Co., a film production company.[9] This article talked of a secret process, not patented, developed by Sarg and his associate Dawley, to synchronize 'the limbs and organs of dumb animals to perform on the screen as if photographed from nature'. It also said that Sarg-Dawley Co. was limiting its production to twelve films per year. This may seem enormous for such a small organization, but one of the characteristics of the silhouette film, as cited by Sarg, is its economy of means: 'I am able, in conjunction with Herbert Dawley, my associate in production, to average 100 feet a day, which ordinarily would represent 960 drawings in celluloid. It is naturally a very much cheaper process than anything hitherto employed.'

At the time the article was published, Sarg was already planning three projects: *The First Circus*, *The Tooth Carpenter* (also known as *The First Dentist*), and *Why They Love Cavemen*, which are mentioned in the piece.

Two more films would be released before the year's end. In 1922, the series was augmented by a further twelve titles, including *Adam Raises Cain*, one of the first films to have been found and restored. The series ended in early 1923 with a final episode entitled *The Terrible Tree*.

Figure 5.2 Tony Sarg, *The First Circus*, 1921.

The series was bravely original, as silhouette films were unusual in the United States, but it was the omnipresent humour that made it work. The recipe was simple: contemporary life transposed into prehistoric times. This kind of situation comedy, reinforced by gags based on anachronistic objects and behaviour, was conveyed in highly polished animation with many examples of visual inventiveness that would not have seemed out of place in a cartoon. Domestic situations, alcohol, cinema, compromises – Sarg and Dawley put all their contemporaries' problems through the prehistoric grinder. Thus, one of the first films, *The First Circus*, brings together – with farcical results – the theory of evolution, Prohibition, and Barnum's circus. The series gained a wide distribution, and not only in the United States.

Herbert M. Dawley took up the torch as soon as *Tony Sarg's Almanac* had come to an end, with a new silhouette series entitled Silliettes, adaptations of classic European tales, for inclusion in the *Pathé Review*. The first episode, also entitled *Silliettes*, was released on 24 March 1923, followed by three other films. The following year, Dawley finished another eight films. After a final episode in 1925, *Jack and the Giant Killer*, the series came to an end.[10]

Let's now examine *Adam Raises Cain*, possibly the most interesting and surprising film among the few that have been preserved.

---

[8] Also known as 'Major Dawley' for his military rank during WWI.
[9] 'Tony Sarg's Invention', *Variety*, 13 May 1921, p. 1, column 4.
[10] The technique used by the two filmmakers is somewhat mysterious. In his *The Silhouette Film* (Le Mani, Genoa, 2004), Pierre Jouvanceau writes:

> In an article of 1921 (*Movies on Strings*, 'Photoplay' n. 21, December 1921, pp. 36 and 114), Tony Sarg lifted the veil on his method to a certain extent: 'The making [of the silhouette film] begins with a rough pencil sketch which I make on paper, of the scene which I wish to represent. I transfer this drawing to cardboard and generally colour the figures black. Then I cut them out with scissors. The next step is to turn the cardboard figures into marionettes by equipping their legs, arms, neck and other parts of their cardboard bodies with tiny hooks and hinges so that they move freely. By means of miniature mechanical contrivances hidden in back of the figures, and worked by buttons, I am able to make them actually seem to be breathing and their eyelids to move.'

The title is based, of course, on a pun, and synopsizes remarkably well the issues and context of the film. At the primary level, the title announces a film about the problems of a puny, retiring man struggling to bring up a difficult baby who is always ready to get into new mischief. This, along with the second meaning of 'raising Cain' – 'creating a monumental scene' – is where the film derives most of its comedy.

Throughout this silent adventure, the main characters open and close their mouths incessantly, using all possible gestures to symbolize their right to speak.

There is Adam, a slight and sickly creature, trying, via a discussion, to stand up to Eve; there is the shrew, Eve, yelling insults and threats at her husband; then there is the doctor, called in as backup, who constantly grumbles about the working conditions he suffers around this infernal family. Monkeys, lions, an elephant, a wasp, poultry, and dinosaurs fill the space with an inaudible cacophony. Even objects have their acoustic place: the plate breaking over Adam's head, the phonograph that he cranks up to settle Cain. The visual suggestion of sound is such that it even seems as if an orchestra is accompanying the performance – at once graceful and comic – of the dancer before Adam.

The latter plays the role of the misunderstood lover, mismatched with his wife, lumbered with a mischievous child, under attack from the vicissitudes of everyday life; a creature full of uncertainties and frustrations, constantly inhibited, though his subversive ramblings compensate for his powerlessness in the marriage. The silhouettes' jumpy movements explain in turn – but always from an exterior point of view – his isolation, his difference, his impotence, and his desire to run away.

Sarg and Dawley bring movement to every slightest detail in the images that have any connection with the supposed emission of a sound – even in the establishing shots where, under normal projection conditions, such movements would be too small to be seen.

The Young Walt Disney

Walter Elias Disney was born in Chicago on 5 December 1901, the fourth son of the Irish Canadian Elias Disney and Flora Call, an Ohio teacher. The Windy City did not stay long in Walt's memory because in 1906 his father moved the family to a farm in Marceline, Missouri, in one

---

Except for the mechanical contrivances, the principle of puppet construction that he describes does not seem too different from that developed by [other silhouette animators]. However, precise as this first-hand account is, it is nevertheless contradicted by what a viewing of Sarg's surviving films would suggest.

It is hard to believe that the suppleness of the silhouettes and the fluidity of their movements could derive exclusively from as rigid a material as cardboard, no matter how numerous and how ingenious these mysterious mechanisms developed by the animator. The dinosaur whose back serves as a toboggan for the characters in *Adam Raises Cain* demonstrates a flexibility such that his neck, his backbone and then his tail become hollow under the presumed weight of the people sliding down; the snake in *The First Circus*, which is attached like a rope between the neck and the tail of a dinosaur to allow a tight-rope walker to demonstrate his art, manifests the same effect; everywhere animal and human silhouettes come and go and pirouette with a surprising ease, with no trace even in their most complex movements of the inevitable jolts that cardboard produces. . . . A frame-by-frame examination of the undulating movements of the massive tails of the dinosaurs demonstrates that the plasticity of the silhouettes, which is at no time below par, could not possibly have been achieved merely by a large number of joints. . . . Sarg and Dawley, unlike most silhouette animators, used a horizontal shooting set-up identical to that used in the shadow theatre, as is demonstrated by a photograph published in *Photoplay*. His silhouettes, placed upright against a translucent screen, obviously needed great solidity. Given these facts, cardboard or any other rigid medium seems unlikely as a material.

So how did Sarg and Dawley make their puppets? Two theories could be advanced.

Either the silhouettes were indeed cut out of cardboard, as Sarg himself maintains, with the body parts that require the greatest suppleness made from a semi-rigid material, which could, without the help of joints, take on any form and hold it for the time it takes to shoot a frame – rubber with a lead wire insert, for example. But the writer does not make any allusion to such a possibility.

Or else – but this contradicts what Sarg has said – he used three-dimensional puppets made of clay or any other material with sufficient malleability – which would explain both their stability and their suppleness.

Two observations tend to give credence to this second hypothesis. In *The First Circus*, the tail of a dinosaur just happens to pass in front of its body during a movement. At the same moment, a ray of light, very noticeable on the blackness of the silhouette, catches the tail and emphasizes its volume. Second, the way characters turn around in *Adam Raises Cain*, when examined frame by frame, demonstrates without any risk of error that at each phase of the movement all the logical perspectives of a three-dimensional body are preserved. However, neither of the two hypotheses can marshal enough evidence to be definitively accepted. Each of them is opposed by factors that could demolish it. It seems that Sarg did not choose to unveil the essential element of his technique, perhaps to avoid competition and – who knows – perhaps to deliberately throw out a few red herrings.

of several attempts to find a better life. The four years spent in the country (the Disneys moved once again in 1910, this time to Kansas City) remained in the future filmmaker's mind as a symbol of childhood happiness. Disney constantly returned to pastoral themes in his films, and he often gave interviewers nostalgic, detailed descriptions of Marceline's paths, willows, and prodigiously large apples.

In 1918, motivated by his desire for adventure as well as by disagreements with his father, Walt decided to volunteer for the Red Cross. Although World War I ended precisely at that time, he was transferred to France with the occupational troops. There, his drawings and caricatures found favour with his fellow soldiers, to the point that, once back home, he decided to become an artist or, more modestly, a 'comic strip artist'. After a brief stay with his family, who had returned to Chicago, Disney moved to the Kansas City of his youth. One of the first people he met was a gifted graphic artist who was working with him at the Pesmen-Rubin Commercial Art Studio, Ub Iwerks. They both loved their jobs: Walt was inventive and enterprising, while Ub was a born animator.

In 1922, Disney founded Laugh-O-Gram Films. Having hired Iwerks and other promising young artists, including Hugh Harman and Rudolf Ising, he began producing fables, such as *Cinderella* and *Puss in Boots*, retold in a comic tone.[11] The young entrepreneur also produced the pilot film for a new series, Alice's Wonderland. The beginning of what seemed to be a bright career, however, was interrupted when Pictorial Clubs from Tennessee, the distributors, remained insolvent. In October 1923, the company was declared bankrupt, while Walt himself had already taken a train for Hollywood with the intention of leaving animation for live-action cinematography. Fortunately, Alice's Wonderland turned out to be a success with a New York distributor, Margaret J. Winkler,[12] whose company had already taken Fleischers' and Sullivan's movies.

In October 1923, Winkler placed an order with Disney for the continuation of his series. In partnership with his brother Roy (Chicago, 24 June 1893–Los Angeles, 20 December 1971), who was to remain his lifelong business advisor, the animator resumed working, this time alone. The series, based on the idea of a live child[13] in a world of animated images, continued for four years.

The first to be hired was a Californian, Rollin Hamilton; then, one at a time, the Laugh-O-Gram veterans joined Disney from Kansas City: Iwerks first, then Harman, Ising and, eventually (but briefly), a friend of Harman's, Isadore 'Friz' Freleng. In 1927, Disney created another character, Oswald the Lucky Rabbit, the protagonist of a fully animated production without live actors. The distribution was entrusted to distributor and producer Charles Mintz, Margaret Winkler's husband and successor, and was supported by Carl Laemmle's Universal. Following the success of Oswald the Rabbit, Mintz managed to hire the studio's best animators, who were resenting Walt's bossy and hot-tempered behaviour. On his side, he had Universal, who owned the copyright for the character. (Mintz's victory lasted only one year, when Universal took Oswald away from him and gave it to Walter Lantz.) Once again, Disney had to start anew. The story goes that after his disagreement with Mintz, Disney sketched the figure of a small mouse and that his wife decided to name it 'Mickey', a much more familiar name than the serious 'Mortimer' suggested by Disney himself. In fact, the credit for Mickey Mouse should be shared equally by Disney, who traced the character's personality, and Ub Iwerks (the only animator who had refused Mintz's offer), who drew the mouse.[14] Ub Iwerks had marked his style in animation: quick, fluid – even gummy – but mechanical and formulaic and based on elementary drawings. Walt's stories and gags were rather good. The young Californians from Kansas City were making the best animated films of their time, second only to the Felix cartoons.

---

[11] These films still have a certain value today. Disney displays his skills as a scriptwriter and his expert sense of rhythm and timing.

[12] A native of Hungary, Margaret Winkler (1895–1990) immigrated to the United States with her family at the age of nine and attended public school, then secretarial school. . . . During her seven years as [Harry] Warner's secretary, Margaret cut her teeth in a decisive way. . . . By 1921, she had amassed a wealth of practical experience and, equally important, a nationwide network of contacts. Armed with these advantages . . . Margaret left the employ of the Warners and went into business for herself.

J. B. Kaufman, *The Live Wire: Margaret J. Winkler and Animation History*, in Maureen Furniss (ed.), *Animation – Art and Industry*, John Libbey/Indiana University Press, New Barnet (UK)/Bloomington, Indiana, 2009.

[13] This role was first played by Virginia Davis, then by Dawn O'Day, Margie Gay, and Lois Hardwick.

[14] From Alice or Oswald to Mickey, the look of the output remains uninterrupted. In the best films of the series about Alice, the girl had a very small role, while the action focused on several animals, particularly a cat named Julius (who looked like a carbon copy of Felix the Cat). As for Oswald, he was a sort of pre-Mickey, albeit less sweet and more adult; he shared Mickey's same gestures and mimicry and even the same . . . desire to kiss his girlfriend whenever possible (*Oh, What a Knight!*, 1928).

6
SILENT EUROPE

The Individualists

At the beginning of the century, Old Continent animation found expression not only through Émile Cohl and the avant-garde painters but also through the isolated artists who worked in Great Britain, Spain, Sweden, Denmark, and Russia. Almost without exception, animators worked either alone or in small groups: no industry, no market outlets, and no careers. In many countries lacking structure and know-how, animation was left to the enthusiasm and extravagance of a few isolated amateurs. Some nations with old cultural traditions, such as the Netherlands, Italy, Hungary, Poland, and Czechoslovakia, produced only occasional films. World War I boosted the market by creating demand for satirical patriotic propaganda films; in several cities, small studios produced advertising reels, film titles, and, sometimes, entertainment shorts.

While live-action cinema was evolving prosperously towards the production of its first masterpieces, animation still laboured to emerge from its 'prehistoric' conditions. Unlike live-action filmmakers, animators remained novices in their field even after cinema had entered the sound age. European production of animated films was slow and continued to be slow until at least the mid-1930s. However, it started to grow in the wake of Walt Disney's international success, with films generally imitating the Disney style. But such growth did not imply artistic quality. Independent contemporary animators were more interesting: They were usually penniless but enjoyed more artistic freedom.

Great Britain

In 1909, Charles Armstrong wrote, directed, and produced two short silhouette films, *The Sporting Mice* and *Votes for Women: A Caricature*, followed, in 1910, by *The Clown and His Donkey*. In 1911, another three films were completed: *M-M!*; *Come Again*; and *Mr. Asquith and the Clown* (a satire on the Prime Minister), followed by the commercial *The Best Cigarette Is a Jones*. In 1914, he made *Isn't It Wonderful?*, followed in 1915 by *Armstrong's Trick Mar Incidents*. All these films were distributed by the Charles Urban Trading Company. For the time being, we have no biographical details.

In *The Clown and His Donkey* (the only surviving film), the figures are white, depicted in profile against a black background. Seven short scenes are separated by black segments of differing durations, with no real narrative, in which a clown and a donkey, sometimes helped by a monkey, do circus tricks, juggle, and play practical jokes while making gestures of complicity towards the audience.

During World War I, lightning sketchers, as well as satirical illustrators and comic strip artists such as Harry Furniss (1854–1925), brought their drawings to the screen. Ridiculing the Germans, particularly the Kaiser, and raising morale at home and on the battle front, Furniss made *Peace and War Pencillings* (1914) and *Winchelsea and Its Environs* (both in 1914). George Ernest Studdy (1878–1948) initiated the series War Studies (1914) and Dudley Tempest made War Cartoons (1914). Lancelot Speed (1860–1931), who was responsible for the series Bully Boy (short satires dealing with current and war events), distinguished himself with *The U Tube* (1917, in which the Kaiser attempts to reach Great Britain by digging a tunnel under the English Channel but goes the wrong way) and *Sea Dreams* (1914, which ridicules the monarch's aspirations of naval power). Dudley Buxton's War Cartoons included *Ever Been Had?* (1917), a work with an extremely elaborate plot for its time and a disturbing atmosphere (it features the 'last man' on Earth, which has been burned by war, and a defeated England; only later does the viewer discover that the drama is actually a film in the making). Jack Dodsworth joined in

1917 with the series Bairnsfather Cartoons and Raemakers Cartoons.

Buxton is also credited with having introduced his friend Anson Dyer (1876–1962) to British animation. For about twenty years, Dyer worked as a painter of stained glass for churches. When he entered the world of animation at thirty-nine, he did not have any specific experience in the field; still, he worked with animation until 1952 and became the most important English producer of animated films in the 1930s. During World War I, in collaboration with Buxton, Dyer gave life to the war patriotic propaganda series John Bull's Animated Sketchbook.

By the end of the war, British animators had acquired a trade, learning new techniques (even though they still preferred the use of animated cut-outs) and experimenting with longer films. Buxton, Dyer, and a few collaborators made a series entitled Kiddigraphs,[1] produced by Cecil Hepworth. Afterward, Dyer worked on adaptations from Shakespeare, while Buxton made two series, entitled Memoirs of Miffy and Bucky's Burlesques. Lancelot Speed worked on still another series, entitled Pip, Squeak and Wilfred. The most successful with the public was George Ernest Studdy (Devonport, 23 June 1878–London, 25 July 1948), with the adventures of Bonzo (begun in 1924), a good-natured puppy that gets into trouble in a middle-class environment. (As a still character, and under the name of 'Studdy Dog', he made his debut on the pages of the magazine *The Sketch* on 2 November 1921.)[2]

Despite economic difficulties affecting the small British film industry, new series were continually in production, and more studios were opening. Joe Noble created Sammy and Sausage about a boy and his dog. Sid Griffiths, who learned the basics of animation by analyzing the movements of Felix the Cat while working as a projectionist in a theatre, also made a series featuring a dog, entitled Jerry the Tyke. Instead of a canine, cartoonist Tom Webster opted for a horse to feature in his *Tishy the X-Legged Horse*. Anson Dyer was the one who left the most noticeable mark on British animation of the 1920s; amid his several engagements as a set designer and educational filmmaker, he spent two years working on *The Story of the Flag* (which was conceived as a long feature but was released in six episodes in 1927). As it happened for British live-action cinema, animation was mostly isolated for domestic exhibition only. The very few films distributed on the continent did not exert any influence on other filmmakers working in Europe at the time.

Ireland

The pioneering work of James Horgan is worth mentioning. Horgan became involved in cinema at the end of the nineteenth century when he acquired a Lumière camera and established his own moving picture exhibition company for the south Munster region. As well as projecting regular international shows, Horgan shot local footage to show to his audiences – mostly religious events. However, soon his eager mind began to look into cinematography in a scientific way and he in fact made some money by patenting a cog for film traction in the camera, which was widely used. He also experimented with Polaroid film. He then began to dabble in frame by frame work – animation – around the year 1909. His most popular piece was his dancing *Youghal Clock Tower* (1910) which lasts only 30 seconds. Here the Youghal's best-known landmark hops into the frame and 'manipulates' itself into its rightful place in the main street. (Youghal, once a walled military port in Cork County, is now a rich seaside resort town). A representation of the clock tower is given as a trophy for best first animation at the Galway Film Fleadh every year.[3]

Frank Leah was born in Stockport, Ireland, in 1886 and died in 1972. He sold his first cartoon to a newspaper when he was twelve years old. Later, he became an art editor of five Dublin journals. He moved on to Calcutta, then London, where he settled in Kensington. Leah was an accomplished landscape and portrait painter who worked with amazing speed. His portraits were generally life size, and he sketched an exact likeness sometimes within nine seconds. In 1917, Frank Leah supplied his drawings to producer Norman Whitten and director Jack Warren for the first Irish animated film, *Ten Days Leave*. The content has not been determined, though the title suggests that it may have been a film about a soldier's home leave.

---

[1] Among these fables, two deserve mention: *Three Little Pigs* (1922) and *Little Red Riding Hood* (1922), both by Dyer.
[2] This series measured up to the standards of its American counterparts for its fluid animation as well as for the use of graphic and cinematographic language. (For instance, when the character notices an odour, it transforms itself into the corresponding object: a sausage, a hare, or an egg).
[3] Steve Woods, *History of Animation*, in http://www.stevewoods.ie/articles.html, retrieved 11 October 2009.

France

Lortac

'In my distant youth, and for long years, I made the animated commercials of Publi-Ciné, which appeared weekly on the screens of France and Italy. . .'[4]

France was the site of the first organized animation studio in Europe. In 1919, Robert Collard (Cherbourg, 19 November 1884–Paris, 10 April 1973), best known under the pseudonym Lortac, founded Publi-Ciné, his own studio of animation in Montrouge, with between ten and fifteen collaborators and five cameras. He also made documentaries and technical and educational films. A fine arts student and later a soldier who was wounded and discharged in 1915, Lortac studied under Cohl and worked with him on short films to be inserted in the newsreels of Éclair. Lortac's team included animators such as Cavé, Cheval, Raymond Savignac (in charge of washing cels, he later became a well-known commercial artist), André Rigal, and (part-time) Émile Cohl himself.

Although the emphasis was on commercials, the studio also made a number of short comic fiction cartoons that were distributed by Pathé. The enormous output of Lortac is usually unacknowledged, since Pathé mostly distributed it in substandard format (9.5 mm) for the home projection market, avoiding cinema theatres. His most famous character was Professor Mécanicas.

In 1922, he became involved in the creation of a satirical supplement to newsreels; its title, 'Le canard en ciné', was a pun referring to the humorous satirical publication *Le Canard Enchaîné*. Brilliant and worth mentioning is the episodic film adaptation he made in 1921 of *Monsieur Vieux-Bois* by the famous Swiss (Genevan) designer and humorist of the nineteenth century, Rodolphe Toepffer (1799–1846).

Lortac animated Toepffer's drawing in collaboration with Cavé using the pasteboard cut-out technique; by cutting images and moving them as they were without any physiognomic changes, he respected Toepffer's work and style. This respect emerges also in the choice of a flowing, narrative structure. Vieux Bois is a clumsy character stuffed with Arcadian readings who lacks any sense of reality. Without fail, he emerges beaten and ridiculed from all kinds of adventures but never gives up and never learns from his experiences. His unique power lies in his ability to continually summon all his courage to begin anew – by simply changing his undergarments. Lortac and Cavé's series represents an example of European-style comic animation, detached from the American slapstick that was soon to dominate. This kind of humour, not founded on rhythm but on character, and with undertones closer to comedy than to the circus, reappeared only in the 1950s in *La bergère et le ramoneur* (Mr. Wonderbird) by Grimault-Prévert. During the 1930s, the Depression slowed down commercial advertising. Lortac closed his studio in 1944 and concentrated on writing scripts for comic books and detective stories, like Bibi Fricotin, Bicot, and Les Pieds Nickelés.

Advertisers and Illustrators

A large number of artists with different backgrounds created advertising films and more ambitious work. Benjamin Rabier (1864–1939) was a brilliant illustrator and cartoonist whose work was published in magazines such as *Gil Blas*, *Rire*, and *Pêle-Mêle*. A specialist in animal stories, in 1916 he worked with Émile Cohl on shorts, the most famous of which is *Les fiançailles de Flambeau* (Flambeau's Engagement), featuring a dog named Flambeau. After leaving Cohl, Rabier made some other films on his own.

O'Galop,[5] who made his debut in the 1910s as an advertising poster designer, worked on a series based on the character of Bécassotte (1919) and on a film adaptation of the fables of La Fontaine. In the early 1920s, Albert Mourlan (1887–1946) created a series dedicated to Potiron. In 1923, he devoted himself to *Gulliver chez les Lilliputiens* (Gulliver and the Lilliputians), a feature film that employed a mixed technique (live action and animation). After one year of work, however, a fire destroyed the negatives and the positive copies of the film. Finally, Didier Daix filmed the series Zut, Flûte et Trotte (1929), featuring Zut as a good-natured hippopotamus.

In 1924, painter Fernand Léger made *Ballet mécanique* (Mechanical Ballet), a potpourri of live-action shots, direct painting on film, classical animation, and special effects, one of the most well-known works of avant-garde cinema of all time. (The American Dudley Murphy[6] contributed with the sequence *Charlot cubiste* [Cubistic Charlie Chaplin], which apparently dated back to 1920–1921.)

---

[4] Letter received by the author from Robert Collard 'Lortac', 18 April 1972.

[5] O'Galop (real name: Marius Rossillon [1875–1946]) was the creator of Bibendum or 'The Michelin Man', the character of the Michelin tyres, one of the most famous icons of the twentieth century.

[6] An undervalued avant-garde filmmaker, Murphy was born in Winchester, Massachusetts, on 10 July 1897 and died in Malibu, California, on 22 February 1968. In the opinion of this writer, his sequence is the only good part of *Ballet mécanique*.

Figure 6.1 Fernand Léger, *Ballet mécanique*, 1924. © 2014 Artists Rights Society (ARS), New York/ADAGP, Paris.

At that time, Léger was interested in objects; he arranged them in his painting in different ways, at times isolated; at other times grouped or contrasting with each other. He wrote:

> This film is above all the proof that machines and fragments, as well as usual mass-produced goods, are *possible* and plastic. The action of giving *movement* to one or many of these goods can make them plastic. There is also the possibility of creating a plastic event, itself beautifully, without the artist being forced to find what it means. It's the *revenge of painters and poets*. In such an art where image had to be all and everything, and where image was sacrificed to narrative anecdotes, we had to defend ourselves and we had to prove that *imaginative art*, relegated among accessories, could build a film by itself, with its own strength, without scenario and considering the *moving image the central character*.[7]

Léger's film must be interpreted as a pictorial and dynamic work in progress and as a linguistic proposal. It had a significant cultural influence (it was circulated perhaps more than any other abstract film of its time) and boosted the development of the French historical avant-garde and of other 'non-aligned' films by Dadaist and surrealist artists.

Fellow artist Marcel Duchamp (1887–1968) also made an animated film (based on vortex-revolving shapes), *Anémic Cinéma*, and so did the American Man Ray,[8] who filmed the Basque *Emak-Bakia* (Leave Me Alone) before working on *Mystères du Château de Dès* (The Mysteries of the Castle of the Dice) and *L'étoile de mer* (The Star of the Sea).

Germany: Animation in the Weimar Republic

Animated films were still made in Germany during the time of the emperor – for instance, a charming sparkling wine commercial entitled *Happy New Year 1910*, directed by the film pioneer Guido Seeber.

With the outbreak of World War I, film imports were stopped, and the number of home-produced live-action films increased tenfold from twenty-five to 250 a year. In 1917, by military government decree, the UFA[9] production company was established. This contributed to a quadrupling of film output in the last year of the war, although the economic situation for Germany deteriorated immensely.

On 1 January 1921, a quota was introduced, allowing imports equivalent to 15 per cent of the total footage of negatives produced in Germany in 1919. It was replaced from 1 January 1925 by a new quota of one imported feature for every German production. The national movie lived its greatest artistic age ever, with such directors as Robert Wiene, Fritz Lang, F. W. Murnau, G. W. Pabst, Paul Leni, and Josef von Sternberg.[10]

Advertising, scientific, and technical films were produced along with the most audacious of avant-garde cinema, and satirical films appealed to wide audiences. The main centres of production were Berlin and Munich.

Julius Pinschewer (Jungbreslau,[11] 15 September 1883–Berne, Switzerland, 16 April 1961) began his career in 1910, addressing his activity exclusively towards advertising. In *Die Suppe* (The Soup, 1911), he mixed object animation with live action. Pinschewer's collaborators included some of the most talented artists of the time, such as Walther Ruttmann, creator of the famous *Der Sieger* (The Victor, 1920); Lotte Reiniger; Hans Richter; Guido Seeber; Oskar Fischinger; Hans Fischerkoesen; and George Pal. Pinschewer gave an artistic direction to German advertising, which continued for twenty years as the most advanced worldwide. After his escape from Nazi

---

[7] Fernand Léger, *Fonctions de la peinture*, Gauthier, Paris, 1965.
[8] Pseudonym of Emmanuel Radnitzky (Philadelphia, 27 August 1890–Paris, 18 November 1976).
[9] Universum Film Aktiengesellschaft.
[10] Most people still call this era 'German Expressionist Cinema', although the only openly expressionist film was Robert Wiene's *Das Kabinett des Doktor Caligari* (The Cabinet of Dr. Caligari, 1919).
[11] Also known as Hohensalza. Today, this is Inowrocław, Poland.

Germany in 1934, he continued his activity in the advertising and educational fields in Bern, Switzerland.

Guido Seeber (1879–1940) was multi-talented as a full-fledged filmmaker, director of photography, designer, editor of technical and trade magazines, inventor, writer of manuals, teacher, and producer. As a director of photography, he contributed to many films, including *Student von Prag* (The Student of Prague, 1913), several films starring Asta Nielsen, and others directed by Georg Wilhelm Pabst. In the field of animation, Seeber created advertising works such as *Kipho* or *Du musst zur Kipho* (You Must Go to Kino-Photo, 1925), a patchwork film produced by Pinschewer for the Berlin Film and Photography Exhibition. In this original work, Seeber combined a vast range of cinematographic tricks with skillful editing.

The Swiss national Rudolf Pfenninger, son of painter Emil Pfenninger, was born in Munich on 25 October 1899. A scenographer, designer, and animator, his talent emerged more through his inventions than through his films (*Largo*, 1922; *Sonnenersatz* [Sun Replacement], 1926). He was particularly notable for his synthetic sound experiments, called *Tönende Handschrift* ('sound writing'), which he conducted between 1930 and 1932. Disappointed by a lack of recognition, he made a few more short films (*Pitsch und Patsch*, *Serenade*, and *Barcarole* with the Diehl brothers). With the rise of Nazism, the artist slid into anonymity. He died on 14 June 1976 in Baldham, near Munich.

In the 1920s, theatres showed the series Kollege Pal and Max und Moritz, as well as films by Hans Fischerkoesen (1896–1973) and Harry Jaeger, Kurt Wolfram Kiesslich (who had made war propaganda vignettes), and Toni Rabold of Dean Film. Louis Seel[12] was extremely active with his *Münchener Bilderbogen*, types of drawn newsreels made in Munich.

The Diehl brothers began their long-lasting career; Lore Bierling, a specialist in Chinese shadows, also made her debut. In 1928, the prestigious painter and satirical caricaturist George Grosz (1893–1959) filmed, for a stage performance by Erwin Piscator, *Die Abenteuer des braven Soldaten Schweijk* (The Adventures of the Good Soldier Schweik). Among production companies, the omnipotent Berlin-based UFA deserves mention as the initiator of the great German cinema, with its future production of special effects, educational films, movie titles, and avant-garde work.

The Matrix

In terms of artistic freedom, Germany and France led the way in Europe. However, it was the avant-garde German film community, unlike its French counterpart, that favoured expressing itself through animated drawings. This preference is perhaps a matter of origins: The French avant-garde was rooted in the Dada and surrealism movements, which drew upon material from real life and turned it inside out. On the other hand, the Germans paid attention to lessons of formal and geometrical rigour taught in part by supremat ism, De Stijl, the Bauhaus, and expressionism. It is not by chance that the German Dadaist Hans Richter turned to films with a post-Méliès slant after having attempted to follow Eggeling's theory of geometry and 'purity'. The pictorial and literary cores of expressionism (represented by Kokoschka, Dix, Toller, and Trakl) lacked direct followers in animation.

Walther Ruttmann

In *Die Niebelungen* (Part One, 1924) by Fritz Lang, the sequence of Kriemhild's nightmare stands out, with flocks of menacing birds flying about in a darkly shaded sky, visiting the queen in her dreams. The author of that suggestive sequence was Walther[13] Ruttmann. Born in Frankfurt-am-Main (28 December 1887), he studied architecture in Zurich and fine arts in Munich while learning to play the cello. Between 1912 and 1918, he painted and engraved, flowing through abstraction and from this moving to a theory of abstract cinema ('painting with time', in his words). After being a lieutenant in World War I, and after a subsequent nervous illness, Ruttmann devoted himself to the realization of his theory. On 27 April 1921, in Berlin's Marmorhaus, he presented his *Lichtspiel Opus I*,[14] which featured a musical score expressly written by Max Butting (1888–1976).

---

[12] Ludwig (Louis, Luis) Seel was born in Wiesbaden in 1881 or perhaps in Deidesheim in 1889. He migrated to the United States and worked as a political cartoonist at the New York *Brooklyn Daily Eagle*, joining in 1915 the group that worked on the Mutt and Jeff series. Back home in 1919, he was one of the earliest producers of German animation. He worked in Austria and in Great Britain, then left for Rio de Janeiro (1927–1939) to eventually return to Nazi Germany and try – rather unsuccessfully – to make his way through the crowd of Goebbels' animators. He survived the war and the de-Nazification and died in Wiesbaden in 1958.

[13] The original spelling was 'Walter' without an 'h'. He added it during his life as an homage to the ancient German tradition.

[14] 'Lichtspiel', which can be translated as 'light play', is also the word for 'movie'.

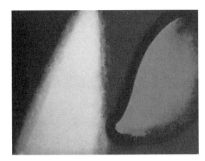

Figure 6.2 Walther Ruttmann, *Lichtspiel Opus I*, 1921.

As the first public presentation of an abstract film, the event was sensationally received by the public and press (newspapers had already reported the praises of previous private showings). *Opus I* is striking not only for its lyrical sensitivity and imaginative capacity but also for its stylistic maturity in technique and form. Amoeboid forms contrast with sharp objects; curvilinear shapes, anticipating those by Oskar Fischinger, cross the screen diagonally, while stripes with a pendulum-like motion seem to keep time. In the following years, Ruttmann produced three other shorts, each called *Opus* and progressively numbered, which were successfully released at home and abroad. The London *Times* wrote in 1925 that Ruttmann's short films would be long remembered.

Ruttmann's contacts within the film industry (besides the sequence for Lang, he had created another nightmare sequence for Paul Wegener's *Lebende Buddhas* [Living Buddha] in 1923), introduced him to Lotte Reiniger's team. Ruttmann collaborated with them on a feature film, *Prince Achmed*, but did not find the experience rewarding. The artist was then entering another stage of his creative evolution: the music of imagery should now have links to history. Having put aside abstractionism, Ruttmann devoted himself to projects (which were improperly classified as 'documentaries'), in which elements of real life combined rhythmically with each other.[15] In 1927, he put his mark on *Berlin – Die Sinfonie der Großstadt* (Berlin, The Symphony of the Great City), which began with thirty seconds of abstract animation – a farewell from the filmmaker to his earlier artistic phase. *Melodie der Welt* (Melody of the World, 1929) was 'possibly the first-ever music video: vaguely a sailor's voyage around the world and his encounters with what we might call today "ethno" music and related dances'[16]; *Wochenende* (Weekend, 1930, a film 'without images'; only the sound track was edited) followed. In other words, Ruttmann was experimenting with the newly useable sound on film. In 1933, Ruttmann went to Italy for the shooting of *Acciaio* (Steel), a hybrid between a documentary and a fiction film based on a text by Luigi Pirandello. Back in Germany, he continued along his path as a rhythmical documentary filmmaker. He contributed as a cameraman to Leni Riefenstahl's *Triumph des Willens* (Triumph of the Will) and also shot war newsreels about the advancing German troops at the beginning of World War II. He died of an embolism on 15 July 1941 in Berlin.

Ruttmann figures as a talented artist and a politically contradictory[17] intellectual (a follower of the left, he later unconditionally supported Hitler). His contributions to animation were limited in number but important in their quality as well as in the influence they exerted on other artists. Some elements of the styles of Eggeling, Richter, Fischinger, and even McLaren can be traced to Ruttmann's pioneering films.

Viking Eggeling

Viking Eggeling was born in Lund, Sweden, on 21 October 1880, the son of a German immigrant and a Swedish mother. After having attended public school without distinguishing himself, Eggeling was forced by economic difficulties to leave Lund for Germany, Switzerland, and Italy (at the end of the nineteenth century, Sweden was an impoverished country with a high level of emigration). For six years, from 1901 to 1907, he lived in Milan, working occasionally and attending the Brera Academy of Fine Arts. He returned to Switzerland, where he taught in a boarding school, and later spent four years in Paris. In 1916, once again in Zurich, Eggeling established contacts with the newly born Dadaism, but he never joined the movement. In Richter's company, he returned to Germany and lived first in Berlin, then in Klein-Kolzig, the home of Richter's birth. When his friendship with Richter ended, he moved once again to Berlin.

After filming a few experiments in 'visual music' that had been made possible by the UFA, Eggeling decided to

---

[15] This change was probably influenced by Ruttmann's admiration for Eisenstein's films and for their 'intellectual editing'.
[16] Ingo Petzke, e-mailed letter to the author, 6 October 2009.
[17] The contradiction is political, not aesthetic. About the inclusion of Ruttmann in the 'reactionary modernism' that was an integral part of Nazi ideology, see Leonardo Quaresima, *Astrazione e romanticismo – Walther Ruttmann e la mobilità del moderno*, in Leonardo Quaresima (ed.) *Cinema, pittura, ars acustica*, Manfrini, Calliano, Trento, Italy, 1994.

continue filming on his own with very limited means. Loans from relatives allowed him to buy a cine-camera, which he installed in his basement apartment. For three years, he carried on his experiments, filming the drawings of his 'long reel' entitled *Horizontal-Vertikal Orchestra*. A few people saw the film, including the Swedish journalist Birger Brinck, who described what he saw as a ten-minute sequence dealing with a rhythmic vertical theme beginning from the top.[18] Reportedly, Eggeling never considered *Horizontal-Vertikal Orchestra* a finished film; unhappy with the results, he abandoned the project and began working on *Symphonie Diagonale*.[19]

With the help of his companion Erna Niemeyer, Eggeling began *Symphonie Diagonale* in the summer of 1923 and completed it one year later after experiencing financial and other difficulties. Friends and collaborators saw the film on 5 November 1924. On 3 May 1925, the film opened to the public with the support of the UFA, which wished to maintain its 'image' as a farsighted film company attuned to the avant-garde. The stellar programme included Hirschfeld-Mack's experiments, Richter's sequences of *Rhythmus*, Léger's *Ballet mécanique*, Ruttmann's various *Opus* films, René Clair's *Entr'acte* (with a screenplay by Francis Picabia), and Eggeling's film. Unfortunately, Eggeling was not able to attend the show. Hospitalized a few months earlier, weakened by deprivation, he died of septic angina at the age of forty-five on 9 May 1925, six days after the premiere.

His remaining film, *Symphonie Diagonale*,[20] is based on the movement and metamorphosis of a white abstract form on a black background.

While the main movement is diagonal, horizontal and vertical movements also take place, contributing to the film's complex content. There is great artistry in *Symphonie Diagonale*. Eggeling's pure graphics move harmoniously and rigorously for seven minutes. The figuration on which *Symphonie* is based presumes a 'time' dimension; the artist unequivocally instructed his friends never to add a musical

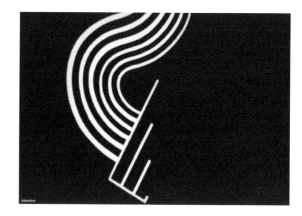

Figure 6.3 Viking Eggeling, *Symphonie Diagonale*, 1924.

score, as the film was music for the eyes already and not part of a synaesthetic project. The film is a painting that lives and develops in time and space and that could not be appreciated when considered in its static fragments.[21]

A hermit with a nearly oriental mysticism, Eggeling thought that art should involve aesthetics, politics, ethics, and metaphysics. His search for purity addressed lifestyle as well as pictorial work. Abstract art was valid because it offered an uncorrupted language through which human beings could communicate. The abstract artist, he believed, gave an unlimited amplification of the human feeling for freedom, and the goal of art was to reflect the spirit of every single individual.[22] A tormented artist, slow to mature stylistically and ideologically, he died too early to be able to fully express his talent.

Hans Richter

Hans Richter (Berlin, 6 April 1888–Minusio, Switzerland, 1 February 1976) was one of the most consistent, tenacious

---

[18] Birger Brinck, 'Linjemusik på vita duken. "Konstruktiv film", ett intressant experiment av en svensk konstnär', *Filmjournalen*, Vol. 5, No. 4, Stockholm, 1923, p. 50.
[19] Original title in French.
[20] In their book *Spjutspets i återvändsgränd* (Spear Points in State of Arrest, Lund, 1997), Swedish film scholar Gösta Werner and musicologist Bengt Endlund prove that Eggeling had structured his film as a sonata, not as a symphony. They conclude that what we have left today is actually only the first part of something that was supposed to be a real four-movement symphony (whose classic structure is: sonata + Lied + minuet + finale). In other words, they maintain that Eggeling's real ambition was to make a feature-length film.
[21] Ingo Petzke notes: I find it noteworthy that Eggeling does NOT use the screen like a screen but rather like a painter would use a canvas: leaving kind of empty stripes along all four sides as if a later framing would occur. Also, Eggeling was influenced by the technique inherent in Chinese scroll paintings. (E-mailed letter to the author, 6 October 2009)
[22] L. O'Konor, *Viking Eggeling 1880–1925 Artist and Filmmaker Life and Work*, Almqvist & Wiksell, Stockholm, 1971.

champions of experimental cinema but at the same time the cause of never-ending misinformation (and probably manipulation). Most critics and historians took his memoirs as gospel, which proved to be inaccurate when tested. He began his career as a cubist painter; later with Tzara and Arp, he contributed to the founding of Dadaism in Zurich. In that ebullient, stimulating environment, he came to feel the emptiness of 'static' painting and the need for something new and rhythmic like music. After having studied the basics of counterpoint under the direction of Ferruccio Busoni, he began painting in black and white in order to reproduce opposites – a fundamental rhythmic principle. Common interests led Richter to befriend Viking Eggeling, who had moved to Zurich during the reign of Dadaism and was involved in similar research. Together, the two artists continued their experiments, first in Switzerland and later in Germany.

The logical development of Richter's research is to be found in three shorts: *Rhythmus 21*, *Rhythmus 23*, and *Rhythmus 25*. They were filmed with the animation of cut-out shapes in years that cannot be precisely identified but are subsequent to what the titles suggest. Squares and triangles in motion appear and disappear, attempting to convey a sensation of purely visual rhythm. Technically, the three *Rhythmus* films were poorly made and do not succeed in capturing the viewer's attention.

In 1926, having overcome the difficulties of the cine-camera and having learned the secrets of lenses, Richter made *Filmstudie*, a complex, articulate work from the standpoint of language and rhythm. Here he used superimposition, various tricks, and geometrical games. For the first time, he also employed a technique that he would use for many years to come: the juxtaposition of live-action shots with animation and that of real people with abstract elements. In *Filmstudie*, for instance, Richter gave equal consideration to human subjects and to some glassy eyeballs that rhythmically grouped themselves together and separated in various forms.

Richter wrote:

The next year was *Inflation*, an introduction to an UFA film, *Die Dame mit der Maske* (The Lady with the Mask), a dance of inflation pictures with the dollar sign in opposition to the multitude of zeros (of the Mark) as a kind of leitmotif. . . . It was certainly not a regular documentary film. It was more an essay on inflation. . . . In 1927–28 I got a little film, *Vormittagsspuk* (Ghosts before Breakfast) done. It was produced for the International Music Festival at Baden-Baden with a score by Paul Hindemith. As it was before the era of sound-film, it was conducted from a rolling score, an invention of a Mr. Blum, in front of the conductor's nose. It did not sound synchronous at all, but it was. The little film (about a reel) was filmed in my artist's studio in Berlin with the Hindemiths and the Darius Milhauds as actors. It was the very rhythmical story of the rebellion of some objects (hats, neckties, coffee cups, etc.) against their daily routine.

Although 'very rhythmic', *Vormittags-Spuk* was no longer an attempt to make music through images, but instead offered a predominantly narrative film characterized by a subtly absurd humour. As with Richter's previous films, this also was composed of heterogeneous elements and employed various kinds of tricks (the single-frame technique was used, too). Unfortunately, the animation of the hats did not succeed; the 'invisible' threads that made the hats dance were clumsily revealed to the audience.

In 1929, Richter released *Rennsymphonie* based on a horse race. In the following years, which he spent as an obscure advertising filmmaker, he decided to leave Germany. After short stays in Switzerland and the Soviet Union, he finally settled in the United States. In the 1940s and 1950s, together with old Dadaist friends and other American artists, Richter contributed to the creation of non-animated, experimental films, such as *Dreams That Money Can Buy*, a feature film made in collaboration with Léger, Ernst, Duchamp, Man Ray, and Calder.

During this activity, Richter only marginally used animation and is most properly placed among the non-conformist filmmakers who technically doodled with motion picture language. As a director, Richter demonstrated neither original vigour nor a well-defined plan of research.

Lotte Reiniger[23]

Born on 2 June 1899, Lotte Reiniger started to work in cinema at an early age. 'It all began in the year 1919', she wrote:[24]

---

[23] By Giannalberto Bendazzi and Ulrich Wegenast.
[24] Letter received by Giannalberto Bendazzi from Lotte Reiniger, 7 November 1972.

I then was an enthusiastic maiden who could really do nothing at all well but cut-out silhouettes,[25] but who desperately wanted to get into films. When I was fifteen years old, I heard a lecture by Paul Wegener, who by this time was the foremost champion for fantastic films in Germany and whose films, the first *Golem* and the first *Student of Prague*,[26] had made a profound impression on me. So I went to this lecture, and that settled it for [the lecture] was dedicated mostly to the fantastic possibilities of 'trick' films, of which very little was known. From this moment onward I had nothing in my mind but to get near that man.

As he was one of the leading actors of the theatre of Max Reinhardt, I persuaded my unfortunate parents to let me go to the acting school attached to that theatre. It was not easy for them for the world of theatre was most alien to them. But they let me go. I was very happy. But as we pupils of the school were not allowed to be present at rehearsals, I did not know how to approach my hero. In order to draw the attention of the famous actors playing there, I began to cut-out silhouettes of them in their roles. These silhouettes were very good and the actors liked them immensely. In 1917, even a book of them was published. Even Prof. Max Reinhardt approved of them and allowed me to be on the stage. I tried very hard to get into a play where Wegener was acting. I cut-out silhouettes of him like mad – and he liked them. His interest in the visual arts was very great and so he helped me enormously and let me also do extras for his films. In 1918, he let me do the captions for his film, *Der Rattenfänger von Hamelin* (The Pied Piper of Hamelin) (in this period the films were shown in reels, and the best films had extra captions for these reels).

In the summer of 1919, when I was in the studio in the garb of a grande dame for *The Galley Slave*,[27] a film of Balzac's novel *Lost Illusion*, Wegener presented me to a group of interesting young men [who] were about to open an experimental animation film studio, as he explained to me, and he said to them 'For heaven's sake help me get rid of this mad silhouette girl. She makes very good silhouettes which cry out for animation. Can't you let her make a film with those silhouettes as they make cartoons?' And they did.

These gentlemen were: Dr. Hans Cürlis,[28] the leader of the group (to be named the Institute for Cultural Discovery) who had studied art history and was often seen in Wegener's surroundings. His friend Carl Koch, studied the same subject, becoming a well-known writer of art books specializing in the Far East. Also present was Berthold Bartosch, an animator who had come over from Vienna where he worked with Professor Hanslick. [Prof. Hanslick] had already founded an Institute like this in Vienna, had made various cartographical films there; these works emphasized the differences between the natural conditions found in Eastern and Western countries. He had come over to form a group with equal ambitions in Berlin. They created an animation table in Berlin and allowed me to have a go there with silhouette tables.

I first helped Bartosch with some geographical films to learn the techniques of animation. I made my first silhouette film on 12 December 1919, a kind of *pas de deux* with two figures and a movable ornament, which followed the mood of the dancers. This was called *Das Orna-*

---

[25] Silhouettes and Chinese (and Malay and Indonesian) shadow plays are two different things that slowly became synonymous in the common European language of the nineteenth century. Silhouettes, illustrations, decorations, and theatre reached their apex by the Belle Époque and were anything but out of fashion in the 1920s, especially in Germany. The silhouette technique/style was always, and still is, an interesting component of animation.

[26] *Der Golem, und wie er in die Welt kam* (The Golem, and How He Came Into the World, 1915, directed by Paul Wegener); *Der Sudent von Prag* (The Student of Prague, 1913, directed by Stellan Rye, starring Paul Wegener).

[27] *Der Galeersträfling* (The Galley Slave, 1919, directed by Rochus Gliese, starring Paul Wegener).

[28] Hans Cürlis is a highly ambivalent figure in German film history, since he followed his goals under four different political systems and smoothly conformed to their ideologies and guidelines [Ulrich Döge: *Kulturfilm als Aufgabe. Hans Cürlis (1889–1982)*, CineGraph Babelsberg, Berlin, 2005].

ment des verliebten Herzens (The Ornament of the Enamoured Heart). The reaction of the audience was so favourable that I went on ever since.

In 1923, a young Berlin banker, Mr. Louis Hagen – who had seen me manipulating my little fairy-tale films in the Institute – asked me whether I would not like to produce a full-length film in this style. This was a big temptation, an unheard of offer we could not resist. Mr. Hagen did not want that work to be produced in the Institute, but offered to construct a studio above his garage, near his house in Potsdam. In the meantime, I had married Carl Koch and we went there and Bartosch went with us, for we had developed a very close friendship to each other and we liked to work together.

Shortly before these happenings, Ruttmann showed his first films in Berlin and we were enthusiastic about them. To my joy, he liked the silhouette films too and we became friends. We all, the so called avant-garde people, always worked outside the industry and only very occasionally were we asked to do some things for commercial films. Bartosch, for instance, made the titles for Wegener's *Golem*, and I did a little short shadow scene for his *The Lost Shadow*.[29] When we were given the chance to produce that full-length film, we asked Bartosch and Ruttmann for their collaboration. They agreed. It was this collaboration which led to the most striking parts of this film (needless to say, it was *Prince Achmed*), for I played my silhouette bits in black and white only and handed them to Ruttmann who on his own animation table composed and executed the fantastic movements of his magic.[30] As far as I remember, it was the earliest time that two animators of a quite different artistic temperament worked together on the same shot. We had negatives and nobody can imagine the tension with which we awaited the marked print.

Alexander Kardan and Walter Türck assisted Reiniger in the animation of the cut-outs, and Bartosch invented various special effects, the most memorable one being the movement of the translucent waves in the Aladdin flight sequence. Although the team was working in the era of silent film, the collaboration with composer Wolgang Zeller was close from the beginning. Zeller took care of some special sound effects, and the crew shot entire sequences in rhythm with the music to obtain synchronization with the orchestra, which was to accompany the film when screened.

Reiniger continues:

> Ruttmann was slightly ashamed to work on such a fairy tale. . . . 'What has this to do with 1923?' he asked me once. I only could say 'Nothing', and it had not. [The film] was finished in [1926].

The feature film (one of the first animation features in the world and the first in Europe) was entitled *Die Abenteuer des Prinzen Achmed* (The Adventures of Prince Achmed). The technique used involved a particular type of cut-out animation; the silhouettes, cut from black paper, portrayed backlit people, animals, and objects. They were also called 'Chinese shadows'. The film had great success, especially in France, where Jean Renoir and René Clair passionately recommended it. Several fables

Figure 6.4 Lotte Reiniger, *Die Abenteuer des Prinzen Achmed*, 1926.

---

[29] *Der Golem, und wie er in die Welt Kam*, 1920, is a remake of the film identified earlier, directed by and starring Paul Wegener. *Der verlorene Schatten* (Lost Shadow, 1921, directed by and starring Paul Wegener).
[30] Ruttmann created the background scenery, while Reiniger filmed the action using silhouettes.

from *The Thousand and One Nights* were adapted for the film in a way that attempted to maintain their gentleness as well as their drama. Chase scenes and escapes by princesses, love stories, and fights between good spirits and monstrous devils are narrated with a refined taste both in figuration and in the movements of filigreed paper actors. The events surrounding this film are tortuous. The bombing of Berlin destroyed the negative and all the positives. In 1954, a positive copy was found in the British Film Institute files, but the fine-grained prints made from it did not permit the reproduction of the original colours (which had been obtained by imbibition). Later, a copy of the technical instructions for the colouring process, written in 1926, was found. Finally, in 1999, the film was satisfactorily restored by the Deutsches Filmmuseum in Frankfurt am Main and released in DVD with the beautiful musical accompaniment by Wolfgang Zeller.[31]

The author of the first monograph on Reiniger,[32] who was judging on the grounds of the perfect, original print, wrote what we would confirm today:

> Some of the architectural backgrounds are cut in so sugary a style as to resemble superbly iced wedding cakes, certain scenes are undoubtedly overloaded with detail, and the pavilion where Aladdin finds the magic lamp is painfully ugly and *kitschig* in contrast to the strands of the creeper by which he descends into the cave.
>
> In spite of that, nothing can detract from the beauty of the scenes where Achmet,[33] hiding behind the trembling leaf of an exotic fern, watches Peri Banu bathing in the lake, where Achmet draws his long bow to shoot down the monster, where the sorcerer visits Aladdin in his booth in the old town, and where the lonely figure of Aladdin sails his bark over the sea. These are the high lights of the film, and in comparison the blemishes are mere scratches on a piece of Meissen.

Formally, too, *Achmet* is not without its weaknesses: for example, the whole of the Aladdin episode as recounted by Aladdin to Achmet forms a loop rather weakly tied on to the main story.

Reiniger's filmic dictionary is minimal: long shots, medium shots plus a couple of disgraceful close-ups, almost no camera movements. Her style is strictly based on theatre and illustration. Characters enter and exit from the wings, the scenery is static and elaborate, and every frame is carefully balanced like a painting (often on the structure of a triangle) and later finely decorated.

Many contemporaries considered the best scene the duel between the Sorcerer and the Witch (much later imitated by Wolfgang Reitherman in Walt Disney's *Sword in the Stone*), but current filmgoers would disagree. The timing is imperfect, and the animation is often stiff. Unforgettable is Peri Banu's[34] bath, instead.

After Bartosch and Ruttmann went their separate ways, Reiniger and her husband Carl Koch worked in Germany, France, and Great Britain, where they had been invited by John Grierson to contribute to the adventurous Film Unit of the General Post Office. Before World War II, the couple made twenty-six films, among them *Papageno* – probably their best known work, based on Mozart's *Magic Flute* – and the insert of silhouette animation in Jean Renoir's *La Marseillaise*.

When World War II broke out, Reiniger was in Rome filming *L'elisir d'amore* (The Elixir of Love). After Mussolini entered the war, too,[35] she and her husband tried to stay in allied but tolerant Italy, where Koch directed two live-action films, *Tosca*

---

[31] The score was originally written for a live orchestra; the actual synchronization took place in 1931 and was carried out in the United States. Wolfgang Zeller (Biesenrode, Mansfeld, 18 September 1893–Berlin, 11 January 1967) would compose film music until 1959, collaborating with such directors as Carl Th. Dreyer, Jean Vigo, Georg Wilhelm Pabst, and Jacques Feyder. Sadly, he also signed the score of the Nazi propaganda film *Jud Süss* (1940).
[32] Eric Walter White, *Walking Shadows*, Leonard and Virginia Woolf/Hogarth Press, London, 1931.
[33] The misspelling is in the original text.
[34] This central character's name is Iranian. Peri means Angel in Persian, and Banu is an extremely respectful appellation for a lady. We thank Javad Khajavi for providing the information.
[35] On 10 June 1940.

(1941) and *Una signora dell'Ovest* (The Girl of the Golden West, 1942). Eventually they had to return to Germany, where they had to endure Lotte's mother's illness, various shortages, and bombings. Reiniger, who had always been a buxom woman, looks skinny beyond recognition in the pictures of the time. An attempt to create a film called *Die goldene Gans* (The Golden Goose) during the war failed.

In 1948, the couple resumed their activities in Great Britain. In the 1950s, they opened the Primrose Productions Company and added about fifteen more works, some of them in colour, to their already rich filmography. One of the first films, based on the silhouette colour technique, was *Jack and the Beanstalk* (1955), followed by *The Star of Bethlehem*. The earlier *The Gallant Little Tailor* won a prize at the Venice Film Festival of 1955.

After the death of her husband, Reiniger did not slow her pace of activity. In 1976, she went to Canada, where she made *Aucassin et Nicolette* for the National Film Board. She also taught seminars for young animators in several cities of the world. She died on 19 June 1981 in Dettenhausen, Germany. Reviewers have unanimously praised the gentleness and precious frailty of her work. The atmosphere that her minute animated silhouettes convey exists as a separate realm that has no relation to a historical perspective, nor to current times (Ruttmann was right in this); her figurines belong to an absolutely calm, abstract world of fantasy that is made nearly dreamlike by the indefinable nature of silhouettes (who can't have facial expressions). Such a choice of figuration may seem eccentric when compared to the major artistic currents of the 1920s. In fact, it belongs to the passage from art nouveau to modernism to art deco, which had the Frenchmen Bourdelle and Maurice Denis (not to mention the brilliant Czech painter and illustrator Alfons Mucha) as its most renowned exponents. Reiniger's techniques have inspired several modern filmmakers, particularly the former East Germans. Even so,

nobody has ever equalled the fluidity of her animation and the plastic finesse of her figures.

Austria[36]

The other German-speaking country inaugurated, during World War I, a series of patriotic satiric cartoons called Österreichische Kriegskarikaturen. They were drawn and directed by poster artist, illustrator, and caricaturist Theo Zasche (1862–1922). Here are some titles: *Als der Russe vor Przemysl stand* (As the Russian Stood Before Przemysl); *Das Neue Dreigestirn* (The Three New Stars, dealing with the axis of Moscow–Paris–London); and the anti-Jewish *Der Zar und seine lieben Juden* (The Tsar and His Dear Jews). In the newsreels, Austrian filmgoers also found drawn inserts depicting civil issues like the hardships of the civilians, especially the ones signed by Otto Dely.

> In the years of 1921 and 1922 the film industry in Vienna was at its peak. Along with the leading film studios, Sascha, Astoria, Dreamland, Listo, Schönbrunn and later Vita-Film, some twenty other companies were producing 70 to 75 full-length productions a year, as well as 50 to 60 one-reel comedies, plus educational, cultural and advertising films.[37]

The previously mentioned Astoria Film company entrusted Ladislaus Tuszynski (Lemberg,[38] 20 May 1876–Vienna, 21 September 1943) and Peter Eng (Peter Engelmann, Olmütz,[39] 21 May 1892–after 1938), both former painters, with the making of animated films (especially commercials). *Die Abenteuer des berühmten Detektivs Harry Packs* (The Adventures of the Famous Detective Harry Packs) was conceived as a series. About the first installment *Die Jagd nach dem Kopfe* (The Hunt for the Lost Head), a report was published in *Der Filmbote* on 3 July 1920:

> Tuszynski's images reveal, through the execution of the figures, in the treatment of the backgrounds, and in the perception of the villain, a subtle execution that

---

[36] By Thomas Renoldner and Giannalberto Bendazzi.
[37] Peter Eng, *Der Trickfilm*, in 'Die Filmwelt' No. 35, Vienna, 1920, quoted in Thomas Renoldner and Lisi Frischengruber, *Animated Films in Austria – Part I*, Asifa Austria, Vienna, no date.
[38] This town stands in Galicia, in the then-Polish segment of the Austro-Hungarian Empire, and was also known as Lwów. Today, this is Lviv, Ukraine.
[39] Today, this is Olomouc, Czech Republic.

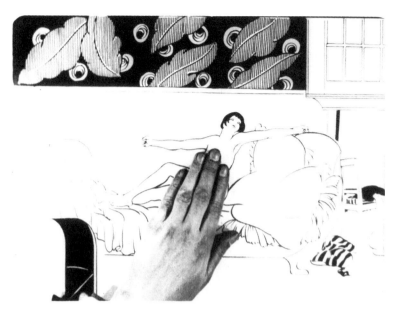

Figure 6.5 Louis Seel, *Wiener Bilderbogen Nr. 1*, 1925.

sometimes leads to a complete illusion of reality. His 'decorations' if one may call them such, are of overflowing richness, the movements of his 'actors' masterfully transposed from real life. In this Tuszynski is inexhaustible in devising original movements and plots and shows himself as master of this new drawing technique.

The film was 500 m long, and its production took a year and a half.[40]

Peter Eng had spent part of his youth in America. Of himself, he wrote in 1920: 'Vienna has a number of noteworthy cinematic draughtsmen, principally Peter Eng, who has worked in Munich, Copenhagen, Berlin and North America, has drawn over eighty animation films for Sascha, Filmag and Astoria.' Eng liked to travel and stylistically was modern and open to the world, in that he distanced himself from any naturalistic tendencies in animation. His theoretical starting point was a preparation for the cartoons that were to dominate during the Disney era. Thus, he wrote in 1920, in 'Die Filmwelt':

> Animation should be an illusion made for cinema, the more simple and 'sketched' the caricature appears, the more amazing and effective the transformation. Filmgoers, tired from the two live-action films of the program, which basically provide photographic entertainment, should find it refreshing to suddenly be confronted with an enlarged piece of paper, just as a city dweller, tired after all the confusing details of the street, may experience the need to look at a humorous cartoon. The viewer must therefore know that we are dealing with pencil and paper. This is perhaps the unconscious, underlying thought from which the great American and Scandinavian artists begin when drawing their moving pictures.

---

[40] Thomas Renoldner and Lisi Frischengruber (*Animated Films in Austria – Part I*, Asifa Austria, Vienna, no date) write:
A second instalment of the series, with the title *Amarantha*, was shown in 1921. A showman's leading attraction, a woman without a lower half, is kidnapped by the ensembles' black dancer and banjo player, who is in love with her. Once again the 'famous detective' Harry Packs is summoned, his 'secret room' being a parody on the expressionist stage design of *The Cabinet of Dr. Caligari*. Harry Packs, hidden in an advertising column, with his dog hunts for the thief Tommy, while the woman without a lower half has already ended up in an antique shop. As a happy ending, the black dancer and his girl row around a desert island, where the viewer can marvel at their happy home and their offspring – two children's heads in plant pots. After these two somewhat dry humoured films, Astoria decided its animation department should attempt something with a more serious note to it. For the film *Kalif Storch* (Caliph Stork, premiered in July 1922), in which live-action and animated scenes were combined, Tuszynski did the animation. The last known, long animation by Tuszynski is *Die Entdeckung Wiens am Nordpol* (The Discovering of Vienna at the North Pole), an advertisement for the Vienna Exhibition, probably from the year 1923. Unlike the detective films, this film features a light, slightly dadaist sense of humour.

Peter Eng was of Jewish extraction. In 1938, he managed to immigrate to the United States, where he died.

The third and last name worth mentioning is Louis Seel, an American globe-trotting producer whom we find from time to time in Germany, Austria, England, and Brazil. In Austria, he produced only one work, the *Wiener Bilderbogen Nr. 1* (Viennese Picture Book No. 1), made on the basis of the *Münchener Bilderbogen* he had made in Germany.

He 'certainly influenced Austrian animators and was possibly sort of a model for them. Seel's mastery of the medium lays in the interaction and dissolving of the "drawn" and the "real" worlds'.[41]

Switzerland[42]

The earliest testified attempt to produce animation in Switzerland is also the oldest physical proof to have survived the test of time to this day: *Histoire de Monsieur Vieux-Bois* (The Story of Mr. Vieux-Bois, 1921), based on the homonymous precursor of graphic novels written and drawn by Genevese scholar, writer, and caricaturist Rodolphe Töpffer in the early nineteenth century. It is the original Swiss content, however, and the origin of the entrepreneurial initiative, that justify the Swiss label, since, as mentioned earlier, the ever-popular satirical tales of Mr. Vieux-Bois' amorous (mis)adventures were actually put to screen by French animation cracks Lortac and Cavé as a commissioned job for the company Pencil-Film, especially founded for the purpose by two young well-to-do Genevese citizens.

The effort prompted a remarkable response from the still-young discipline of film critique, not only unusual in its analytical appreciation but also for the category of animation as such, and turned into a long-running public success in its hometown as well: After its initial commercial release as three sequels of ten to twelve minutes early in 1922, the full half-hour show kept up a presence in special screenings until 1936, whereas little to nothing is known about its screen performance elsewhere in Switzerland or any other European country. Afterwards, the material fell into oblivion until it was rediscovered and restored in 1971.

Denmark[43]

Danish animation began as early as 1907 with the trick films *Tryllesækken* (The Magic Sack, 1907) and *Heksen og Cyklisten* (The Witch and the Biker, 1909), produced at Nordisk Films Kompagni in Copenhagen. This company had a worldwide distribution of silent movies and made a number of trick farces between 1907 and 1910. However, the audience quickly lost interest for this naïve type of movie, and production stopped.

The actual founding father was Robert Storm Petersen.

An early animator was Sven Brasch (1886–1970), internationally famous for his artistic commercial posters. Brasch made an animation film from a series of quite static metamorphic drawn pictures. The title was *Som det er – Som det føles* (A Rather Good Intention), and the film premiered in 1919.

Some puppet films were produced at Nordisk Films Kompagni by Christian Maagaard Christensen (1892–?), including *Letmatrosen* (The Ordinary Seaman, 1919); *Den skønne Irmelin* (The Beautiful Irmelin, 1920); and *Dukkemagerens Drøm* (The Puppet Maker's Dream, 1918).

Animated commercials became very popular during the 1920s, and artists such as Alfred Skibstrup and Aage Lippert made a good amount of funny and quite artistic productions, many of which are still in existence.[44]

Storm P.

Robert Storm Petersen (1882–1949) was a unique artist among his contemporaries. In his nonsensical and often baroque humour lay a deep compassion and social understanding of the outcast. Born in an innocent time, he experienced the rough turn of the century, when nationalism raised its voice in Europe and reached its climax with World War I. Deep down, Storm P. (as he called himself) was a philosophical man who believed in the good side of humanity and felt genuine sorrow when he experienced the opposite. His father was a butcher, but teenager Storm, far from following in his footsteps, displayed a great

---

[41] Thomas Renoldner and Lisi Frischengruber, *Animated Films in Austria – Part I*, Asifa Austria, Vienna, no date.
[42] By Rolf Bächler.
[43] By Annemette Karpen.
[44] Many of these commercials are kept in the Danish Film Archive. They still have a remarkable freshness.

sense of humour and a strong talent for drawing. He began to draw cartoons for the newspapers and worked in various theatres in Copenhagen with lightning sketches as his specialty. From 1906, he painted sets – and worked as a silent actor – at Nordisk Films Kompagni. In 1913, he invented his characters *De Tre Små Mænd* (The Three Little Men). That same year, he married Lydia Sørensen, who was more than twenty years his elder.

He became very interested in drawn animation and experimented for several years before opening his own production studio at Nordisk Films Kompagni. Around 1919–1921, he started making films on his home-constructed trick table.[45] *Øen* (The Island)[46] and *Tre små mænd* (Three Little Men) are both from 1920.

Storm P. got more ambitious with his next film, *Gaasetyven eller Et Ande-Eventyr* (The Goose Thief or a Duck Story), which premiered on Christmas Day 1920. It is a nonsensical story about three little men who later became regular characters in Storm P.'s films.

He portrayed himself in a character that had to deal with the three little men during a duck-hunting expedition. After these followed a few comical films, such as *Storm P. tegner de tre små mænd* (Storm P. Draws The Three Little Men, 1920); *Professor Steinacks Metode eller Foryngelseskuren* (Professor Steinack's Method or The Rejuvenation Cure) and *Jernmixturen* (The Iron Elixir) both from 1921; and *Fastekuren* (The Fasting Cure) from 1922. Storm P. displayed a crisp and self-confident style of drawing. Together with photographer Karl Wieghorst (1871–1953), Storm P. invented his own trick table, and the two of them were jointly responsible for the animation.

After this time, Storm P. lost interest in animation production, although his characters were seen in many commercials during the 1920s. In 1930, he abandoned moviemaking and devoted his time to comedy acting and making daily cartoons for newspapers.

In an interview with the Danish newspaper *Politiken* on 22 December 1920, he said: 'I am totally absorbed in this type of new work. From now on I will let the three little men dance out in the wide world and be my emissaries.'

In 1919, Storm P. travelled to the United States to promote his films and ideas. The trip, however, was a fiasco. He found the Americans superficial and only liked the Native American he met. After three months, he returned in a depression. He made a series of animated films using drawn animation and cut-out techniques and finally recovered from the depression. As Storm did not know the cel process, he got tired of the repetitious work and painting. In 1925, his wife died. After a year of grief, he married Ellen Margrethe Jakobsen, who was ten years younger than him. They remained married until his death.

After 1930, he made scenes for a ballet, *Benzin*, and was extensively used as a comedy actor at the Royal Theatre in Copenhagen. However, Storm was an improviser by nature and after some time quit the theatre, as he did not have the patience for learning long texts by heart and rehearsing. He

Figure 6.6 Robert Storm Petersen, *Three Little Men*, 1920.

---

[45] Nordisk Films Kompagni is today called Nordisk Film. We can still find the wooden building where Storm P. had his trick table. The ceiling was made higher so his trick table could function comfortably. From outside, it looks like a small tower.
[46] *Øen* (The Island, 1920) was left unfinished by Storm P. But Lars Jakobsen, a Danish animator, did finish it for his DVD compilation *Eventyret om dansk tegnefilm* (The Tale of Danish Animation, 2008). *Storm P. tegner de tre små mænd* (Storm P. Draws the Three Little Men, 1920) lasts thirty seconds. Storm P. is seen live sitting by his easel with his drawing pad. He draws the three little men and leans back. They come alive and greet him while he remains in the picture. It is quite a sophisticated technique for a beginner.

devoted his time to painting in oil, often with crass social realism and a latent symbolism; his works were exhibited in both Denmark and abroad. He made daily cartoons for the newspapers and wrote some philosophical essays until his death in 1949.

Storm P. has a museum dedicated to him and his work, Storm P. Museet. His films are kept in the Danish Film Archive.

Sweden[47]

Grogg the Sailor Man

Victor Bergdahl (Österåker, 25 December 1878–Stockholm, 20 January 1939) was an outstanding representative of Swedish animation. A comic artist and a cartoonist, Bergdahl followed the same path as his American colleagues by animating his comic strip characters.

His activity as an animator lasted about fifteen years from 1915 to 1936. He focused on the character of Captain Grogg, a sailor, fisherman, and seafarer, and developed his naïve adventures brilliantly.

Bergdahl made thirteen films starring Captain Grogg and committed much of his career to the development of this character. His work is an important example of methodical production: Captain Grogg was in fact the first animated series of the Old Continent to have a constant character who was presented with recurring elements to help the audience know him through and through. Many of these elements were derived from Bergdahl's personal experiences, so it is possible to speak of the Captain as his alter ego. The passion for the sea, and the difficult relationship with a bigot wife who hated smoking and drinking, are the most obvious common elements between the artist and his creation.

Before becoming an animator, Bergdahl had boarded as a sailor, coming up to Australia, and this is why we see so many exotic animals and people in his films. The long voyage he undertook also offered him the opportunity to sharpen his drawing technique as a result of an accident that forced him to remain immobile for a long time, and the opportunity to study the wave motion of the ocean, which Bergdahl reproduced in his films with a skill and an unparalleled poetry for the time.

After returning from Australia, he became a cartoonist for newspapers in Sweden and then an animator, driven by his innate curiosity and his insight towards the potential of the new medium. His first four movies contain the issues that Bergdahl developed later: The effects of drinking and smoking are the real protagonists of *Trolldrycken* (The Magic Brew, 1915) and of the three movies on the Cirkus Fjollinsky. Opportunities and situations, however, are borrowed from authors who Bergdahl had the opportunity to appreciate at the time: James Stuart Blackton and Winsor McCay. The real innovations at the thematic level came with the Captain, while his research at the technical level and his significant contributions had always been a constant since the early years of his work.

The scenes of sea in *Kapten Grogg på Stora Oceanen* (Captain Grogg on the Big Ocean, 1920) are worthy of those that Winsor McCay drew for *The Sinking of Lusitania* (1918). The waves are reproduced in a full-bodied and realistic way, although this does not prevent fantastic elements from being introduced, such as the Captain's accomplished pirouettes by boat on the stormy sea. The shorts *Kapten Groggs underbara resa* (Captain Grogg's Wonderful Journey, 1916); *Kapten Grogg och Kalle på negerbal* (Captain Grogg and Kalle at the Darkies' Ball, 1917); *Kapten Grogg gifter sig* (Captain Grogg Gets Married, 1918); and *Kapten Grogg bland vilda djur* (Captain Grogg among Wild Animals, 1919) are some of the most representative titles of the issues dear to Bergdahl.

The dramaturgy is often compelling and the stories well narrated. The constant factors are the sea, the Captain's loyal friend and shipboy Kalle and, of course, the

Figure 6.7 Victor Bergdahl, *Captain Grogg's Wonderful Journey*, 1916.

---

[47] By Valentina Pezzi and Giannalberto Bendazzi.

bottle: the magic that helps the protagonist recover from any difficult situation. In *Kapten Groggs underbara resa*, we find the Captain and Kalle busy stowing supplies for a voyage on a small sailing boat. Beer and spirits are very much part of the load. In this adventure, crossing a sea in storm and calm, Grogg and Kalle are able to see a mermaid, a shark, and a swordfish until they arrive to a faraway village where they conquer beautiful women, but not before defeating a lion. In *Kapten Grogg bland vilda djur*, Grogg studies the law of animals in the jungle: eat or be eaten. In addition to huge snakes and kangaroos (clearly recalling Bergdahl's stay in Australia), the hero gets acquainted, in *Kapten Grogg bland andra konstiga kroppar* (Captain Grogg Among Other Strange Bodies, 1921), with a nice female centaur. This element points out the ambivalence of Bergdahl's worlds: the exotic and the fantastic. The two films that show the duality of the Captain bring us back to the real world. He is tied to a brutal woman who doesn't share his interests, just like what has happened to Bergdahl, a jovial and gregarious man thwarted by his wife's bigotry.

Indeed, compared to other pioneers of the early days, Bergdahl distinguished himself as one of the most innovative artists. He invented a particular model of an animation table with underlighting, and he also created a new method of cut-out based on the juxtaposition of shapes of paper and cut-outs of scenarios. However, his most innovative solution was the invention of the pre-printed background that consisted of printing the detailed drawn background, in which blank spaces were left on which to place the animated characters.

With his passion for inventions, Bergdahl enriched his shooting techniques with a whole variety of improvements but never discovered the advantages of transparent celluloid sheets. His work, which he carried on in solitude, even learning the techniques and mechanisms of animation on his own by simply observing movies, was characterized by significant manual as well as intellectual effort. Still, he maintains his inspiration – with wit and humour. Bergdahl's work is a combination of high-class design and animation (note, for instance, the 'blur' effect that accompanies rapid movements) and naivety and roughness, especially when it comes to the rules of the cinematographic language, like crossing the proscenium.

När Kapten Grogg skulle porträtteras (When Captain Grogg Was to Have His Portrait Done, 1917) is a masterpiece: a mixture of animation and live action, with all the technical and artistic qualities we have already mentioned. Captain Grogg goes to a painter to have his portrait done; the painter is Victor Bergdahl himself. Bergdahl plays with Grogg, teases him by drawing a big or bottle-shaped nose, chases him, and finally shuts him in a drawing canvas. In the chase scenes, Bergdahl also used the then-unknown technique of pixilation, obtaining an effective movement of himself.

In the 1920s, the audience began to become disillusioned with these adventures; in the last movie, *Kapten Grogg har blivit fet* (Captain Grogg Has Become Fat, 1922), he seems fat and bitter, a distant memory of the adventurer of the first films. From this moment on, Bergdahl returned to animation only four more times, three times for advertising and the last time in 1936 to participate in a project of sexual education with the information movie *Från cell till människa* (From Cell to Man, 1936).

In December 1938, a month before he died, Bergdahl wrote an article for the Swedish evening newspaper *Nya Dagligt Allehanda* to sum up his life on his sixtieth birthday. He had just seen Walt Disney's *Snow White and the Seven Dwarfs* and was deeply impressed. In the article, Bergdahl expressed enthusiasm but also a hint of bitterness about what he might have done if he had had the ability and courage to move away from the burlesque; he also perhaps had a feeling that a new panorama, with a new undisputed star, was coming into a world of animation in which he could not participate.

Other Swedish Animators

Émile Åberg (1864–1940) and Rudolf Mauritz Liljeqvist (1888–1973) made similar efforts but were less successful. The best film of Åberg was *Lille Kalle dröm om sin snögubbe* (Little Kalle Dreams His Snowman, 1916), clearly inspired by Winsor McCay. R.M. Liljeqvist is remembered for *Negern och hunden* (The Black Man and the Dog, 1916), an eight-minute film, rather elementary and naive in terms of its graphic and narrative treatment.

From 1917 on, Swedish newsreels featured lightning sketches, too. Paul Myren (1884–1951) began as a newsreel illustrator and then made animated inserts for the live-action film *Skärgården i Robinson* (A Modern Robinson, 1920), directed by Rune Carlsten.

Advertising was another fertile ground for the early leaders and also a more profitable one. Arvid Olson (1886–1976) was the most prolific artist in this field, mainly working for Stomatol, a manufacturer of products for oral hygiene. His funny and well-made commercials made animation rather popular and were associated with high audience expectations.

Norway[48]

Animation in Norway dates back to the mid-1910s when cartoonists such as Sverre Halvorsen, Thoralf Klouman, and Ola Cornelius made their first short caricature-based animated drawings.

Sverre Halvorsen (1892–1936) made his first time-lapsed drawings with chalk on a blackboard in 1913. *Roald Amundsen paa Sydpolen* (Roald Amundsen on the South Pole) was the first and the only one that still exists. It is not a real animated cartoon, but a lightning sketch where Halvorsen is seen making a drawing of the polar explorer Amundsen with the Earth as his body. Halvorsen made several other similar films in the mid-1910s but gave up since he couldn't make a profit.

Well-established newspaper cartoonist Thoralf Klouman (1890–1940) made three film cartoons in 1914. The most popular was *Hedin rider kjephesten* (Hedin Rides the Wooden Horse) about the Swedish explorer Sven Hedin. All three films are lost, but according to an article in the Norwegian trade journal *Film og Kino*, it's obvious that the amount of animation in these films was sparse; it is likely that they were lightning sketches like Halvorsen's films. The caricatures were 'presented to the public so that they could see how the drawing was made, then it was shown on the screen for a minute, and then it was gone'.[49] For the 1917 film *Admiral Palads* (Admiral Palace), Klouman made fifty drawings, some of which he used several times, to make a film about the American President Woodrow Wilson. This was hardly a fully animated cartoon either, but it might have been the very first animation made in Norway. It premiered some months before the film *Fanden i nøtten* (The Devil in the Nut, 1917) by Ola Cornelius (1890–?), which is generally considered the first proper Norwegian animated cartoon.

Fanden i nøtten is based on a Norwegian folk story, the first of many such animated adaptations of the rich Norwegian folklore literature. The seven-minute film was produced by Eivin Ovrum, who had learned modern advertising in the United States and had established an advertising studio and agency when he came back to Norway. Eager to explore the possibilities of animated cartoons, he hired Ola Cornelius to make the drawings for the film. He was assisted by Marie Valle, a rare female animation pioneer. The film earned good reviews in the press, and it was even screened abroad in Stockholm and Copenhagen. Half of the film still exists as a cinema commercial for the margarine brand *Melange*, which was probably made into an advertising film in the first half of the 1920s.[50]

Halvorsen, Klouman, and Cornelius claim in articles in the film trade press in the late 1910s to have been the first to have made film cartoons in Norway. Depending on how you define the animated cartoon, they can all be right. We know that Victor Bergdahl's *Kapten Grogg* and Bray's *Colonel Heeza Liar* (called Mentulant in Norway) were very popular around 1917 when Klouman and Cornelius made their films. Together with Ovrum and Halvorsen, they were central members of the trade/art organization *Tegnerforbundet* (The Cartoonist Society), which was founded in 1916. This association had some very active years in the late 1910s due to its extensive contact with colleagues in Sweden, where the members likely came into contact with Victor Bergdahl.

In the early 1920s, Sverre Halvorsen made a few short film cartoons with animated segments. The cinematographer Hans Berge (1895–?) had worked with Klouman and Cornelius on their pioneering films. His company, Fram Film, is credited as having produced *Heimebrennerens mareritt – Drikkens følger* (The Moonshiner's Nightmare – The Results of Drinking, 1924). The film is lost, and the censorship card, unfortunately, reveals nothing about the content of the film. But since it was made during the prohibition period in Norway, it almost certainly satirized the misuse of alcohol, which was common in many early Scandinavian animated films. The same theme is central in Sverre Halvorsen's *Det nye aar?* (The New Year?, 1921), produced by the company Bio Film.

In the period from 1913 to the early 1920s, at least sixteen film cartoons were made. Many of the leading Norwegian cartoonists attempted to succeed as animators and film cartoonists, but it was too much work for too little money. Cinema commercials were still not established properly as a way of making money.

The big change happened in the late 1920s. In the years 1927–1929, about a hundred animated cinema commercials were made by several competing studios in Oslo. Ottar Gladtvet, who had produced Sverre Halvorsen's *The New Year?*, made many of them. Niels Sinding Hansen and Ths. W. Schwartz made several as well. Many of these were made for the tobacco company J. L. Tiedemann. In

---

[48] By Gunnar Strøm.
[49] 'Raymond', *Norges første filmtegner. Skuespiller Thoralf Klouman*, 'Film og Kino' No. 3, 1917.
[50] For more details on silent Norwegian animation, see Gunnar Strøm, 'Caricatures, Cartoons and Advertisements: The Pioneers of Nordic Animated Film', in John Fullerton and Jan Olsson (eds.), *Nordic Explorations: Film Before 1930*, John Libbey, 1999, pp. 114–136.

addition, prominent Scandinavian animators like Victor Bergdahl and Storm P. made cinema commercials for Norway in the 1920s. Gladtvet also worked with German advertising film producer Julius Pinschewer. Many of these advertising films still exist. They can be several minutes long, and many of them are fascinating remnants from a very busy period of early Norwegian animation.

Unfortunately, all the studios closed in 1929 and did not make it into the sound era. They also could not compete with the quality of the new output coming from Disney and the other American cartoon studios.

Finland

In 1914, Erik Wasström (1887–1958) filmed, in an imitation of Blackton, a 'magic pen' drawing of current events. Ten years later, Karl Salén and Yrjö Nyberg (who changed his name to Norta in 1934) made the animated film *Aito sunnuntaimetsästäjä* (A True Sunday Hunter). The film was released by Lahyn Film, a Turku-based production company that also produced animated advertising. In the late 1920s, caricaturist and cartoonist Ola Fogelberg (1894–1952) shot a five-minute-long film based on the character Pekka Puupää (Peter Woodenhead), while animator Hjalmar Löfving (1896–1968) made his debut and continued to create fifteen animated films over the course of his career.

Hungary

The pioneer of Hungarian animation was Kató-Kiszly István[51] (Budapest, 1895–1963), who made his debut with *Zsirb Ödön*[52] (1914) using cut-outs. During his long career (he retired in 1957), the filmmaker produced hundreds of animated films for all purposes, from entertainment and advertising to education and newsreels. Kató-Kiszly began in a most empirical way, working on the roof garden of a cinema, using the sunlight and measuring exposure times with a metronome. His adaptation of Petőfi Sándor's poem *János vitéz* (János the Knight, 1916) and a silhouette film entitled *Rómeó és Júlia* (Romeo and Juliet, 1921) merit acclaim.

Spain

One of the finest artists of early animation was the Aragonese Segundo de Chomón (Teruel, 17 October 1871–Paris, 2 May 1929), an excellent cameraman and creator of special effects.

His first film, *Choque de trenes* (Train Collision, 1905, approximately 60 m) marked the beginning of the use of models in cinema. Chomón's *El hotel eléctrico* (The Electric Hotel, also filmed in 1905 – or 1907) was 'a masterpiece, honourably competing with the animation of real objects, in later years, by masters such as Walt Disney or by McLaren in *Neighbours*' (Francisco Macián).

Chomón's contribution to cinema involved not only animation but also filmmaking as a whole. As a film director and director of photography, he worked in Barcelona, Paris (Pathé), and Turin (for Itala Film[53]). He was, above all, a major director of photography and a tireless inventor of devices such as the dolly and of equipment that allowed the motion picture medium to develop its expressiveness. As for the frame-by-frame technique, Chomón considered it one element of the whole language of moving images – no more than one of the many tricks he created or perfected. It is said that he refused offers to direct animated feature films because of the economic risks and effort involved.

Caricaturist Fernando Marco attempted to follow the path of cinema only once, with *El toro fenómeno* (The Phenomenal Bull, 1917, first screened in 1919). Marco worked on the images, while Luís Tapia wrote the text in nimble verse. Despite its simple plot (an accident-filled run by a bull with huge horns), the film became popular.

Figure 6.8 Segundo de Chomón, *El hotel eléctrico*, 1908.

---

[51] Surnames first, given names second, according to Hungarian customary usage.
[52] This is the name of the protagonist, the sound of which in Hungarian means 'keg'.
[53] In Turin, he directed the live-action film *La guerra e il sogno di Momi* (The War and the Dream of Momi, 1917), which incorporated a frame-by-frame sequence. Momi, a child, receives a letter from his father, who is on the front in WWI. Slowly he falls asleep and dreams of a battle among puppets (the object animation sequence). Eventually he wakes up, pricked by a bayonet, which is actually a rose thorn. This virtually faultless work, remarkable in its fluid, expert animation, was the first 'Italian' example of animation to impress audiences.

Figure 6.9 Segundo de Chomón with his wife and son at the vertical frame-by-frame camera set in Itala Film Studios, Turin.

Portugal[54]

It's commonly acknowledged that the first animated film of the country was *O pesadelo de António Maria* (António Maria's Nightmare, 1923) by Joaquim Guerreiro.

A black pencil draws, on a white background, the six-time Portuguese Prime Minister (from 1910 to 1926) António Maria Da Silva, who comes home, takes his hat and clothes off, and goes to bed, but while sleeping he has a nightmare: An angry crowd in the street demands the end of food scarcity and cries out for freedom. Joaquim Guerreiro was the editor of the magazine *A Sátira* (Satire)

Figure 6.10 Joaquim Guerreiro, *O pesadelo de António Maria*, 1923.

and worked as cartoonist for many others (*O Século, Ilustração Portuguesa, A Tribuna, O Zé*). *O pesadelo de António Maria* was first shown on 25 January 1923 in the Eden Teatro in Lisbon as part of the revue *Tiro ao Alvo* (Shoot the Pigeon) by Luís de Aquino, Xavier Magalhães, and Laurenço Rodrigues (this can be considered the first Portuguese multimedia show[55]). It was screened again in February in the Águia d'Ouro Theatre in Oporto, where the actor Manuel Santos Carvalho voiced the film live.

It's possible, but not certain, that a short commercial had been filmed in 1920 by the then–13-year-old designer Luís Nunes and the cinematographer Manuel Luís Vieira: Influenced by the well-known drawing *His Master's Voice*, the quiet dog finally becomes animated after years of listening to the gramophone. Fred Netto was another pioneer: Around 1925, he produced *Tip-Top*, a short filmed with a Kynamo camera that he had previously modified that was screened in the Salão Central in Lisbon. *Uma história de Camelos* (A Camels' Tale, also known as *Os Camelos* [Camels]), directed by João Rodrigues Alves and filmed by Vitorino Abreu, was shown on 11 November 1930 in Cinema Lys in Lisbon on occasion of its opening. A newspaper of the time reported that the 'subtitle [was] written in verse by famous poet Rui Correia Leite' and that the film was an 'excellent musical adaptation'.[56]

---

[54] By Alberto Rigoni.

[55] Fernando Mateus and Paulo Cambraia, *80 anos do cinema de animação em Portugal*, Centro Nacional de Banda desenhada e Imagem, Amadora, 2003.

[56] António Gaio, *History of Portuguese Animation Cinema*, Nascente – Cooperativa Acção Cultural/Ministerio da Cultura/Instituto do Cinema Audiovisual e Media/Cidade de Espinho, Portugal, 2002.

A Lenda de Miragaia (The Legend of Miragaia), by Raul Faria de Fonseca and António Cunhal, premiered on 1 June 1931 at the Jardim Cinema in Lisbon. Black silhouettes on a white background tell us the tale of King Ramiro's fight to win over the moor King Alboazar the love of Queen Gaia, in the end giving the name Miragaia to a district in Oporto. *A lenda* is thought to be the first animated silhouette film in Portugal. According to Cunhal: 'Making a paper horse trot is much more difficult than teaching a real horse some tricks.'[57] Another pioneering Portuguese silhouette movie was *A Balada da Fonte* (The Ballad of the Source, 1933) by João Carlos.

The last 'first Portuguese animated film' was *Semi-Fusas*, whose premiere was scheduled in Cinema Olímpia in Oporto in February 1934. It was made by Hernani Tavares Seravat, and it was one of the last Portuguese silent films – sound cinema arrived in the country in 1931.

The Rest of Europe

The history of **Belgian** animation began in the 1920s when the Houssiaus, a Brussels-based father and son team, produced some advertising films. **Polish** animation's pioneer was philosopher and journalist Feliks Kuczkowski (1884–1970), who in 1917 filmed *The Chairs' Flirtation* and *The Telescope Has Two Ends*. 'They were based on a small number of drawings by his friend, painter Lucjan Kobierski', Marcin Gizycki said. 'The first film consisted of 38 drawings, which means that it wasn't "true" animation.'[58] In 1918, Kuczkowski created a film (the title of which has been lost) with animated objects. The work was the practical rendition of what he called 'visual filming', a sort of improvisation in front of the camera. In the 1920s, he made *The Orchestra Conductor*, a second 'visual film' using clay. Another pioneer was Stanislaw Dobrzynski, who made a few films from 1918 to 1924.

Aurel Petrescu (1897–1948) pioneered the field of animation in **Romania** by working, in solitude, on about forty films, the most famous of which were *Pacala in the Moon* (1920) and *Pacala in Love* (1924). A journalist, graphic artist, director, comic illustrator, and the first film critic of his country (he wrote a column from 1915 thereafter), Petrescu remained without imitators or followers. With a few exceptions, his films were lost during the war, and his premature death prevented the new generation from benefiting from his technique and artistic experience. Another multifaceted, disorderly genius was artist, painter, writer, and teacher of film direction, Marin Iorda. *Haplea* (1927), featuring the popular character of the title, was his only animated short. In **Italy**, Tiziano Film of Turin produced in 1920 *Baby . . . e la 'Lucrezia Borgia'* (Baby . . . and the 'Lucrezia Borgia') by the Bolognese artist Carlo Amedeo Frascari, known as Zambonelli (1877–1956).[59]

Russia/Soviet Union

Ladislas Starewich[60]

Lucanus cervus, commonly known as the stag beetle, is famous for being an oversized insect (up to 10 cm) with stunningly large mandibles. However, *Lucanus cervus* was also the subject that showed the world the artistic talent of Ladislas Starewitch.

This filmmaker, whose original name was Wladyslaw Maryan Aleksandrowicz Starewitch, was born on 8 August 1882 in Moscow to Polish parents.[61] After his mother's death, he spent his childhood in Kovno[62] with his grandparents.

Little Ladislas demonstrated great talent in graphic arts. He liked drawing and staging projections with the magic

---

[57] 'Cinéfilo', 1930, now in António Gaio, *History of Portuguese Animation Cinema*, Nascente – Cooperativa Acção Cultural/Ministerio da Cultura/Instituto do Cinema Audiovisual e Media/Cidade de Espinho, Portugal, 2002.

[58] Letter received from Marcin Gizycki, 1 March 1986. Much of the information on pre-war Poland reported in this chapter is based on this source.

[59] This film was sort of a legend, until Alessandro Cavaleri (*Un'ombra dal passato: Carlo Amedeo Frascari – Zambonelli*, Dissertation, Università degli Studi di Milano, supervisor Giannalberto Bendazzi, Milan, 2006) demonstrated that it actually existed, although no copy still remains.

[60] By Fabia Abati.

[61] Aleksandr Starewicz and Antonina Legiecka came from a village near Kovno, Lithuania, which was a region of Poland at that time. Poland, in her turn, was a nation of the tsarist Russian Empire, and the family had Polish nationality within the Empire. The filmmaker's name can be spelled either Vladislav Starevich (transliteration from the Russian Cyrillic alphabet), Wladyslaw Starewicz (Polish), or Ladislas Starewitch (French). A Polish national, he was born a subject of the tsar when the Russian Empire incorporated his country; in 1918, Poland was born again and he became a citizen; eventually he moved to Paris where he found his shelter and set his studio up. He never gave up Polish citizenship and only by the late 1920s mastered the French language, but this writer chose to use the French spelling of the name throughout the book, as most of Starewitch's output – and his fame – is linked to France.

[62] Today, this is Kaunas, Lithuania.

lantern for his little familiar audience. His books were decorated with drawings to flip at the bottom of the pages. His deep interest in science and entomology caused him to collect butterflies and insects his whole life.

Starewitch attended the secondary school in Dorpat[63] and began to earn some money: He painted postcards and illustrations for local magazines. Collaboration with an entomology journal satisfied his interest in this subject. Despite protests from his family, he persisted in his artistic vocation and attended a painting school. In the meantime, his fame grew, and new commissions arrived: He was asked to paint images for churches and design theatre sets.

He eventually found a job at the Count Court without giving up his interests and in fact cooperating with the natural history museum. He took pictures of insects and animals until a new idea appeared in his mind: making movies about the lives of insects. Wouldn't it be nice to show them to the visitors of the museum?

His first films (1909) were live-action documentaries that he financed himself. Then he decided to shoot the duel of male stag beetles to conquer the female. But as Starewitch turned the light on upon the coleoptera, they froze in fear and began moving again only when the lights were off.

While living animals are not always tameable, puppets are. Starewitch remembered some movies, like *Les allumettes animées* by Émile Cohl, where objects are animated with the frame-by-frame technique. He guessed that he could also move puppet insects with legs supported with wire:

> In the mating season, beetles fight. Their jaws remind one of deers' horns. I wished to film them but since their fighting is nocturnal, the light I used would freeze them into total immobility. By using embalmed beetles, I reconstructed the different phases of that fight, frame by frame, with progressive changes; more than five hundred frames for thirty seconds of projection. The result surpassed my hopes: *1910 – Lucanus Cervus* (10 metres long) – the first three-dimensional animated film [Author's note: Starewitch was unaware of the previous puppet and object animated films].[64]

Before shooting the beetles, he drew each position of their movement, and then he composed each position and shot them frame by frame. The high frequency of frames per second (sixteen, the maximum at the time) proves the great quality of the animation. Starewitch himself was amazed by the harmony and fluency of the beetles' actions, as he wrote in his diary:

> When I saw the movie, I was surprised by the fluidity of movements. That fight was beautiful, maybe too much. . . . When we see a movie that represents a horse running, we note that, at least one frame on three, the position of its legs is ungraceful. . . . Actually, if he draws the same horse running, the artist will try to avoid the poses that disturb his sensitivity, and will introduce a sort of harmony between each phase of movement. So, even if they show the same subject, the drawing will be different from the pictures for its particular elegance.[65]

After the success of *Lucanus Cervus* (1910) and *Prekrasnaya Lukanida* (The Beautiful Leukanida, 1910), in 1911 Starewitch moved to Moscow, where he collaborated with the well-established pioneer film producer Aleksandr Khanzhonkov.[66] That same year, Starewitch won a prize from the tsar for *The Grasshopper and the Ant*. With the live-action film *The Terrible Vengeance*, he introduced a talented new actor, Ivan Mozzhukhin.

Starewitch kept working on the subject he knew and loved the most: insects and animals. His knowledge about their habits and his skill in drawing and photography made him consider them real actors playing a role, on scenery specifically devoted to them. The subjects of Starewitch's movies found an unlimited source of ideas in the European folk tale tradition, from Aesop to oral storytellers to La Fontaine, although some stories were his own.

Strekoza i muravey (The Dragonfly and the Ant, 1911) achieved great popularity both home and abroad, and even the tsar praised it. It tells the old story of the lazy dragonfly who doesn't care about the future and just sings all day, while the active ant collects food and wood for the winter. The dragonfly will be punished: When the winter comes, it will ask in vain for help.

The real protagonist is the vicious dragonfly rather than the hardworking ant. Starewitch doesn't hesitate to describe every single action of the insect, whose movements are

---

[63] Today, this is Tartu, Estonia.
[64] Irène Starewitch, *Hommage à Ladislas Starewitch*, Unpublished manuscript provided to Giannalberto Bendazzi by the writer, Paris, no date (perhaps 1973).
[65] Léona Béatrice and François Martin, *Ladislas Starewitch 1882–1965*, l'Harmattan, Paris, 2003, pp. 41–42.
[66] Aleksandr Khanzhonkov, the founder, had gained fame for having interviewed the ill-tempered Tolstoy shortly before the writer's death.

similar to those of a human. The dragonfly plays the violin and drinks wine, moving its legs just like a drunk person. At the same time, its feelers move up and down just like those of a real dragonfly. Starewitch focuses on its amusement to make the ending even harder: When the dragonfly lies on the ground waiting for a deadly cold winter, the audience remembers how it was happy when it was playing violin a few minutes before and feels sympathetic.

Mesty kinematographicheskogo operatora (The Cameraman's Revenge, 1911) is probably the most famous animated film of his Russian period. The plot is a familiar *ménage à trois*: Mr. and Mrs. Beetle, bored by family life, look for distractions. Mr. Beetle goes to night clubs, where he finds a gracious dragonfly, a dancer. To conquer her, Mr. Beetle has to fight with another lovesick potential partner, a grasshopper; when the battle is won, Mr. Beetle can finally amuse himself with such a beautiful partner. He doesn't know that the grasshopper is a cameraman and is outside the door preparing its revenge: It shoots all the happenings in the room.

When he goes home, Mr. Beetle is welcomed by an unexpected surprise: His wife is having fun with a young painter. After showing him the door, he forgives his wife and decides to go with her to the cinema to celebrate the peace. The movie shown on the screen is exactly the one shot by the grasshopper. Mrs. Beetle isn't happy at all to find out about her husband's infidelity and doesn't hide her disappointment. The exciting day ends in a prison cell.

The Cameraman's Revenge is a perfect example of young Starewitch's unsentimental, unmoralistic style. The story is perfectly suited for animal characters. As in Aesop and Phaedrus' fables, it is universal because its protagonists are animals – i.e. symbols. Mr. and Mrs. Beetle are a typical middle-class couple bored by family life. Starewitch's characters are also good actors: The spectator has fun and indentifies himself in the incoherent and very realistic Mr. Beetle. His acting is, again, a balanced mix between human and animal action: His human feelings are clear but, at the same time, his features and anatomical structure are scientifically correct.

In 1913–1914, Starewitch set up his own film company, but by the summer of 1914 World War I had started and the thirty-six-year-old anti-militarist filmmaker was at risk of being drafted. The Skobelev Committee[67] let him continue his career although there were difficult wartime conditions. In 1917, after the Revolution, he directed the didactic *K narodnoy vlasti* (People's Power) to explain to the population how to vote at the November elections for the Constituent Assembly. But the Bolsheviks continued climbing to power, and civil war ensued.

In 1918, the filmmaker moved from Moscow to the more secure Yalta, where in the same year he directed *Stella Maris*,[68] which both he and his producer (Khanzhonkov again) considered his live-action masterpiece. In 1920, after having spent some time in Italy, Ladislas Starewitch docked in France.

He certainly didn't leave newly born Soviet Russia because he was a reactionary. Had he been interested in politics, he would probably have been labelled a Jacobin. But a ferociously individualistic, ideologically non-aligned foreigner wouldn't have been welcomed by either Lenin or Stalin – and above all, he wouldn't have been allowed to make films. Poland had no film industry. So he continued his career in France, creating his own studio in Fontenay-Sous-Bois in the suburbs of Paris.

During the 1920s, he produced the most interesting part of his work. While he continued adapting popular fables for the screen, such as in *Les Grenouilles qui demandent un roi* (The Frogs Who Wanted a King, 1922), he wrote and directed movies that alternated live action and animation scenes (*La Voix du rossignol* [The Voice of the Nightingale], 1923; *L'Horloge magique* [The Magic Clock], 1928). His favourite actress was his daughter Nina Star (Janina/Jeanne Starewitch), who was happy to be part of the fantastic world created by her father.

The Voice of the Nightingale was successful with audiences and made Starewitch a household name all over Europe and even in the difficult American market. It tells the story of a girl who finds a nightingale and keeps it in a cage. During the night, the nightingale sings sweet melodies that make the girl dream. When she wakes up, she realizes that she has stolen freedom from a creature that needs to go back home to feed its chicks. She then sets the nightingale free. The bird, grateful to the girl, gives her its beautiful voice.

The subject sounds horribly corny, but the film is not. Starewitch's approach is classically Slavic/mitteleuropean: disenchanted, dry, even in the wildest melodrama.

---

[67] Originally a charitable institution for orphans and widows of the 1905 Russian-Japanese War, this committee set up a Military Film Section in March 1914 before the outbreak of the war. It produced newsreels and fiction films.

[68] The film is based on a novel by British writer William John Locke (1863–1930). Stella is a paralyzed but wealthy girl whose parents protect her from the outside world. She falls in love with an unhappily married family friend who, after many melodramatic tangles, and a salvific surgery, marries her. Oddly enough, in the same year, 1918, American star Mary Pickford interpreted a film directed by Marshall Neilan by the same title and based on the same subject.

Ladislas Starewitch achieved great popularity during his life. His animation technique, so precise and spectacular, amazed the public of his time, and he is still admired today. The refinement of his movies comes from a culture that included technical and practical knowledge: graphic arts, entomology, science, and photography. He loved experimenting with different techniques[69] and could choose how to use them according to his intent. The results he achieved were particularly advanced, and he always tried to improve them. His weakness (if any) was his luxurious imagery: backgrounds, costumes, faces, and bodies are so detailed and overabundant that the eye is often not able to fully enjoy them. But one thing must be emphasized: Although for many years only black-and-white copies have been available, each and every Starewitch film of the 1920s was coloured with various techniques.[70] Colours certainly emphasize the clarity of the images.

His characters are lazy, active, tender, and stupid: In one word, they are human. Starewitch was aware of the importance of the actor on the screen to tug at the audience's heartstrings: to make the audience laugh with the *Cameraman* or cry with the *Nightingale* it is necessary that all the puppets (and the human actors, too) on the screen naturally play their roles.

After the Revolution

Despite a unique cooperation among the different artistic fields in one of the most creative periods of the century, animation played a marginal role in the world of a cinema dominated by Eisenstein, Pudovkin, Dovzhenko, and Dziga Vertov.[71] Soviet animation included quality works but remained a less-developed field than those of real-life cinema, theatre, literature, and painting:

The popular tale, the modern tale, the surrealist tale, the musical comedy based on current events, the political and social satire, and pamphlet – these were the themes of Soviet animation in the beginning.[72]

Soviet animation originated directly from political manifestos and satirical vignettes. Dziga Vertov[73] started with *Segodnya* (Today, 1923), directed by himself and animated by Ivan Belyaev, and continued with *Sovetskie igrushki* (Soviet Toys), along with artists Aleksandr Ivanov and Aleksandr Bushkin.

As it is a political satire – i.e. a topical work – *Soviet Toys* is incomprehensible to anyone who is alien to the topic. Actually, Vertov makes a visual libel against the New Economic Policy (NEP), the bland privatization that Lenin started in 1921, and that many ideologically dogmatic fellow communists opposed. In the film, we are introduced to the caricatures of a fat man, two priests, a soldier, a peasant, a worker, and a rich woman. Subsequent events show the bourgeois' greed, dishonesty, and moral decay; finally, they are all hung on a Christmas tree as ornaments ('toys' in Russian). The drawings and technique are crude, but the film is precious as a document of its time.

Figure 6.11 Dziga Vertov, *Soviet Toys*, 1924.

---

[69] We know that there is no such a thing as a real 'first inventor' in history; nevertheless, we must acknowledge Starewitch with the frequent and consistent use of the so-called two-dimensional puppets (one side flat, the other side volumetric), much easier to animate than the complete figure in a set. Many people give credit to Czech Břetislav Pojar, who reintroduced the process more than three decades later.

[70] Just to name one, the coloured version of *Le Rat de ville et le rat des champs* (The City Mouse and the Country Mouse, 1926) is far better than the black-and-white one. In the 1990s and 2000s, Léona Béatrice Martin and François Martin, proprietors and curators of the Starewitch estate, have restored in colour all the films of the 1920s (except *La Petite Parade* [The Little Parade], 1928). Many festivals have projected the restored copies in their retrospectives.

[71] While Vertov did experiment with animation, he never took to the medium very seriously (see http://animator.ru/db/?ver=eng&p=show_person&pid=2912 for his films), Dovzhenko and Eisenstein started off as caricaturists but did not go on to pursue graphics in their pure form. However, both Eisenstein and Pudovkin wrote keenly about animation in their theoretical works and acknowledged the medium early on.

[72] Ivan Ivanov-Vano, *Risovannyi Film* (The Animated Film, Moscow, 1950).

[73] With the given name of David Abelevitch Kaufman (1896–1954), he was an important revolutionary film theorist, documentarian, and newsreel producer. His best-known film is *Chelovek s kinoapparatom* (The Man with a Movie Camera, 1929).

The already-mentioned Aleksandr Bushkin (Balasov, 1 April 1896–Moscow, 5 June 1929), a painter and poster artist, arrived in Goskino[74] in 1922 from Kiev. He made films using the technique of animated cut-outs, including *V mordu Vtoromu Internacionalu* (In the Face of the Second International, 1924) and *Karera Makdonalda* (McDonald's Career, 1925). Bushkin died too young to be able to fully express his talent, but he had the time to publish the first Soviet book on animation: *Tryuki i multiplikatsya* (Tricks and Animation, 1926).

During the same years, sculptor Nikolai Khodataev (Rostov, 9 May 1892–Moscow, 27 December 1979) and painters Zenon Komissarenko (Simferopol, 10 April 1891–Moscow, 1980) and Yuri Merkulov (Rasskasovo, 28 April 1901–Moscow, 3 February 1979) founded an Experimental Animation Workshop at the school of cinematography GTK and began working. After *Mezhplanetnaya Revolyuciya* (Interplanetary Revolution, 1924), which was intended to partly resemble Mayakovsky's *Comic Mystery* and was partly a parody of the science fiction film *Aelita*, by Protazanov, they released *Kitaj v ogne* (China in Flames, 1925), dedicated to the revolutionary struggle of the Chinese. That same year, they shot *1905–1925*, covering the period between the first Russian insurrection and the events of 1925.

Irina Margolina kindly provided the following insight into this relevant artist of early Soviet animation.

Nikolai Petrovich Khodataev (1892–1979) was born on 9 May 1892 in the Cossack village of Konstantinovskaya where, among the cherry orchards, the quiet was disturbed only by the whistles of passing steamers. It was fortunate that his father had a secure job in the tsar's civil service and could not only feed his children but was also able to give them all an education and pay for a music teacher; all kinds of canvases, colours, and paint brushes for Kolya (Nikolai Petrovich); and a good library. In 1898, the family moved to Moscow: Kolya was six years old. In 1912, Kolya travelled to the Caucasus. He was physically strong and daring. The various adventures he had there only serve to underline his basic character traits: He was headstrong, independent, and bold to the point of recklessness. Once he fell down a steep slope into a mountain river, only managing by some miracle to save himself by grabbing the bough of a tree. Another time, he nearly died when he went off alone into the mountains. Kolya, Nikolai Petrovich, was not a good pupil at secondary school, but from childhood on he loved drawing and was extremely talented in this area. He declared that he wanted to become an artist, and for that he had to be accepted by the School of Painting, Sculpture and Architecture. He received good tutoring and, having passed his exams, donned a beautiful green and gold uniform. As a youth, he was highly strung, prickly, very self-assured, and impatient. He could not acknowledge that anyone might be superior to him, especially in the area of art. He could accept no affection, even from his parents. He did not believe in God and did not go to church. In his art, he was hardworking and tenacious, devoting himself heart and soul to his practice. He loved music and often sang. He worked a lot on improving himself and finally came to grips with life skills before many others. Because of this, he accepted the revolution more easily and painlessly. Thus, Nikolai Khodataev graduated from VKhUTEMAS (Higher Art and Technical Workshops) with a diploma in fine art but continued his studies in the same institution in the architecture department, after which he worked for the State Committee for the Preservation of Ancient Monuments. Then, in 1924, in the 'rooms of the former restaurant Yar, a group of young artists – Zenon Komissarenko, Yuri Merkulov, and Nikolai Khodataev set up an experimental animation workshop and started shooting the first Soviet animated fantasy film, *Interplanetary Revolution*'. Khodataev, Merkulov, and Komissarenko used the cut-out technique for their film. Moving the paper figures boldly and energetically under the camera, they were in a hurry – not because they did not have enough time, but because they were anxious to see their own fantasy take off. They were in such a rush that we can see their hands in the shot. A little earlier, Yakov Protazanov had begun shooting his feature film *Aelita*. The novel had only just appeared, offering a broad range of possibilities for the screen. *Interplanetary Revolution* was conceived as a parody of Protazanov's costumed hit and, at the same time, a satire in the style of the *mistero buffo*. It was ironical that behind the wall (literally) of their studio, in a different part of the complex, Mezhrabpomruss also had studios and Protazanov was there, shooting *Aelita*. Ivanov-Vano recalled:

> Life on the other side of our studio wall was making a great din. Silent films were made very noisily. Actors and extras would constantly be coming to look into our quiet abode. Exotically-dressed 'martians', breathless with curiosity, would observe our strange work. It all seemed like black magic and sorcery to them, and they related to us with a special understanding. And the animators examined with great interest their 'martian' costumes, made of silk and silvery cellophane, designed by the artist Alexandra Ekster.

---

[74] Founded by Lenin in 1919, the Gosudarstvennyi Komitet po Kinematografii (State Committee for Cinematography) soon abandoned its supervising function and became the country's most important production company.

The first Soviet animators were delighted by the results of their labours.

Yuri Merkulov wrote:

The battling rocket squadrons and the flight into the starry cosmos all seemed to us the most surprisingly beautiful, merry and witty spectacle. Amazed and stunned, we laughed happily, rolling around the floor, waving our legs in the dark, empty room. We fancied ourselves as the Columbuses of animation.

The next subject which the team opened up for the country, and discovered for themselves, was China. The theme of nations in dire need of help. It was a burning socialist issue. A neighbour in need of help, a neighbour who was different, with a different-coloured skin and – the main thing – a different culture . . . A black man or a Chinese – these were icons of oppressed races, a socialist cliché. . . and from this perspective animation stops being comedy and satire and becomes serious. It even touches on feelings.

Interplanetary Revolution was funded by Khodataev, from earnings on an architecture project, but *China in Flames* was state financed. It was the first feature film. In it, each of the artists was able to demonstrate his personal style. So one could at least make a guess as to which episode was drawn by Zenon Komissarenko, which by Ivanov-Vano.

Khodataev wrote:

Movement has its own drawing technique. Drawing in movement. . . . The animators gradually began to expand their artistic ambitions. Then it became clear that they were on the threshold of a great art, with great possibilities. All this time (from 1924), the art of animation was seen as a slightly makeshift production technique, and only slowly and with great difficulty was experience accumulated, while the animators' drawing skills developed. There were times when we had nothing to be proud of except our inexhaustible energy and our brave struggle to conquer the technology of this young art, so unfamiliar to us.

Khodataev's next film was *One of Many*. This, again, was a comedy. Khodataev wrote a lot about animation. He analyzed its artistic and social possibilities, calling it 'dynamic graphics'. He did not idealize his first efforts, considering them rather primitive, and wrote that what was most successful with primitive movement in animation was satirical and comic subjects. An example was the film *One of Many*, about the dream of a Komsomol (Young Communists) member, in which she visits Hollywood and has unforgettable meetings with well-known actors. Khodataev very much wanted to convey feelings and emotions in his animation. In painting, this was possible. He wrote:

In *The Samoyed Boy*, my group used a more realistic approach – though without going into the psychological aspects and using quite stereotyped images – for certain scenes which were particularly risky in animation, such as the meeting of the mother with her son, whom she had thought to be dead. The almost realistic emotional tone of *The Samoyed Boy* even gave us reason to think that with this film new horizons were opening up for animation in that it had now conquered serious genres and even tragedy.

These were Khodataev's words. The film *Terrible Vavila and Auntie Arina* (1928) is about women's issues. It was the first to deal with equal rights for women and was dedicated to 8 March, Women's Day. The 1927 agitprop film *We Must Be Vigilant* is an early demonstration of Khodataev's internal struggle between the artist and the citizen. He did not like animated agitprop, for he felt the genre an unworthy occupation for an artist. And even agitprop pieces were beginning to fall foul of the censors. They were already getting nervous about satire and even in propaganda films they wanted only comic storylines. The film *The Music Box* was a breakthrough, manifesting a plasticity of animation movement and the filmmaker's ability to nudge animation towards real art. He invited his sister Olga Khodataeva and Daniil Cherkes to work on the film. Unusual and memorable heroes appeared. He called the faceless characters of the then-current Soviet animation 'murzilki'. Yet *The Music Box* was unnoticed. It was not banned, but no one paid the film any attention. Yet it was a significant work. 'Arriving from obscurity, I am departing into obscurity', wrote Khodataev. After *The Music Box*, he made one more film, *Fialkin's Career*. Again, the animation itself, and the movement, are splendid – but the film is nothing special; irony was deployed in a not very serious cause.

It was hard for me to leave animation. I thought about coming back, but I realised that as an artist I was catastrophically divorced from reality . . . I could not snap out of that feeling of devastation which had been tormenting me recently . . . What has the film business done to me?

The first to analyze Soviet animation, a talented artist, a very intelligent, educated person, he made the film *Pushkin's New Home*, probably to a certain extent drawing an analogy between the fate of the poet and his own life and destiny. At that time, he thought a great deal about the place of the artist in history. The film was banned and that served as a further impetus when making his decision – to leave animation forever. Nikolai Petrovich continued to draw and took up sculpture and easel painting. He lived in absolute anonymity until 1979. He called his favourite cat Foma Fomich Pushkin.

Filmography: *Mezhplanetnaya revolyutsiya* (Interplanetary Revolution), 1924; *Kak Avdotya stala gramotnoi* (How Avdotya Learned to Read), 1925; *Kitai v ogne* (China in Flames), 1925; *Start* (Start), 1925; *Kak Murzilka pravilno pisal adresa* (How Murzilka Wrote Addresses Correctly), 1926; *Budem zorki* (We Must Be Vigilant), 1927; *Dayesh khoroshi lavkom* (Let's Make the LavKom Good), 1927; *Odna iz mnogikh* (One of Many), 1927; *Grozny Vavila i tetka Arina* (Terrible Vavila and Auntie Arina), 1928; *Desyat pravil kooperatsii* (Ten Rules of Cooperation), 1928; *Dnem s ognem* (By Day with a Flame), 1928; *Samoyedski malchik* (The Samoyed Boy), 1928; *Novoselye Pushkina* (Pushkin Moves House), 1928; *Avtodorets* (The Car Lover), 1931; *Razoruzheniye* (Disarmament), 1932; *Organchik* (The Music Box), 1934; *Karyera Fialkina* (Fialkin's Career), 1934; *Kinotsirk* (Cinema Circus), 1942 (animator, with Lev Amalrik directing).

Irina Margolina kindly provided the following insight into this relevant artist of early Soviet animation.

Zenon Petrovich Komissarenko (1891–1980) was an enigma. His fate is well known, but his life was not. His registration card says he was an animator. We do not even know whether Zenon was his real name or a pseudonym. It is quite possible that he assumed it later in life.

Komissarenko was interested in the possibility of venturing into a new art.

He worked with Protazanov on the film *Aelita*. A student of Malevich, he was ahead of his time.

The episode with the moving fragments of glass in *Aelita* is an example of stop motion animation, not particularly original, and was Komissarenko's first experience with animation.

Sergei Komarov recalls that he was a strange person, with strange tastes. He had no interest in human beings as the object of art.

It was Komissarenko who brought Khodataev into animation. It was he who excited Khodataev with his living graphics – 'dynamic graphics', as Khodataev called it. It was Komissarenko who invited Khodataev to work on the film *Interplanetary Revolution* (1924).

The theatre costumes designed by Komissarenko originated as sketches for the next film they made together, *China in Flames*.

He himself wore the same one jacket throughout his life, but on paper he was a daring, liberated artist – or, as we would say today, designer. He was born too early: At that time in Soviet Russia, a different kind of art was required, comprehensible to illiterate viewers. He perceived the world in terms of the music of colour. He painted in gouache because oil paints were expensive and also because they did not convey the richness of the world of colour that was rampaging around his consciousness.

The artistic style – or rather styles – of the film *China in Flames* was mostly down to Komissarenko, although we can divine a varied stylistic, for various artists worked on the film, each with a different vision and a different artistic taste.

One of Komissarenko's student contemporaries tells of his appearance at the time: his head thrust proudly upwards, his hair crew cut, with a small, auburn moustache, his shirt always hanging out of his wide breeches, puttees on top of shoes you couldn't quite identify, laconic, quiet, courteous in conversation, languid; it was plain that his innermost desire was to give himself greater significance and to be the leader of any new project.

A magical China was dreamed up by the filmmakers. The scenery and topography were drawn by the Brumberg sisters, Ivanov-Vano, and Komissarenko.

During the war, Komissarenko, with the rest of the Soviet film industry, was evacuated to Tashkent. Here he devoted more and more time to painting, producing magnificent graphics. Some of his works remained in the collection of the Tashkent Museum, but they were destroyed in a fire.

From 1928 to 1933, he worked at the Red Army's Gosvoyenkino studio.

During the 1950s, he worked at the Glass Institute, where he made stained glass windows (none of which have been preserved). We can only guess how they looked.

Zenon Komissarenko was intrigued by the cosmos and even gave his paintings cosmic titles: *Venus*, *The Universe*, *The Milky Way*.

He had an exhibition at the Sorbonne, but the exhibits were lost for years until they turned up in the attic of the Cinema Veterans' Retirement Home at Matveyevskoye, where Komissarenko lived out his final years.

This is what Jacques Marcadé wrote of Komissarenko's painting:

Officially acknowledged as the founding father of Soviet animation, who had taken part in all the landmark events of the 1920s, Zenon Komissarenko, having paid his dues to the general craze of the time for utilitarian art and waited till he was of retirement age, revealed himself as one of the most brilliant artists of the post-war period. His art was decidedly abstract, i.e. an orchestration of colours to the rhythm of a beating, interior, spiritual pulse. His colour fairy tales are scintillating explosions of light.

Zenon Komissarenko utilized the well-known 'flipbook' method of animation, still used today, whereby both characters and backgrounds are redrawn for each frame. (Previously, figures had been cut-outs and it had been hard to place them accurately.) He died in 1980 at Matveyevskoye in the Cinema Veterans' Retirement Home.

Filmography: *Aelita*, 1923; *Mezhplanetnaya revolyutsiya* (Interplanetary Revolution), 1924; *Kitai v ogne* (China in Flames), 1925; *Uchis strelyat na 'yat'* (Learn to Be a First-Class Marksman), 1928; *Pervaya pyatiletka* (The First Five-Year Plan), 1929; *Russkaya vintovka* (The Russian Rifle), 1929; *Pulemet Maksima* (The Maxim Gun), 1929; *Takticheskoye nastupleniye* (Tactical Offensive), 1929; *Podvodnaya lodka* (The Submarine), 1930; *Korabli* (Ships), 1930; *Razvedka* (Intelligence), 1931; *Tryapye* (Rags), 1933.

The Experimental Animation Workshop lasted only one year, but it was the cornerstone of a professional, long-lasting Soviet/Russian animation.

In 1927, Khodataev directed an all-woman crew with his sister Olga Khodataeva (1894–1968) and Valentina and Zinaida Brumberg; together they created the already mentioned *Odna iz mnogih* (One Among the Others) about the dreams of an adolescent girl in love with movies and (American) movie stars. The film, which mixed animated passages with shots of the blond protagonist, was narrated in a moralistic, yet amused, tone. In 1928, the same group signed *Samoedsky malchik* (The Samoyed Boy) about the Siberian boy Chu who kills a big bear, unmasks a tricky shaman, and eventually is taken to Leningrad on a ship.

Yuri Merkulov became the boss of the group Politsatira, hosted by Goskino/Sovkino, and among his political satires made *Propavshaja gramota* (The Lost Diploma) in 1927, where he stood godfather to a young animator bound to a great future: Aleksandr Ptushko.

Aleksandr Ivanov (Rasskasovo, 5 June 1899–Moscow, 13 March 1959), who we have already mentioned as Dziga Vertov's collaborator, organized an independent group and produced some commercials, the best known being the one for Vinsindikat (the State Union of Wine Workers). Along with cinematographer Boris Frantzisson, he then made quite a few political satires until his client Sovkino (under the new name of Goskino, 1926) entrusted him with the organization of an animation department. The team consisted of Aleksandr Ivanov himself, artist Panteleimon Sazonov (1895–1950), and technician Nikolai Voinov (1900–1958); they called themselves Group IVVOS (**Iv**anov, **Vo**inov, **S**azonov). In 1927, Ivanov produced his first film for children, *Tarakanishe* (The Big Beetle).

In 1927, Yuri Zhelyabuzhsky (1888–1955) directed *Katok* (The Skating Rink), based on a subject by Nikolay Bartram, with drawings by Daniil Cherkes and Ivan Ivanov-Vano. The film features an urchin who sneaks into a skating rink and behaves mischievously but in the end wins a race. The story, entertaining and well animated, is based on excellent black-on-white artwork, simple, dry, and extremely expressive in its unadorned style. Cherkes (Moscow, 31 August 1899–10 June 1971), who had worked as a theatrical set designer with Meyerhold and had collaborated on political films, made a couple more animated films before devoting himself to painting in the 1930s.

Irina Margolina kindly provided the following insight into this relevant artist of early Soviet animation.

Daniil Yakovlevich Cherkes (1899–1971) was an artist-animator and fought in two world wars. Born in 1899 into a lawyer's family, he inherited his passion for drawing from his father, an amateur artist, collector, and connoisseur. It was thanks to his father's collection that Cherkes was able to survive and to feel relatively free, for during his headstrong years he sold off the collection, enabling him to pursue his favourite activities.

Cherkes loved the sea and he loved painting. Choosing the latter, he went to study in the fine arts faculty of VKhUTEMAS (Higher Art and Technical Workshops). There he worked in the studio of Malyutin, whose assistant was Pavel Korin.

Cherkes's father worked as a manager in the Yava tobacco factory. In 1937, he was sent to one of Stalin's prison camps, where he died of a heart attack.

Cherkes was fascinated by Vsevolod Emilyevich Meyerhold, by the man and by his work, and took a job as designer for Meyerhold's theatre.

This was a new kind of theatre, happening in the street. Verkharna's play *Dawns*, with Cherkes as designer was, in this genre, a public spectacle among many produced at the time.

In 1919, Cherkes interrupted his studies at VKhUTEMAS to volunteer for the Red Army and was assigned to train for the command personnel.

He took a good while to find his calling. Returning from the front, he went back to VKhUTEMAS and completed his studies in the studio of Petr Konchalovsky. After graduating, his career was fairly varied: He worked both at the Mosgiz and at the Molodaya Gvardiya (Young Guard) publishing houses.

In 1925, he took up animation, making his film *Senka the African* with cameraman Leonid Kosmatov. The film was based on the Kornei Chukovsky story *Crocodile*.

Ivan Petrovich Ivanov-Vano, who worked with Cherkes, recalled:

It was hard to link up the drawn characters with the live-action. In some situations we managed with photographs as backgrounds, but it was particularly hard to mix drawn characters with live-action shots in the same frame. We built an animation stand with a sheet of glass, which we covered with barium salt and placed underneath it a special mirror, which ensured that the image on the glass would not move around. We were pretty nervous, but in fact the result was splendid. Children easily grasped the convention. Some film historians think we used rear-projection and multiple screens, but neither of those was even suggested at the time.

The crowd scenes in *Senka the African* seem to be drawn from life from the life of that period.

Cherkes made his next film with Nikolai Bartram, a researcher and collector of children's wooden toys from Sergiyev-Posad.

Yuri Zhelyabuzhsky, Gorky's adopted son, and Nikolai Bartram worked with Cherkes on the film *The Skating Rink*. Ivanov-Vano recalled:

The film *The Skating Rink* appealed to young viewers, both in the drawing technique and in the graphic treatment of the characters, in the naïve style of children's drawings. The film was tailored to a child's understanding. To make the film easy on children's eyes we decided against a blinding white background and instead drew white lines on a black background. That way the line read better, more vividly and more expressively.

The animation of this film is supple, in the style of American characters such as Koko the Clown, by the brothers Dave and Max Fleischer.

Cherkes himself was an outstanding draughtsman. He exercised enormous influence on the colleagues he worked with and on the whole animation industry of the period.

Cherkes made another film with that same trusted group. Ivanov-Vano recalls:

Again we turned to the adventure genre. We searched long and hard for the right subject, finally settling on *The Adventures of Münchhausen*. The baron's fantasies suited the specifics of animation perfectly. Unlike *The Skating Rink*, this film was done with a black line on white paper. Working with Daniil Cherkes was of great benefit to me. A magnificent draughtsman, he instilled in me a love of drawing and did much to improve my skill in this area. We loved this work and put particular care into the scenes with horses. Cherkes found, in a shop somewhere, a wooden model of a horse, held together with mechanical hinges, and we could move it into the most expressive poses. That was the best visual aid.

The documentary film *The All-Union Powerhouse* – about the Donets Basin – was done in the style of Dziga Vertov. Here, Cherkes was experimenting with mixing documentary and animated images. Cherkes's career, like that of Nikolai Khodataev, coincided with the period of the most stringent arts policy on the part of the Soviet authorities.

On the film *The Music Box*, directed by Khodataev, Cherkes was the designer, along with the well-known book illustrator and engraver Georgi Yacheistov. This film became a classic, though it was never shown to an audience. Saltykov-Shchedrin's satire was too incisive and too topical, and his books would soon be removed from libraries and forbidden. There was no talk of releasing the film: For all intents and purposes, it was banned. *The Music Box* was a great and significant work, and the fact that it was not seen by audiences was a massive blow to Cherkes. He decided to abandon animation, especially since the period of political terror was approaching: Churches were being blown up and, for a man of culture, it was the beginning of a very difficult period.

Cherkes's unreleased film of 1934, *Look Up*, had the working title of *Little Hero*. By some miracle, the film's negative was preserved by Cherkes's friend Leonid Nikolayevich Lazarev. The film critic Ross tore the film to pieces in the *Cinema Gazette*, saying that it diverged from the script, was not understandable by its intended audience and, furthermore, that it was badly drawn. The film was about the Pioneer youth movement participating in safeguarding the harvest. Even this kind of innocent film could, it seems, incite a storm of invective from critics. After this last unsuccessful attempt, Cherkes abandoned animation for good.

After 1934, Cherkes dedicated himself to painting. He loved the sea and was always drawing boats: they enthralled him throughout his life, as did his missed career as a sailor. But he was never depressed, remaining optimistic till the end, ever cheerful and smiling. He wrote to one of his students: 'When you draw from nature don't be fearful and don't rely on your memory. The main thing is not to grumble and to see the best in everything, not the bad side of life.'

In 1957 he suffered his first heart attack but did not stop working.

He was always drawing. He used various techniques: He boiled up both paint and glue on a kerosene stove; worked on damp paper, which he covered with drawing; cut himself little quill pens; and all in all greatly tried the patience of his loving household. But for them, as for him, his work was the most important thing. In 1958, he received grateful thanks from the naval high command for his work on naval subjects.

He wrote in one of his last notebooks: 'Life is wonderful, not because it is always good, but because life is a struggle, with circumstances, with oneself, with hardships, with our ailments, a struggle for the right to do what you enjoy.' Cherkes died in June 1971.

Filmography: *Senka-Afrikanets* (Senka the African), 1927; *Katok* (The Skating Rink), 1927; *Agitka – Pervoye maya* (Agitprop – The First of May), 1929; *Knizhnaya polka* (The Bookshelf), 1929; *Pokhozhdeniya Myunkhgausena* (The Adventures of Münchhausen), 1929; *Kooperatsiya na relsakh* (Cooperation on the Rails), 1930; *Glyadi v oba* (Look Up)/*Malenki geroi* (Little Hero), 1934; *Organchik* (The Music Box), 1934 (designer).

Ivan Ivanov-Vano (Moscow, 27 January 1900–May 1987) instead pursued a long-lasting career in the field of animation. With Cherkes, Ivanov-Vano co-directed *Senka-afrikanec* (Senka the African, 1927). While these events were taking place in Moscow, other young people were busy in Leningrad.[75]

Students Aleksandr Presnyakov (1902–1953) and Igor Sorokhtin (1898–1959) made an animated segment at the Institute of Cinematographic Art for the documentary *Sem' let Oktjabrja – Sem' let pobed* (Seven Years from October – Seven Years of Victories, 1924), produced by the City Committee of People's Deputies of Leningrad.

A year later, Sorokhtin and other associates were given a regular place to work, and with their savings (difficult at a time when there were serious shortages) they produced the satire *Alimenty* (Nourishments, 1925) and *Dal' zovyot* (Distance Calls, 1926; never screened). The group was then enrolled in the Leningrad Sovkino studio, becoming its animation and special effects department. In 1927, illustrator Vladislav Tvardovsky (1888–1942) joined the company as a director; more importantly, Mikhail Tsekhanovsky (Proskurov, 6 June 1889–Moscow, 22 June 1965) joined the studio as well.

Tsekhanovsky, a painter and book illustrator, had no experience but had a beautiful mind and learned quickly. In 1929, he directed *Pochta* (Mail), probably the masterpiece of nascent Soviet animation. Based on a popular text for children by Samuil Marshak, the film described mail carriers from all over the world. Re-edited in 1930 in a sound version, *Mail* is well designed and well paced, has a good-natured atmosphere, and contains the most beautiful frame of all silent animation: a tunnel turned into a vortex symbolizing excitement, speed, and depth. It also became popular outside the Soviet Union; the American critic Harry Alan Potamkin praised it highly, while architect Frank Lloyd Wright showed it to Walt Disney as an example of thought-provoking animation.

Another important figure in Leningrad was caricaturist Boris Antonovsky (1891–1935), who drew and directed *Zri v koren*/*Krestovy pokhod* (Go to the Roots of Things or The Crusade, 1930). The subject was very popular in Soviet Union then, as the Catholic Pope from Rome was calling upon the faithful to start a crusade against the communists.

Ukraine

This is one of the least well-known countries in Europe, and probably in the world. Its history goes back to the ninth century, but for more than 1,000 years it was neglected as a 'nation without a state', and its territory varied greatly. To make things even more complicated, the cradle of the *Russian* nation was the Kievan Rus, a state based on the *Ukrainian* city of Kiev. From the ninth to the twelfth centuries, the Kievan Rus spearheaded the various nations of Eastern Slavs. To most foreigners, the Ukrainians appeared then – and later – as just a Russian tribe speaking a peculiar dialect, despite many failed attempts at reaching independence. During World War II, many nationalist Ukrainians joined the Nazi forces, preferring Germany to Russia, and after World War II the nationalist guerrilla never ceased. Just before the fall of the Soviet Union in 1991, the crowd shouted to visiting American President George Bush, Sr.: 'You don't know it, but we are no less a nation than France!'

World War I ushered the country into an eight-year period of official warfare and then civil warfare until the Ukrainian Socialist Republic declared itself a founding member of the Union of Soviet Socialist Republics on 30 December 1922. Until 1991, its history was a section of USSR history.

The founder of Ukrainian animation, Viacheslav Levandovsky, was born in Odessa on 24 February 1897 and died in Kiev on 18 April 1962.

A talented artist, he started his cartoon-making career in Odessa and continued after having moved to Kiev. In Odessa, Levandovsky made the first Ukrainian cut-out animation film *Skazka o solomennom bychke* (The Fairy Tale about the Straw Bull, 1927); in Kiev, he made *Skazka o belke khoziaushke I myshke zlodeike* (The Tale about the Squirrel Hostess and the Mouse Villain, 1928).

Like each and every animation pioneer, Levandovsky did everything by himself and continued working in his hometown Kiev until 1936. He enjoyed such estimation among colleagues that many years later (1980), Ivan Ivanov-Vano said that he could only be compared to Yuri Norstein.

---

[75] Founded by Tsar Peter the Great as Saint Petersburg in 1703, the city became the capital of Russia in 1712. In 1914, with the war against Germany, it was renamed Petrograd, more Russian sounding a word; it became Leningrad after the communist leader's death in 1924 and until 1991; today it is Saint Petersburg again.

7
SILENT ASIA

Japan[1]

As soon as the first cartoons by Émile Cohl and John Randolph Bray were shown in Tokyo around 1914, some of the local artists tried to imitate them as animators. The Japanese animated films (which in the beginning were called *senga eiga*, or 'films with designed lines') boast three pioneers: Shimokawa Hekoten, Kitayama Seitaro, and Kouchi Sumikazu. All three of these artists made their debut in 1917 within a few months of each other and were in close contact with film production companies from the very start.

The Tenkatsu Production Company contracted the popular cartoonist Shimokawa for *Imokawa Mukuzo genkanban no maki* (Imokawa Mukuzo the Concierge, taken from a character from his mangas), which entered history as the ancestor of Japan's animation cinema since it was the first to be shown to a public audience.

Shimokawa Hekoten (Miyakojima, prefecture of Okinawa, 2 May 1892–26 May 1973) was working as a caricature cartoonist for the satirical paper the *Tokyo Puck*; he did not know the production procedures of animation, which he attempted to learn by observing foreign products. In the beginning, he tried to introduce a design technique using chalk on a blackboard; he then proceeded to paper by preparing several copies of the backgrounds[2] on which he drew the characters and erased the superimposed parts thanks to a primitive light table of his own invention. In this fashion, he produced the aforementioned film, shown for the first time in January 1917. It seems that he was not happy with the quality of this work. Later, he produced other short films still centred on the same character – even though no fragment has remained of these efforts. At any rate, he was forced to retire from animation because of problems with his eyes (perhaps due to the use of light tables) and returned to his original profession.

Kitayama Seitaro (3 March 1888–13 February 1945), after studying Western painting and working for an art publishing company, began his career in cinema, writing subtitles for silent movies with the Nikkatsu Mukojima Studio. Unlike Shimokawa, he proposed producing an animated short to the film company. *Saru kani kassen* (The Crab Takes Revenge on the Monkey) was actually the first animated film to be produced in Japan. However, on account of several delays, it was shown to the public only on 20 May 1917, a few months after Shimokawa's work. His *Momotaro* (Momotaro, the Peach Boy) became the first Japanese animated cartoon to be shown abroad in France. Despite being a self-taught man, with a totally artisan style, he was a prolific artist – indeed, he produced ten films in 1917 alone – also thanks to the collaboration of the assistants he had as a painter. Among his pupils were Kanai Kiichiro and Yamamoto Sanae. In 1921, he quit Nikkatsu to open a studio of his own, the Kitayama

---

[1] By Lisa Maya Quaianni Manuzzato.

[2] Tsugata Noboyuki states: Shimokawa adopted printing backgrounds only four years after Bray's conception of the technique. From these, it would be hard to say that Japanese animation lagged behind that of other countries in the same period. Rather, it might be more apt to assert that there were signs of independent development in later times (Research on the achievements of Japan's first three animators, 'Asian Cinema', Spring/Summer 2003, p. 24).

Surnames first, given names second, according to Japanese customary use.

Eiga Seisakusho, an independent animation company with which he was able to organize the production work in a more industrial manner. Moreover, he discovered several promising talents. The subjects of his films are often traditional fables, even if we find commercials, animated sequences for reality films, and films of propaganda and education in his filmography. Kitayama initially used drawings on paper; later, he forayed into cut-out animation. In the article *Seneiga no tsukurikata* ('How to Make Animated Films'[3]), he openly revealed that he had been influenced by foreign animation, even though he did not give any further details.[4] His work was undermined by the devastating Kanto Earthquake in 1923.

The third pioneer was Kouchi Sumikazu[5] (prefecture of Okayama, 15 September 1886–6 October 1970). He studied painting first and then worked as a satirical cartoonist at the *Tokyo Puck*. On commission from the production house Kobayashi Shokai, he produced *Hanawa Hekonai Meito 'shinto' no maki* (Hanawa Hekonai, the New Sword), which was first shown on 30 June 1917.[6] The film shows a samurai – the protagonist – being swindled into buying a blunted sword. It was the first national animated film to be reviewed in Japan: In September, the film magazine *Katsudo no sekai* pointed out the superior quality vis-à-vis the contemporary works by Shimokawa and Kitayama. Kouchi used the cut-out technique, frequently utilized in Japanese animation until the mid-1930s (because of its simplicity and reliability). Following a series of works taken from popular tales, he went on hiatus for a few years. In 1923, he ventured into political advertising by founding Sumikazu Eiga Sosakusha. In the early 1920s – together with his colleagues Kanai Kiichiro and Yamamoto Sanae – he introduced some grey shading in the animated designs, which until then had been drafted with china ink. He ended his career with the film *Chongire hebi* (The Cut-Up Serpent, 1930) to return to manga permanently.

Another important figure is the already-mentioned Yamamoto 'Sanae' Zenjiro (6 February 1898–8 February 1981) who, having been deeply impressed by the viewing of an animation film, became an apprentice with Kitayama before directing the worthwhile *Usagi to kame* (The Rabbit and the Tortoise) in 1924, taken from one of Aesop's fables and characterized by a rather realistic design. In 1925, he founded the Yamamoto Manga Seisakujo; in the same year, he produced *Obasute yama* (The Mountain Where Old Women Are Abandoned) and *Tsubo*, which was commissioned – as were many of his films – by the Education Ministry. In 1927, he produced *Ushiwakamaru* (Ushiwakamuru, the Little Samurai). In 1928, in collaboration with Kanai Kiichiro, he directed *Shitakiri susume* (The Sparrows with the Forked Tongue) and *Issunboshi* (The Tiny One Makes It Big,[7] 1929). He continued to direct films until the mid-1940s; in the years after the war, he dedicated himself to production.

Murata Yasuji (Yokohama, 24 January 1896–22 November 1966) worked with the Yokohama Cinema Shokai – a company producing educational films – where he worked with subtitles for American animated films, which he was able to study; in the meantime, he learned animation techniques from his boyhood friend Yamamoto and debuted as a director in 1927. He was the first Japanese director to use the technique of total animation; he contributed to the development of this art by installing an engine, thanks to collaboration with the projector producer Takamitsu Kogyo, on a three-foot camera. Thus, it was possible (beginning with *Kaeru wa kaeru* [A Frog Is a Frog] in 1928) to perform all the shooting in one sitting, resolving problems with inefficiency and the exposure of the film. Murata was a master of cut-out animation, thus equalling, from a technical point of view, animation with celluloid. A prolific director (between 1927 and 1935, he directed no less than thirty films), he used a caricature style and many zoomorphic characters such as ducks, monkeys, and pigs, often with characters taken from cartoons, illustrated books, and tales. His best films include *Tako no hone* (The Octopus Bone, 1927) and *Tsukinomiya no ojosama* (Princess of the Moon Palace, 1934). He also dealt with sports themes in very popular films, such as *Oira no yakyu* (Our Baseball Match, 1930).

---

[3] Published in '*Zen Nihon katsuei kyoiku kenkyukai*' ('Basic Facts for Film Education'), 1930.

[4] Still, in this context, he dwelt on the mission of animation:

> With animation, we should do things that can't be expressed with live-action film, or which require a considerable amount of money to express, and even then, aren't very effective. When expressing complex content, in a very simple manner, I want to use animation. The mission of animation is to express things impressively, strongly, deeply, and extremely simply.

[5] This animator's name is often transliterated as Kouchi Jun'ichi.

[6] A copy of this film (at times called *Namakura-to*), together with a copy of *Urashima Taro* (1918) by Kitayama Seitaro, was found in 2009 by Matsumoto Natsuki; these constitute the most ancient findings of Japanese production.

[7] Another possible title may be *Issunboshi no shusse*.

Generally speaking, the amount of films made during these years is considerable, particularly in comparison with other countries. The best films produced in the world (including animated films) were shown in Japan. This appealed to both would-be animators and the public at large. The recurring subjects of animation at the time were traditional tales and the mangas that appeared in the dailies. Therefore, for present-day viewers, especially foreign ones, it can be difficult to understand the works of that time.

Japanese animation suffered from foreign competition. Distributors did not want to risk too much in small local productions, giving preference to foreign products, which were more economical and sophisticated and better appreciated by the public.

Therefore, well into the end of the 1930s, the only important sponsor was the Ministry of Education, which was interested in producing educational animations.

It is not surprising, therefore, that the style, the technique, the narration, and the rhythm of most of the films of the time appear to be weak. After all, most of the animators were unsophisticated professionals who worked from home and were paid by cinematographic production companies.

The Narrator

An integral part of the experience of a silent film, the *benshi* embodied the role of the narrator by supplying the 'verbal component' to cinematic entertainment until the final victory of the sound film (around 1939). The figure of the *benshi* was an essential part of cinematic viewing, and it is considered one of the reasons why sound took so long to be developed in Japan compared to other parts of the world.

The *benshi* was able to play his role before, during, or even after the cinematic showing. In the beginning, he appeared before the film to summarize the film for the audience. In Western productions, the *benshi* explained the 'exotic' cultural content.

His role evolved further when, in addition to providing an introduction to the film, the narrator began to perfect his voice in order to accompany the film images. For foreign productions, a single *benshi* explained what was taking place on the screen; for Japanese films, a veritable performance role called *kowairo setsumei* (voice colouring) came into being: A group of artists – from four to six – carried on a kind of direct voiceover for the figures on the screen outside the spectators' view. Little by little, for Japanese films as well as foreign films, these artists began to utilize an imitative voice.

Attempts on the part of the avant-garde of the cinema of the Pure Film Movement to attack the *benshi* institution proved ineffectual, even though the Japanese cinema had not as yet adopted narrative techniques that were already being used by Western directors. However, on account of these criticisms, the occupation of the *benshi* underwent further changes: The introduction before the film disappeared, as well as the groups of *kowairo setsumei*, leaving only a single narrator who commented on and carried out the dialogue during the presentation. This period, which was called the Golden Age of the *Benshi* (1925–1932), transformed these voice artists into veritable stars to become the presentation's centre of attention. It should also be noted that in Japan the projections were also accompanied by music, which had a symbiotic nature with the *benshi*.

8
SILENT LATIN AMERICA

Mexico

According to the *Índice cronológico del cine mexicano*,[1] the first animated film of the country is *Mi sueño*, made in 1915 by an unknown author. The first animator whose name we know is Miguel Angel Acosta[2] (or Alcorta), who animated some cut-outs in 1929 (Luis Strempler mentions 'more than two hundred productions of animated films of about thirty seconds each').[3]

According to Manuel Rodríguez Bermúdez,[4] we must also mention painter and poster artist Juan Arthenack (1891–1940) among the pioneers. Arthenack collaborated with various magazines and developed some successful comic strips, such as *Don Prudencio y su familia* and *Adelaido el conquistador*. In 1919, he directed (and starred in) the live-action film *El rompecabezas de Juanillo*, which contained a frame-by-frame sequence in which letters combined until they created the word *excélsior*.

In addition to these nearly legendary artists, the true pioneers of Mexican animation were Salvador Pruneda, Bismarck Mier, Salvador Patiño, Alfredo Ximénez, and Carlos Manriquez.[5] They learned their trade in the United States during the 1920s at the studios run by the Fleischers, MGM, and Disney and in the 1930s tried to create animation studios in their home country.

Salvador Pruneda (1895–1986) had a complicated political life and quite often had to find shelter across the border. There he met Bismarck Mier, a young Mexican of German descent (1906–1962), and Salvador Patiño. In the 1930s, back from the umpteenth exile, he founded a studio in Mexico City, producing newsreels, titles, and trailers. In this studio, Salvador Pruneda adapted for the screen the comic strip *Don Catarino y su apreciable familia* that he and Mier had drawn ten years before. According to Moisés Viñas, *Don Catarino* was screened in 1934, but more likely it remained unfinished. Carlos Sandoval, who in those times frequented Pruneda and his collaborators, maintained that no more than ten seconds were actually made, although the magazines published photographs of at least four scenes.[6] Another Pruneda project was an animated sequence for the live-action film *Revista Musical*, but this one sank, too, due to financial problems.

Colombia[7]

In this country, animation started at the beginning of the twentieth century, with small incursions in contexts like newsreels and the use of very simple techniques such as frame-by-frame object movement. An example of this type of animation is *Garras de Oro* (The Dawn of Justice), a movie produced in 1926. This silent black-and-white film features the separation of Panama and Colombia, ratified in November 1903, and shows, in a quick scene of a few seconds, a hand-coloured national Colombian flag.

---

[1] Moisés Viñas, *Índice cronológico del cine mexicano (1896–1992)*, Unam, Mexico, 1992.
[2] See, for example, Juan Manuel Aurrecoechea, *El episodio perdido: Historia del cine mexicano de animación*, Cineteca Nacional, Mexico, 2004, p. 15, and Manuel Rodríguez Bermúdez, *Animación: Una perspectiva desde México*, Centro Universitario de Estudios Cinematográficos, Unam, Mexico, 2007, pp. 124–125.
[3] Manuel Rodríguez Bermúdez, *Animación: Una perspectiva desde México*, pp. 79, 124.
[4] Manuel Rodríguez Bermúdez, *Animación: Una perspectiva desde México*, p. 124.
[5] Juan Manuel Aurrecoechea, *El episodio perdido: Historia del cine mexicano de animación*, p. 15.
[6] Juan Manuel Aurrecoechea, *El episodio perdido: Historia del cine mexicano de animación*, p. 15.
[7] By Francesca Guatteri.

Brazil

O Kaiser, by caricaturist Seth (Álvaro Marins),[8] is considered the first Brazilian animated movie. First shown in January 1917, this very short satire against the war targets Kaiser Wilhelm II. The German leader first dreams of dominating the world but is later swallowed by the globe itself. It may be helpful to mention that Brazil sided with France, Great Britain, and the United States in World War I. A few months later, on 26 April 1917, Kirs Filme released the country's second animated film, *Traquinices de Chiquinho e seu inseparável amigo Jagûnço* (The Escapades of Chiquinho and His Inseparable Friend Jagûnço). The filmmakers were not acknowledged in the film credits. *Avênturas de Bille e Bolle* (The Adventures of Bille and Bolle) by Gilberto Rossi and *Fono* (Eugênio Fonsêca Filho) followed one year later in 1918. The film features two characters, Bille and Bolle, who were modelled after Bud Fisher's Mutt and Jeff, arriving in São Paulo by plane and having adventures there.

For about ten years thereafter, animation was produced only in advertising, mainly by Seth, who had switched to this field.

Chile

Chilean animation was related to Chilean political satire, similar to the animation in Argentina. The first attempt to make a film with illustrations came in 1921. *La Transmisión del Mando Presidencial* (The Transfer of the President's Power) was made by Alfredo Serey, an illustrator for the daily *Las Últimas Noticias*. The silent film was nothing more than a series of still frames featuring the new president Arturo Alessandri, who is shown watching a safe with cobwebs that illustrate the fiscal deficit. This short lasted about ten minutes.

Three years later, *Vida y Milagros de Don Fausto* (Life and Miracles of Don Fausto), a film 'with a million cartoons' based on *Amenidades del diario vivir*,[9] was published in the magazine *Topaze*. During a time when copyright fees could hardly be applied for, especially in a distant country like Chile, the director Carlos Borcosque simply took the character of Don Fausto, martyred by his wife Crisanta, and adapted his adventures to local realities.

The film *15.000 Dibujos* (15,000 Drawings) premiered in 1937 and was more akin to the Disney style. The short was directed by Jaime Escudero and Carlos Trupp and starred an anthropomorphic condor whose name was Copuchita and approached the prototype of the Chilean *roto*.[10]

Argentina: The World's First Animated Feature Film

During the first three decades of the twentieth century, Argentina's economy was one of the most successful and promising in the world, and its society one of the most advanced and cultivated. However, it was certainly marked by limits and inequalities, especially between elegant Buenos Aires and the rest of the country. The Argentinean cinema industry, on the contrary, reached its most significant stage primarily in the 1930s.

It is a surprising and rare phenomenon that a still little-developed film industry, affected by technological limitations and import and export troubles, could achieve the prolific rate of inspiration that the Argentines did in the difficult field of animated feature films.

Quirino Cristiani

On the fringes of the main cultural industries and currents of the time, Argentina owed its production of animated films mainly to the Italian-born Quirino Cristiani (Santa Giuletta, Italy, 2 July 1896–Bernal, 2 August 1984), who moved to Argentina at the age of four. At a very young age, Cristiani attracted attention with his caricatures, which were published in the daily papers of the capital. When producer Federico Valle (Asti, Italy, 1880–Buenos Aires, 1960) wanted an experimental political vignette 'in action' for his newsreel *Actualidades Valle*, he hired the then–twenty-year-old Cristiani. After having learned the basics of animation from a film by Émile Cohl from Valle's collection,[11] Cristiani filmed *La intervención a la provincia de Buenos Aires* (Intervention in the Province of Buenos Aires), an approximately one-minute sketch that made fun of the provincial governor Marcelino Ugarte.

---

[8] We know Seth's real name from a short autobiography published on Rio de Janeiro's *Gazeta de Notícias* on 27 July 1947.
[9] *Amenidades del diario vivir* is nothing else than George McManus' *Bringing Up Father*; Don Fausto is Jiggs, and Crisanta is Mary.
[10] *Roto* means ragamuffin.
[11] The film was probably Cohl's *Les allumettes animées* (Animated Matches) of 1908, since in his old age Cristiani remembered that the film he saw featured 'moving matches'.

Following the success of the film, Valle decided to produce a full-length animated political satire. Alfonso de Laferrère wrote the text, while Quirino Cristiani took care of the animation and what today would be called the direction; Andrés Ducaud built the models for the impressive sequence of the Buenos Aires fire. In order to attract more publicity to the venture, Valle hired Diógenes 'El Mono' Taborda, one of the most famous caricaturists of the time, for the creation of the characters.[12] (In fact, Taborda worked only partially on the film, bored by the meticulous, slow workmanship needed in the frame-by-frame process.)

El Apóstol (The Apostle) was first projected at the Select Suipacha Theatre on 9 November 1917. Lasting a little more than an hour, *El Apóstol* was the first animated feature film ever made. (No copy of this film exists today, and we must rely on a few written sources and Cristiani's memory. Whether or not *El Apóstol* was actually a feature film is still uncertain[13].) The plot was quite linear, albeit complicated by several digressions: Angered by the Argentines' moral decay, elected president Hipólito Yrigoyen[14] dreams of rising to Olympus, dressed as the apostle of national redemption. After several political discussions with the gods, the president obtains Jupiter's lightning and burns Buenos Aires in a purifying fire. He is about to build his perfect city on the ashes of the corrupt one when he awakes and returns to reality. Although poorly distributed, the film enjoyed great success with the public, and the newspapers of Buenos Aires pointed to it as an example of the progress of the national cinema.

Cristiani took advantage of his success to leave Valle and work on another feature film based on an episode of the then-raging World War I.[15] Entitled *Sin dejar rastros* (Without Leaving a Trace, 1918) the film was shown for only one day; confiscated for political reasons, it disappeared in the basement of some government office. In the following years, Cristiani became involved with a variety of projects, from advertising to educational-scientific shorts, such as *Rinoplastía* (Surgery of the Nose) and *Gastrotomía* (Surgery of the Stomach) of 1925, to institutional and comic shorts. These last were, as usual, linked to current events: boxing matches with heavyweight Angel Luis Firpo (*Fir-pobre-nan* and *Firpo-Dempsey*, 1923) or the visit to Argentina by the handsome young Italian prince Umberto di Savoia (*Humbertito de garufa*, 1924).

Along with Cristiani, Andrés Ducaud deserves our attention, although there is only scarce and uncertain information on him. After having worked as a scene designer for Cristiani's *El Apóstol*, Ducaud continued his collaboration with the producer Federico Valle. In 1918, he directed *Abajo la careta* or *La república de Jauja* (Down with the Mask or The Republic of Plenty), a satiric feature film on the old conservative oligarchy. The tepid reaction of the press was justified by the slow action and overall ennui that characterized the film. Shortly afterward (the precise date is unknown), Ducaud filmed another feature-length satire on the high society of Buenos Aires. Entitled *Carmen criolla* (Creole Carmen) or *Una noche de gala en el Colón* (Gala Night at the Colón Theatre), it was a combination of drawings and puppets, with characters by Diógenes Taborda. The film failed because of its dull, drawn-out pacing and technical imperfections.

---

[12] Diógenes Taborda (1890–1926) was a real pillar of Argentine modern humorous drawing and comics. He was nicknamed 'El Mono' (the monkey) because of his ugliness.

[13] Printed documents state that the film was screened for seven months, seven times a day, but we can't deduce the running time from that, as we don't know the opening/closing time of the theatre.
On the other hand, one who wants to get free from the concept of running time could take into consideration that *El Apóstol* was the sole subject of the daily projections and that the definition of a feature film is 'the main film on a cinema programme' (*Longman Webster English College Dictionary*, Longman House, Essex, UK, 1984).

[14] Hipólito Yrigoyen (1852–1933) was elected in 1916 as the first radical (populist) president after decades of conservative leadership. His election was received with hope but also scepticism.

[15] The German secret service had tried to provoke Argentina's entry into the war as a German ally by torpedoing a merchant ship from Rio de la Plata and accusing the English and the French of the act. Although the mission was supposed to 'leave no trace' (in Castilian, *sin dejar rastros*), it was discovered and became a major issue in Buenos Aires. Yrigoyen expelled the German ambassador but avoided any other action that could have undermined the country's neutrality.

9

SILENT AFRICA

Union of South Africa[1,2]

The Artist's Dream/The Artist's Inspiration (1915) is considered the first animated film made in South Africa and was produced by African Film Productions. Directed by the American Harold Shaw,[3] it tells the story of an artist's animated drawings and includes cartoons and live action. The protagonist was Dennis Sentry (a cartoonist for the *Rand Daily Mail* and the *Sunday Times*), along with star actress Mabel May. Sarienne Kersh describes it as 'a sophisticated drawtoon about an artist who draws a beautiful woman in a park. He then dreams a subsequent series of events in which his drawings come to life'.[4] It is a self-reflexive work that challenges viewers' perceptions of reality and illusion and invites them to question the notion of authorship. This sophisticated 'drawtoon' (or lightning sketch/chalk talk) strongly echoed the modes of production and style used by many of the early American animators, such as Winsor McCay and James Stuart Blackton. The film was produced by Isidore W. Schlesinger (1871–1949), Mabel May's husband and the father of the cinema production and industry in South Africa.[5] He is credited with the establishment of the earliest documented native film production house, which was founded in 1915, called African Film Productions, and was created from the fusion of the African Theatres Trust (theatre management and administration) and the African Film Trust (import and distribution).

In 1917, African Film Productions released four more animated shorts directed by cartoonist and scriptwriter Norman H. Lee, entitled *The Adventures of Ranger Focus*, *Don't You Believe*, *Crooks and Christmas*, and *The Adventures of Ben Cockles*. Regrettably, no remnants of these films exist, and only a few still photographs survive.

---

[1] By Shanaz Shapurjee Hampson and Giannalberto Bendazzi.

[2] On 13 May 1902, the treaty that ended the Anglo-Boer War was signed at Vereeniging; it signified a new era of cooperation between English and Afrikaner living in Southern Africa. By 1910, the two Afrikaner states of the Orange River Colony (*Oranje Vrij Staat*) and Transvaal (*Zuid Afrikaansche Republiek*) were joined with Cape Colony and Natal as the Union of South Africa. The repression of black Africans became entrenched in the constitution of the new union (although perhaps not intentionally), and the foundations of grand apartheid were laid.

[3] Harold Shaw (1876–1926) began his career in film as an actor with Edison in 1908, quickly graduating to a live-action film director and then moving to the IMP Company. His best known work from this first period is the haunting fantasy film *The Land Beyond the Sunset* (1912). Shaw moved to Britain in 1913 to work for London Film Productions and made a name for himself with (for instance) *The House of Tempered* (1913) and *Trilby* (1914). In 1916, he ventured out with his actress wife Edna Flugrath to South Africa, where he had been hired by African Film Productions. His first film there, *Die Voortrekkers* (1916), which starred Flugrath, was sensationally successful locally and gained some screenings overseas (in the United States, this was known as 'Winning a Continent'). The scenario was written by historian Gustav Preller, and its version of the Great Trek emphasized the common destiny of Britons and Afrikaners (the Anglo-Boer War was long past and the political stress was now on the Union) and the 'savagery' of the native people (who, the film argues, were led to rise against the Boers by Portuguese traders). Newspaper reports of the time stressed the authenticity of the props and costumes and the huge numbers of extras, black and white, many of them mine employees. The completed film ran for some two hours. Shaw and Flugrath then made a melodrama about stolen diamonds, *The Rose of Rhodesia* (1917), and a horse-racing drama entitled *Thoroughbreds All* (1919). After having returned to Britain, Shaw went to the Soviet Union to film *Land of Mystery* (1920), a melodrama loosely based on the life of Lenin. Shaw made more films in Britain before returning to America to direct for Metro. He died in a car accident in 1926.

[4] Sarienne Kersh, 'History of South African Animation', *Screen Africa*, 20 November 1996, p. 36.
[5] Schlesinger was an American, too; he was born in New York and never gave up his original citizenship. Originally a developer, he embraced the film business in 1913. In the Johannesburg suburb of Killarney, he founded Killarney Film Studios. Killarney was one of Schlesinger's real estate properties as a developer. The housing that made Killarney a full-fledged Johannesburg suburb started only in the early 1930s.

10
SILENT OCEANIA

Australia

Australian cinema dates back to 1896 with the production of documentaries. The very first feature film in living memory is Charles Tait's *The Story of the Kelly Gang* (1906). That florid age ended with the arrival of the sound track, and except for one or two unusual films, the Australian filmmaking industry did not regain prominence until the 1970s and 1980s when government agencies offered opportunities to talented actors and directors.

During World War I, Harry Julius animated political vignettes with cut-outs for the newsreel the *Australian Gazette*. These one- or two-minute films exhibited better-than-average drawing and technique and, presumably, Julius incorporated such skills into the lightning sketches he created for his later films. Other animators worked during the 1920s and 1930s, leaving no record except for some advertising spots and a few vignettes on daily events, such as cricket matches.

More About It

This is the appreciation Pierre Jouvanceau gives in his *The Silhouette Film* (Le Mani, Genoa, 2004, pp. 150–153):

> Exhausted by his journey, Prince Achmed walks along the water's edge under the great palms which encircle a lake. We feel the calm of the place. There is a flapping of wings and three magnificent birds land on the bank. Achmed hides in the foliage. The winged silhouettes strip off their bird costumes, revealing lithe, young, female bodies. The tallest of them, and the most beautiful, is Peri Banu, Queen [of the country]. Thinking they are alone, the naked girls step into the water, watched by a Prince already madly in love. Is the following scene shown through the eyes of Achmed, in a 'point-of-view' shot? The framing closes in, the set fades and the image shows the condensing that is characteristic of telephoto lenses, those instruments so loved by voyeurs. While the set had been complex a moment before, imitating the natural beauty of the environment in which the protagonists found themselves, suddenly there is no longer any background. There is no separation of water and sky and everything seems to have dissolved into pure light. Nothing is left of the luxuriant foliage except a few leaves in the foreground – the ones that are supposedly hiding Achmed. It is as if the scene were concentrated on the bewitching nudity of the bathers. Nothing matters any more except the spectacle of the naked bodies. Even the water, in which they are partly immersed, is invisible. A surprising image, all bathed in light, for a scene which is supposed to be happening at night. Some other shots in *Prince Achmed*, a feature whose sets are among the most complex in the history of silhouette cinema, are similarly stripped of detail. But none demonstrates as forcefully as this one the potential of a temporary rejection of décor. Peri Banu bathing in 'non-water': this is the dissolution of all representation, the reduction of the film's world to a few indications, the subjugation of the set to the animated silhouettes. It is also the suggestive power – here at its strongest – of the light, the great return of the silhouettes to bathe in the purifying power of immaculate white. It is no mere chance that this scene coincides with a pause in the unbridled rhythm of the events that are pushing Achmed towards an ever-receding goal. This special moment when the hero's heart opens up to love is also, quite naturally, complemented by a visual halt. Forgotten is the luxuriance of the extraordinary landscapes where black magic is constantly brewing, forgotten the extreme rapidity of the action. The set has disintegrated, the rhythm has slowed, all peripheral vision – which could have distracted attention from the bathers who are so bewitching Achmed – is eliminated. Thanks to this focusing on the void, the Prince's dazzlement has also become palpable to the viewer. Apart from the physical details of the scene, this pause is reminiscent of the sexual act (of the phallocentric variety). Moreover, does not Achmed, having hidden Peri Banu's feathered finery and thus prevented her from escaping, indulge in something that looks like a kidnapping? The erotic charge generated by the scene is undeniable, and it features several of the genre's

conventions. There is the bathing, which justifies the state of undress – and thus dispels its morally obnoxious aspect – and at the same time legitimises the insistent framing on the naked bodies; the carefree behaviour of the girls, who do not know they are being spied on; the voyeurism of the hero, which doubles of course for the viewer's; and the theft of the clothes which signifies, for the girls, both the sudden awareness of a hitherto unsuspected presence and also the impossibility of recovering their previous state, their lost innocence. The eroticisation of the bodies, in this precise scene, happens via a mutilation of the silhouettes. It is a mutilation in the literal sense, an amputation done with scissors to the cardboard figures. The water, the element of décor whose representation is, paradoxically, refused us in the very shot where it becomes narratively indispensable, is actually suggested in a manner which seems very strange – but is in fact the only one possible. We must remember that because of the back-lighting and the effect of translucency no silhouette element can be masked by a décor element that is lighter in tone than itself. This is why, as they wade deeper into the invisible waves, the feet, then the legs of the naiads are cut off at the supposed point of their contact with the water, and little moving pieces of black card, suggesting the reflection of the body, complete the illusion. This progressive amputation continues until the wading comes to a stop, indicating the presumed depth of the lake. Even if invisible in form, the lake is there. The silhouettes alone, though at the cost of their physical integrity, have rendered it perceptible. The pure light has transmuted into water.

THE THIRD PERIOD

The Third Period includes the years when Walt Disney dominated the industry and the development of film animation as a primary form of entertainment, acclaimed by critics and beloved by audiences throughout the world. An appropriate denomination of this period is 'The Golden Age (1928–1951)'.

11
THE GOLDEN AGE (1928–1951)

What for animation was the Golden Age covers one of the worst ages in modern history. In October 1929, the Wall Street stock market crashed. The Great Depression followed, hit the whole planet, and lasted a long time. In Russia, Spain, and Germany, countless people were murdered out of political dogmatism. China was involved in a civil war, which didn't stop even during the bloody Japanese invasion of 1937. World War II led to more than 50 million casualties. After its end, the Cold War started.

To nobody's surprise, in such a situation the Dream Factory bloomed. A spectator could buy a cheap ticket and then watch a feature film, one or two short comedies (often cartoons), and a newsreel: a luxury.

In 1939, World War II started, and Hollywood turned out *Gone with the Wind*, *The Wizard of Oz*, *Stagecoach*, *Mr. Smith Goes to Washington*, and *Ninotchka*. In December 1941, Pearl Harbor was bombed, and Preston Sturges' *Sullivan's Travels* hit movie theatres.

The message of this latest *conte philosophique* disguised as a light film comedy has seldom been emphasized. A Hollywood director of 'escapist' comedies (Joel McCrea) wants to become a serious intellectual and depict 'a true canvas of the sufferings of humanity'. In order to learn how to do so, he mingles with the poor, the tramps, and even (unwillingly) the jailed. One night, among his fellow citizens condemned to hard labour, he attends a screening. Watching a funny film,[1] these desperate people at long last have a laugh.

This description is an idealized depiction of the situation; the actual reactions of the audience and the style and content of the films being made during those times did not always live up to this ideal.

French cinema was ruled by master directors Jean Renoir, Jean Vigo, René Clair, and Marcel Carné; in 1934, Robert Flaherty made *Man of Aran*; Ozu Yasujiro was active in Japan; and after World War II, Roberto Rossellini, Vittorio De Sica, and Luchino Visconti produced the best works of Italian neorealism.

The 1930s and 1940s were, in a way, the last hurrah of the Western modernity fighting with itself. The original ideal of civilizing and expanding had become the obsession of taming and subjugating. The oligopoly of nations didn't result in a mutually advantageous agreement: politics is not economics. By 1945, only the United States and the USSR would be standing up, and modernity would slowly die, making room for the ideological clash between liberalism and communism.

For animation, these were the years of wine and roses. The Golden Age affected society as well. For the first time in history, animation was influencing feelings, tastes, and common language. The shapes of Mickey Mouse, Donald Duck, Bugs Bunny, Tom & Jerry, Sylvester the Cat, and Woody Woodpecker became the common iconic heritage of various peoples of the world and would continue to do so for decades. This also turned them into very effective ambassadors of their home country way of life abroad.

Steamboat Willie
Sync or Sink

On Sunday, 18 November 1928, filmgoers were slowly filling the New York Colony Theatre. A broke Walt Disney was among them. He had been in town for almost three months, trying and trying, and had eventually found an ally in Harry Reichenbach, the Colony manager, who had acceded to bet on – by then – the long-withering genre

---

[1] Just to stay in tune with the subject of this book, this was Walt Disney's *Playful Pluto* (1934).

that was animation. The feature film was *Gang War*, starring Jack Pickford and Olive Borden. People remember it because people forgot it. The audience only watched the cartoon.

The cartoon was *Steamboat Willie*.[2] On a riverboat, a mouse dressed in short trousers works as the factotum of the captain, a large cat. His female counterpart is a girl mouse who comes aboard carrying some sheet music and a guitar. A goat devours both of these, but the couple is still able to have fun and play the popular song *Turkey in the Straw*; eventually the captain punishes the timewaster and sends him to peel potatoes. The little film had a perfectly synchronized score (the latest fashion – sound – plus the novelty of synchronization) and was centred on Mickey Mouse (an unpretentious and fresh protagonist).

Maybe not overnight, but in a few months, a global star was born, and animation rose again from the dead.

Walt Disney's extraordinary success completely changed the rules of the game. The older animators found themselves confronted with the choice of either learning up-to-date techniques or retiring. The market expanded, and sales revenues and employment increased. In the gloomy years of the Depression, young artists found opportunities in animation, which in turn was enriched by their leading-edge talent.

Overall, it was a giant step ahead for an industry that, according to a 1931 issue of *Popular Mechanics*, could have been bought for US$250,000 just a few years before.[3]

The Non-Concurrence Factor

It is inaccurate to say that the novelty of sound was the cause, or at least the only cause, of such a sensation. In fact, the Fleischers had already released sound cartoons; a couple of months before *Steamboat Willie*, Paul Terry distributed his *Dinner Time*.

The film itself was far from perfect – perfunctory personality animation, no dramatic climax, a weak ending: In most aspects, it was a recipe for mediocrity. The one novelty it did have, however, was synchronized sound.

Although we will never be able to verify *Steamboat Willie*'s sound design as the element that triggered the public's subsequent enchantment with the character, we must

Figure 11.1 Walt Disney, *Steamboat Willie*, 1928. © Disney

pause to consider its stylistic value to animation history and especially focus on the way its synchronized sound was used.

In the very first frame, we see the steamboat moving along – but the sound we hear is that of a steam locomotive pulling along its heavy load. Later in the film, Mickey beats on the teeth of a cow and we hear the notes of a xylophone.

As he pulls a tail or strangles a whole menagerie of characters, we hear the various instruments of a band, and a little concert results. There is a non-concurrence between what we see and what we hear. Although hardly surprising today, this was an astonishing acceleration of filmic language in 1928.

One of the best-known theoretic essays in all of cinema history is *Statement on Sound* by Sergei M. Eisenstein, Vsevolod Pudovkin, and Grigory Aleksandrov, which was published in August 1928.[4] Among other issues, it asserted that 'the first experiments in sound must aim at a sharp discord with the visual images' and that

> Sound, treated as a new element of montage (as an independent variable combined with the visual image), cannot fail to provide new and enormously powerful means of expressing and resolving the most complex problems, which have been depressing us with their insurmountability through the imperfect methods of a cinema operating only in visual images. The contrapuntal method of structuring a sound film not only does not weaken the international nature of cinema, but gives to its meaning unparalleled strength and cultural heights.

---

[2] Curiously, *Steamboat Willie* was released at the same time another musical show set on a river triumphed on Broadway: Jerome Kern and Oscar Hammerstein's *Show Boat*.
[3] Leslie Cabarga, *Fleischer Story*, Nostalgia Press, New York, 1976, p. 27.
[4] *Zayavka* (Statement), in 'Zhizn' iskusstva' (Living Art), Leningrad, 5 August 1928.

When the essay came out, Disney, who couldn't have read the Russian even if he were interested in theory, had already finished his film. Working without 'theory', what the three world-famous film directors and theorists[5] wished for as a hope for the distant future, the then-almost-unknown American animator had already achieved by himself. Did this make Walt Disney an avant-garde artist? Most people would have scoffed at the idea, as most certainly would have Walt himself. As so often happens, the point is terminological, just as in those other instances when we have to deal with such abused and hazy words as 'non-representational art', 'art of research', 'experimental art', 'non-objective art', and so on.

Steamboat Willie was decidedly groundbreaking in animation history. In the field of audiovisual language, Disney and his crew had achieved what only some Soviet dreamers had longed for and big-budget companies hadn't even yet imagined. At the same time, it was just entertainment, show business, after all: Walt was using the non-concurrence factor as a way to make better products that he could sell more easily. The idea of using film techniques to express inner emotions or offer up his view of the world would not even have occurred to him. 'Avant-garde' is actually a term that should apply to the audience, not to artists.

Sound

Until the late 1920s, films themselves, aside from a few earlier experiments, did not provide sound.[6] Typically, they were accompanied by live music performed by pianists, organists, or sometimes orchestras. In 1923, American inventor Lee de Forest (1873–1961) projected some shorts with his Phonofilm process in New York, a direct sound-on-film system that had only brief success because of its poor fidelity.[7]

Historians conventionally agree that the 'first' film with synchronized music and dialogue was Alan Crosland's Warner Bros. feature *The Jazz Singer*, starring Al Jolson (1927). Initially, the producers opted for the Vitaphone system based on one-sided phonograph disks: These were played on turntables mechanically connected to the projector so that the film and the disc were started together and played in sync. The system was, however, soon abandoned in favour of the competing optical sound-on-film method.

Optical sound is imprinted along one end of the film between the frame area and the sprocket perforations. Looking at a piece of film, we see a parallel stripe of fluctuations in light and dark patterns. This is the optical sound track, which is analogous to the sound wave of the original recorded sound and is reproduced by projecting light through the film from an exciter lamp and detecting the transmitted fluctuations in intensity with a solar cell, which electrically converts the changes of brightness to audible changes in volume and pitch.

Two optical sound track processes in common use were: 1) variable density, which was used in the de Forest and Fox Movietone systems, in which sound was represented by continuous gradations in light-to-dark tones (ultimately, this was not as successful: If a print of the film was not perfect, the variable-density sound track would be unable to be listened to); and 2) variable area, which is still used today; an example is the RCA Photophone.

---

[5] To be precise: a genius (Eisenstein), a brilliant mind (Pudovkin), and Aleksandrov.

[6] The idea that motion pictures could talk had occurred as early as Edison's development of his Kinetograph which, from the start, he had conceived as a visual accompaniment to his phonograph; with his employee W. K. L. Dickson, Edison created a rough working prototype of synchronized sound as early as 1889. Numerous other inventors and studios made their own attempts, including, notably, Georges Demeny, August Baron (in France), and William Friese-Greene (in England). Several other prototypes were exhibited at the Paris World Exposition of 1900, including Léon Gaumont's Chronophone system, which would subsequently also enjoy a limited run with exhibitors in England. Other early systems included Oskar Messter's Biophon (circa 1903 in Germany), Cecil Hepworth's Vivaphone (circa 1910, also in England), and (in the United States) Edison's Kinetophone and, later, Cinephonograph (circa 1911). Because these first systems attempted to synchronize with the film sound recorded on separate phonograph discs, they were awkward to use and invited synchronization problems.

[7] Inventors before de Forest had experimented with various sound-on-film processes, including Eugen Augustin Lauste (circa 1904–1907 in Britain); Katherina and Ferdinand von Madaler (circa 1916 in the United States); and Josef Engl, Joseph Massole, and Hans Vogt (1919 in Germany). However, de Forest's patent of the Audion three-electrode amplifier tube (in 1907), enabling sound amplification that could be heard in a theatre auditorium, likely ensured his system's early success.

12 AMERICA LAUGHS!

Walt Disney the Tycoon

Steamboat Willie was not the first film of the new Mickey Mouse series. The first one was *Plane Crazy*. Following Lindbergh's transatlantic flight, an enthusiastic Mickey decides to become a pilot; involves farm animals in the process; and even brings his fiancée, Minnie, with him into the sky; they crash but end up safe and sound. The film featured some impressive close-ups, although it did not surpass the quality level of the previous productions; in fact, it was based on the previous *The Ocean Hop* (1927) starring Oswald the Lucky Rabbit. Mickey was no more charismatic than Oswald; he looked and behaved very much like him and, from a purely graphic viewpoint, neither character amounted to much.[1] Disney trademarked Mickey Mouse's name and held on to it tightly.

When Al Jolson had begun to sing and talk in the screen production *The Jazz Singer* (1927), Disney had sensed that an industrial revolution, rather than a passing fad, was taking place: Cinema was to become irrevocably oriented towards sound. Assisted by Wilfred Jackson,[2] a just-hired young collaborator of his who had some knowledge of music, Disney set up a makeshift synchronization system.

Recording took place in New York. After several technical and logistical problems with the sound system and its provider, Pat Powers, whose rights to the process were reportedly dubious, and possibly even illegal,[3] success arrived. Disney had ensured himself the collaboration of a resident musician, Carl Stalling (also from Kansas City), who wrote the music of the first Mickey Mouse cartoons. The strong-minded musician argued immediately with Disney's imposition of rhythms, effects, and synchronization, which he felt conflicted with the methods of musical composition. The two reached a compromise: While music would remain in the background in Mickey's comic films, in the series entitled Silly Symphonies, it would dominate over the images, which would largely illustrate it. *The Skeleton Dance* (1929) was the first of the 'symphonies', a sort of *danse macabre*[4] created by Ub Iwerks[5] to Stalling's music.[6]

After Stalling's departure, the Symphonies used music just the way any other cartoon did until the series ended in 1938. The most famous of these extravaganzas, or sometimes short tales, was *Three Little Pigs*; the theme song, *Who's Afraid of the Big Bad Wolf?*, by Frank Churchill, became one of the most popular American tunes from

---

[1] The second film of the series was entitled *The Gallopin' Gaucho*. Originally made as silent films, these first two titles were released after *Steamboat Willie* in post-synchronized versions.

[2] Wilfred Jackson (Chicago, 24 January 1906–Balboa Island, California, 7 August 1988) would become a great Disney director, gaining three Academy Awards for *The Tortoise and the Hare* (1935), *The Country Cousin* (1936), and *The Old Mill* (1937) for Walt Disney.

[3] Powers's system was very similar to, if not an infringement of, Lee de Forest's Phonofilm process; de Forest likely lacked the wherewithal to sue him.

[4] The music for *The Skeleton Dance* has nothing to do with Camille Saint-Saëns's *Danse Macabre*, as some books report; it is a composition that used elements of Grieg's *March of the Dwarfs*.

[5] As for Iwerks's fate, see the paragraph concerning him.

[6] Carl Stalling (not to be confused with animator Vernon George Stallings) left Disney after only one year. He gave the best of himself at Warner's, where he composed more than 600 music scores for cartoons.

1933 on.[7] The film won an Oscar, the second for Disney after the award-winning *Flowers and Trees*, the first *Silly Symphony* in colour.[8] Disney won thirty Oscars overall by the end of his career in several categories.

In just a few years, Mickey Mouse became the object of an incredible phenomenon of collective love all over the world. In 1930, Mickey's comic strips, drawn by Floyd Gottfredson,[9] began publication, followed by the merchandising of handkerchiefs, T-shirts, combs, watches, and dolls, all bearing the mouse's image.

The Fixed Star

For such a successful animated character, however, Mickey had a surprisingly short life. Born in 1928, he in effect concluded his theatrical career in 1953, after 121 short movies (in his last regular appearance, *The Simple Things*, he went fishing with Pluto).[10] Most relevant, his lack of action as a protagonist began in the early 1930s. 'Mickey is not a clown', Ted Sears (1900–1958), director of the script department, remarked in a memo directed to his collaborators:

> He is neither silly nor dumb. His comedy depends entirely upon the situation he is placed in. Mickey is most amusing when in a serious predicament is trying to accomplish some purpose under difficulties or against time.

It was soon clear that such a well-behaved and groomed mouse could not include comicality among his qualities. It was necessary to surround him with less respectable co-stars who were capable of providing laughter. In the end, these same characters – the hot-tempered Donald Duck, the dull Goofy, and Pluto the clumsy dog – took on all the action for themselves, reaching a stardom of their own and achieving top billing in their own cartoons beginning in 1938.

Mickey and his mates entered the world of colour in 1935 with *The Band Concert*. It was a momentous film, not only because it was funny and imaginative – and certainly one of the best American animated cartoons ever – but also because, here, the flirtation between animation and synchronized music was at its apex. Indeed, in this case, the flirtation is a full-fledged marriage: Music is the hub of the action and even dictates the screenplay. First, Donald Duck misleads the band (which is meant to play the *William Tell* overture) into *Turkey in the Straw*; second, an actual tornado breaks out at the notes of *The Storm* (again from *William Tell*). Interestingly, Walt's beloved Mickey already enjoys a new finesse in character animation, thanks to the vital influence of studio art instructor Don Graham (see the discussion on Graham later in this section), while the band characters still depend on Ub Iwerks's 'rubber hose' approach, and the performance of the newcomer, Donald, is also rough.[11]

After a brilliant role in the *Fantasia* segment *The Sorcerer's Apprentice* (1940), Mickey made less and less frequent appearances. As director Frank Capra once remarked, if nobody has ever succeeded at building or imposing stars, it is because stars are born by themselves – Mickey Mouse was such a phenomenon.

According to supervising animator Fred Moore (1911–1953), Mickey was the typical good boy: clean, happy, polite, and as smart as necessary.

Mickey was still the best actor.[12] In addition to the aforementioned films, other works deserving mention include the precocious *Just Mickey* (1930, featuring the violinist

---

[7] According to several people, a Roosevelt-inspired optimism was present in both film and song. Disney's biographer Richard Schickel argues instead that they mirrored Herbert Hoover's beliefs: Disasters happen because of improvidence, while a solid, traditional house does not collapse when the wolf blows. Politically, Disney pronounced himself a Republican, at least from the 1940s on.

[8] In 1932, Disney signed a contract that gave him the exclusive animation rights, for three years, to the new trichromic Technicolor process.

[9] For a few months, Disney wrote the scripts, while Iwerks sketched in pencil. Floyd Gottfredson (1905–1986) drew Mickey's cartoons from 1930 to 1975; he stood out among the other comic strip artists who worked on Mickey for his imagination. Among the specialists working on Donald Duck comics, the best was Carl Barks (1901–2000), a Disney gagman and scriptwriter who became a comic strip artist in 1942.

[10] Mickey would make several later revival appearances, as in *Mickey's Christmas Carol* in 1983, *The Prince and the Pauper* in 1990, and *The Runaway Brain* in 1995; these, however, were exceptions: Mickey would not again return regularly to the screen.

[11] The duck in this film was animated by Dick Huemer (1898–1979), a New York veteran who had joined the studio in 1933. He was an excellent story man and director.

[12] Writer Giacomo Debenedetti, an Italian gentleman, was chatting once on a train with a French lady. 'The greatest film actor is Meek-aeh', she asserted. He couldn't figure out who that man was. 'Meek-aeh is not a man, *c'est une souris*, it's a mouse!' The negligible misunderstanding led him to realize that 'Mickey is even *the only* sound actor: the only one whose concreteness is both visual and acoustic' (lecture, Milan, 1931, in Giacomo Debenedetti, *Al cinema*, Marsilio, Venice, 1983).

mouse playing solo); *Brave Little Tailor* (1938, a clever tale); and *The Pointer* (1939). A handicap to his acting, in his early films, was the bond to sound: People wanted a musical Mickey, and he was forced by scriptwriters into dancing, singing, instrument-playing scenes. By the mid-1930s, however, he was a full-fledged comedian. The character's charm was also due to his voice, which, until the end of World War II, was given to him by Walt Disney himself.[13]

Human or Animal?

In fact, Mickey, born a mouse, became a person in his seventh or eighth short film, *The Plow Boy*, because 'the public was willing to accept Mickey, a pseudo-mouse, as a boy, and Goofy, a pseudo-dog, as a man'.[14] These fantastic creatures lived in an equally fantastic environment, a beyond-the-looking-glass[15] caricature world, interlaced with normalcy and magic. The mouse-boy, the dog-man, the duck-youngster became credible because of their acting, which largely followed the same principles as that of live actors. Disney focused on his 'drawn actors', which he carefully studied for their facial mimicry, gestures, and acting expedients. Each character needed his own personality; a way of gesturing consistent with his appearance and psychology; and a body with properly located bones, muscles, and joints. No longer pure graphics, animation had become a real world in caricature, which obeyed logical laws. In 1940, Don Graham wrote: 'A natural action must be caricatured to constitute acting. Action as a thing in itself has little sustaining interest for an audience. When action, portrayed graphically, is ordered – caricatured – it becomes a new form of acting.'[16]

In his excellent essay, *Disney Design: 1928–1979*, John Canemaker quotes a note written by Disney in 1935: 'The first duty of cartoons is not to picture or duplicate real action or things as they actually happen – but to give a caricature of both life and action . . . I definitely feel that we cannot do the fantastic things, based on the real, unless we first know the real.'[17] Disney distanced himself from defining animation as a 'copy of reality' or as exclusively graphic research, opting instead to call it 'plausible impossible'.[18] Such a concept marked the beginning of what was later defined as Disney's 'realism'. Given this, it is easy to see how the weak point of Disney's movies has always been said to be the more 'realistic' – i.e. least caricatured – human characters that tend to be underdeveloped, such as Snow White, Cinderella, and the Prince.

In later years, Disney's 'realism' became more and more dominant, particularly with the use of the multiplane camera and the narrative requirements of feature-length movies.[19] Many sequences became minute, decorative copies of reality, breaking the basic unwritten rule of animation: never to challenge live-action cinema in its own territory. Multiple examples can be cited in which the audience's attraction to the Disney character depends more on the classical dramatic patterns (suspense, choreography, 'romantic moments') than on the dreamlike, imaginative qualities created by the animated drawings. According to Disney's recipe, in front of a believable character, acting in a believable way and in a plausible environment, viewers

---

[13] Ollie Johnston, a veteran at Disney, wrote:

> In my opinion, Walt was synonymous with Mickey, and when he lost interest and stopped doing the voice things changed. No one else ever had the ability to project personality into that high falsetto voice that he did. One man [James MacDonald, 1906–1991] did it for many years after Walt stopped and did a great job, but how can you expect anyone to have the same feelings as the creator?
>
> (Ollie Johnston, letter to author, 8 November 1982)

[14] Don Graham, 'The Art of Animation' (unpublished manuscript, property of Walt Disney Productions, 20 July 1955, courtesy of John Canemaker).

[15] Perhaps not by chance, Disney often returned to the theme of the walk-through mirror and to Lewis Carroll's work.

[16] Don Graham, 'Animation: Art Acquires a New Dimension', *American Artist*, December 1940, p. 12.

[17] John Canemaker, 'Millimeter', *Disney Design 1928–1979: How the Disney Studio Changed the Look of the Animated Cartoon*, Vol. 7, No. 2, February 1979, p. 107.

[18] As for the aesthetic creed of Walt Disney, see the memo he dictated in 1935 for Don Graham, quoted in its entirety in Shamus Culhane's *Talking Animals and Other People* (St. Martin's Press, New York, 1986, pp. 117–127). It is one of the most remarkable documents in animation history.

[19] This massive device was used for the first time in the *Silly Symphony The Old Mill* (1937); it was also used partially in *Snow White* and extensively in later feature films. Characters and background scenery were placed on superimposed glass planes so that a three-dimensional composition appeared in front of the vertically positioned camera.

feel perfectly comfortable and accept even the most impossible dream as normal behaviour.

Years of Expansion

Following the success of Mickey, for the first time in his life, Disney had money and used it to expand his projects and his company. From the six people employed in 1928, the enterprise grew to include 187 employees in 1934 and more than 1,600 in 1940. The studio, which had been on Hyperion Avenue, Hollywood, since 1925, experienced enormous growth and, throughout the 1930s, it expanded to include new buildings and additions. As for his staff, initially Disney included the best animators available on the market, particularly those from New York. However, it soon became clear that these skilled collaborators had little inclination to adapt to Disney's philosophy of work and to his brand of innovations. As early as 1929, Walt made a deal with the Chouinard Art School for his people to take a night drawing class a week – but the old-timers failed to show up. Consequently, the company hired beginners and trained them in a new 'school' that first took shape under the spontaneous impulse of animator Art Babbitt, then officially, since November 1932, under Chouinard instructor Don Graham. In seven years, it screened 35,000 applicants.

The new methods of production (of which Walt was openly very proud) followed a Tayloristic rationalization of labour: Specialized teams worked on animation, scene design, special effects, layouts, or scripts; inking, colouring, and filming were also separated. The storyboard, a sort of drawn script, helped keep the theme of a film under control. In fact, the company's structure was like an extension of its founder's personality. Having hired animators who adopted his method but had better creative or technical skills than his own, he took upon himself the task of organizing and motivating them, often correcting and reproaching, occasionally giving praise. His employees agreed that he had a difficult, often tart character, but also a magnetic personality. He also must have had an extraordinary charm to manage so many remarkable personalities, some of them for over forty years.

Disney had the same impact on American animation that the discovery of sound had for the rise of the industry of cinema as a whole: All of a sudden, he made obsolete every production created in the old way and put it out of circulation. In fact, much of the praise he received from critics, especially in the early 1930s, was due to his visual inventiveness as well as to his ability to bring the 'image-sound' relationship into the grammar of cinema (at that time, a controversy surrounded sound, which was seen by many as the destroyer of the visual language of silent cinema).

The Ones Who Made the Magic

In addition to the artists cited throughout this chapter, the following deserve mention: Ben Sharpsteen (1895–1980, director of *Dumbo*); James Algar (1912–1998, director of *The Sorcerer's Apprentice* segment of *Fantasia* and creator of the True-Life Adventures documentaries series); Clyde 'Gerry' Geronimi (1901–1989, co-director of *Cinderella* and various other feature films; his original name was Clito, and he was born in Chiavenna, Italy); Hamilton Luske (1903–1968, co-director of *Pinocchio* and many more feature films); Earl Hurd (1880–1940, the inventor of the cel technique, who spent his last years at Disney as a storyboard man); Hugh Hennesy (1891–1954, layout artist of *The Band Concert*, art director of *Snow White and the Seven Dwarfs*); Albert Hurter (1883–1942, sketch artist highly influential in *Snow White* and *Pinocchio*; born in Zurich, Switzerland, he moved to the United States around 1912); Joe Grant (1908–2005, character designer and story artist who created the Queen in *Snow White*); Jules Engel (1909–2003, choreographer of the *Mushroom Dance* in *Fantasia*, destined to become an abstract animator); Les Clark (1907–1979, animation director of short and long feature films from 1935–1955); Don Da Gradi (1911–1991, a layout artist in the 1940s who became a scriptwriter for *Alice in Wonderland* and *Peter Pan*); Al Eugster (1909–1997, who brought to the studio the experience he had accumulated since his teens as an assistant to Otto Messmer for Felix the Cat); Grim Natwick (1890–1990, who gave the Snow White character a touch of true femininity); James 'Shamus' Culhane (1908–1996, cultivated and intellectually curious animator, then director, then producer); T. Hee (1911–1988, character designer, animator, and director of *The Dance of the Hours* segment of *Fantasia*); William Cottrell (1906–1995, possibly the ace of Disney's story artists; developer of the Disneyland park); Mary Robinson Blair (1911–1978, inspirational artist and designer in the 1940s to early 1950s; also wife of Preston Blair's brother, Lee); Perce Pearce (1899–1955, story man, director, and eventually producer of the first live-action films, commencing in 1950 with *Treasure Island*); Zack Schwartz (1913–2003, art director on *Fantasia* and *Bambi*); Bill Peet (1915–2002, high-quality, prolific story man); Ken Anderson (1909–1993, a versatile talent, the sole art director and production designer on *One Hundred and One Dalmatians*); Judge Whitaker (1908–1985, the man who made an actor out of Donald Duck); Dick Lundy (1907–1990, another Donald specialist); Charles A. Nichols (1910–1992, director of many episodes of the Pluto series and of the famous *Toot, Whistle, Plunk and Boom*); Bill Justice (1914–2011, a great animator during his long career, who then turned to imagineering for the Disney theme parks); Isidore Klein (1897–1973, sometimes known as 'Isadore' or 'Izzy'; in his short tenure at Disney in the 1930s, he contributed a special touch of Jewish humour); Cy Young (1900–1964) and Ugo d'Orsi (1897–1964; Young and d'Orsi together formed the Chinese-Italian team who developed the special effects for *Snow White*); and Charles Philippi (1898–1954, art director of *Pinocchio*). The voiceover artists include Clarence Nash (1904–1985: Donald Duck)[20] and Pinto Colvig (1892–1967: Goofy),[21] who also worked as a gagman. Among musicians, outstanding were the aforementioned Frank Churchill (who, in addition to *Who's Afraid of the Big Bad Wolf?*, also composed such songs as *Some Day My Prince Will Come* and *Whistle While You Work*); Leigh Harline (1907–1969: *When You Wish Upon a Star*); Paul Smith (1906–1985, Academy Award for best original score in 1940 for *Pinocchio*); and Oliver Wallace (1887–1963, Academy Award for best original song in 1942 for 1941's *Dumbo*). We ask for forgiveness from the many other distinguished artists we are omitting here.

Another Disney Folly

On 21 December 1937, during a gala, Disney showed his latest daring enterprise: an animated colour feature film entitled *Snow White and the Seven Dwarfs*. Despite some initial scepticism by the spectators who believed that animation had to be comical, the adventures of the princess, persecuted by her stepmother and protected by the dwarfs, poisoned by an apple and brought back to life by the Prince's kiss, conquered all audiences. Stories about the film premiere abound. John Barrymore was said to have tears in his eyes, while Disney, incapable of dealing with the emotion, waited outside wondering, at the first outbursts of laughter, whether the audience was laughing at him or with him. It is also said that, for once in his life, Roy Disney did not yield when, a few days before the release, his brother insisted on remaking a scene that had been spoiled by a small flicker. After a three-year-long search for perfection, *Snow White and the Seven Dwarfs* (begun in 1934 with a budget of US$250,000) ended up costing US$1,488,423. The young producer's creativity was clearly motivated by a strange mixture of perfectionism and risk taking. Disney came close to bankruptcy during the filming of *Snow White*, as he had with *Steamboat Willie* (after the war, he even borrowed against his life insurance policy in order to build his amusement park, Disneyland). In a very short time, however, *Snow White* grossed more than US$8,000,000. The critics were unanimously favourable, and Disney's love affair with his audiences reached its apex.

Snow White's solid narrative structure was dominated by the classical unities of time and action. To avoid the risk of boring the spectators with a one-and-a-half-hour-long feature of elementary drawings, Disney painstakingly connected the events of the story to its moods (from romantic to comic, to dark, to pathetic). Colours were distributed harmoniously throughout the movie.

The songs were given narrative or psychological functions. It was Disney the revolutionary at his best. In every musical, until then, songs and choreographies had frozen the action so that the story advanced by stops and starts. (According to theatre scholars, the 'first' Broadway musical to have songs and dances fully integrated into the plot was Rodgers and Hammerstein's *Oklahoma!* But that was March 1943: five-and-a-half years after *Snow White*).

As for characters, the dwarfs were the best: magnificently animated, each with his own name and personality (in contrast to Grimm's original text, where they were portrayed as an indistinct group).[22] Even years later, *Snow*

---

[20] Although fundamental in creating the character's charm, his quacky delivery was almost incomprehensible. This created problems of dialogue and action. 'It was the bane of my existence', director Jack Hannah would comment after his retirement.

[21] A skilled clown, musician, actor, and cartoonist, Vance DeBar 'Pinto' Colvig had also been a pioneer of American animation. In the late teens, he had set up Pinto Cartoon Comedies Company in San Francisco, and there he created one of the first animated films in colour: *Pinto's Prizma Comedy Revue* (1919).

[22] Much of the credit belongs to Vladimir 'Bill' Tytla (1904–68), a highly praised New York animator of Ukrainian origin.

White can be said to be one of the best musicals in Hollywood history.

The film – a fairy tale – also definitely marked Disney's choice for a children's audience. From then on, the company's output would be aimed at children, at 'children from eight to eighty', or at 'the child which is inside all of us'. It was an innovation in Western (and probably global) film production: pure entertainment for children, without hidden pedagogical, educational pedantry. Audiences flocked.

Besides *Snow White*, Disney's best-remembered feature films are *Pinocchio* (in which the animation is undeniably superb) and *Dumbo*, a fine, compact work. Among short films, the number of notable works is greater, especially in the first seven to eight years of sound cinema, when the character of Mickey was rendered more powerful by a certain irreverence, a vague sadism, and even a rustic inelegance. The other stars of animation, Donald and Goofy, were at their best in the next decade, under the care of Jack King (1895–1958), Jack Kinney (1909–1992), and the genial Jack Hannah (1913–1994).[23]

As for the Silly Symphonies, despite their immediate success, they did not stand up as well to the test of time. To different degrees, they all suffered from the problem of 'cutesiness', which affected a large part of Disney's production from the mid-1930s on. Exceptions to this rule were *Three Little Pigs*, *The Tortoise and the Hare* (1935), and *The Country Cousin* (1936).

Disney's most sophisticated work was *Fantasia*. Created as an illustration to eight pieces of classical music, this full-length *Silly Symphony* was spectacular because of the animators' magnificent virtuosity, but it drowned in its pictorial and graphic choices. Caricature drawings and animation, which would typically accompany popular songs, clashed in a trite manner with music by Beethoven, Bach, and Stravinsky (Stravinsky's *The Rite of Spring* became a history of the world with toy dinosaurs and syrupy lava). The relation between serious music and art-in-movement demanded more powerful artistic temperaments (a comparison can be made with the film *Night on Bald Mountain*, the extraordinary gothic world created seven years earlier by Alexandre Alexeïeff).[24]

Figure 12.1 Walt and Roy Disney, Academy Award. © 1932 Disney.

The Pillar Brother

Roy Oliver Disney (Chicago, 24 June 1893– Burbank, 20 December 1971) was a brilliant businessman and financier. The man who would find the money and save it. The one who made all the dreams viable. An unselfish, protective older brother who could be stubborn and firm, quarrel with and not speak to Walt for months but never compromise his loyalty. Merchandising of the Disney characters began in 1929, by way of licensing with a stationery company to imprint the newly born Mickey Mouse on school writing tablets. It was Roy who made merchandising a major source of income – and who chased infringers all over the planet. It was Roy who guided the company's going public on April 1940, when a lot of investment was needed but all the power had to be kept.

He would candidly, self-effacingly portray himself to biographer Bob Thomas:

> If I contributed anything, I contributed honest management for [Walt]. It wasn't that he wasn't smart enough if he applied himself. He was always disinterested in figures, legal work, and all that stuff. . . . So he'd have been easy prey for somebody to twist him and take him.[25]

---

[23] Jack Hannah should not be confused with William Hanna of the Hanna and Barbera team. Jack Hannah managed to stop the decline of Donald Duck in the 1950s by putting him in comic situations and by having him confront other antagonists, particularly the rodents Chip and Dale.

[24] In *Fantasia*, the less pretentious sequences are the best; for instance, Dukas's *The Sorcerer's Apprentice* musically accompanies one of Mickey Mouse's most clever performances.

[25] Bob Thomas, *Building a Company: Roy O. Disney and the Creation of an Entertainment Empire*, Hyperion, New York, 1998.

> Roy Oliver Disney was the father of Roy Edward Disney, who we'll meet in the next chapters of this book.

More years of expansion, reorganization and, in Disney's words, confusion, followed. In 1940, when the studio produced *Pinocchio* and *Fantasia*, they moved the company to larger and more impersonal headquarters in Burbank. In the meantime, with World War II, the vital European market was shut. *Fantasia* failed at the box office. In 1941, the company, which had always been characterized by a spirit of enthusiasm and collaboration, was severely affected by an animators' strike, spurred by disagreements over contracts and wages, which lasted from 28 May to 29 July. Walt considered it a personal attack; there was even a hint of physical confrontation between him and the strikers. An agreement was reached by Roy Disney. An angry Walt immediately left for South America on a government-promoted goodwill tour. Because of the changed mood inside the company and the American intervention in the war, several excellent artists left, including the strike chiefs Art Babbitt (1907–1992) and Dave Hilberman (1911–2007); and animators Vladimir William Tytla (1904–1968), John Hubley (1914–1977), and Walt Kelly (1912–1973).[26]

Disney's trip to South America had been promoted by Nelson Rockefeller, then the Coordinator for Inter-American Affairs in Washington. In an international scene dominated by World War II (from which the United States was still abstaining), the American government wanted to reinforce its bonds with its neighbours and counted on the immense popularity of Mickey's 'father'. After the Japanese attack on Pearl Harbor, on 7 December 1941, Disney's studio in Burbank established a very intensive relationship with the government, the army, and the navy. Educational, technical, and training films were released in a continuous cycle, more than quintupling annual production.[27] This huge effort (which, in the year 1943, represented 94 per cent of the company's activity) was considered a patriotic duty by Disney and was furnished at cost only. In turn, this public service permitted Disney to keep his offices open and his skilled animators active.

During this war period, the entertainment section continued to produce full-length feature films, including *Dumbo* (1941), *Bambi* (1942), *Saludos Amigos* (1943), and *The Three Caballeros* (1945); these last two derived from Disney's visit to Latin America. The production of shorts included anti-Nazi propaganda films, such as *Der Fuehrer's Face*, *Education for Death*, and *Reason and Emotion* (all in 1943). *Victory through Air Power* was another expression of Disney's participation in the war effort. Convinced of the decisive role played by the Air Force, Disney produced, at his own expense, this full-length film supporting Major Alexander de Seversky's drive to build more bombers.[28]

---

[26] Kelly left cinema for comics, starting the comic strip *Pogo* (1942). Kelly (who had participated in the animation of the 'Pastoral' episode in *Fantasia*) left before the strike, turning from cinema to comics and starting his long-running and much acclaimed comic strip *Pogo* (1942).

[27] It should be kept in mind that these films required limited, simplified animation.

[28] *Victory through Air Power* is by far the least Disneyesque, least successful, and least known of Walt's feature films (although a DVD version was released). The faithful Wolfgang Reitherman, who was a skilled pilot and reached the rank of major during World War II, blamed de Seversky for having played on Walt's feelings: 'That story had been settled already two years before that. There wasn't any doubt that we were going to have airpower.' ('Woolie Reitherman Interviewed by Thorkil B. Rasmussen on 24 February 1978', in Didier Ghez (ed.) *Walt's People: Volume 2*, Xlibris, Bloomington, Indiana, 2006). This is the review of one of the best film critics of the times, James Agee (*The Nation*, 3 July 1943):

> I only hope Major de Seversky and Walt Disney know what they are talking about, for I suspect an awful lot of people who see *Victory through Air Power* are going to think they do. Certainly I am not equipped to argue with them. I have the feeling I was sold something under pretty high pressure, which I don't enjoy, and I am staggered by the case with which such self-confidence, on matters of such importance, can be blared all over a nation, without cross-questioning. Beyond that, I can only talk of it as a certain kind of moving picture.
>
> When Disney is attending strictly to mechanics and to business, it is good poetry and, barring its over persuasiveness, good teaching. When, instead, he is being poetic, or cute, or in this case funny, it is neither. Such images as that of the Nazi wheel are vivid and instructive.

Disney's Animation Declines

At the end of the war, America went through a time of prosperity never seen before, but for Disney's animators the booming 1930s never came back. Short films suffered with the new fashion of showing two feature films rather than the usual single feature, cartoon, and newsreel. Furthermore, animated feature films could not be improved because of skyrocketing costs. Disney began looking towards other kinds of production, such as nature documentaries, live-action movies for children, and television shows, where he became a forerunner among Hollywood producers. Above all, he concentrated on his ever-larger amusement park project, Disneyland, leaving more and more responsibility for the production of feature films to his veterans from the golden age. One year after Disney died in Burbank on 15 December 1966, *The Jungle Book*, the last film on which he had directly worked, was released. Walt Disney Productions continued operating with large profits, due especially to its amusement parks (Disneyland and the more recent Walt Disney World in Florida), and more movies were made in the now well-established Disney style under the management of Wolfgang Reitherman (1910–1985). A new momentum was given to Disney animated feature films in the late 1980s by a completely new generation of animators (which we discuss later in the book).

The personal Disney will always be difficult to define (he was 'a very complicated man', in his collaborators' unanimous opinion). Some accused him of being a harsh speculator or just a manager who was unable to draw. With his employees, he was often impenetrable, distant, and brusque and considered those who left or who opposed his will to be traitors. Conversely, he was a faithful husband and an affectionate father, so nostalgic for childhood that he had a giant toy train built in his backyard. He was also generous towards his old friends and those who had worked with him during difficult times. Never a rich man, at least by Hollywood standards, he did not demand quantity, but rather quality, from his collaborators. His ambitious enterprises kept the company in a perilous state of indebtedness, which lasted until his death, when prosperity came with a more conservative management.

Despite the large investments towards the continuous race for perfecting new and improved technologies, Disney never lost his awareness of the fact that he was just making products directed towards a consumer's world. This commercialization catered to the largest number of buyers and, as a consequence, was ultimately limiting for the films, the producer, and the public. Although this 'entertainment' cinema could be made 'artistically', Disney himself recoiled from the idea of 'art' cinema, defending his choice and describing his movies as being made without cultural or intellectual ambition and totally out of place in art theatres ('I sell corn, and I love corn').

As a middle-class, small-town Midwesterner (he always considered himself a Kansas City boy), Disney shared the aesthetic aspirations as well as the social origins of his audiences.[29] *Funny Little Bunnies*, one of the most mannerist Silly Symphonies, gave a simple-minded vision of Eden, with limpid brooks, green hills, and smiling little animals

---

Such images as that of the bird which nests in a Maginot gun mouth are the defective side of this notably split talent or composite of talents. The human animations, like all of Disney's, are so bad they become interesting as misanthropic footnotes. The real poetic energy in Disney's films has always come of the children and grandchildren of his basic metaphors – the sounds and images of impingement, for instance, as the Nazi wheel is assaulted – and usually these are finely detailed and polished. Here they are not much more than roughed-in. The non-musical sound is good without his occasional brilliance; the music is a loss. The colour undersea (as in Disney's forest glades, etc. – there is something fishy about either him or me) is subdued and quite pretty; the extroverted colour is so much loud candy, if candy were to develop aesthetic pretensions. The patronizing comic cuteness with which early aviation is treated and the gay dreams of holocaust at the end seem to me as ill-advised as the finely mechanized expository stuff between them is new and correct.

I noticed, uneasily, that there were no suffering and dying enemy civilians under all those proud promises of bombs; no civilians at all, in fact. Elsewhere, the death-reducing virtues of De Seversky's scheme – if he is right – are mentioned; but that does not solve the problem. It was necessary here either (1) to show bombed civilians in such a manner as to enhance the argument, (2) to omit them entirely, or (3) to show them honestly, which might have complicated an otherwise happy sales talk. I am glad method 1 was not used, and of method 3 I realize that animated cartoons, so weak – at least as Disney uses them – in the whole human world, would be particularly inadequate to human terror, suffering, and death. Even so, I cannot contentedly accept the antiseptic white lies of method 2. The sexless sexiness of Disney's creations has always seemed to me queasy, perhaps in an all-American sense; in strict descent from it is this victory-in-a-vacuum which is so morally simple a matter – and so salubrious for the postwar if only it were true – of machine-eat-machine.

[29] In any industrial sector, dependence on a mass market implies a reduction of creativity. In Hollywood cinema, the caution imposed by 'decency', as well as by the fear of offending ethnic or religious minorities, has led to both anecdotes and sociological dissertations. Disney accepted these limitations more than other animators.

Figure 12.2 Walt Disney's nine old men. From left to right, standing: Ollie Johnston, Eric Larson, Frank Thomas, Marc Davis, Milt Kahl. From left to right, sitting: John Lounsbery, Ward Kimball, Les Clark, Wolfgang Reitherman. © 1972 Disney.

depicted painting opulent Easter eggs. Gradually, Disney's 'good' characters acquired ever more rounded forms and newborn-like features, with large heads, overdeveloped eyes, short arms, and showy buttocks. Their baby-like traits moved adults and reminded children of their dolls and teddy bears,[30] while the neat lines, mixed with soft nuances, created a look as polished as the most perfectly kept home.[31] (Disney reacted angrily when, during a visit to the studio, architect Frank Lloyd Wright suggested that he film the lively pencil sketches rather than the buffed cels.) In the long run, this kitsch became the worst, most insinuating enemy of Disney and his collaborators.

For a long time, Disney was the only standard: Not only did he defeat competition, he also erased it because, in the mind of his viewers, his animation was accepted as the defining example of the animated film. On the negative side, his work fed the general public's reluctance to accept alternative proposals for a more cultured, stimulating, or simply different animated cinema. Disney himself contributed to reinforcing his 'cartoon monopoly' by publicly describing animation and by theorizing about it as if it had never existed in any other form but those he himself had created – needless to say, his keen sense of public relations assisted him in his quest for animation superiority.

Disney was the most important Hollywood producer of animation in the 1930s and 1940s, on par with the live-action producers Irving Thalberg and David O. Selznick. As a 'founder of an empire', he belonged to the all-American group of 'emperors' that included J. P. Morgan, Henry Ford, Thomas A. Edison, William Randolph Hearst, Florenz Ziegfeld, and P.T. Barnum. His cinema is 100 per cent Hollywood – founded on the star system, oriented towards the luxurious packaging of mass products,

---

[30] An ethological analysis of this tendency towards puppy-like shapes has been suggested by Stephen Jay Gould in 'Mickey Mouse Meets Konrad Lorenz', *Natural History*, Vol. 88, No. 5, May 1979.

[31] What Norman Mailer wrote about Marilyn Monroe, another cinematic myth loved by the same public, can be applied to this phenomenon: '[She had] all the cleanliness of all the clean American backyards' (Norman Mailer, *Marilyn: A Biography*, Coronet, London, 1974, p. 15).

and based on broad stereotypes. On one hand, he was hailed as the animator 'par excellence', the Burbank magician, the twentieth-century Aesop. On the other hand, he was criticized as the one who destroyed the graphic freedom of animation in favour of live-action-style realism or as the sly propagandist of American ideology all over the world. No matter: A critical history of cinema cannot overlook the ideological weight that Walt Disney's work had, and still has, on audiences and animators alike.

The Twelve Rules of the Nine Men

The Disney 'Nine Old Men' originated as an informal group in the early 1950s. The term had long existed as the nickname of the panel of judges (nine, in fact) of the Supreme Court of the United States. 'Hey, I have my Nine Old Men, too', Walt Disney quipped one day and prepared a list. They were all under fifty; they were 'old' in the sense of 'old friends'.

Here are their names in order of birth: Eric Larson (1905–1988), Les Clark (1907–1979), Milton Kahl (1909–1987), Wolfgang Reitherman (1910–1985), John Lounsbery (1911–1976), Frank Thomas (1912–2004), Ollie Johnston (1912–2008), Marc Davis (1913–2000), and Ward Kimball (1914–2002).

Two old men in particular were friends for life: Frank Thomas and Ollie Johnston. They were to systematize and disseminate, in their wonderful book *Disney Animation: The Illusion of Life* (1981), the workshop secrets created in that unique moment coinciding with the creation of *Snow White and the Seven Dwarfs*.[32]

As always, the secrets, once stated, became rules – iron for the mediocre who followed them blindly, gold for the intelligent who knew how to interpret and often subvert them.

The rules were numbered from one to twelve: 1) squash and stretch, 2) anticipation, 3) staging, 4) straight-ahead action and pose to pose, 5) follow-through and overlapping action, 6) slow in and slow out, 7) arcs, 8) secondary action, 9) timing, 10) exaggeration, 11) solid drawing, and 12) appeal.

1. Squash and stretch: 'By far the most important among the discoveries that we did', said Thomas and Johnston. Here, the classic example is the rubber ball. In real life, its deformation at the time of bouncing is less than a millimetre and therefore invisible. Animation, however, engages with our brains, not only with our eyes. To be credible, the bouncing ball must expand to the ground as if it was squashed and then throw itself up with the oblong (stretched) shape of a projectile. The principle of squash and stretch, which also applies to other malleable organic forms, such as the face and body, brings a feeling of life and vitality to characters and their movements.

2. Anticipation: Renowned animator and director Richard Williams describes this principle as 'the preparation for an action . . . It communicates what is going to happen'. An action must be 'presented' to the viewer in order to be clearly visible and thus significant. Classic examples are: a baseball player winding up for the pitch, an arrow pulled back before being released from a bow, etc.

3. Staging: An action is staged so that it is fully understood, the behaviour of a character is staged in a way that is recognizable, a facial expression so that it is easily seen, an emotion or state of mind in a way that touches the viewer. In essence, it is the general principle of show business. On a theatre stage, for example, the characters, scenery, props – the observable elements on which the scene is built – are carefully arranged within the scene so that the characters' physical relationship or hierarchy in relation to each other, or within their environment, most clearly conveys, from moment to moment, what

---

[32] It must once more be emphasized here that the innovators who identified and codified the principles were the group that preceded and mentored the Nine Old Men, such as Ub Iwerks, Norman Ferguson, Fred Moore, Hamilton Luske, Grim Natwick, Dick Lundy, Richard Huemer, Art Babbitt, Vladimir Tytla, and Walt Disney, among others. As Frank Thomas and Ollie Johnston write in *Disney Animation: The Illusion of Life*: 'Under the leadership of the Nine Old Men, the original principles were refined, perfected, and extended.' The Nine continued to use the principles forged by others in sophisticated and subtle ways that were totally integrated into a performance.

is at stake in the scene: the emphasis, mood, or whatever may be important for the audience to register at that moment of the story.

4. Straight-ahead action and pose to pose: These are the two ways of animating characters. In the straight-ahead method, the animator starts by making a first drawing and goes forward, drawing by drawing, improvising movements little by little. Pose-to-pose animation, however, is when the animator has previously designed the action and already determined what the first storytelling drawing and last storytelling drawing of the action are (the 'extreme' poses). The best overall method is to work straight ahead between each of the extreme poses.

5. Follow-through and overlapping action: Follow-through is when the character stops after a movement but, to be credible to our mind, the soft parts of his body – or loose appendages such as ears and tail – continue moving in a secondary action after the main action, from a minimum of a few frames to a maximum of a couple of seconds more; otherwise, he would look very stiff.

Overlapping action is when parts of the body move sequentially at different times, such as a fat character rising from a chair. The belly and torso might come up later than the head and chest.

6. Slow in and slow out: The animator typically starts a movement slowly, then speeds it up during its course, and then eventually decelerates it at the end (unless that particular scene requests something else, of course). This way, the movement will look credible and not begin or end abruptly.

7. Arcs: All living things, when performing a movement, naturally follow a rounded path or 'arc'. In a simple walk, the body arcs up and down as the arms and legs form separate arcs in their movements. An animated character must move in these arcs to give a sense of its form and natural rotation at its joints.

8. Secondary action: An animator, both for a sense of realism and visual interest or counterpoint, incorporates into a scene layers of simultaneous actions, large and small, typically with varied rhythms. A classic example would be Pluto the dog tracking a scent: the broader, slower, primary action of his prowling legs is accompanied by the much smaller and quicker 'secondary' action of his sniffing nose.

9. Timing: We must approach this word with care, as it has at least two similar but distinct meanings. In the sense of the ninth Disney rule, timing means the construction of the internal rhythm of a given action – in other words, the spacing of 'inbetween' drawings from one key pose to the next. A more common, universal meaning applies to the 'timing' of the movements or the happenings on stage relative to each other. We laugh or are terrified or moved, but only if the gag or scream or sigh arrives in the exact moment it has the best impact. The performer who misses the timing ruins the show.

10. Exaggeration: Even some Disney men of the 1930s misunderstood this word and believed that they had to distort the drawings and create super-violent action. This exaggeration is simply to take the caricature to sufficient extremes to make it clear and expressive.

11. Solid drawing: The animator must look for a figure that moves well, that has volume but still is flexible, that possesses strength but at the same time agility: a 'plastic' shape. In other words, a Disney character must be credibly volumetric.

12. Appeal: This term might (misleadingly) evoke cute kittens and cute bunnies. The Disney films were anything but free of mawkishness – but 'appeal' here means something higher. 'For us', said Thomas and Johnston, 'it means anything a filmgoer likes to see, a charm, an attractive design, simplicity, communicativeness, magnetism'. The villains have to have appeal, too. It is no accident, we can add as an example, that Shakespeare's *Merchant of Venice* only perfidious Shylock has become a memorable figure.

The common purpose of these rules – and of many other measures that were adopted – was to obtain, as the title of Thomas and Johnston's book puts it, the illusion of life. (The illusion, not the representation: Virtually all Disney animation is a caricature, and when it is not – witness the Prince in *Snow White* – it is weak.) Just in order to avoid misunderstanding: The twelve rules that we have listed here are not meant to apply to all types of animation. They are important only for character (or personality) animation – for animation the Disney way.

Animation Heads West

In the course of a few years, American animation followed in the footsteps of live-action cinema and moved its operations from New York to Hollywood. Many animators left the East Coast, attracted by Walt Disney's reputation and expansion. Charles Mintz's studio was relocated; Pat Sullivan also planned to move, although he never actually did so. Other studios were founded directly in California. By the end of the 1930s, only Paul Terry kept his headquarters in the east in New Rochelle, New York. He was joined in 1942 by the survivors of the Fleischer Group, which had returned to Manhattan from Florida. Every major Hollywood company had its own animated fillers to be distributed with its live-action features. These fillers were mainly bought through distribution contracts with small animation production companies. At times, large companies opened their own animation departments, as Metro-Goldwyn-Mayer (MGM) did in 1937. This financial link between producers and distributors was an important reason for their geographical proximity.

Animation was thus influenced by its wealthier counterpart, mainstream cinema. The theme of the 'magic', which had been a constant suggestion in the first two decades of the century, vanished suddenly; cartoons became *films*, leaving behind their origins as drawings that came to life. Following the rules of the Californian 'dream industry', animation also relied on the star system. Producers directed all their efforts towards creating stellar characters. They also became involved in a race for colour, music, depth of field, and sumptuous animation but, still, characters remained the centre of attention. Only after World War II (with the exception of a few works released by Screen Gems in 1941), did formal and colouristic interests get the upper hand in UPA productions. As for visual style, animated films lost the graphic stamp that had been their distinctive mark. Camera movements, framing, and cutting strove to imitate live-action cinema. Comic inventions were drawn ever more often from situations and accidents rather than metamorphoses or the sudden activation of inanimate objects.

Due to the new marketplace, many old animators became scriptwriters and gagmen, leaving the drawing to more artistically gifted newcomers. Other gagmen came from the variety theatres. Although the comic solutions they invented were not inappropriate for animation, their new style was decidedly oriented towards *action* and gave rise to a new generation of slapstick comedy in which Donald Duck and Bugs Bunny imitated Charlie Chaplin and Buster Keaton. The era of a villain squeezing a school building in order to catch the children, or big toes transforming into ballerinas at the sound of a flute, was over.[33]

Hollywood cinema influenced cartoons in still another way by becoming itself a source of inspiration – in satire. Several animated shorts were parodies of famous films, others hosted the caricatures of current stars, and still others comically hinted at the current events in the world of cinema, including other animation; one of Schlesinger director Frank Tashlin's characters, for instance, ate spinach, saying that if it was good for Popeye, it should work for him too.

Concurrently, animation loosened its ties with comic strips. In the years preceding World War II, only Popeye moved successfully from the comic strip page to the screen; the few other cartoons based on strips had short lifespans. By that time, characters were specifically designed for the needs of animation. If anything, the reverse process took place, when almost every hero of the screen – from Mickey Mouse to Betty Boop, Porky Pig, and Woody Woodpecker – was given a second life in print. The evolution of American comic strips into adventure themes, with non-caricatured characters such as Alex Raymond's *Flash Gordon*, did not influence animators, with the exception of a short-lived rendition of *Superman* by the Fleischer brothers.

Following the example of Disney, many companies gradually departmentalized labour. Figures, dimensions, gestures – all the principal traits of characters – were fixed on a model sheet that served as a reference to each animator and director. In this way, the cartoon character would not suffer from changes in physiognomy or personality, even when it was assigned to different teams. The old-time anarchy was replaced by an organization in which several teams worked under a director, with separate groups

---

[33] One notable exception: Tex Avery's Warner and, later, MGM cartoons, which continued to draw freely on such surreal invention, frequently exaggerated to extreme, comic proportions.

writing scripts and gags. With no exception, the cel process was the chosen technique, as it allowed the distribution of tasks among director, scene designer, chief animator, animator, 'inbetweener' (who did the transitional drawings between two extremes set by the animator), and the departments responsible for colouring and buffing the cels.

The new importance given to 'acting' over simple action decreased the opportunities for ad libbing and diminished the whimsical development of action during production; the technique of inbetweening depended precisely on the need to predetermine every detail. Earlier practice, in which often the animated sequence was largely invented even while it was being created, was soon shelved.

One aspect that has been stigmatized by modern scholars is the lack of veracity in the credits. The names appearing in the head titles were often chosen not to indicate the people who actually worked on a particular film but to 'compensate' those animators who were next in line in rotation; sometimes credit was taken by those who had the power to do so (this happened with some producers). This questionable practice had its own rationale. The screen credit was a privilege reserved for only a few in the Hollywood system; in several instances, screenwriters (to mention only one category) did not receive any credit for major works, while smaller contributions were recognized. Furthermore, the production companies, which were large melting pots of talent, produced good, albeit homogeneous, results. Without dwelling on the theories of mass communication or mass production, assembly-line animation and market demand undoubtedly affected these productions. To a greater or lesser degree, every short was the subproduct of a greater work produced by all the creative people engaged in it at that time. To search for individual creative responsibilities becomes a mirage, more seductive than practical. With no regrets, artists gave up their graphic personalities and reached a sort of common dialect of the pencil, a standardized formula. Their expertise in the trade was such that they were able to switch between animation of different characters, move from one studio to another, and work on different projects simultaneously without causing inconsistencies visible to the general viewer. (Clearly there were variations from artist to artist, which the specialist is able to discern and thus can even recognize the work of individual artists; however, since these idiosyncrasies were not typically requested, or even welcome, such an approach, rather than serving a helpful critical function, risks becoming an intellectual guessing game.)

The characters of American animation at that time, whether human or zoomorphic, did not differ much from one to the other, as far as plastic choices were concerned. These last were far from the level demanded by a perfectionist: Drawings were elementary, and the palette and background took no more from art history than a few suggestions from fairy tale illustrations. In fact, what counted was not the drawing in itself, but animation, or the drawn movement. Norman Ferguson (1902–1957), a veteran at Disney who was considered the best animator of his time by many colleagues, drew only middlingly well but was able to 'capture' movement like nobody else. Animation meant to invent and hone the mimicry of face and body, set a rhythm, give life to what needed to have life on the screen. Then, as now, these characteristics determined who was a good animator.

If drawings were to be uniform for everybody, a higher level was reached with the adoption of a 'common dictionary' of physiognomic traits. In a how-to manual, Preston Blair (1908–1994), at that time one of the best character animators for Disney and later for Metro, gave some suggestions: The 'cute' type needed the basic proportions of a child, plus a shy and timid expression; the 'screwball' required exaggerated traits, such as a long head, thin neck, and big feet. A 'goofy' character needed a long neck, humped back, and curved shoulders; he should also have a beak nose; no chin; long, swinging arms; and sleepy eyes. The 'heavy' type should be characterized by a big chin and jaws; a large trunk and chest; and long, heavy arms with large hands and short legs.[34] Many protagonists from different series can be easily identified with these archetypes.

This animated comedy is close to the ancient *commedia dell'arte*. The dumb, quarrelsome, and scatterbrain types are brothers of the smart Harlequin or the greedy Pantalone. They have a well-defined psyche and are ready to jump into a series of adventures, improvised or even suggested by current events. As in the *commedia dell'arte*, this comedy also returns again and again to set routines, which play on the very fact that the audience is already familiar with them and is just waiting to see the slight twist that will make *that* variation on the routine pay off differently from those before. Such comedy poses a razor's-edge challenge, since the audience might very well react: 'Again and again? Can't they invent something new?'

Those who criticize these films for their mediocre drawing should keep in mind that the value of a comic character does not reside so much in its features as in its actions and in the rhythm with which those actions occur.

---

[34] Preston Blair, *Learn How to Draw Animated Cartoons*, Foster, Tustin, 1949.

Round contours invited deformations and accidents; in the post-war era, when more sophisticated drawing prevailed, the impetuous comedy of slapstick began to wane. Moreover, not much of the 'pretty' production (the Silly Symphony series and the like) of that age has survived today's tastes.

The Roosevelt years, dominated by economic crisis, social demands, and international isolationism, were not markedly reflected in cartoons. A few exceptions include Disney's *Three Little Pigs*, in which the characters have been seen as the representatives of national hope, and the restless bunnies, ducklings, dogs, cats, and mice of Warner Bros. and MGM at the end of the 1930s suggested a frenetic activity ready to burst after a ten-year-long sleep. Those same years were also a time of research, artistic experimentation, and stylistic developments for American intellectuals. At this time, American avant-garde artists released their first animated films.

The Masters' Master

Donald Wilkinson Graham (Fort William, Ontario, Canada, 17 June 1903–Gig Harbor, Washington State, 19 October 1976) was the man who taught them all. If the Golden Age of American animation had a basic, common stylistic standard, one of the reasons was Don Graham's direct or indirect influence (the other reason being the eagerness to copy the Disney formula).

This former engineering and painting student settled in Los Angeles in 1930 to teach at his former school, the Chouinard Art Institute. In 1932, he met Walt Disney and, along with him, developed the new artistic approach to animation that eventually led to *Snow White* and to the concept of 'plausible impossible'. Intermittently, he collaborated with Disney until 1955, at the same time continuing his work teaching other animators at Chouinard. By the end of his life, he (jokingly) calculated that he had taught at least 25,000 animators.

His extraordinary legacy survives in his only book, *Composing Pictures, Still and Moving*, first published in 1970 by Van Nostrand Reinhold, New York, and in many texts and manuals written by people who had learned from him.

Lantz from the Rabbit to the Woodpecker

After his arrival in Hollywood, Walter Lantz briefly served as a gagman for live-action short comedies at Hal Roach's and Mack Sennett's studios, then worked for Charles Mintz. One day, Carl Laemmle, the founder and boss of Universal Pictures, got fed up with the manoeuvring over a cartoon character to which his company owned the copyright: Oswald the Rabbit. Charles Mintz had cheated Disney over the character in 1927; now some of Mintz's animators were, in turn, trying to cheat Mintz. Laemmle knew Lantz and knew a talented and honest man when he saw one. He entrusted him with the bunny and put him in charge of a newly created Universal animation department of more than 100 employees. Assignment: twenty-six cartoons a year. Lantz enlisted Bill Nolan as a fellow director and the nine-year-old star Mickey Rooney as Oswald's voice; except for a short alliance with United Artists, Lantz would never leave Universal until his retirement.

Among the new department's first duties, one was thrilling: an animated insert for an ambitious project, *The King of Jazz* (1930), starring Paul Whiteman,[35] which was to be filmed in Technicolor on bichromic (two-colour) stock. Although the film was undeservedly unsuccessful, the animated insert (also in Technicolor) was very well received, and Whiteman's arranger, Jimmy Dietrich, stayed on as the studio's composer – adding even more talent to the animated enterprise. It was not a time of masterpieces. Oswald was a cute but insubstantial character in need of heavy gags and funny situations to avoid becoming boring; it is not by chance that in his most famous movie, *Confidence* (1933), he had only a minor role. *Confidence* was a true example of political propaganda, depicting the ghost of the Depression with its economic and social problems, and showing Oswald running to Franklin Delano Roosevelt for a remedy. The newly elected president offers a dose of 'trust', which Oswald injects into everybody with a syringe.

In 1934, the colour series Cartune Classics was introduced with the intention of competing with Disney's Silly Symphonies. The series lasted until 1942 but was revived in 1953–1957. In 1935, Bill Nolan left for Mintz and later for the short-lived Skippy Studio; eventually he accepted an offer from the Fleischers in Florida. At the same time, during a reorganization of Universal, Lantz decided to establish his own business, Walter Lantz Productions. The

---

[35] To the dismay of many jazz purists, this popular orchestra conductor (1890–1967) was really nicknamed the 'King of Jazz'.

operation was almost invisible, as nothing changed except on paper. Offices, facilities, furniture, and people just took the new name on 16 November 1935, producing the same films and selling them to the mother company through a solid distribution contract.

Oswald underwent a couple of restylings, first wearing gloves, a T-shirt, and shoes, then even changing from a black to a white rabbit (*The Case of the Lost Sheep*, 1935) and accentuating his physiognomy as a rodent. This expedient served only to delay the wear and tear on the star, who finally disappeared in 1938.

Walter always knew he needed to invent some new characters. After several efforts (including the doggy Pooch the Pup and the three little monkeys Meany, Miny, and Moe), it was time for Andy Panda. According to Leonard Maltin[36]:

> Lantz was constantly searching for animals that had not been used as cartoon stars before. . . . The panda was a novel idea, sparked by the national attention given to the donation of a panda to the Chicago Zoo.

While Lantz's unusual choice may have indeed been rooted in that current event, the long-lasting success of the character was due to the artist's ability to appeal to children. Gracious and polite, Andy was nevertheless always ready to correct his clumsy father, leaving children with a feeling of power. Andy Panda debuted in 1939 in the cartoon *Life Begins for Andy Panda*, directed by Alex Lovy (1913–1992).

The year 1940 was an ominous one for Walter Lantz and his crew. The new Universal managers thought that they could do without animated cartoons and told Lantz so. On 31 January 1940, they even renounced the copyrights of all the animated characters and gave them to Lantz and, by the end of February, the studio was closed. However, thanks to Walter Lantz's stubbornness (he mortgaged everything he owned) and his employees' loyalty (they decided to work for free for a while), it was soon reopened, and a few months later, on 25 November, a short called *Knock Knock* (directed again by Alex Lovy) was released. It featured the characters Andy Panda and his father but, above all, it hosted an obnoxious bird that would become the long-awaited big star of the studio: Woody Woodpecker.

Woody was basically created by story man Ben 'Bugs' Hardaway (1897–1957), a refugee from Warner's who had previously worked on other pests such as Bugs Bunny and Daffy Duck.[37]

Distraught, delirious, even dangerous, the very first Woody exhibited brutal features, feverish eyes, and two pendulous teeth in his beak. Gradually, his appearance and manners improved, but the character remained a constant pain in the neck, with an idiotic laugh that was destined to become famous. Just like Bugs Bunny, Donald Duck, Tex Avery's characters (see later in this section), Chuck Jones's Minah Bird, Walt Disney's Aracuan Bird,[38] or the earlier version of Daffy Duck, Woody embodied an uncontrolled force, typical of the American cartoons of the 1940s.

In his studio, Lantz sometimes directed the films, coordinated the work, and hired people, having the rare merit – for a manager – to know all the secrets of the job; in short, he functioned as a Disney on a smaller scale, yet with a more affable personality. It is difficult to state the degree of his actual participation in the creative process of production and to point out the amount of credit that other artists deserve. Without any doubt, his films can be easily recognized by their style, although at times they suffered from poor timing. Quality was sacrificed for speed, and the characters' sense of decorum often lapsed into mannerism. (Not by chance, Woody Woodpecker was Lantz's best product, a restless character whose manners could be blunted but never completely controlled.) It should be noted that the peak of Woody's popularity coincided with the arrival in the studio of the already-mentioned Shamus Culhane, a veteran of many production companies who switched to directing after working on films such as *Snow White* and *Gulliver's Travels*. A person with vast cultural interests and a predisposition for music, Culhane directed the very entertaining *Barber of Seville* for Lantz in 1944.

Another shock arrived in 1949, when the studio had to stop working again. But by late 1950, the resilient producer and his crew reopened it and kept it alive until 1972.

Among Lantz's collaborators are also worth mentioning: his longest-standing associate, director Paul J. Smith (1906–1980), and such talented wanderers as Burt Gillett, Preston Blair, Dick Lundy, Tex Avery, Jack Hannah, and LaVerne Harding (1905–1984), possibly the only woman

---

[36] Leonard Maltin, *Of Mice and Magic*, New American Library, New York, 1980, pp. 163–164.

[37] Walter Lantz always maintained that he had been inspired by a spiteful, noisy woodpecker that had kept him and his second wife, actress Grace Stafford, awake during a night on their honeymoon trip. The marriage took actually place one year after Woody's first short. Stafford voiced the character (whose voice initially was provided by Mel Blanc) beginning in 1950.

[38] From *The Three Caballeros* (1944).

in Hollywood to reach the highly valued rank of animator in those times.[39]

Ub Iwerks

Ub Iwerks was born in Kansas City on 24 March 1901. Since his original Dutch name, Ubbe Eert Iwwerks, did not sound pleasant to American ears, he simplified it in the 1920s. In 1919, he held a job as a publicity graphics technician at the Pesmen-Rubin Commercial Art Studio, where he met Walt Disney. The first part of Iwerks's career developed at Disney's side. The two artists worked almost uninterruptedly together until 25 January 1930, when Iwerks accepted an offer from producer Pat Powers to open a studio in his own name.[40] Aside from the flattering thought of his own studio, Iwerks had several other reasons to split with Disney. Once successful, Disney tended to limit his collaborators' individual creativity, even when they were his oldest, most loyal friends, such as Iwerks. Furthermore, Disney's idea for a 'new' kind of animation clashed with Iwerks's, who was strongly anchored to the style developed in the 1920s.

At his studio, Iwerks retrieved a character he had sketched in 1928, Flip the Frog. Originally designed with very frog-like features, the frog, because of marketing reasons, later became more anthropomorphic, to the point that it almost looked like a Mickey Mouse without ears and a snout (the fact that the animation of both characters had been the work of the same hand undoubtedly accentuated the similarity). When the anticipated success did not come, Iwerks abandoned Flip after thirty-six episodes. In 1933, he released a new character, Willie Whopper, a child with a blond forelock and a tendency to tell lies, who only lasted one year. The series ComiColor Cartoons followed in the vein of Disney's Silly Symphonies and was made with the two-colour technique of Cinecolor. From his bankruptcy in 1936 to 1940, Iwerks worked as a subcontractor for Warner's and for Charles Mintz Screen Gems. In 1937, he directed *Merry Mannequins* for Mintz, which can probably be considered his best work.

Finally, faced by a lack of opportunities and fascinated more and more by the technical aspects of animation (in the 1930s, Iwerks had created a sort of multiplane camera, built with little money and much ingenuity), Iwerks returned to Disney, working on special effects and new machinery from 1940 until his death on 7 July 1971. In 1959 and 1964, he won Oscars for his inventions. Of the artist's relation with Disney after his return to the studio, there are only rumours; though the two men had been on the same wavelength in their younger days, Iwerks reportedly came back to the studio as simply an employee – with no remaining evidence of the old friendship.

The failure of Ub Iwerks as an independent artist was due in part to his lack of entrepreneurial skills and in part to his limitations as a director. He lacked that instinct for stories and plots that was Disney's strength. His films were loosely built, unentertaining, revolving around characters with weak personalities. Moreover, even his later drawings and gags were clearly products of the 1920s, irretrievably outdated and scarcely competitive. This notwithstanding, Iwerks's talent as an animator, a colourist, and a gagman stands out in sequences that often outdo the films of which they are parts.

Mintz, Krazy, and Columbia

Universal's requisition of the copyrights for Oswald the Lucky Rabbit did not leave Charles Mintz resourceless. Wishing to make it in the market, he moved from New York to Los Angeles, bringing along the best of his small studio.

Distributed by Columbia, the new Krazy Kat shorts were made, as usual, by Ben Harrison and Manny Gould, but the design underwent a further remaking. The protagonist of this new series was a far cry from George Herriman's anthropomorphic lunar male/female cat who wandered in Coconino County through a constantly changing background while being struck by the bricks thrown by his beloved Ignatz the Mouse.

The new Krazy Kat was merely one of the numerous imitations of Mickey Mouse, lacking not only a personality of its own but also those features that characterized the original version of the cat, except for the bow knotted behind the neck. The last episode, 'Krazy's Shoe Shop', was released on 2 October 1939.

---

[39] The first woman to reach the animator rank in a US studio (in 1933) was Lillian Friedman at Fleischer Studios in New York (Karl Cohen, 'Milestones of the Animation Industry in the XX Century', *Animation World Magazine*, No. 4.10, January 2000, http://www.awn.com/mag/issue4.10/4.10pages/cohenmilestones2.php3).

[40] Powers (1870?–1948), who had provided Disney with his sound recording system, was in 1930 the distributor of Disney's shorts. Powers would abandon both Iwerks and moviemaking in 1936.

With Krazy Kat, Mintz released another series featuring a little boy named Scrappy, his ever-present dog, and his female counterpart. Mintz did not involve himself with the artistic aspects of production, leaving his animators with full autonomy. This philosophy worked with some productions; the series with Scrappy, for instance, had fine episodes and improved animation in imitation of Disney's. However, Mintz lacked ambition as far as quality was concerned; as a consequence, several artists, such as Dick Huemer, Al Eugster, and Preston Blair, left the company at the first opportunity. In 1934, he began his Color Rhapsodies, characterized by the same imperfections and highlights as the rest of his production.

Mintz died in 1940, shortly after the Columbia Distribution Company took over his firm. Afterwards, the studio was affected by the constant change of artistic directors (seven in eight years). It had a brief golden age under Frank Tashlin, in 1941, who not only imposed his original taste but also recruited talented artists from Disney who had been disappointed by the strike at Disney and its outcome. The new arrivals included Zack Schwartz, Dave Hilberman, and John Hubley, who would later become outstanding personalities at UPA. Some productions, particularly *Prof. Small and Mr. Tall* (1943), were forerunners of the graphic and pictorial revolution that took place after World War II. The studio also released a clever pair of new characters: the Fox and the Crow (the fox was the predestined victim of the scatterbrained, spiteful crow). Tashlin's tenure lasted only a few months. Afterwards, the studio showed little promise of profitability and closed in 1948.

Van Beuren

Tom and Jerry (not to be confused with the much more famous cat and mouse by Hanna-Barbera for MGM) were the first characters created at the studio of Amadée J. Van Beuren (1879–1938). After 1929, when Paul Terry left with a good number of animators to open his new company, Van Beuren remained with a reduced staff and with the rights to *Aesop's Fables*. As an entrepreneur, he had made his fortune dealing with peep-show machines (individual viewers for short, sometimes spicy, films mainly destined for amusement parks). Like Mintz, and unlike the typical bosses of American animation, he was a businessman turned filmmaker. An ambitious man, Van Beuren made every effort to develop his company, abandoning the updated *Fables* (which, by 1930 and under the direction of John Foster and Harry Bailey, had turned into a shameless, bad-taste copy of Disney's shorts, with two leading characters who looked exactly like Mickey and Minnie Mouse) and hiring Vernon George Stallings and George Rufle (1901–1974).

In 1931, Stallings and Rufle helped to create the youngsters named Tom and Jerry, the former tall and dark, the latter short and blond. The debut film, credited to John Foster (1906–1971) and George Stallings, *Wot a Night* (1931), was a playful, creative mixture of the comical and the horrific, in the best tradition of American cinema, be it live action or animation. The episodes that followed were less successful, and the series was stopped in 1933. Van Beuren turned to Otto Soglow's Little King, a well-known character from comic strips, and even to the famous radio serial *Amos 'n' Andy*. This, however, did not produce much better results since the animators of the studio were only capable of utilizing outdated, ten-year-old styles and techniques. The use of talented but young and inexperienced artists such as Frank Tashlin, Joe Barbera, Pete Burness, Bill Littlejohn, Shamus Culhane, and Jack Zander did not help matters, and the films remained substantially poor in spite of a few good ideas. Still undaunted, Van Beuren attracted Burt Gillett, director of *Three Little Pigs* at Disney, evidently a key player in animation at that time. Gillett's changes and improvements included a rapid conversion to colour, a much more refined animation, and the release of Rainbow Parade, a new successful series from 1934.

Two major problems, however, weighed heavily on the studio: Gillett's mercurial behaviour, which estranged many employees (much later, Shamus Culhane described Gillett as a man just one step away from the madhouse) and the inability to create a character that could effectively appeal to the public. An attempt to revive Felix the Cat, in 1936, failed. Additionally, in 1935, Van Beuren, who was in poor health, suffered a stroke, which confined him to a wheelchair. When the RKO Distribution Company withdrew its support from Van Beuren's studio and gave it to Disney in 1936, the studio closed. Van Beuren died in 1938 of a heart attack.

Terrytoons and Mighty Mouse

Paul Terry (founder of Terrytoons, in partnership with Frank Moser from 1930) is currently referred to as an example of resistance to the innovations taking place after the introduction of sound. Parsimonious and afraid of novelties, Terry was extremely diligent in his productions and in maintaining deadlines (he behaved less properly in 1936, when he managed to kick out Frank Moser in order to remain sole owner of the company). Favouring independent episodes, the producer yielded with reluctance to the fashion of eponymous characters; only in 1938 did he produce his first one-character series (featuring the silly Gandy Goose, a cross between Donald Duck and Goofy). The first colour short of his studio was released in 1938, and the bulk of production was converted to colour only in 1943. Terry's creations, however, should not be underestimated. Although not particularly attractive in graphics and animation, they often displayed good gags and a sense of irreverence, which contrasted pleasantly with the simpering of other contemporary productions. As Terry once remarked, with Disney, it was form that counted; with him, it was ideas.

Neither Kiko (1936) – a kangaroo who wanted to be a boxer and who walked like a clown, using its tail as a third leg – nor Gandy Goose were able to achieve perennial fame, but Mighty Mouse (1942), a cross between Mickey Mouse and Superman, became a success. In spite of his being little more than a unifying element for a series of gags, the character pleased the public, probably because of the contrast between his reduced dimensions and huge strength (it should be noted that Terry exclusively addressed an audience of children). Primitive mimicry did not prevent Mighty Mouse from becoming a character of comic strips or from having a long career, which culminated with TV appearances in the 1960s. The Mighty Mouse shorts had a basic structure, relying on suspense or so-called Griffith-style conclusions: In a dangerous situation, will the superhero manage to arrive in time to reestablish law and order? How will he do it?

After the attack on Pearl Harbor, in December 1941, Terrytoons contributed to America's role in the war by providing patriotic propaganda films as well as other productions commissioned by the US government.

The Fleischers: Betty Boop, Popeye, and Two Feature Films

A surprising mixture of impetuous growth and stylistic, as well as organizational, carelessness characterized the development of Fleischer Studios. Despite the fact that the organizational structure of the studio continued to rely more on improvisation than on planning, personalities such as Betty Boop and Popeye enjoyed an extraordinary success.

The film *Minnie the Moocher* (1932) became a masterpiece of American animation; Max Fleischer's technique of shooting with enhanced depth of perspective (the stereoptical process) preceded Disney's multiplane camera by two years, and his *Gulliver's Travels* (1939) was the second American feature-length animated film.

Still, the studio created a story department, headed by Bill Turner, only in 1931. When the department was finally opened, it was merely embryonic, and the animators largely continued to create their own stories. The role of a director, also, was never officially established. Dave Fleischer, who appropriated for himself the right to sign as the director of each film, in fact held the responsibility for motivating the various teams, insisting on the already outdated formula of appealing to the public with a machine-gun-like fire of gags. This inclination was, after all, his very strength; as Shamus Culhane, at that time an employee of the studio, remembers, Dave Fleischer was able to provide his crew with an ever-constant flow of new gags. From 1930 to 1932, the design of characters such as Betty Boop or the dog Bimbo underwent constant unexplained changes until their features were finally established with a model sheet. Even a technical event such as the invention of sound – which was supposed to reawaken at least the interest of the family inventor, Max – was dealt with casually, even awkwardly; for a long time, the Fleischers mixed the now standard, and more refined, practice of recording the voices first with a great deal of post-dubbed recording – which allowed Jack Mercer[41] and other voice actors to ad lib additional dialogue (hence the frequent lack of synchronized mouth movements for Popeye). Nonetheless, the studio's animation evolved.

Although animators in New York were still far, if not totally alienated, from the attention Disney paid to mimicry and action, they tried to undertake a psychological study of their characters, defining attitudes and mannerisms. Each character acquired its own typical movements, which were kept under control (as opposed to the perpetual motion of the early Fleischers' production). Betty Boop had many fathers, animator Ted Sears being the most outstanding one, and was animated sensitively and with a good dose of realism by Myron 'Grim' Natwick, a

---

[41] Mercer (1910–1984), who provided Popeye's voice for most of the series, was also an animator and a story man.

116   Chapter 12: **Walt Disney the Tycoon**

Figure 12.3 Max Fleischer with Mae Questel, Betty Boop, and Bimbo.

senior animator who had studied painting and anatomic drawing in Europe and who had become a specialist in female characters (a sort of George Cukor of animation).[42] Betty was the typical flapper of the just-ended Jazz Age. A curly-haired brunette with two deceptively naïve eyes, she wore a black dress that exposed arms, shoulders, legs, and a garter on her left thigh. Aware of her sex appeal, she was capable of flirtation as well as self-irony. Among the mice, ducks, rabbits, dogs, and children crowding the cartoons of the times, she was almost subversive. To help mitigate her personality, she was given two companions: first Ko-Ko the Clown, with his buffoonesque comedy, and the dog Bimbo.

In 1934, following the enforcement of the Code of Motion Picture Production,[43] the peppy character was drawn with more chaste clothing, and her attention was turned towards domestic tasks and to loving animals. Thus censored, Betty Boop lost much of her appeal and disappeared from the screen in 1939. A significant aspect of the character's charm was her voice, a mischievous and

---

[42] Natwick played a leading role in the animation of the title character in Disney's *Snow White* and, after his return to Fleischer Studios, of Princess Gloria in *Gulliver's Travels*.

[43] The Motion Pictures Producers and Distributors Association (MPPDA) adopted the Code (also known as the Hays Code) in 1930 but put it effectively into action in 1934. It remained in force until 1968.

childish falsetto given to her by several performers, the best of whom was Mae Questel. Betty's voice was precisely the element that prompted the singer Helen Kane (on whose personality Betty had actually been modelled) to file suit for plagiarism against the Fleischers. The case was dropped with the revelation that Kane herself had actually imitated another singer's style.

Minnie the Moocher, featuring Betty Boop and animated by the talented Willard Bowsky,[44] is probably the masterpiece among the productions of Fleischer Studios. Dense with action and atmosphere, the film is based on a song by Cab Calloway, who appears in person in the opening scene,[45] and revolves around a runaway girl, telling of the ghosts and fears she encounters during her trip into the unknown. Although the film has a conformist ending – the girl and her companion Bimbo return home – the visions and allusions to danger and sex demonstrate the rare power of a *totentanz*, a dance of death.

Popeye the Sailor (1933) marked the cinematic debut of the character created in 1929 by cartoonist Elzie Crisler Segar. Popeye represented another untraditional choice by the studio. He was an angular, grouchy, selfish character, difficult to understand, surrounded by a true menagerie of characters: the gluttonous Wimpy, the clumsy Olive Oyl, and the primitive giant Bluto. Popeye, a stone thrown into the quiet pond of melodies, symphonies, rhapsodies, and harmonies, made a splash. In 1935, a poll taken among American children surprisingly revealed that Popeye was more well liked than Mickey Mouse. His charm could probably be traced to his innocent, uninhibited use of strength: When facing a bully or danger, the sailor would eat spinach, gain a Herculean strength, and reverse the critical situation.[46] However, Popeye, too, underwent a gradual process of refinement by animator Dave Tendlar (1909–1993) and voice actor and story man Jack Mercer (who gave the character his typical mumbling speech).

Among the numerous episodes featuring Popeye, three lush specials, each on two reels and produced in colour, cannot be forgotten: *Popeye the Sailor Meets Sindbad the Sailor* (1936), *Popeye the Sailor Meets Ali Baba's Forty Thieves* (1937), and *Aladdin and his Wonderful Lamp* (1939). The second film of this group is undoubtedly the best for its inventiveness and richness of drawings and background. The refinement of the quarrelsome sailor occurred when the Fleischers surrendered to the domineering influence of Disney. In 1934, with Color Classics, they attempted to imitate the Silly Symphonies by mixing their propensity towards action, the grotesque, and the absurd with sentimentality and gracefulness. The result was a hybrid product, although some shorts did have some flavour. *Educated Fish* (1937) is the well-told adventure of a naughty little fish that hates school but runs back to it after having saved himself by the skin of his teeth from a fisherman; *Hunky and Spunky* (1938) features a mother donkey and her baby fighting against an evil miner who wants the baby to work for him. Both shorts were nominated for Academy Awards, mainly due to their animation director Myron Waldman (1908–2006), probably the most Disneyesque among the Fleischers' artists.

The same hybrid style returned in *Gulliver's Travels* (the first feature film produced by the Fleischers), dumbfounding many viewers. The path leading to this project had been long. In 1937, the Fleischers had to face a strike – one of the first strikes affecting an American studio – that ended after nine months of intransigence on both sides. The event convinced Max that it was time to leave heavily unionized New York for a more friendly area. Max had been after Paramount, which did business with his company, to back a feature for years. According to animation historian Mark Langer, he actually 'made the two-reel colour Popeyes in a fruitless attempt to demonstrate to Paramount that longer animated films would be profitable'.[47] When Disney's *Snow White and the Seven Dwarfs* came out, Paramount finally relented, although, according to Langer, there remained considerable doubt as to whether the Fleischers had the wherewithal to make a feature. With their characteristic rashness, the Fleischers moved to newly built headquarters in Florida and started to build their dream.

While some artists lacking in corporate spirit returned home to the Hudson, the others began working strenuously on *Gulliver's Travels*. The staff of artists grew beyond measure to include about 100 animators from California, among whom were the prodigal sons Shamus Culhane, Grim Natwick, Al Eugster, veteran Bill Nolan, and scriptwriter Tedd Pierce. Young people from the Miami Art School were hired for those tasks requiring less

---

[44] Born in 1907, he enlisted for the Second World War and was killed in action in France on 27 November 1944.
[45] Because of their close relationship with Paramount, the Fleischers were able to use the singers who were under contract to the company.
[46] The expedient of eating spinach, which had been only episodic in the strips, became a tradition on the screen. Crystal City, Texas, centre of the canned vegetable industry, erected a statue to Popeye.
[47] Mark Langer, e-mail message to author, 2005.

responsibility. The artists, however, not used to working together, produced mediocre results characterized by a few high points (such as the opening scene featuring Gulliver's ship being tossed by the storm) and many clumsy sequences. Gulliver, a character drawn with human features and animated with the rotoscope, stylistically clashes with the Lilliputians, who are represented by caricatures and who, in turn, contrast with the half-realistic, half-caricatured traits of Prince David and Princess Gloria. The plot itself is scarcely enthralling. Overall, the only truly original character is the muddling town crier Gabby (an entire series was later based on him). Presented to the public on 18 December 1939, *Gulliver's Travels* did rather well at the box office, even though it suffered from the closing of the European markets due to the ongoing war.

The second feature film by the Fleischers was *Mr. Bug Goes to Town* (UK title: *Hoppity Goes to Town*). The title was clearly a play on Frank Capra's *Mr. Deeds Goes to Town*. The plot revolved around various New York insects searching for a quiet home and a couple (Hoppity, a male grasshopper, and his girlfriend, Honey Bee) living their love story, opposed by the rich and cruel C. Bagley Beetle.

This second production was released only after the ruin of the studio. 'In order to get the loan to make *Mr. Bug*', writes Mark Langer,

> both Max and Dave had provided Paramount with signed, undated letters of resignation. The two brothers stopped speaking to each other over Dave's affair with his secretary, but there had been serious tension for years, as Dave felt that Max was hogging all the credit. Things came to a head when Dave insisted that he was going to compose the score to *Mr. Bug*. Max wrote a letter to Paramount saying that he could no longer work with Dave. Dave, who was still co-owner with Max of the Fleischer Studios (Paramount simply lent them production money and distributed their films) left and signed up with Columbia. This left Paramount in a position where the 50% owner of the company producing their animation was working for a competitor, and with the Fleischer Studios in administrative chaos. The letters of resignation were then produced.[48]

Storyboard artist Izzy Sparber, business manager Sam Buchwald, writer-director Dan Gordon, and Seymour Kneitel (1908–1964, Max Fleischer's son-in-law and one of the leading animators) went to New York and, after several meetings with Paramount brass, worked out a new agreement to bring the studio, reorganized as 'Famous' (but not owned by Paramount until 1954) back to its original seat. Gordon left shortly after. Famous continued producing films featuring Popeye and the Fleischers' newest star, Superman.

Max and Dave Fleischer still attempted to survive in the entertainment world; however, they never again achieved the success they once had.

Warner Bros.

After their defection from Disney and a subsequent separation from Mintz, Hugh Harman (Pagosa Springs, Colorado, 31 August 1908–Beverly Hills, 25 November 1982) and Rudolf Ising (Kansas City, 7 August 1903–Newport Beach, California, 18 July 1992) decided to work on their own. Having invented a character as similar as possible to Mickey, an African-American boy named Bosko, the two artists made a pilot film entitled *Bosko the Talk-Ink Kid* and tried to market it. Their best bidder was Leon Schlesinger, chief of Pacific Art and Title, a company specializing in film title cards. Schlesinger also enjoyed a good relationship with Warner Bros., as they were distant relatives; he also had helped them financially at the time of their daring conversion to sound. Schlesinger drew up a distribution contract and instantly became a producer of animated films. After Disney, Schlesinger (1884–1949) was probably the most farsighted American producer of his field. Although his employees described him as a bland person, detached and mercenary, he deserves the credit for having established an extraordinary group of artists in the course of several years and for having managed it without hindering their fantasy.

Initially, Harman and Ising were put in charge of the films. In 1930, they began the series Looney Tunes, featuring Bosko, who was soon accompanied by a girl named Honey and by the dog Bruno (the vowels of whose name remind one of Pluto). Although Bosko lacked both personality and mimicry, Harman and Ising themselves had the makings of entertainment moguls: Their ambition did not stop with the creation of a standard product, and their sense of comicality went far beyond the usual tricks of animation. The two became successful only after they quit their jobs at Warner's in the middle of 1933, by which

---

[48] Mark Langer, e-mail message to author, 2005.

time Harman had already left his mark on the highly professional Looney Tunes and Ising had done the same in the sister series Merrie Melodies (created along the lines of the Silly Symphonies, featuring music that the mother company had already launched in its musicals).

Harman and Ising's request for larger investments in the quality of products led to a clash with Schlesinger. The two artists left, taking Bosko with them. They made a couple of shorts for Van Beuren; then, MGM offered them an advantageous distribution contract. Schlesinger turned to two directors at Disney, Jack King and Tom Palmer,[49] but he soon got rid of them, hiring instead two newcomers with promise, Tex Avery and Frank Tashlin. He also promoted chief animator Friz Freleng to director. A new character (a boy named Buddy who was nothing more than a white version of Bosko) temporarily filled the vacuum left in the production.

In the long run, the studio's most profitable idea was the contemporaneous launching of a series of new characters, some of which were short lived, but others became long-lasting stars of the animated world. From 1935 to 1940, Porky Pig, Egghead, Elmer Fudd, Daffy Duck, and Bugs Bunny made their debut in some of the best films of comic cinema. It would be misleading to attempt to determine the individual creators or the precise dates of birth of these characters, since they developed over the course of years, undergoing many alterations in their physical aspects, manners, and personalities. Porky was a stammering piglet, innocent but not without vanity, who was doomed to be a victim of circumstance and of the other protagonists. He soon became a second fiddle to Daffy Duck, a black duckling characterized (in his first phase, which lasted until the post-war era) by a frenzy and an impudence that made him the prototype of the scatterbrain, as described in Preston Blair's manual. Daffy's lack of cruelty made him likable: His continual pestering of others was just a consequence of his predictably illogical response to whatever situation he was in that determined his every action and which viewers came to recognize and accept. On the contrary, Egghead was a human, like Elmer Fudd,[50] the grumpy, foolish adversary of Bugs Bunny.[51]

Finally, Bugs Bunny was perhaps the most accomplished animated version of what nineteenth-century Jewish comedy theatre (mother of much humour in American cinema) defined as a *schnorrer* – the loner, characterized by facile speech, a mocking coldness, and the irresistible ability to dazzle others with his shrewdness and chatter. As far as his acting was concerned, Bugs Bunny mastered the use of the slow burn – the comical convention in which a character reacts to the most serious provocations with faultless composure. When facing death, the bunny toys with the ever-present carrot while amiably asking, 'What's up, doc?' When provoked, he clarifies: 'Of course, you realize that this means war' before counter-attacking and zeroing in on his enemy. All things considered, Bugs Bunny is a sort of frame-by-frame Groucho Marx.

Tex Avery[52]

Frederick Bean 'Tex' Avery (Taylor, Texas, 26 February 1908–Burbank, California, 26 August 1980) subverted the rules and meanings of animated pictures as soon as he joined Warner Bros. After renouncing his early ambitions as a comic strip artist, this young, talented entertainer started at Mintz's and spent a few years (1929–1935) working for Walter Lantz at Universal, first as an inbetweener and then as an animator: 'He was a hard worker', Lantz said.

> He was naturally talented and had a deep sense of humour. He was a cruel joker. Everyone created the gags, but Tex was the best and funniest of all. He soon became an excellent animator, but that wasn't enough, he wanted to be a director.[53]

---

[49] This Tom Palmer was an Italian-American New Yorker by the original surname of Pipolo and should not be confused with the homonymous comic book artist of the 1960s.

[50] The appearance of both characters – short, round, bulb-nosed – is very similar, and many people, including this writer, were convinced that Egghead had metamorphosed into Elmer Fudd. However, reliable scholar Mike Barrier writes: 'Actually, no . . . Egghead and Elmer were always distinct characters' (e-mail message to author, summer 2011).

[51] In spite of its nickname 'Bunny', the character is more of a hare than a rabbit. Allegedly, 'Bugs' comes from the nickname of Ben 'Bugs' Hardaway, a respected Schlesinger animator, writer, and director. The studio's character designer, a Canadian by the name of Charles Thorson, drew the rodent and wrote 'Bugs's Bunny' on the model sheet.

[52] By Federico Rossin.

[53] *Tex Avery: un univers en folie*, documentary, written and narrated by Patrick Brion, Warner Home Video, France, 2003, DVD.

Avery worked mainly on the Oswald the Rabbit series and probably directed some of them. Leon Schlesinger hired him almost by chance and put him in charge of a small team of animators who were too rebellious to collaborate with their colleagues: among them, Chuck Jones, Bob Clampett, and Bobe Cannon, who would later have brilliant careers. The small, wild bunch settled into a cottage, detached from the main body of the studio, which was renamed 'Termite Terrace', and started working on their creations. Clampett said of the building: 'The wood crunched and you could pass your hand through the walls.'[54] Even though Avery did not reach the height of his accomplishments until he was at MGM, it was at Warner's that he developed his original style. A genius at exaggerating and turning things upside down, he pushed the techniques of deformation of a character's physiognomy to their limits, and he often used a parody of an existing film or a film genre as a structure around which he could spread all his imaginativeness. His exploding gags undermine the conventions of the main filmic genres, as in his *Detouring America* (1939), *Cross-Country Detours* (1940), and *Aviation Vacation* (1941), in which he made fun of the tired movie travelogue format, pairing an archetypical pompous, offscreen narrator with crazy gags and an iconoclastic shattering of the 'fourth wall'. For Tex Avery, the world in itself is crazy, and so are human beings and animals: *The Isle of Pingo Pongo* (1938), *Believe It or Else* (1939), and *The Land of the Midnight Fun* (1939) are perfect examples of these irrational mock documentaries.

Musicals (*I Love to Singa*, 1936) and gangster films (*Thugs with Dirty Mugs*, 1939) were two other targets, but his favourite parody was dedicated to fairy tales. He started at Warner Bros. with *Little Red Walking Hood* (1937) and *Cinderella Meets Fella* (1938) and made a first masterpiece with *The Bear's Tale* (1940), in which he mixed and shook together *Goldilocks* and *Little Red Riding Hood*, starting a deconstructive and self-reflexive fairy tale production that would flourish later at MGM.

Although he made many cartoons featuring Porky Pig, Daffy Duck, and Elmer Fudd and significantly shaped each one of them, Avery was not very interested in continuing characters: His preference was for 'single', non-serial films. Except for Droopy, Avery's personae were short lived (one of them, the crazy Screwy Squirrel, was even killed on the screen). Furthermore, Avery's dogs, cats, canaries, bears, and wolves were not markedly different from the graphics of other characters of the same species. He gave the definitive personality and details (the 'What's up, doc?' catchphrase, the carrot, etc.) to Bugs Bunny in *A Wild Hare* (1940) but he himself stated:

> I've always felt that what you did with a character was even more important than the character itself. Bugs Bunny could have been a bird. . . . It isn't what you see on the screen, it's what they say and do that builds up their personality.[55]

The important elements were not so much the characters as their actions. In other words, what counted were pure comedy and the timing and rhythm of the gags. Avery distinguished himself even from his most eminent colleagues, such as Hanna and Barbera, Clampett, Jones, and Freleng, by rejecting generalities and by considering every film as a work in itself, though strictly connected to the artist's opus. He was the one-man band of animation at Warner Bros. But he also had the privilege of working with other great artists: Carl Stalling, who composed the music of the cartoons using experimental pastiches and avant-garde musical textures, and Mel Blanc, who was in charge of character voices and lent his incredibly flexible throat to Porky Pig, Daffy Duck, and Bugs Bunny. Later, at MGM, Avery worked with Scott Bradley, another master of mixing sounds and noises together and switching from one tune to another.

In 1941, Tex Avery left Warner Bros. and, after a short period at Paramount, joined MGM, where he stayed until 1955. Most of his Warner Bros. cartoons, according to Warners cartoon

---

[54] *Tex Avery: un univers en folie*, documentary, written and narrated by Patrick Brion, Warner Home Video, France, 2003, DVD.

[55] Joe Adamson, *Tex Avery: King of Cartoons*, Da Capo Press, New York, 1975, p. 162.

historian Greg Ford, are now considered 'as privileged "flash-forwards" or preparatory "teasers" for the remarkable series of MGM cartoons to shortly follow' and which are 'more valuable for the ways in which their madcap structures and surrealist juxtapositions anticipate the films that he would later direct at MGM'.[56] In 1942, after seven years at Warner Bros., Avery's style had become astounding and ultra-rapid. At Warner's, he learned lessons that he would be able to apply at MGM:

> I think I started that faster trend. We started filling in more gags. . . . I found out the eye can register an action in five frames of film. Five frames of film at twenty-four a second to register something, from the screen to your eye to the brain. I found out, if I wanted something just to barely be seen, five frames was all it needed. What would ruin it would be two or three seconds of film.

Like Warner Bros., MGM had its own animation department, headed by Fred Quimby who, according to director Michael Lah, was 'strictly a businessman, [who] knew nothing about stories or gags or whatnot', preferring the comedy of Hanna and Barbera. 'Tex's arrival was like an avalanche', said Lah.[57]

His first MGM film was *Blitz Wolf* (1942): an explosive anti-Nazi propaganda cartoon employing the old fairy tale of the three little pigs as a dummy plot. Avery portrayed Hitler as a wolf, a character that would become a star of his films and, through speed, pushed the gags to their limits. His histrionic skills and subversive humour emerge most strongly in the six fairy tale parodies featuring, in the Red Riding Hood role, a voluptuous, red-headed pin-up girl who performs in front of a lascivious wolf, driving him crazy with sexual excitement (*Red Hot Riding Hood*, 1943; *The Shooting of Dan McGoo*, 1945; *Swing Shift Cinderella*, 1945; *Wild and Woolfy*, 1945; *Uncle Tom's Cabaña*, 1947; and *Little Rural Riding Hood*, 1949). The sexy girl, a human character beautifully animated by Preston Blair (*Pinocchio, Fantasia*), contrasts strongly with the wild and herky-jerky behaviour imposed on the horny wolf: His eyes pop out of his head, his tongue rolls out on the floor, his jaws drop open, he chews his paws out of sexual hunger, and he literally falls to pieces. The setting of these fairy tales is often a sparkling big city full of luxurious night clubs and overrun with hyper-long limousines: Avery introduces a refreshing modernity and an adult vision of sex in the cartoon world – until then, almost completely dominated by a childlike imagery.

> I guess I leaned more toward an adult audience, even with the early Bugs Bunnys. I tried to do something I thought I would laugh at if I were to see it on the screen, rather than worry about 'Will a ten-year-old laugh at this?' Because we couldn't top Disney, and we knew he had the kid following, so we went for adults and young people.[58]

Self-reflexive gags were other means he used. *Red Hot Riding Hood*'s first scene, for example, is a comical false start: The wolf, Red, and Red's grandma refuse to reenact the same fairy tale for the umpteenth time. By affirming directly to the camera that they are cartoon characters, they point out to the director – and thus to us spectators – that what we are watching is nothing but a film. Avery made similar gags to the ones he had invented at Warner Bros. in order to include the viewers, to break the suspension of disbelief, and to undermine linear narrative: For example, his characters may interact with a spectator in the movie theatre (who is depicted as a shadow silhouette against the screen) – see *Daffy Duck and Egghead*, 1938; *Cinderella Meets Fella*, 1938; and *A Feud There Was*, 1938. The famous gag of an animated hair bobbing up and down in the projection gate until one of the characters finally grabs it and pulls it out was used in both the Warner and MGM years (*Aviation Vacation*, 1941; *Magical Maestro*, 1952). Another alienating gag is the onscreen imposition of road signs and other labels to make verbal commentaries ('Corny Gag, Isn't

---

[56] Greg Ford, 'Tex Avery Program Notes', in Zagreb Animafest festival catalogue, Zagreb, 1978.
[57] Joe Adamson, *Tex Avery: King of Cartoons*, Da Capo Press, New York, 1975, p. 167.
[58] Joe Adamson, *Tex Avery: King of Cartoons*, Da Capo Press, New York, 1975, p. 187.

It?' says a sign commenting on another sign shown just before): With this, writes film reviewer Ronnie Scheib, Avery underscored 'the director-audience complicity in awareness of the cartooniness of the cartoon'.[59]

Avery's MGM characters run so quickly when they hunt each other that they sometimes trespass the frame limits, letting us see the sprocket holes of the film (*Dumb-Hounded*, 1943); they even happen to cross a drawn line announcing the end of Technicolor and fall into a black-and-white world (*Lucky Ducky*, 1948): In his intellectual understanding of cinematographic fiction, Avery was second only to Buster Keaton and his *Sherlock Jr*. He broke almost every Hollywood filmic convention and dissolved most of the classical narrative rules of the screen. As a prophet of the most fantastic paradoxes, he created a world in which all that is impossible hangs, without explanation, like a perpetually hovering cloud. Like Mel Brooks a few decades later, Avery counted on excessive laughter, considering it supreme comicality, the most beautiful monument to liberating mirth.

One of the dangers of discussing Avery's filmmaking is to intellectualize this seemingly spontaneous, popular artist. In fact, the apparent lack of sentimental, political, or ideological content in his work forces this critic to consider the artist as he actually was, an extraordinary explorer and manipulator of filmic and comic languages. Avery's poetics is laughter itself, a simple content expressed in a language that is groundbreaking even today. Undoubtedly, Avery belongs to that very limited group of movie artists (Chaplin, Keaton, Laurel and Hardy, the Marx Brothers) who built the twentieth century's visual comedy from scratch, inventing procedures and styles that have since become common currency. Instead of focusing on stereotypes as the basic elements of serial movies, Avery preferred to touch on the commonplace – which he overturned and used as an occasion for the absurd. For instance, in *Symphony in Slang* (1951), a man arriving in heaven tells the story of his life using slang expressions and metaphors, such as 'the dress fit her like a glove', which are illustrated literally.[60]

An easy critical expedient is to depict Avery as an anti-Disney – violent and surrealistic, just as Disney was sweet and realistic. In fact, Avery learned from Disney's lesson and brought it to completion. Disney created an art grounded in a believable reality, in a solid credibility: Avery adopted this foundation *in toto* in order to subvert its logical, physical, and metaphysical laws: The existence of a Disneyesque reality made it possible for Avery to overturn it completely. In Averyland, there is no gravity, no causality, and no time-space continuity as we know them: Everything is submitted to a shock that dissolves every psychological and narrative expectation, a shock that sets a new reality made of crazy associations and crashing speed, anarchic violations, and astonishing reversals. Disney always tried to adopt an animation style made of continuity and fluency of movements and gestures because he wanted animated films to be as realistic as live-action films. Avery started from this point, introducing (according to Ronnie Scheib) 'a radical discontinuity in the visible process of production and allowing the audience to experience movement and change as an open process rather than as an irreversible organic becoming'.[61] It was thanks to the combination of these two artists' approaches that personality animation – cinema with drawn actors – came to be identified with the Golden Age of American comic animation. Certainly, Avery's drawn characters were not merely graphic signs, but great actors and mimes, despite their living in a distraught, exaggerated world: They grow bigger and bigger (*King Size Canary*, 1947) or shrink (*Big Heel Watha*, 1944); they are blown to pieces and then reconstituted (*Garden Gopher*, 1950); or they simply disappear from the screen (*The Screwy Truant*, 1945). No moral precept is possible for them because they are driven by hunger (*What's Buzzin' Buzzard?*, 1943), sexual desire (the tales with Red), and paranoia (*Northwest Hounded Police*, 1946).

---

[59] Ronnie Scheib, 'Tex Arcana: The Cartoons of Tex Avery', in Gerald and Danny Peary (eds.) *The American Animated Cartoon: A Critical Anthology*, Dutton, New York, 1980, p. 119.
[60] The gimmick was brilliant, although not new: None other than Émile Cohl had inaugurated it.
[61] Ronnie Scheib, 'Tex Arcana: The Cartoons of Tex Avery', in Gerald and Danny Peary (eds.) *The American Animated Cartoon: A Critical Anthology*, Dutton, New York, 1980, p. 114.

In the early 1950s, competition from television and the dismantling of the old vertical studio monopoly (production–distribution–exhibition) confronted MGM with a new economic crisis: The animation department was closed. After leaving MGM in 1953, Avery worked for a few months with his old employer, Walter Lantz, for whom he directed four good cartoons and created a new character (the penguin Chilly Willy). Later, he worked on TV commercials and spent his last years in the script department at Hanna-Barbera Productions.

Bob Clampett[62]

Bob Clampett (San Diego, California, 8 May 1913– Detroit, Michigan, 2 May 1984), together with Tex Avery, gave the Looney Tunes their looniness. Despite all the efforts he made to promote his image, he has not yet received the recognition he deserves.

As a child, Clampett drew comics, some of which were published. He was also interested in puppets and put up some puppet shows for the kids of his neighbourhood. He joined Warner Bros. Cartoons in 1931. In 1935, he was assigned, with Chuck Jones, as animator to Avery's unit at 'Termite Terrace'. In 1937, he was promoted to director and started making low-budget Looney Tunes starring Porky Pig (whom he claimed he created in 1935). In 1941, when Avery left Warner's, Clampett took over his unit.

Clampett was a versatile talent who practiced every aspect of his art: directing, drawing, writing, creating gags, voice acting, and even writing music. He had a passion for all forms of popular culture. His cartoons constantly refer to movie stars, radio programs (notably Orson Welles's *War of the Worlds* in *Kitty Kornered*, 1946); comic books (*Dick Tracy* in *The Great Piggy Bank Robbery*, 1946); and jazz (*Coal Black and de Sebben Dwarfs*, 1943; *Tin Pan Alley Cats*, 1943). Very often they are parodies. *A Corny Concerto* (1943) is a spoof of Disney's *Fantasia*. *What Price Porky* (1938) is about a mock World War I.

It could even be said that all his films are parodies, since they make fun of the cartoon conventions on which they pretend to be based. Clampett's Looney Tunes are spoofs of the Looney Tunes. Their characters, like Avery's, frequently display an awareness of being in a cartoon – a self-consciousness best exemplified by Bugs Bunny who, in *What's Cookin' Doc?* (1944), proclaims that he deserves an Academy Award for his past performances.

A striking aspect of Clampett's work is its youthful exuberance. He doesn't hide a willingness to show sexual desire and to make more or less disguised dirty jokes as often as possible. There is a meanness that makes him a predecessor of the 'sick comedians' of the 1950s. He is the creator of Tweety who, in his hands, is an angelically sadistic baby bird. And there is, like Avery again, an eagerness to break all rules, a passionate yearning for a freedom, even anarchy, which gives the feeling that anything can happen.

More often than not, it does happen: In his very first Looney Tune, *Porky's Badtime Story* (1937), Porky's garage is ripped inside out like a glove by the speed of the car coming out of it. Clampett's early masterpiece, the surrealistic *Porky in Wackyland* (1938), is described by Leonard Maltin as 'an eye-popping tribute to the unlimited horizons of the animated cartoon, a perfect example of what the medium could do with just some imagination and a lot of talent'.[63]

Clampett does not care about credibility, nor does he give too much attention to the coherence of personalities. Sometimes his hero becomes downright mean: In *Hare Ribbin'* (1944), Bugs Bunny kills a dog by shooting him in the mouth (this scene was not released, but the director's cut is available).

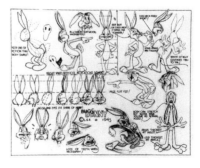

Figure 12.4 Bugs Bunny model sheet, 1943. Model sheet drawn by Bob McKimson.

---

[62] By Silvano Ghiringhelli.
[63] Leonard Maltin, *Of Mice and Magic: A History of American Animated Cartoons*, New American Library, New York, 1987, p. 237.

Sometimes the roles are inverted and the persecutor is persecuted, like Bugs Bunny in *Falling Hare* (1943).

As a director, he gave his animators total freedom (thus obtaining from them their best work). As a consequence, there are contrasts in the animation of different scenes, or even within one scene, since he would sometimes switch from one animator to another in the middle of it. This is obvious in the colour cartoons, with the work of Bob McKimson and Rod Scribner: While McKimson's style is solid, credible, realistic, Scribner's is wild, made of extreme exaggerations and deformations. (It is noteworthy that Scribner's work for other directors is much more mild mannered.)

The heterogeneity of Clampett's cartoons generates an exhilarating sense of freedom, but the overall effect is not always as convincing as individual scenes.

Clearly, it is no easy task to mould ill-assorted elements into a meaningful whole. Apart from some early masterpieces, it is mainly in the cartoons he directed during his last year at Warner's that he found the right balance and attained a truly convincing aesthetical coherence.

But Clampett's main contribution to the art of animation stems from his will to expand the expressiveness of bodies and to transcend physical limitations. For Avery, he animated Daffy Duck's crazy ballet in *Porky's Duck Hunt* (1937), and that wild style became the trademark of his own cartoons. He expanded on the old 'rubber hose' animation, and his characters literally have a rubbery complexion – in *Porky's Tire Trouble* (1939), a dog drinks a 'rubberizing solution' that makes his body elastic, deformable, bouncy; in *The Daffy Doc* (1938), an artificial lung causes Daffy's and Porky's body parts to inflate like balloons. Animation director John Kricfalusi writes: 'His characters were living[,] throbbing vessels of cartoon protoplasm.'[64]

The Great Piggy Bank Robbery (1946) epitomizes the qualities of Clampett's cartoons. It is focused on Daffy Duck and his obsession with Dick Tracy. The whole cartoon represents Daffy's mindscape, from the disquieting introduction in an obliquely shaped rural landscape to the surreal hallucination in the gangster's hideout. It is masterfully directed, with exquisite timing, excellent use of sound and music, and such unsettling devices as unusual angles and jump cuts. The animation is appropriately delirious. Daffy's beak suffers absurd deformations whenever he speaks. Rubber Head, a villain with an eraser head, literally erases him. Daffy's body parts separately squiggle out of an amorphous bunch of villains in which they were caught and recompose him.

Clampett left Warner's in 1945. The following year, he directed a single cartoon for Republic Pictures: *It's a Grand Old Nag*. In 1949, he started working for television, for which he created a very successful puppet show, *Time for Beany*, which featured Cecil, the Seasick Sea Serpent (a puppet character he had invented as a kid), and also produced an animated series based on the character. He continued to work in television for the rest of his career.

Friz Freleng (Kansas City, Missouri, 21 August 1906–Los Angeles, 26 May 1995) was already a veteran in the 1940s, having started with Disney in the years of silent cinema; in 1929, he returned to his hometown to work in advertising, then went back to California to join Harman and Ising. He worked for Schlesinger and, briefly, for MGM. In 1940, he returned to Warner's. He had all the skills of the great cartoon directors: a sense of comedy and timing, a taste for the characters' personalities, and experience as an entertainer.

As with Chuck Jones, Freleng's golden years came after the war. The years between 1942 and 1946 were characterized by a sort of 'republic' of equals, where each director gave his best, but where no one in particular emerged as a leading personality. Leon Schlesinger, who had always maintained a low-wage policy, compensated his crew with fast careers and the most complete freedom at each stage of creation. With the same foresight, Schlesinger gave his artists, animators, and designers the support of two experts in the use of

---

[64] John Kricfalusi, 'Porky and Daffy – Innovative Wackiness – The Double Bounce Butt Walk', John K. Stuff!, 5 March 2008, http://johnkstuff.blogspot.com/2008/03/porky-and-daffy.html.

sound: musician Carl Stalling and voice actor Mel Blanc (1908–1989). The latter, gifted in making a surprising number of voices with unexpected caricaturistic powers, gave Warner's animals and people much of their personalities and liveliness.

Of all major companies, Warner Bros. served as a Rooseveltian stronghold, reflecting, in its films, the social and political spirit of the New Deal. With the advent of World War II, the company increased its political involvement, taking sides even in its cartoons. Freleng's *Daffy the Commando* (1943) and *Herr Meets Hare* (1944) and Tashlin's *Plane Daffy* (1944) mocked the Nazis, while Freleng's *Bugs Bunny Nips the Nips* (1944) was a ferociously anti-Japanese film. The studio also produced films on behalf of the US government. A series of short comedies (three to four minutes long) featuring Private Snafu were exclusively directed to a military audience.

Although this company's films were made by prominent filmmakers and thus often represent excellent creative work, they were also a series of productions in which quantity counted at least as much as quality: It was never the studio's ambition to produce a masterpiece. A few shorts – e.g. *Gold Diggers of '49* (1936), *A Wild Hare* (1940), and *Coal Black and de Sebben Dwarfs* (1943) – are notable for historical or artistic reasons. The first film, which marks Tex Avery's debut, shows the artist's developing style; with the second film, Bugs Bunny's personality was substantially forged; the third, directed by Bob Clampett (and despite racial stereotypes startling to us today), was indeed a good film, a sort of animated *Hallelujah!* starring an all-black cast.

On the whole, however, series production, having existed for decades in animation and in the other fields of mass culture, became the consciously adopted genre by Warner's – as well as MGM – and each episode belonged to a saga without beginning or end. Recurring themes, such as the one-on-one chase or fight (hunter and hare, cat and mouse, cat and canary, and so on) were no longer straitjackets but, rather, aspects of a total narrative genre consisting of skilled variations on its own formula. A limited number of mannerisms and idiosyncrasies of the characters were manipulated, in a virtuoso manner, within a unity of time, place, and action. Despite a few exceptions (above all, the irrepressible Tex Avery), the style of each film was established more by the animated protagonist than by the artist-director. This substantial homogenization, another characteristic of mass production, emerged not only when economic pressure exerted influence on freedom of expression – as was the case for Warner Bros.' animated films.

Carl W. Stalling, Musical Animator

The first movie I ever saw was *The Great Train Robbery*. I saw it in a tent at a street fair in Lexington, around 1903. It made such an impression on me that from then on I had only one desire in life: to be connected with the movies in some way.[65]

Carl Stalling was born in Lexington, Missouri, on 10 November 1891.[66] As a young man he moved to Kansas City, where he got his start as a pianist in the silent-era movie theatres. Here, in the early 1920s, he met Walt Disney, who was impressed by his skill in improvising and in irreverently combining jazz, classical music, and folk songs. In 1928, Disney hired Stalling, who signed the score of *Steamboat Willie* and, in 1929, gave birth to the Silly Symphony series with the masterful *Skeleton Dance*.[67] In 1930, the musician left to wander from one studio to another.

He settled in 1936 at Schlesinger's, working on the Warner Bros. cartoons along with such directors as Friz Freleng, Bob Clampett, and Chuck Jones. He would stay there until 1958.

By 1936, Stalling had developed an animator-like mentality: that one second is a long time, with twenty-four whole frames to fill. Some seconds of a march plus some seconds of jazz plus some seconds of a symphony, seasoned with sound effects[68] and, obviously, tightly connected with the action: This

---

[65] Mike Barrier, 'An Interview with Carl Stalling', *Funnyworld*, Vol. 13, Summer 1971. *The Great Train Robbery* was directed in 1903 by Edwin S. Porter.
[66] According to other sources, in 1888.
[67] As we have already pointed out, some sources wrongly reported that the score was based on Camille Saint Saëns's *Danse Macabre*. It is actually a foxtrot combined with a quotation from Edvard Grieg's *The March of the Dwarfs*.
[68] The sound effects man was Treg Brown (1899–1984), who was given an Academy Award in 1965 for the sound effects of the live-action film *The Great Race* directed by Blake Edwards.

was Carl Stalling's recipe. Working for Warner's was easier than for almost anybody else, as the company owned a large library of songs that the musician could use as he pleased.

Despite his inclination for pastiche, most of his output was original, and as Stalling later said: 'It had to be, because you had to match the music to the action, unless it was singing or something like that'.[69] In fact, Chuck Jones pointed out, '[his music] was never ornamental or merely supportive to the imagery, but integral'.[70] His originality lies in the fact that he just behaved as an animator: He squashed and stretched the pentagram, distorted, emphasized – in short allowed himself all the liberties that would have scandalized a 'decent' composer.

Obviously what he created was film music, functional to action, story, characters, and mood. But it was music, full stop, too.

'Stalling didn't just break the rules', wrote Jason Ankeny, 'he made them irrelevant . . . Stalling introduced the avant-garde into the mainstream, and as popular music continues to diversify and hybridize, his stature as a pioneer rightfully continues to grow'.[71]

Pierre Schaeffer, the French founder of *Musique concrète*, wrote in 1948: 'We have called our music concrete because it is composed by pre-existent elements, borrowed from any kind of acoustic material, either sound or traditional music'. Without having ever been praised as an innovator, Carl Stalling had been doing just this for twenty years.

Actually, wrote composer John Zorn:

> Stalling was one of the most revolutionary visionaries in American music – especially in his conception of time. In following the visual logic of screen action rather than the traditional rules of musical form (development, theme and variations, etc.), Stalling created a radical compositional arc unprecedented in the history.[72]

This master, whose lesson few people understood and almost none learned, died near Los Angeles on 29 November 1972.

Metro-Goldwyn-Mayer: Cat, Mouse, and Tex

From 1930 to 1934, Ub Iwerks supplied animated short subjects to Metro. In 1934, he was supplanted by Harman and Ising, who launched the Happy Harmonies series (which lasted only a few years) and reintroduced, albeit not too convincingly, their star from Warner's, Bosko. The two artists' success with Metro lasted three years and was due particularly to the strong personality and intellectual ambitions of Harman. Then, what had happened at Warner's occurred again: The artists' financial requests for a work that would compete with Disney were considered excessive. As the most important film company, MGM at this point felt that it was able to afford its own department of animation without having to depend on small external production companies. Fred Quimby, an administrator with little originality but a good sense of organization, was named chief of the new department (1937).

As a newcomer to animation, Quimby groped for a few years until, in 1939, he played it safe by returning to Harman and Ising, who had formed their own studio and were basically freelancing. In 1939, Harman directed *Peace on Earth*, a 'serious', pacifist film featuring a Christmas night, honoured only by animals since the humans on the earth had exterminated each other in wars. The film was very well received by critics and audiences; it was even rumoured that Harman was being considered for the Nobel Peace Prize. Meanwhile, Ising was able to satisfy his old ambition of creating a truly popular character. *The Bear That Couldn't Sleep* (1939) featured the bear Barney, whose popularity would last for the next four or five years. In 1940, Ising became the first, after his former employer Walt Disney, to win an Oscar for animation. The award-winning film, entitled *The Milky Way*, was a fable taking place in space – a praiseworthy film, but overly drenched with the mannerist loveliness dictated by the taste of the times. The entertainment industry phase of Harman and Ising's careers ended around 1942 when Ising was named officer in charge of animation at Fort Roach (Hal Roach Studios). For the next decades, the duo concentrated on training and educational films, going into semi-retirement by the mid-1950s.

---

[69] Mike Barrier, 'An Interview with Carl Stalling', *Funnyworld*, Vol. 13, Summer 1971.
[70] Joe Carrol, 'Sound Strategies', *Animatrix*, No. 7, 1993, p. 36.
[71] Jason Ankeny, Album Review, *The Carl Stalling Project – Music from Warner Bros. Cartoons 1936–1958*, Apple iTunes, accessed 15 March 2012, http://itunes.apple.com/us/album/the-carl-stalling-project/id272506574.
[72] John Zorn, *Carl Stalling: An Appreciation*, liner notes, *The Carl Stalling Project*, Vol. 1, Warner Bros. 26027, 1990, CD.

The year 1940 was important for Metro, as it marked the beginning of the adventures of the cat, Tom, and the mouse, Jerry, in the film *Puss Gets the Boot*. The primary credit for the movie rested with two young animators who had received their training inside the studio: William Hanna and Joseph Barbera. Hanna (Melrose, New Mexico, 14 July 1910–North Hollywood, 22 March 2001) studied journalism and engineering. He moved to California in order to find employment as an engineer. As times were hard, he looked into other fields and found a job with Harman and Ising. Barbera (New York, 24 March 1911–Studio City, California, 18 December 2006) was a bank employee who soon tired of his job and tried his hand in comic strips. Attracted to animation by the charm of Disney's *Skeleton Dance*, he worked as an apprentice for Van Beuren when, in 1937, he moved to the promised land of California.

Hanna and Barbera worked in the same studio for two years before deciding to form a creative team. The success of their first film strongly influenced their careers and, for the next fifteen years, the two artists recounted all possible variations of the struggle between the cat and the mouse, winning seven Oscars. Later, they founded and directed one of the world's most gigantic companies of animated television series. In the beginning, the grey cat Tom differed greatly from the red mouse Jerry. Tom was ferocious and violent; Jerry represented shrewdness opposed to brutality. Later, when the two characters were more developed, the two roles mingled, and Tom and Jerry spent much of their time attempting to hurt each other as much as they could. As a general rule, Tom was the one who suffered the most, since he was not able to hide his wickedness behind an angelic mask, as did the small and apparently defenceless mouse. In the end, as with all the pairs of implacable enemies who are incapable of exterminating each other, a sort of solidarity was established: The existence of the one appeared justified by the other, and the reciprocal attempted murder seemed to become a precious common heritage.

The team, soon directed by Hanna and Barbera, achieved Disney-like perfection. Barbera would write the stories, make sketches, and invent gags, while Hanna was chiefly responsible for the direction. Together, the two would orchestrate an actual pantomime for each short for the benefit of their animators and would later be extremely demanding in quality. The series reached its highest level of excellence when its creators found themselves in competition with Tex Avery, who had moved to Metro in 1942. In Avery's work, violence had always been instrumental in an unlimited vision of comicality; its characteristic tendency towards paradox, therefore, combined harmoniously with every other possible exaggeration. Hanna and Barbera captured and reproduced this same concept but concentrated it into the smallest situations. (In fact, the entire saga of Tom and Jerry rarely went beyond the confines of the dining room and the formal living room.) So much violence was related in the explicit rule that in animation any catastrophe can be solved in a few frames; Tom (almost always the victim) was thus massacred, twisted, flattened, and worked into every conceivable shape. In the long run, the fun disappeared and the formula became mechanical due to the characters' substantially poor acting.

Tashlin the Wanderer

Frank Tashlin (Weekhawken, New Jersey, 19 February 1913–Hollywood, 5 May 1972) was born into a French-German family (the Taschleins). At the age of fifteen, he found a job as an errand boy with Fleischer Studios in New York and later worked as an animator for Van Beuren. Finally, attracted by the Mecca of cinema and the California sun, he moved to Hollywood (a spurious anecdote recounted that he arrived there on the most rainy day of the year without a raincoat).

Once in Los Angeles, Tashlin covered a lot of ground. From 1933 to 1935, Tashlin joined Leon Schlesinger at Warner's, after which he performed a brief stint with Ub Iwerks. He returned to work for Schlesinger and was promoted to director. From 1938 to 1941, he worked for Disney. He moved to Screen Gems and later, for the third time, he returned to Warner's. About 1945, Tashlin quit animation to become a scriptwriter for live-action feature comedies. Finally, in 1951, he became a film director. His works include *Son of Paleface* (1951), starring Bob Hope; *Artists and Models* (1955), starring Jerry Lewis; and *The Man from the Diner's Club* (1963), with Danny Kaye. In addition, Tashlin drew his own comic strip in 1933 ('Van Boring' was a caricature of his ex-employer Amadée Van Beuren) and wrote and illustrated four comic books.

Tashlin has yet to be honoured with the esteem he deserves; undoubtedly, his fragmentary career makes it difficult to single out a common thread in his work. Still, some elements of his style emerge constantly: a preference for fast, 'cinematographic' editing and difficult framing; a slapstick-like inspiration (it was believed that Tashlin secretly studied the old films of Keaton and his peers); an ironic perspective of everyday superficiality; and, finally, a predisposition (as had Avery) to disclosing the filmic facade by involving the spectator directly. A moment of fame came to him towards the end of the 1950s through his work with Jerry Lewis. Usually, his live-action films were affected by his training as an animator as much as his animated films showed his ambitions as a movie director. Tashlin was a well-rounded filmmaker – one of the few; he was also one of the very few artists who left a mark in each field in which he worked.

The American Avant-Garde

As European cinema absorbed Disney's teachings and tried to appeal to a larger public, European-inspired experimental animation landed in the United States and found room to grow within the independent, non-conformist cinema. These filmed live-action experiments – similar, in their non-conformity, to those of the French movements of the 1920s, were to prepare the road for the 'second avant-garde' of the 1940s, with Maya Deren, Gregory Markopoulos, Curtis Harrington, and Kenneth Anger. They were also the foundation for the underground movement of the 1960s. The number of grants offered by 'cultural' institutions to independent artists increased, and a flourishing cultural circuit of 16-mm films grew in universities, museums, libraries, and film clubs. Animation offered the most flexible medium to those who wanted to free fantasy and to present views unknown to regular cinema; in such an environment, abstract cinema became ever more important.

Following a course parallel to the Hollywood dream industry, the live-action avant-garde found expression in films by Robert Florey (*Life and Death of 9413*, *The Loves of Zero*, *Johann the Coffin Maker*), by the Webber-Watson duo (*The Fall of the House of Usher*, *Lot in Sodom*), by photographer Rolf Steiner (H_2O), and by poet Emler Etting (*Oramunde*, *Poem 8*).

Mary Ellen Bute (Houston, Texas, 21 November 1906–New York, 17 October 1983), after having studied painting in Texas, left for the East Coast and, at the suggestion of composer and musical theorist Joseph Schillinger (1895–1943), started researching the connection between image and music. She collaborated with Schillinger himself and filmmaker and cinema historian Lewis Jacobs (1906?–1997) on the failed project *Synchronization* or *Synchrony* (1933), but in 1934 was able to produce *Rhythm in Light*. The film was based on Grieg's *Anitra's Dance*. This time she had at her side Melville Webber (1871–1947), the co-director of the aforementioned *Fall of the House of Usher* (1928) and *Lot in Sodom* (1933). Later, Bute made *Synchromy No. 2* (1935); *Escape* (1938, an illustration of Bach's 'Toccata and Fugue'); *Tarantella* (1939, with music by Edwin Gershefsky); and *Spook Sport* (1940, based on music by Saint-Saëns, with animation by Norman McLaren). Bute's camera operator and, later, producer was Ted Nemeth (1911–1986), who became the artist's husband.

A pert, diminutive, highly cultivated lady, Mary Ellen Bute was a major figure in American arts for forty years. She was much less elitist than most of her colleagues and contemporaries, as she managed to have her films often screened in regular theatres to average filmgoers instead of secluding herself in a circle of specialists. She courageously approached live action and as difficult a subject as James Joyce, with *Passages from Finnegan's Wake* (1967), aiming at a public who was not, in her opinion, necessarily loathe to culture.

'Seeing sound' was her mission and, in order to achieve such a result, she felt free to combine various techniques: drawing, painting, coloured lights, inks flowing into water, cut-outs. Her abstract films were nevertheless stylistically consistent and original, always full of liveliness and sometimes gaiety.

Douglass Crockwell (Ohio, 1904–Glens Falls, New York, 1968) earned his living as an illustrator and designer of magazine covers.[73] In 1938, 1939, and 1940 he made *Fantasmagoria I*, *II*, and *III*, respectively. Here, he adopted a technique used later on by Oskar Fischinger, which involved photographing the composition and modifying a painting on glass in its succeeding phases. In 1946, he released his most famous film, *Glens Falls Sequence* and, one year later, *The Long Bodies*, an assembly of the experiments he had made over several years. In his own words, the long

---

[73] Crockwell, according to the website *American Art Archives*,

> had a knack for getting the kind of assignments that were Norman Rockwellesque. His name was even similar to Rockwell's; too much, Crockwell thought, so he'd sign his name to hide the rhyming similarity: 'Douglas', 'DC', or simply 'D'. Crockwell had his own style, however, and his incredible realism and facility with subjects ranging from war to illness to family reunions made him one of the most popular artists of the 1940s and 50s.

('Douglas Crockwell', *American Art Archives*, http://www.americanartarchives.com/crockwell.htm, retrieved 25 December 2011)

bodies are the four-dimensional traces objects leave in space during the course of their existence.

Dwinell Grant (Springfield, Ohio, 1912–Doylestown, Pennsylvania, 1991) moved to abstract animation in 1940 after working as an abstract painter. Until 1948, he produced films with the title of *Compositions*. Then he devoted himself to educational films, returning only sporadically to art cinema. Francis Lee (New York, 1913–1998) made his first film as a reaction to the Japanese attack on Pearl Harbor. Entitled *1941*, the film gave an abstract interpretation of war. After having worked as a cameraman on the European front, Lee filmed *Le bijou* (The Jewel) in 1946 and *Idyll*, in 1948. Later, he devoted himself to studies of painting and Chinese civilization, on which he based the film *Sumi-e*. In 1940, the Californian brothers John and James Whitney debuted in what turned out to be a long and productive career.

Canada

Other than Raoul Barré in New York, Walter Swaffield and Harold Peberdy in Toronto, and Loucks and Norling in Winnipeg (on whose work only sketchy information exists), the early history of Canadian animation is best epitomized by Bryant Fryer (1897–1963). A native of Toronto, Fryer developed his skills in Paris, London, and New York, where he worked for John Randolph Bray. Returning to Toronto in 1927, he attempted to create a series with silhouettes entitled The Shadow-Laughs. He completed only two episodes, *Follow the Swallow* and *One Bad Knight*. In 1933, Fryer tried again with *Sailors of the Guard*, *Bye Baby Bunting*, and *Jack the Giant Killer*. But this time, the endeavour was beyond him. Although Fryer never achieved the same heights as Lotte Reiniger, writes Louise Beaudet, 'the care he put in scanning movements and in the effects of perspective is absolutely remarkable'.[74]

The actual birth date of Canadian animation coincides with the arrival of Norman McLaren. Invited in 1941 by John Grierson to the National Film Board of Canada, the Scottish filmmaker initially worked alone and, subsequently, with a team of young artists he himself hired and trained, including George Dunning, Jim McKay, René Jodoin, Jean-Paul Ladouceur, Evelyn Lambart, and Grant Munro.

The early films were influenced by McLaren's desire to obtain maximum results with limited means, as well as by the unavailability of means themselves. The young artists devoted their efforts towards sober and inexpensive

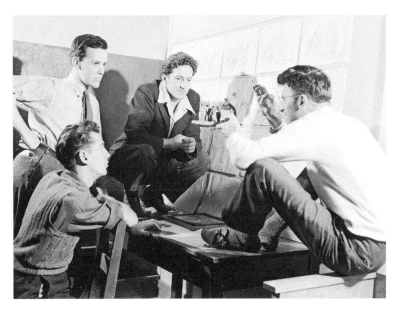

Figure 12.5 René Jodoin, George Dunning, Jim MacKay, and Norman McLaren, 1943. © 1943 National Film Board of Canada. All rights reserved.

---

[74] Louise Beaudet, 'L'animation', in *Les cinémas canadiens*, in Pierre Véronneau (ed.) Lherminier-La cinémathèque québécoise, Paris, 1978.

'experimental' animation. Aware that he had to avoid a heavy-handed influence on his followers, McLaren encouraged them to search for their own individual styles.

Due to the war, the majority of the work was directed towards propaganda films. The small group was also involved in preparing graphics and animation for the Film Board's other projects. When the time came to redirect production towards peacetime activities, a statute was drawn to address the Board's new priorities: to make Canada familiar to Canadians and foreigners alike, to promote technical research, and to act as state consultants for the field of cinema. The animation department was one of many branches of the organization, though not the most important from an economic and productive standpoint. Yet, it soon became the most acclaimed abroad for its innumerable works of high quality. In 1966–1967, so as to meet the demands of the French-Canadian minority, the department split into English- and French-speaking divisions.

Among the initial members of the group, the most talented was George Dunning. Born in Toronto in 1920, Dunning graduated from the Ontario College of Art and went directly to the National Film Board. After directing a few educational films, he made *Grim Pastures* (1944), *Three Blind Mice* (1945), and his first significant work in collaboration with Colin Low, *Cadet Rousselle* (1946). Based on a popular song, *Cadet Rousselle* was one of the first films using animated cut-outs created with a magnetized base and metal cuttings. In 1948, Dunning went to Paris, where he met Alexeïeff, Bartosch, and Paul Grimault. Back in Canada, he did not return to the Film Board but instead co-founded the production company Graphic Associates in Toronto with his former colleague Jim McKay. In 1956, after a short stay at Bosustow's UPA studio in New York City, Dunning went to London to open a local branch of the production company. The following year, he opened his own production company.

Jim McKay (Beaverton, 1916–Oakville, 2002), formerly a caricaturist, worked on a 'popular song' series and gave a good account of himself with *En roulant ma boule* (1943). Having co-founded Graphic Associates with Dunning, McKay worked on commissioned films after his partner left for London.

Jean-Paul Ladouceur (Montreal, 30 December 1921–Laval, 21 November 1992) played one of the main characters in McLaren's *Neighbours* (1952). Shortly after completing the movie, he left the Film Board for the Canadian Broadcasting Company (CBC). His co-star in McLaren's film was Grant Munro (Winnipeg, 1923), an expert technician and animator who filmed *The Daring Young Man on the Flying Trapeze* (1945). Munro left the Board but returned in time to be 'animated' in *Neighbours*.

13
EUROPE

Great Britain

In the 1930s, the majority of British animators worked in advertising, with only a few involved in the production of entertainment films. Anson Dyer returned to animation after some years of activity with live-action cinema and documentaries. In 1935, he founded Anglia Film, hoping to compete against American predominance in the area of cartoons. After a first attempt to animate musical works (such as *Carmen*, in 1935, which was released in 1936), he turned to a character already familiar to the English public: Sam Small, a foolish little soldier, who often served as a scapegoat for other snappish characters, and whose first adventures had been told by comedian Stanley Holloway on the stages of music halls and, later, on the radio.

Holloway recorded eighteen monologues for Dyer's films, the first of which was *Sam and his Musket* (1935). Wanting to make a breakthrough, Dyer decided to work in colour. The result was aesthetically acceptable – although the narrative and the cinematographic ideas did not mesh well with Holloway's skilled, yet slow, presentation and the film did poorly with audiences. After five episodes, Dyer's backers pulled out; but with unusual generosity, they let the filmmaker keep the equipment, and he was able to reopen a small studio for the production of advertising films. Among these, *The King with the Terrible Temper* (1937) was a funny short with a mere trailer at the end for advertising.

In 1936, Roland Davies (1904–1993), a cartoonist with the *Daily Express*, attempted to animate the adventures of one of his comic strip characters, the horse Steve (which had appeared in March 1932 in the *Sunday Express*). The result was a failure in every respect: Davies's graphic style was insignificant, his choice of black-and-white was obsolete, and even the inventions and plots were linked to an old-fashioned concept of animated film. The public did not show any interest. While lacking native artists (McLaren's unique talent was still in the making), Great Britain became a destination for foreign animators, including Lotte Reiniger, Hector Hoppin (teamed with British Anthony Gross), John Halas, and Len Lye.

The major novelty in 1940 was the founding of two studios, Halas and Batchelor, and Larkins. Both studios worked mainly on commission during their first years of activity. Halas and Batchelor produced more than seventy shorts for the War Office, the Ministries of Information and Defence, the Central Office of Information, and the Admiralty. Bill Larkins opened his own business after a short-lived partnership with veteran Anson Dyer; the studio produced many educational works and survived even after its founder left. With Peter Sachs and Denis Gilpin, Larkins created graphically advanced films that led some to claim that the British had preceded the UPA in revolutionizing style. As for Dyer, he produced and directed a few anti-Nazi propaganda films and, later on, entertainment movies such as the three-part serial *Squirrel War* (1947). He retired in 1951, when his animators left to found their own production company.

In 1944, a group of animators formerly connected to the production company of J. Arthur Rank founded G.B. Animation. The group, which started with few ambitions, quickly expanded into what many saw as the British challenge to Disney. David Hand (1900–1986), director of *Snow White* and *Bambi*, was named head of the studio. A good manager, he lacked the vision of a Hollywood-style producer. A growing number of young people, recently returned from military service, took the company's admission tests, which were similar to those given by Disney in the 1930s, and the studio announced its intention to employ 2,000 specialists. Through an imposing training plan, Hand undertook the task of teaching artists the secrets of Don Graham's animation, such as design and character acting. But the series Animaland, featuring Ginger Nutt the squirrel and its mate Hazel, flopped, despite its high technical achievements. As Hand himself admitted, these films were not as amusing as the filmmakers had expected. It should be added that personality animation, applied to characters without personality, is a flaw instead of a merit. Some animators contended that the group should have continued along the path of British tradition rather than attempting to translate a foreign style. The group dissolved in 1949 and Hand returned to the United States.

Another American, Fleischer alumnus George Moreno, produced some shorts featuring a London taxi driver and his car. Entitled Bubble and Squeak, the series lasted only five episodes.

Gerard Holdsworth, a former officer of the advertising agency J. Walter Thompson and a collaborator of George Pal's in the 1930s, worked in the field of puppet animation. With the help of Dutch animators he had brought in, Holdsworth began working on commission. *His Story of Time* (1951), made for Rolex, is still popular today. But a failed screen adaptation of Saint-Exupéry's *The Little Prince* was fatal to the production company.

Len Lye

An eccentric genius, Len Lye was born in Christchurch, Southern Island, New Zealand, on 5 July 1901. He tells how, at the age of three, while he was scuttling around during a winter afternoon, he kicked a kerosene can.

> I kicked that can around to make the most god-awful racket my lungs and kicks on can could. I can still feel the impact of my kicks on that can and hear an echo of tinny clashes. But what is most clear is a great flash of quivering sunlight that came from the can. I stood stock still. I don't know what I did next. I think I went over and sat on a long and looked at the can. We're all stopped short by wonder some time, and that's when it first stopped me in my tracks.[1]

A romanticized anecdote, no doubt, but be it at age three or at fifteen, this discovery nonetheless struck the colonial boy: Movement was the most modern of the artistic languages of his times. Said Lye:

> Every painter, every artist, I think, is making a discovery in just trying to isolate images that convey what he thinks is significant. I had my own pet little subject, which was motion. So I was incessantly inventing my own exercises for this kind of development.[2]

At the age of seventeen, he made his first kinetic sculptures, utilizing pulleys and cranks applied to fruit crates. His interest was exclusively directed towards the problems of form; consequently, film seemed to him the ideal instrument to 'control movement'.

In 1922–1923, in Australia, Lye learned the basics of classic animation. He soon abandoned his attempts to paint films directly on stock and went in pursuit of hundreds of other ideas. He dreamed about Moscow and Meyerhold's theatre but moved to the Samoan islands; after two years in paradise, he left the South Seas, moved by the urgency to create. ('I couldn't do much work there', he recalled. 'It was too wonderful for a young person'.)[3] Still wishing to go to the USSR, he decided to stop first in London, where he planned to learn Russian; there, in 1927, he found a job as a theatrical assistant. As critic and filmmaker Edgar Anstey wrote:

> In his earlier days Len Lye had been something of a rolling stone in art, journalism, poetry and philosophy, a gay troubadour of the intellect, ready and indeed eager to plunge into current aesthetic and philosophical controversy at the drop of his gay check cap, and never known to plunge without returning to the surface with some rare fish, or, at worst, a sizable red herring.[4]

With financing from the London Film Society, in 1929 Lye shot a nine-minute film using traditional

---

[1] Roger Horrocks, *Len Lye: a Biography*, Auckland University Press, Auckland, 2001, p. 7.
[2] Gretchen Weinberg, 'Interview with Len Lye', *Film Culture*, No. 29, Summer 1963, p. 41.
[3] Len Lye, letter to author, 1975.
[4] A. Mancia and W. Van Dyke, 'The Artist as Filmmaker: Len Lye', *Art in America*, July–August 1966, p. 101.

animation techniques. Entitled *Tusalava*, which in Samoan means 'things go full cycle', the film received good reviews but could not stand a comparison to Disney's fireworks; according to Alberto Cavalcanti, it was an out-of-fashion bagatelle. Cavalcanti also recalled how Lye needed all his personal charm to convince John Grierson and Cavalcanti himself, then directors of the General Post Office Film Unit, to produce a film by painting directly onto stock. Lye's charm worked and, in 1936, he released the five-minute *A Colour Box*. That same year, Gerald Noxon produced Lye's *Kaleidoscope*, four minutes long and made with the same technique. The two abstract films were acclaimed, albeit only within the limited circle of experimental filmmakers.

'Every film I got from the GPO, I tried to interest myself in by doing something new. Every film I did was something not previously done in film technique.'[5]

In 1936, in collaboration with the great documentary filmmaker Humphrey Jennings, Lye made a puppet film, *The Birth of the Robot*. In *Rainbow Dance* (1936), he used the human image, made abstract by special colour effects. 'This is my quirky film', Lye wrote later, 'quirky is how it makes me feel – in a kind of pop-art way. . . . All the stuff was shot in black and white, and transposed into three primary colour separations for the final colour print'.[6] *Trade Tattoo*, of 1937, was followed by a series of war propaganda films, made for the British government.

Len Lye's film *Swinging the Lambeth Walk* (1939) has commonly been confused with another film, *Lambeth Walk Nazi Style* (circa 1941), a sardonic, wartime propaganda short made by optically reprinting footage of Hitler and goose-stepping Nazi troops who appear to be dancing, Ziegfeld-like, to an eponymous popular tune.[7] This other (apparently uncredited) film was not by Lye – who speculated that it was the work of his friend and early collaborator Jack Ellitt;[8] it has also been attributed to Charles A. Ridley of the British Ministry of Information.[9] In a letter to this author, Lye denied that the two films could reasonably be confused: 'My *Lambeth Walk* is an abstract colour film with OK accompaniment for guitar and double bass (neither instruments ever having heard of the madman Hitler).'[10] Lye's film, which was not war propaganda, was sponsored by the British Council for the Travel and Industrial Development Association.

In 1940, Lye filmed *Musical Poster*, very dear to him, for which he employed many techniques. The film was used as a 'curtain raiser', attracting viewers to the films produced by the government in order to support the war effort.

In 1944, invited by the production company responsible for the March of Time newsreels, Lye moved to New York. He won an award at the Festival of Brussels in 1958, with *Free Radicals*, a five-minute-long, black-and-white film referring to some electronic particles (free radicals) which according to Lye, moved in a way similar to his painted forms.

For political reasons, however, this little film did not please the millionaire from whom Lye had sought financial support. Later that year, Lye resumed his activity as a kinetic artist, making sculptures that moved electrically and produced sounds. In 1979, as he sensed his impending death, he honed and completed *Free Radicals* and *Particles in Space* (the latter filmed in the 1960s). Lye died on 15 May 1980, in Warwick, Rhode Island.

---

[5] Gretchen Weinberg, 'Interview with Len Lye', *Film Culture*, No. 29, Summer 1963.
[6] Len Lye, 'Caption for Rainbow Dance', unpublished manuscript, circa 1972.
[7] *Lambeth Walk*, named after a district in London, was an exceedingly popular song before and during World War II.
[8] Jack Ellitt was born in 1902 in Manchester (England) as Abraham Isaac Elitzki. Three years later, he was brought to Sydney, Australia, where he made close friends with Lye upon his return from the Samoa Islands. In 1926, Lye went to London, urging Ellitt to join him, which he did in 1928. Having studied music and being interested in experimentation, Jack Ellitt became Lye's sound editor and, at the same time, an avant-garde composer. The two men parted in 1939, and Ellitt made a career for himself as a composer, sound editor, and documentary director. In the early 1970s, he went back to Australia and died in Wyong (North of Sydney) in 2001 at the age of ninety-eight.
[9] 'The Lambeth Walk', *Wikipedia*, last modified on 13 March 2012, http://en.wikipedia.org/wiki/The_Lambeth_Walk.
[10] Len Lye, letter to author, 31 July 1972.

Chapter 13: Great Britain

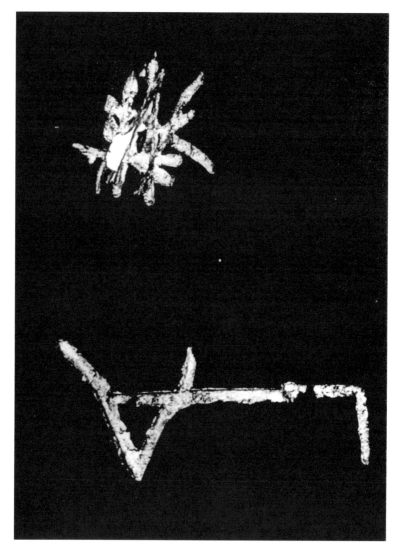

Figure 13.1 Len Lye, *Free Radicals*, 1958. Credit: Frame enlargement, Stills collection, Nga Toanga Sound & Vision. Courtesy of the Len Lye Foundation.

His films can be classified into three main groups. Some revolve around the exploration of colour and graphics (*Rainbow Dance* was probably the finest). Others centre on texture, colour transparency, and on the interrelationship between these two elements. (The unusual palette includes unsaturated colours, dusk and periwinkle blue; the masterpieces of this group being *Trade Tattoo* and *Color Cry* (1953).) Finally, a third group, which includes Lye's last films, makes a masterful use of 'graffiti' on black stock, creating three-dimensional exploration (*Free Radicals*, *Particles in Space*, and the posthumous *Tal Farlow* [1981]). The major contribution of this genial New Zealander was his audacious inventiveness, which allowed him to film abstract cartoons (*Tusalava*), to give up the camera (*A Colour Box*) and to combine, as never before, abstract drawing with live-action images (*Trade Tattoo*).

The first breakthrough from the confines of the traditional 'I' came in the Renaissance when painters started developing imagery of three dimensions, which is a bodily sensory thing of spatial relationships. . . The early post-Impressionists tried to simulate the everyday physical things of the vibrations of light by juxtaposing little stipples of colour. . . The artists were exhilarated by the sensory exploration of the physical world. You could emphasize it with your bodily senses rather than perceiving it by your brain.

The film area exists in the sensory side of art. There's a whole lot of areas that we experience that we have not words for. . . . All these physical things that we do we take for granted and all these are related to movement.

My terms of reference are 'individuality'. The experience of individual being, of heightened states of being, is what we're trying to get at in art. One of the ways of getting to it is by the process of feeling yourself in the shoes of another image, by empathy.

I don't know what an audience is. It's a whole lot of other people who are basically a unique version of individuality like me, so I'm only interested in me. Art is a question of you being me.[11]

What interested Lye was the composition of movement: Animation techniques are methods of controlling the movement on the basis of its composition. As for the connection between his activities as a filmmaker and as a kinetic sculptor, he wrote that he wanted to communicate nothing, or at least, nothing to the 'new brain'.[12] His images came from the primitive 'old brain' to the body and to its sense of kinetic presence.[13] Lye's films, as Cavalcanti remarked in the 1940s on the occasion of a retrospective, are like Mallarmé's poems or Picasso's paintings: People may or may not like them, but those who like them can understand them. Or maybe there is nothing to understand: One has only to enjoy them.[14]

Lye's production is limited as far as quantity is concerned; nonetheless, his works are among the best in the history of animation. One sees, in the vibrations of his textures and in the popular rhythm of the music he chose to accompany them, a perfect, dynamic self-portrait – an extravagant portrait of mankind.

However, it would be a mistake to look at Len Lye's films in isolation from his kinetic sculptures, his writings, and his painted batiks. He was not a filmmaker who enjoyed hobbies. More than any of his colleagues and his contemporaries, he expressed himself with no language boundaries. He spoke to the primeval brain, via motion, getting inspiration from his inner self and from Polynesian art.

He, arguably, was not strictly a professional. He gave up abstract filmmaking out of sheer whim, and never missed it. Among so many 'experimental' artists, he was the one for whom every creation had to be also a challenge or a riddle. A gregarious man, he was yet the loneliest one of all. His physical presence was visible in cinema, visual arts, literature circles, yet we find virtually no traces of his name in cinema, visual arts, and literature. In a century full of manifestoes and movements, he joined nobody; outwardly, he could belong to the futurists, but he abhorred their idol, the machine.

Len Lye was a rootless wanderer and hence an undisciplined, erratic creator to whom pundits couldn't easily attach a label. His relative obscurity, given the acknowledged genius of his work, would be the eventual price for his liberty.

France

The popularity of Disney's movies led some animators and producers towards American-style animation. A short-lived example of this was Dessins Animés Européens (DAE), which was founded in Paris (1934), by Leontina 'Mimma' Indelli and Lo Duca.[15]

---

[11] Gretchen Weinberg, 'Interview with Len Lye', *Film Culture*, No. 29, Summer 1963.
[12] Len Lye, letter to author, 31 July 1972.
[13] In the cryptic language of Len Lye, the 'old brain' is the one that performs at the level of sensory perceptions; the 'new brain' is the one that actuates conceptual thinking.
[14] Alberto Cavalcanti, 'Presenting Len Lye', *Sight and Sound*, Vol. 16, No. 64, Winter 1947–1948, p. 136.
[15] A controversial journalist and film critic, Giuseppe Maria Lo Duca (Milan, 1905–Fontainebleau, 2004) migrated from Italy and shortened his name. He later was among the founders of the legendary magazine *Cahiers du cinéma*.

'DAE began work on *La découverte de l'Amérique* [The Discovery of America], *Dorothée chez les fantômes* [Dorothy and the Phantoms], and *La conquête de l'Angleterre* [The Conquest of England, ca. 1938]', wrote Lo Duca.[16]

The first film was completed. Its animator was Pierre Bourgeon. We will mention neither the operator, nor the colouring process of the film. Together, they caused DAE to go under: the operator did not notice a defect in the camera, while the inventor had not yet perfected his process.[17]

Mimma Indelli (Signa, Italy, 7 December 1909–Marseille, France, 2 January 2002) had only one complete film under her belt, the fresh and funny *La découverte de l'Amérique* (1935) but was anyway one of the very few European women to have directed an animated short. In 1942, she tried again with *Le coche et la mouche* (The Stage Coach and the Fly, based on La Fontaine's fable, made in collaboration with Paul de Roubaix),[18] but the work was destroyed in a fire. She left cinema to become a successful painter and to win the world championship of underwater fishing (Campomoro, Corsica, 1952).

In France, animation survived primarily because of cinematographic advertising, but other attempts were made. André Rigal (1898–1973) was responsible for the humorous insert of the *France-Actualité* newsreel that began in 1933 with the title *France bonne humeur* (France in a Good Mood). During the years of German occupation, he directed some short films including *Cap'taine Sabord appareille* (Captain Sabord Gets Underway), *Cap'taine Sabord dans l'île mystérieuse* (Captain Sabord in the Mysterious Island), and *V'la le beau temps* (Here Is the Good Weather). For many years, Rigal collaborated with Jean Régnier, director of *Les joies de l'eau* (The Pleasures of the Water, 1932).

Russian expatriate Bogdan Zoubowitch (1901–1999), a collaborator of Ladislas Starewitch, also made films of his own. His *Histoire sans paroles* (Story without Words, 1934) was sort of a cinema geopolitical newspaper opinion column, made with animated puppets, and its fame is based more on its unusual subject (the Japan-China War, which started in 1931 and was certainly far from the French public interest of the 1930s) than on its quality. *La Fortune enchantée* (The Enchanted Fortune, 1936) was a combined-techniques work (a counterfeiter and some children – either drawn or live action, abundantly masked – act in an absurd comedy that openly belongs to the avant-garde), signed by that Pierre Charbonnier (1897–1978), who would later enter film history as Robert Bresson's background artist.

Filmmaker and scientist Jean Painlevé (1902–1989) animated clay figurines made by sculptor René Bertrand in a successful version of *Barbe-bleue* (Bluebeard, 1938). Four years earlier in 1934, comic artist Alain de Saint-Ogan (1895–1974) created drawings for *Un concours de beauté* (A Beauty Contest), in collaboration with Jean Delaurier.

In 1930, Delaurier (Aurillac, 1904–Chatillon, 1982) met Jean Varé, an Anglo-Swiss artist whose real name was Maurice Hayward (1914–40). Together they completed *Meunier tu dors* (Miller, You Are Sleeping, 1931). In 1935, Delaurier made *Couchés dans le foin* (Asleep in the Hay), illustrating a then-fashionable song by Mireille and Jean Nohain.[19] The film, which included a few daring scenes, was not liked by Mireille, who prohibited its distribution.

Arcady (Arcady Brachlianoff) made his debut in the field of popular songs too. A Bulgarian (Sophia, 2 January 1912–Paris, 12 November 2001), he wrote the music for some of Charles Trenet's[20] lyrics before moving to animated advertising. In the 1940s, working in the unoccupied part of France, he made some short films, including *Pym dans la ville* (Pym in the City), *Les aventures de Kapok l'esquimau* (The Adventures of Kapok the Eskimo), and *Le carillon du vieux manoir* (The Bells of the Old Manor), all in 1943.

Assisted by animation director René Bertrand (the director of *Bluebeard*), painter and illustrator André Marty (1882–1974) signed *Callisto, la petite nymphe de Diane* (Callisto, the Little Nymph of Diana) in 1943. The film is more elegant than interesting, and Jacques Kermabon writes:[21]

To use a recognized artist to raise the artistic level of a film is a common temptation. . . . To use André Marty goes in this direction. The artist had reached his sixties, he enjoyed certain notoriety. . . . The *Encyclopedia Universalis* spent a brief article that started this way: 'The drawings of André Marty, little master of fashion illustration, belong to the Art Déco aesthetic, but his

---

[16] This film was based on a copy that no less than Émile Cohl had previously drawn of the Bayeux Tapestry, in half scale and full colour. (Lo Duca awarded the old master the role of co-director.)

[17] Giuseppe Maria Lo Duca, *Le dessin animé*, Prisma, Paris, 1948, p. 40.

[18] The original French title of this film is part of a metaphoric idiom. In French, to 'act like a fly in a stage coach' means to buzz around or to be a busybody. Thus, the title might very well be rendered *The Busybody*.

[19] Mireille (Mireille Hartuch, 1906–1996) was a singer and composer; Jean Nohain (Jean-Marie Legrand, 1900–1981) was her lyricist.

[20] World-famous singer and composer (1913–2001). Among his hits: *La Mer*, *Douce France*, *Y'a d'la joie*, and *L'Âme des poètes*.

[21] Jacques Kermabon, 'Callisto, la petite nymphe de Diane – 1943', in Jacques Kermabon (ed.) *Du praxinoscope au cellulo – Un demi siècle de cinéma d'animation en France* (1892–1948), CNC, Paris, 2007.

personal vision, full of kindness for pretty women and elegant children, makes him a very endearing artist.'[22]

Illustrator, painter, and poster artist Albert Dubout (1905–1976), assisted by animator Jean Junca, attempted to make a series based on his character Anatole; *Anatole fait du camping* (Anatole Goes Camping) and *Anatole à la Tour de Nesle* (Anatole at the Tour de Nesle) were filmed during the war and distributed in 1947. Antoine Payen (1902–1985), a veteran from the 1920s, made two short films in 1946: *Cri-Cri, Ludo et le soleil* (Cri-Cri, Ludo and the Sun) and *Cri-Cri, Ludo et l'orage* (Cri-Cri, Ludo and the Storm). Finally, it must be remembered that artists such as Alexeïeff and Bartosch continued working in France during the 1930s and 1940s.

An important event in this period was the debut of Paul Grimault. Born on 23 March 1905 in Neuilly-sur-Seine (100 ft and five years away from Jacques Prévert, who later became his very close friend and artistic collaborator), Grimault attended the School of Applied Arts and later found employment arranging displays for a department store.[23] Pierre and Jacques Prévert, Jean Aurenche and Jean Anouilh all advised him to turn to animation. In 1936, in partnership with André Sarrut, Grimault founded Les Gémeaux, an advertising and technical animated film production company. After working on commissioned films and on *Monsieur Pipe*, an art film project that remained unfinished, Grimault created his first art short film in 1941 by utilizing what was left from an old project financed by Air France. Entitled *Les passagers de la Grande Ourse* (The Passengers of the Great Bear), the film was the first manifestation of the author's vigorous caricature drawings, his sober sense of colour, and his delicate touch. Grimault died in Mesnil-Saint-Denis on 29 March 1994.

Jean Image, née Hajdú Imre,[24] was born in Budapest on 26 January 1911.[25] The son of a bank manager, he attended the Applied Arts Academy of Budapest and concluded his studies in Berlin. His following stop was Paris, where he made a name for himself as an advertising poster designer. After a two-year internship in London (1936–1937) to learn the technique and the trade of animation, he returned to Paris and created various commercials and some shorts. His 1939 short *Le loup et l'agneau* (The Wolf and the Lamb) was a metaphor of the Nazi politics and occupation of Czechoslovakia, and was destroyed in the early 1940s after the German invasion of France. When peace returned, the filmmaker created his own company, Les Films Jean Image (1948) and, two years later, released the first drawn-animation feature-length film of the French cinema: *Jeannot l'Intrépide* (Grand Prix, children film section, Venice Film Festival, 1951).[26]

Anthony Gross

The Englishman Anthony Gross (Dulwich, 19 March 1905–8 September 1984) found his artistic homeland in Paris. In partnership with American financier and photographer Hector Hoppin (Washington, DC, 12 March 1906–Sarasota, Florida, 28 January 1974), he founded the production company Animat (1932). The company's small but functional staff quickly produced two good shorts: *Jour en Afrique* (A Day in Africa) and *Les funérailles* (Funeral Ceremonies). It was the third work, *La joie de vivre* (The Joy of Living, 1934), which confirmed Gross' skills. An example of art nouveau floral ballet, *La Joie de vivre* features two girls, a blonde and a brunette, running through a varied countryside; they are chased by a boy who wishes to return the shoe that one of the girls has lost. In the end, all three happily disappear into the sky on the boy's bicycle. After the success of this short film, Hoppin and Gross were invited by Alexander Korda to London, where they animated the brilliant *The Fox Hunt* (1936) in colour. Perpetuating his taste for ballet, Gross played on the choreography between the dull hunters and the smart fox, which manages to escape even in traffic. Back in Paris, the two partners viewed *Le jour et la nuit* (Day and Night), filmed during their absence by the Animat crew under the direction of David Patee.

After changing the company name, in 1937, to Société Hoppin et Gross, they began a new adventure: a feature film entitled *Le tour du monde en 80 jours* (Around the

---

[22] Guillaume Garnier, 'Marty André Edouard (1882–1974)', Encyclopedia Universalis, retrieved 3 March 2012, http://www.universalis.fr/encyclopedie/andre-edouard-marty/.
[23] Date of death: 29 March 1994, in Mesnil-Saint-Denis.
[24] Surname first, given name second, according to Hungarian customary usage. The pseudonym 'Image' came from the addition of Im(re) + Haj(du).
[25] He died in Paris on 25 October 1989.
[26] This is the plot: Jeannot (Little John) and his brothers are lost in the forest. After a long march, they arrive at the ogre's palace, where they are captured and put into a machine that causes them to shrink. Reduced to the size of insects, they are shut up in a cage, but Jeannot manages to escape. He arrives in the Village of Insects, where he saves the queen bee from the invasion of hornets. In gratitude, the entire beehive launches an attack on the castle of the ogre. The latter is thrown into the machine to shrink and placed in the cage, while Jeannot and his brothers go through the same machine in reverse and return to their normal size.

World in 80 Days). Once again, however, events conspired against the birth of the European animated feature film: World War II broke out in 1939, and Nazi troops entered Paris on 14 June 1940. Gross, who escaped to England, lost all traces of his film. At the end of the war, the old 1939 stock was found in the archive of Technicolor and returned to its creator. With the help of the British Film Institute, Gross reorganized his work, adding some transition sequences. The film was thus released in 1955 as a short, entitled *Indian Fantasy*, featuring Phileas Fogg preparing for his trip and the episode in which he saves the Indian Princess from her death at the stake. *Indian Fantasy* was the last animated work by Gross, who then retired from cinema and devoted himself to painting.

A true *joie de vivre* characterizes Gross's work, instinctive and spontaneous, uninhibited and nearly pagan (in a conversation with this writer, the artist defined himself as a 'dionysian'). A refined sense of humour is also present, directed against everything that is pompous, artificial, and opposes free fantasy. As for style, the floral creations of this pliant choreographer move in a lively and graceful manner. The colour, also, is original, emphasizing a game of whites and reds, in contrast to the broad palette used by many contemporaries.

Berthold Bartosch

Berthold Bartosch was born in 1893 in Polaun, then Austrian Bohemia (today, this is Polubny, Czech Republic). In 1911, he moved to Vienna to study architecture; there he became friends with Professor Erwin Hanslick, his teacher at the Fine Art School and a leftist, who exerted great influence on Bartosch. When Bartosch finished his studies, Hanslick suggested a collaboration to create educational animated films 'for the masses'. Bartosch accepted. Some of his earlier works were strictly educational (such as his geographical films); others, such as *Communism and Humanity*, or the ones illustrating Tomas Masaryk's[27] theses (*Der Tschechoslowakische Staat*, The Czechoslovak State, 1918), were obviously politically oriented. These 'non-artistic' works constituted Bartosch's sole apprenticeship. An individualist with an inborn passion for inventions – two requirements for becoming a true animator – he did not learn technical procedures from anybody, preferring to manage on his own.

In 1919, he moved to Berlin to open a branch of Hanslick's production company. There he met Eggeling, Richter, Ruttmann, Lotte Reiniger and, later, Jean Renoir, with whom he established a lasting friendship. He also befriended Berthold Brecht, then a young, still unknown writer. In Berlin, Bartosch continued creating educational films; he also collaborated with Lotte Reiniger on *Prince Achmed*.

In October 1930, Bartosch was approached by the Flemish Frans Masereel (1889–1972), then a famous illustrator, who proposed to turn one of his books into a film. One month later, the deal was made: Alexander Werth-Regendanz,[28] Masereel's publisher, agreed to back the project.

Having moved to Paris along with his newly-wed Maria Ebel, Bartosch began working in a little (and inconvenient) room near the Northern Cemetery. Unfortunately, Masereel's wood engravings, which were beautiful on paper, were too rigid and heavy for the screen and very hard to animate. On his own, Bartosch organized the work and began filming, combining three-dimensional images with shaded backlighting provided by a machine of his own invention. In order to create the depth of field that is not offered by simple drawings, he placed the motion picture camera vertically above a working surface formed by several levels of glass plates.[29] On each of them, he would arrange scenographic elements or cut-out figures with the illumination coming from below. In an attempt to soften the hard lines of the drawings and the rigidity of the animation, he created a muffled, opalescent atmosphere by blurring the glass plates with common soap, while also making frequent use of superimposition. In January 1932, he and Maria moved to a small apartment above the Vieux Colombier.[30]

---

[27] This sociologist and philosopher (1850–1937) was the founder and first president of Czechoslovakia (1918). His son Jan (1886–1948) was minister of foreign affairs after the Nazi invasion was over. He was found dead in 1948 on the eve of the Communist Party coming into power.
[28] This man was the owner of Transmare Verlag, associated with Kurt Wolff Verlag, which had originally published Frans Masereel's books. Kurt Wolff was the first publisher of Franz Kafka.
[29] This technique is now called 'multiplane'.
[30] A legendary theatre on the Left Bank, where writer-director Jacques Copeau renovated French theatre at the beginning of the twentieth century.

Figure 13.2 Berthold Bartosch, *L'Idée*, 1932. © Jeff Guess/Re:Voir.

When the film entitled *L'Idée* (The Idea) was finished in 1931, it was a creation by Bartosch, retaining little of Masereel's original mark. The 8 January 1932 issue of *Le Peuple* (The People) reported:

> Some of us went to look at *L'Idée*. Born of the brain of a man, worker, artist – it is not known and it is not necessary to know – the Idea, born of love and revolt, dominates. As pure light, it accompanies workers in their painful march toward freedom, and nobody can kill it. Everybody tries, though, since [the Idea] upsets their calm digestion. But neither the industrialist nor the judges in his service, nor the soldiers working for the ruling class are able to destroy it. When the man who generated [the Idea] is shot, the bullets pass through [the Idea] without touching it. How much did I regret that this beautiful work by Bartosch could not have been (will it ever be?) shown to the audience of workers for which it had been conceived. We have censorship. The work is so movingly beautiful that at a second viewing – when attention is no longer so strongly directed toward the surprising novelty of the technical creation – emotions are purified. One is even more moved by the wonderful story, dedicated to all the martyrs of this Idea, which honours the world of labour.[31]

The plot of *L'Idée* is scanty. A man conceives of the 'Idea' of a beautiful and pure creature, represented by a naked girl. Although the conservatives try to destroy her, dress her (thus making her impure), or coerce her to their ends, the Idea turns only towards the exploited. Even when her creator is executed by a firing squad, she continues to live and becomes a fixed star in the sky. The syncopated editing and dramatic superimpositions of the film can still captivate the modern viewer. This is one of the rare films in which political commitment does not conflict with lyricism, similar to such films of the times as those by Pudovkin, Eisenstein, and Dovzhenko.

The film, which took months to complete, was not released, and Bartosch did not earn anything from it.[32] It was the English live-action film director and critic Thorold Dickinson who, impressed

---

[31] For the time being, there is no actual evidence of the financial backing of the German or the French Socialist Party, although such support was considered common knowledge by everybody in the milieu (including Maria Ebel Bartosch herself, in response to this writer's questions). The film is in fact structured in such a way that a lecturer (i.e. a political preacher) is needed to fully understand its symbols, allegories, and admonishments. It was typical of productions that political propagandists would use in the 1920s and 1930s.

[32] *L'Idée* was a protest film in the tradition of German socialism. It is not improbable that, in the scene portraying the workers' defeat, Bartosch intended to depict the defeat of the Spartacist uprising of 1918. The film had distribution problems, confirmed by the existence of two versions of the title cards, an original version and a second one, cautiously edited by an anonymous Englishman who made an illegal copy of the film.

Original introduction (translated from the French):

Some men live and die for an Idea/but the Idea is immortal./One can persecute her/judge her/prohibit her/condemn her to die/but the Idea continues to be alive/in the souls of men./She is everywhere, she is in our presence/side by side, in misery and struggle./She rises here/and there, She continues/her walk through the centuries./Injustice trembles in front of her./To those who are exploited she shows the path/toward a better future./He whom she penetrates/does not feel isolated any longer/because she is, above everything else/THE IDEA.

Counterfeit introduction:

The female image appearing/as unifying symbol throughout/the film is the Idea/which reaches every creative artist,/to the poet she is inspiration/to the sculptor, form/to the novelist, theme/to the patriot, the ideal.

by Bartosch's work, saved the artist by offering him financial help for the creation of another film.

Bartosch's second film was a poem 'against the war', filmed in colour and involving the use of a laborious procedure. Each image had to be shot three times on three film stocks, sensitive to the three different colours of the three-colour process. The exposed films were to be developed in London, since Paris lacked a suitably equipped laboratory. When the filming ended, just before the war, Bartosch began editing the 900- to 1,000-m film, which was to be released with music by Arthur Honegger (who had also composed the soundtrack for *L'Idée*). However, all negative and positive stocks were destroyed in the war, with the exception of a few centimetres. Years later, Maria Bartosch, the artist's widow, wrote, 'Only three people saw the anti-war film: my husband and I in Paris, and Thorold Dickinson in London.' The work did not even have a final title, being called from time to time *Cauchemar* (Nightmare) or *Saint François*.

Bartosch emerged from the disasters of the war without even a nationality. After obtaining French citizenship in 1950, he began research for a third film about the cosmos. In his small study, he tried to give life to a sort of poem of light ('Light, always this search for light obsessed him', his wife Maria recalled). Because of his deteriorating health, however, he was not able to work at his machine, which required standing for many hours at a time; in his last years, Bartosch devoted himself to painting. He died in 1968, telling Alexandre Alexeïeff, who frequently visited him in the hospital, about his project for the film: 'It must be very simple. It is difficult to be simple; but it is necessary. I learned much in the years I worked.'[33]

André Martin, after visiting him in 1959, wrote:

> Bartosch works as a poet who does not even wonder whether he will be read. Those who want to know cinema from A to Z must fall into the habit of recognizing the importance of films which have become invisible, of abandoned projects and impossible cinema. In the age of expensive art and sciences, controls, governmental agencies and the hyperbole, Bartosch stubbornly settles down, committing the upsetting crimes of non-conformity, the crime of poetry.[34]

Alexandre Alexeïeff

Aleksandr Aleksandrovich Alekseev (later, as a French citizen, Alexandre Alexeïeff) was born on 18 April 1901 in Kazan, in tsarist Russia. He was the third and last child of Maria Polidorova, a headmistress, and Aleksandr Alekseev, an officer in the imperial navy. Aleksandr's brothers' names were Nikolay and Vladimir. One year later, Aleksandr Alekseev accepted the post of naval attaché at the Russian embassy in Constantinople (then capital of the Ottoman Empire and now known as Istanbul), and his family moved with him to the shores of the Bosphorus. Constantinople was a happy time for the boy, as he enjoyed the best affective and material conditions that anyone could wish for.

Yet it came to a tragic end in 1906, when his father died in strange circumstances, in all likelihood murdered, in Baden-Baden, Germany, while on a diplomatic mission. The family had to return to Russia and manage a difficult existence in Saint Petersburg.

Though this initial chapter of the artist's life might seem a mere simple melodramatic anecdote, it is of decisive importance in understanding his future inspiration. That interrupted bliss gave rise to a perennial *forma mentis* – sowing in him the need to cling to the moment, to conserve the taste of every joy experienced – and cemented a nostalgic character.

In those days, Saint Petersburg was brimming with writers, painters, musicians, scientists, and thinkers; its theatre scene was buzzing, its elegant life shone. However, Alexandre barely got a whiff of what his new city had to offer. His time was given over to reading and to study, to training and to drawing in the Cadet Academy where his position as an officer's son entitled him to a place. Once again, an event in the early years of his life was to leave an indelible mark on the artist's career: His drawing master at the

---

[33] Alexandre Alexeïeff, letter to author, no date.
[34] André Martin, 'Berthold Bartosch immobile', *ACA*, No. 5, March–April 1959.

Cadet school influenced him categorically by letting pupils explore their potential for fantasy, far beyond the constraints of traditional academic copies from nature. From now on, Alexandre Alexeïeff would never use models except on one occasion, when he turned to his wife Claire for help, using her face to illustrate Malraux's *La condition humaine*.

In 1914, Russia, allied with France and Great Britain, went to war with Germany and the Austro-Hungarian Empire. This was World War I, in which the Russian soldiers, facing a German army that was well equipped, well trained, and well managed, fell apart disastrously. The 1917 Revolution put an end to czarism and set off a civil war that was to last for three years.

In the most chaotic situation imaginable, those sixteen-year-old cadets were caught between the orders from their superiors and their own desire to conduct themselves like self-sufficient adults, between the dizzying hopes of a radical reconstruction of society and of humanity and the daily horror, the killings, the robberies, the violence.

During the summer of 1917, when the politics of Russia was steadily deteriorating, Alexandre was sent by his mother to the town of Ufa as a guest of her brother, Anatoly Polidorov, a socialist lawyer who successfully defended peasants and workers against the arrogance of the rich and powerful. His uncle asked him about his plans for the future, and Alexandre replied that he wanted to be an engineer. 'I thought you wanted to be an artist', quipped his uncle. Alexandre, fired with revolutionary ideas, said that the country needed engineers in order to build a society that was new, prosperous and advanced. 'You disappoint me', concluded Anatoly. Alexandre reconsidered his future and took art classes for the rest of the time he was stationed in Ufa. In autumn, he joined his fellow cadets in Orenburg. Later he learnt that his uncle had been killed by the Bolsheviks, who were somewhat less than accommodating when it came to rival ideas on the left. From that point on, Alexandre steered well clear of ideologies and all that lurked behind them.

Three freezing months later, the cadets – those who were able to – reached Vladivostok, the furthermost tip of eastern Siberia, from which they departed on board a warship, but it was several months before they were told that the civil war was over. After a year of aimless drifting, and still dreaming of painting, Alexeïeff chose France (whose language he had already mastered) as his new home. He landed at Cassis, near Marseilles and, with the help of a letter of introduction, he had been given in Vladivostok[35] to set designer and fellow Russian expatriate Serge Sudekin, he settled in Paris in 1921.

'At the time', he remembers, 'it was believed that three hundred thousand Russians lived in Paris; among them were the major forces of the theatre. There was Diaghilev's famous ballet, there was Pitoeff, there was Sudekin, there was Alexandre Benois'.[36]

For a few years, he worked as a set designer while taking painting and drawing lessons at the Académie de la Grande Chaumière in Montparnasse.

In 1925, he devoted himself to illustrating high-quality books and to etching, an activity that ensured him some economic security. But, at the age of thirty, Alexeïeff went through a stage of dissatisfaction:

> I had the feeling I had tried everything . . . everything I was capable of. I illustrated books, and that gave me money; thus everything was going well. But I kept repeating to myself that this was no longer an art, just a trade like others. That was the time of *Caligari*, *Circus*, Chaplin's tramp and Eisenstein's films. Cinema certainly deserved the interest which my writer friends gave to it. I told myself: I will make some cinema. By myself. I don't want a large crew, I don't want Eldorado. Mine shall not be a product, but a work of art.[37]

At that point, the idea of the 'pinscreen' was born. As an engraver, Alexeïeff knew how to express

---

[35] During his short stay in Vladivostok, he had managed to show his drawings to the famous illustrator Ivan Bilibin (1876–1942). Favourably impressed, Bilibin wrote a letter of recommendation.
[36] *Portrait d'Alexeïeff*, post-production script of television documentary produced by ORTF (French Television), directed by Maurice Debèze, 1971.
[37] *Portrait d'Alexeïeff*, post-production script of television documentary produced by ORTF (French Television), directed by Maurice Debèze, 1971.

himself through the use of chiaroscuro, nuances of grey and complex images. They were images requiring a unique dynamism compatible with their style, so complicated as to discourage any animator who used traditional animation techniques. It was therefore imperative for Alexeïeff to discover a way to animate engravings: 'I had to find a way to work by myself, in my art studio, and to create by myself images exactly as I wanted them.'[38]

He designed a white screen on which thousands of retractile pins were mounted perpendicularly so as to form a mesh. If two light sources were set at the sides of the screen, each pin would cast two oblique shadows on it; the sum of all the shadows together would make the screen completely dark. At that point, if certain groups of pins retracted, their shadows would shorten and the corresponding area would lighten. Full retraction of the pins would produce no shadows, only the white of the surface. In this way, the artist would be able to obtain any figure and to utilize the complete palette of greys. A film of animated engravings would then become possible if the artist gradually changed the images and photographed them frame by frame at each new stage.

This idea would have remained in its conceptual stage (Alexeïeff had considered an animated version of Mussorgsky's music), but for Claire Parker (born in Boston on 31 August 1906). Like many young Americans of the 'lost generation', Parker lived in Paris. Having seen the books illustrated by Alexeïeff, she wrote to him expressing her admiration and asking him for lessons. The event marked the beginning of a long lasting artistic and personal relationship. With the support of Parker, Alexeïeff decided to go on with the project.

In 1932, the two artists began shooting *Une nuit sur le mont chauve* (A Night on Bald Mountain) and worked on it uninterruptedly for eighteen months. Having listened again and again in the dark to Mussorgsky's music, Alexeïeff built the film in his own mind, frame by frame.[39] With his pinscreen technique, it was not possible to make preparatory drawings, and mistakes in shooting could be corrected only by starting all over again. In 1933, the film was completed. When shown to friends and experts, it obtained great critical success, but the distributors objected that the only way to reach profitability was to produce a dozen films per year. Disappointed, Parker and Alexeïeff left art cinema and turned to advertising.

At the time, advertising was still in its infancy, and artists enjoyed a large degree of freedom. Claire and Alosha, as he was called by his intimates, worked with a group of friends, including Alexandra de Grinevsky, Alexeïeff's former wife. Together they produced a few small masterpieces, especially valuable for the precision of set design, the detailing of light tricks, and the use of varied techniques (which, however, did not include the pinscreen). *La belle au bois dormant* (Sleeping Beauty), made for a wine firm, deserves praise; Alexeïeff's contribution to the film is clearly recognizable over those of the other artists.

With the outbreak of World War II, the Alexeïeffs left Paris for the United States, where they encountered difficult work conditions. Large animation corporations, with their assembly-line production, did not hold any interest for the mastery of the Russian-French émigré. With a larger, more perfected pinscreen, Alexeïeff made *En passant* (Passing By, 1943), for the National Film Board of Canada. Based on a song from French-speaking Quebec, this very short film was the first example of 'free work' produced by Alexeïeff after ten years of silence.

In America, Alexeïeff also continued his activity as an engraver, developing a technique that allowed him to obtain colour engravings. Shortly after the end of the war, the couple returned to Paris.

In 1951, a period of abstract experimentation began: the animation of illusory solids; that is, of solids that are traced on the frame by a moving light source after a long exposure time. Alexeïeff decided to connect these tracing sources (usually metallic spheres, properly illuminated), to composite pendulums, whose oscillations could be mathematically

---

[38] *Portrait d'Alexeïeff*, post-production script of television documentary produced by ORTF (French Television), directed by Maurice Debèze, 1971.

[39] The symphonic poem in one part, *A Night on Bald Mountain*, evolving around one basic theme, was composed by Mussorgsky in 1876. It referred to the legendary witches' Sabbath, which supposedly occurred every summer solstice (on the night of the 24 June, the feast of St. John the Baptist) on Mount Triglav, near Kiev.

Figure 13.3 Alexandre Alexeïeff and Claire Parker working on *En passant*, 1942.

computed, and which could therefore be planned. By adjusting the various forms traced by the light source, he was able to 'animate' these nonexistent solids. 'This is the second stage of movement', he claimed. Using this technique, called 'totalization', he shot some advertising films, including *Fumées* (Vapours), winner of a special award at the cinema festival of Venice, in 1952.

In 1962 Orson Welles, who had admired one of Alexeïeff's books of illustrations, invited the artist to make the prologue of *Le procès* (The Trial), a film based on Kafka's novel.[40]

---

[40] This is an account of the event in his own words (from Peter Bogdanovich and Orson Welles, *This Is Orson Welles*, Jonathan Rosenbaum (ed.), Harper Collins, New York, 1992):

(Peter Bogdanovich) – How did you manage to get the story illustrations for the prologue?
(Orson Welles) – They're images made with pins, thousands of pins. I found these two old Russian [*sic*], completely crazy, cultivated, elegant, fascinating. It was Alexandre Alexeïeff and Claire Parker, husband and wife. They sat down and stuck pins in a big board. The shadow of the pins made the chiaroscuro. They were two of the kindest and happiest people in the world. In my opinion, those images are extraordinarily beautiful.
– Yes, they're really beautiful. How did you find them?
– I don't remember. I must have seen something on television or somewhere. They were working on a film, I think they'd been working on it for the last sixty years. I went to see them and I persuaded them to interrupt their work for five months (not long, by their standards) and stick pins for me. They did it, and they did it superbly.
– Yes. It's one of the moments of the film that I like most.
– We should have made the whole film with pins! With no actors. A film without actors, what you and Alfred Hitchcock like!
As Claire Parker told this writer, the encounter had funnier touches:

After a couple of calls from the producer, Orson Welles came to our studio. He started to look around everywhere, at all our equipment, getting more and more surprised. At first he spoke to me in English, then he realised that Alosha also spoke the language well. From that moment he forgot my presence and addressed himself solely to him. It was entertaining to see these two creative giants trying to seduce each other, to win each other over. Eventually they reached an agreement about how many images were needed, how much time was needed, about how much money was needed. Then, before leaving, Welles said to Alosha: 'Could I come here when you're working? I'll just be sitting in a corner, I won't talk, I won't distract you. I'd like to see how the prints on the pinscreen are created'. Alosha looked at him, and his voice became even more baritone: 'One cannot refuse Orson Welles anything – he replied as if he were pronouncing a sentence – but I know my work would suffer!' So he parted with a resigned smile, and we never saw him again. We found out, many months later, that he was very pleased with the work.

By using the pinscreen, Alexeïeff created some pictures that he filmed one after the other, without animation. Many reviewers wrote that the prologue was of a better quality than the film itself.

In 1963, Alexeïeff and Parker filmed *Le nez* (The Nose), based on the short story of the same name by Nikolay Gogol. In 1972, they completed *Tableaux d'une exposition* (Pictures at an Exhibition),[41] a work that was for several reasons connected to *A Night on Bald Mountain*. Based on the music which Modest Mussorgsky had expressly composed to 'suggest images to painters', it was intended as the first part of a trilogy that was to include all the *Pictures* by the Russian composer. Due to practical problems, the project was left unfinished. Then, in 1975, Alexeïeff provided drawings and scene designs for *Finist*, a Russian fable produced by Corona Cinematografica of Rome and animated by the Italian Giorgio Castrovillari.

In 1977, on a new screen of pins built the preceding year, Alexeïeff and Parker began *Trois thèmes* (Three Themes), based on three more *Tableaux* by Mussorgsky. Alexeïeff wrote:

> The terms *adagio*, *maestoso*, *lento* have not yet found their place in animation, which is limited to *scherzo*, excluding elegy, eclogue and other lyrical terms. This happens because it is difficult – if not impossible – to 'slow down' animation. Well, this is what I am trying to do.[42]

Three Themes opened in Milan, Italy, in March 1980, during a triumphant soirée honouring Parker and Alexeïeff. It was also the filmmakers' swan song: Parker died in Paris on 3 October 1981, while Alexeïeff's death followed less than one year later, on 9 August 1982.

Élie Faure, a French poet and art critic who loved prophecies, wrote:

> You know, these animated drawings, still so barren, so stiff, so meagre, that are projected on the screen and that are, if you will, as the forms I imagine a child's graffiti drawn on a blackboard are to Tintoretto's frescoes or Rembrandt's canvasses. Suppose that three or four generations of people are harnessed to the problem of animating these images in depth, not by surfaces nor lines, but by thicknesses and volumes; of modelling, by values and half-tones, a series of successive movements that by long practice would gradually become habit, almost a reflex, so that the artist comes to using it at his pleasure for drama or idyll, comedy or poetry, light or shade, forest, city, desert. Suppose an artist is so armed with the heart of Delacroix, the passion of Goya and the strength of Michelangelo; he will throw on the screen a cineplastic tragedy entirely his own, a kind of visual symphony so rich and so complex, opening, by its rush through time, perspectives of infinity and the absolute which are both exalting by their mystery and more moving by their tangible reality than the symphonies in sound of the greatest musicians. There, that is the distant future which I believe in but which I do not know can be achieved.[43]

It did not take three or four generations, but eleven years. *A Night on Bald Mountain* was screened in 1933, while Faure was still alive (he died in 1937). In spite of the pompous prose and name-dropping, Faure's text was actually prophetic, showing how Alexeïeff's work led to a sudden leap in the art of animation.

A master of the fine arts, a friend of writers such as Soupault and Malraux, and a 'careful' participant in the surrealist and avant-garde movements ('careful' because his inborn aversion for clamour and publicity never made him a protagonist), Alexeïeff was considered an experimental filmmaker, whose value had to be judged in terms of the novel linguistic contributions he made to the history of cinema. *A Night on Bald Mountain* was, and still is, considered a solution to the old problem of

---

[41] Mussorgsky composed *Pictures at an Exhibition* in 1874. They refer to the paintings of Viktor Hartmann, a friend of the composer, whose work had been exhibited posthumously in St. Petersburg. Originally written for piano, the music was transcribed for orchestra in 1922 by Maurice Ravel. The music, which guides a hypothetical visitor through the exhibition, is divided into fourteen passages, spaced by a *promenade* that is repeated four times in variations.

[42] Alexandre Alexeïeff, letter to author, 14 February 1978.

[43] Élie Faure, 'De la cinéplastique', in *L'Arbre d'Eden*, Crès, Paris, 1922.

agreement between the music of sounds and the music of images; Alexeïeff's animated engravings are seen as a proposal of the linguistic potential of the cinematographic medium. The critics are certainly correct, but experimentalism was only a secondary facet of Alexeïeff's prismatic activity. The artist invented the pinscreen not for the sake of invention, but in an effort to make an instrument for himself, the only instrument capable of producing his fantasy.[44]

A Night on Bald Mountain is an exceptional poem of images, an inexhaustible source of lyric suggestion, rich with ambiguous hints. The music functions as a text, to which the fluidity of images continuously refers, but without any mechanical linking of rhythm and timbre. Images enrich music and music enriches images, in an evocative process which allows both artistic expressions to maintain their individual vitality and mutual respect. Looking for suggestions, the filmmaker turned to the musician who was for him a spiritual guide and with whom he shared a common ethnic origin (Alexeïeff always had a place in his heart for great Mother Russia).[45] Alexeïeff's figurations also derived inspiration from Mussorgsky's notes to the musical piece Gogol's *The Night of St. John* and some poems by Pushkin. For his creative work, Alexeïeff adopted the following method: He encountered a text, a memory, or a word and then liberated his fantasy. The images of *A Night on Bald Mountain* are subtle, voluminous, and often intertwined; far from being simple 'animation' or simple 'animated engravings', they are a window open on a fantastic universe.[46] Fantasy takes shape, thanks to the infinite shades of greys: 'The artists of my time', Alexeïeff stated more than once, 'used surfaces and lines. I wanted shades. They played the trumpet; I wanted to use the violin'.

Clearly, the attitude of this poet of images differed from that of his friends, writers, or painters, who were striving towards less artistic, more cultural, and more intellectually oriented research. Perceived as an experimentalist, he was criticized by many reviewers for his lack of self-renewal, for the similarity of his films – particularly his last releases. Such an accusation is valid only as far as technique is concerned. In both *Pictures at an Exhibition* and *Three Themes*, Alexeïeff still used the pinscreen, exactly as he had done for *Passing By* and *The Nose*. But the inner, poetic evolution is very clear. From the anguished, aggressive, 'gothic' vision of the 1933 film, the artist moved to the all-consuming childhood memories as well as Russian legends of *Pictures*. The complex, sinuous rhythms of the two pinscreens rotating in front of each other act as mediators for a world which does not exist anymore and for traditions which can no longer be found.

> While making *A Night on Bald Mountain*, I believed I was showing the struggle between Good and Evil, between Night and Day. Much later, I discovered that I recounted the drama of my father's death and the metamorphosis of my mother, who became depressed. But it was involuntary; I did it without knowing. I understood it twenty years later. I was thirty. I had then to demonstrate that it is possible, for a human being, to make a picture in movement. I am seventy as I start the *Pictures*. I believe that now I have to demonstrate that animation can also be poetic, to prove that cinema can abandon 'photography', to look for a certain grammatical form of dialogue: something like a sonata with two themes, on two alternating pinscreens. After all, like every other artwork the *Pictures* are the portrait of their author, Mussorgsky. Clearly, the film will also be my self-portrait. But what the film will be in the end I cannot know, and I will never know.[47]

---

[44] The painting *Vaste Ocean* of 1964 (Art Institute of Chicago) by German artist Günther Uecker, should be mentioned here. Uecker's painting is a large white canvas on which nails have been affixed to create the appearance of waves. Alexeïeff's procedure was very similar.
[45] It is perhaps significant that Mussorgsky was also educated at the Cadets' school in St. Petersburg.
[46] It is possible to track down some visual memories of *Faust* (1926) by F. W. Murnau: the flight through the clouds, the flight over reconstructed model countryside, the grey husks, the character who 'takes off his head' when he takes off his hat.
[47] Alexandre Alexeïeff, letter to author, 25 October 1971.

Shortly afterward, he wrote:

We saw copy number zero of the *Pictures at an Exhibition*, on 17 December. I believe that this film equals *A Night*, although it is very different. One has to see this film twenty times before understanding it: this is true for good poetry.[48]

If there is a division between narrative and poetry, this is represented by the adjustment of language to the logical principle deriving from daily sensory experience. The narrative medium always keeps in mind a before and an after, reality and fantasy, a cause followed by an effect. Not so for the poetic medium, which substantially is atemporal, having an inner time and space, expressing itself with images liberally created by the poet's mind, then integrating and structuring itself not according to logical laws, but according to the emotional response of the person who enjoys them. Because of the close connection between narrative and the world of daily and sensory experiences, cinema – which is born from the filming of current events and is linked to the sensory world it photographs – absorbs the logical categories of this world and becomes the central place of narrative. After Eisenstein's failed attempt at an 'intellectual editing' (for instance, *October*), the only cinema that could free itself from its obligations to prose was the one that had for its object the intellectual creations of the author rather than the surrounding reality.

This occurred in the cinema of Eggeling and Ruttmann. The rhythmic flowing of abstract images produced something that could equal the rhythmic flowing of abstract sound or music. To create poetry, some images were needed which were figurative, loaded with meaning, and it was necessary to give them a rhythmic formalization. With his delirious figurative fantasy and with his powerful style, Alexeïeff was able to fulfil these requirements. His chiaroscuros were his past recollections, nightmares and visions of the legends of pagan Russia, as well as images of the loved and lost native country. All these were strongly autobiographical elements, as Alexeïeff himself remarked, which made his work into a lyrical anthology.

Up to a certain point, one can speak of decadence, keeping in mind the historical notion of the term rather than the current pejorative meaning. As far as decadence and romanticism have been absorbed by the avant-garde movements of the beginning of the twentieth century, Alexeïeff's art can be considered avant-garde. Alexeïeff observed and learned many things, but seemed almost afraid of being overwhelmed by a zeal for research and experimentation that could drain the artistic expression of any human content.

Alexeïeff's art was strengthened by the artist's isolation, by his quiet awareness of not belonging to any fashionable currents and by his consequent renunciation of the praise of a large public. His art is refined, sometimes aristocratic, but never 'cult'. Hoffmann and Poe, Dostoevsky and Pasternak, were travelling companions rather than models for a filmmaker who never had masters other than himself and whose art was not born from his books but from his life.

Alexeïeff's two poetry works, *Night* and *Pictures*, contrast with the more lengthy narrative of *Passing By* and *The Nose*. *The Nose* derives from a short story by Gogol about a barber who finds a nose in a loaf of bread, a young man who wakes up without his facial ornament, and the nose itself, which seeks a life of its own. The film is related to Alexeïeff's other activity as a book illustrator: Without literally following the text, Alexeïeff the illustrator entered the spirit of the book and rewrote it through images. *The Nose* does not repeat Gogol's plot, but creates a poem in its own right, a 'salute to Gogol'. It is an interweaving of the few events making up the story with delicate images of nineteenth-century Russia; flash-like syntheses of space and time; metamorphoses of objects; constructions; living beings; dark, mysterious figures rising from the pavement and then disappearing after having communicated nothing but their presence. The film is a splendid example of modern and surrealist narration, created by a man 'who had learned spontaneity' from surrealism.

---

[48] Alexandre Alexeïeff, letter to author, 19 December 1971.

The prologue Alexeïeff created for *The Trial* can also be connected to book illustration. Images are fixed, following one another on the screen like pages turned by hand. The only changes consist of the passing from a lighter to a darker tone, obtained during the film developing. The value of such experience suggests a careful examination of Alexeïeff's fascinating work as an engraver. It was tightly linked to his activity in cinema, to the point that he theorized and applied a real montage to this art form: in the relation between printed pages and illustrated pages, in the number of consecutive illustrated pages, and in the number of printed pages separating the illustrated ones. Such an analysis, however, deserves a separate essay.

Three Themes, created in Alexeïeff's old age, is almost a goodbye and a will. In the first segment, very slow images are superimposed like final memories of the Russian countryside; the second summarizes several framings from *Pictures*, in a sort of self-quotation serving to reaffirm the artist's own inspiration; and the third segment features Goldenberg and Schmuyl, the former heavy and rich, ready to produce coins by striking his hammer, the latter in the form of a fluttering bird, poor and creative. Schmuyl resembles Mussorgsky and, in Alexeïeff's words, symbolizes 'the artist as opposed to those who own money'. It is impossible not to notice also an autobiographical portrait of Alexeïeff, who throughout his life rigorously rejected the influence of commercialism. Although these observations have stressed Alexandre Alexeïeff's masterful creativity, Claire Parker's role should not be overlooked. An inspirer and supporter, she was gifted with a lively sense of movement – the couple loved to define themselves as 'the artist and the animator'. Able by logic to catalyse the most daring dreams of her companion, Claire deservedly co-signed every film. In the course of friendly conversations, the two wondered, 'What would have happened had we operated separately?' When asked alone, Claire Parker never had a doubt. 'He is the genius', she used to say.

Belgium

In 1932, Ernest Genval (1884–1945) directed *Plucki en Egypte* in collaboration with A. Brunet, Leo Salkin, and M. Van Hecke. From 1935 to 1937, Roger and Norbert Vanpeperstraete made *Tout va très bien, madame la marquise* (Everything Is Well, Madame la Marquise) and *Couchés dans le foin* (Asleep in the Hay), puppet films disliked by the censorship committee for their 'licentious' themes. Edmond Philippart also made puppet films: *Chansons de Charles Trenet* (Songs of Charles Trenet), *Style imagé*, and *Images mouvantes* (Moving Images).

In 1940, during the German occupation, journalist and photographer Paul Nagant (1914–1967) founded a studio, the Liège-based Compagnie Belge d'Animation (Belgian Company for Animation [CBA]), which produced *Zazou chez les nègres* (Zazou with the Black People) and *Ma petite brosse à rimmel* (My Little Mascara Brush, 1940–1942). When the building that housed the studio was destroyed by fire, Nagant built another one in Brussels, where he produced *Le chat de la mère Michel* (Mother Michael's Cat, 1943) and *Le petit navire* (The Little Boat, 1944).

In Antwerp, producer Wilfried Bouchéry, in collaboration with Marc Colbrandt and Henry Winkeler, completed *La naissance de Pim* (Pim's Birth, 1945) and *Le forgeron Smee* (Blacksmith Smee, 1945), while two feature films in progress were destroyed by a fire in July 1945.

Liège was also home of Albert Fromenteau (born in 1916), director of *La captive de Frok Manoir* (The Captive of Frok Manoir, 1944); *Le voyage imprévu* (The Unexpected Trip, 1944); and *Wrill écoute la BBC* (Wrill Listens to the BBC, 1945).

Immediately after the war, Claude Misonne (1914–1973, already well known as a writer) began to direct puppet films. In 1947, financed by Wilfred de Bouchéry, she released the first Belgian feature film, entitled *La crabe aux pinces d'or* (The Crab with Golden Claws). Based on Hergé's comic strip character Tintin, this slow-paced movie had little success at the box office. The studio, however, continued production, in collaboration with the newly born, state-funded television.

The Netherlands

In the Netherlands, animation began with *De moord van Raamsdonk* (Raamsdonk's Assassination, 1930), a film of animated silhouettes made by Otto Van Neijenhoff (1898–1977), in collaboration with famous puppeteer Frans ter Gast. The film tells of the atrocious crime described in a popular song, as told by an organ grinder. The music was by Karel Hartman.

During the 1930s, Dutch frame-by-frame cinema was represented with honour by the Eindhoven-based group directed by George Pal. After the Hungarian-born Pal moved to the United States, the studio closed and the group dissolved. In 1941, Johan Louis 'Joop' Geesink continued the Dutch tradition of animated puppets. An ingenious businessman and a great organizer, Geesink (The Hague, 28 April 1913–Amsterdam, 13 May 1984) founded a small advertising company shortly after the beginning of World War II. In 1941, he made *Pierus*, his first animated film, commissioned by the railroad company, followed in 1943 by *Serenata nocturna* (Evening Serenade), Geesink's first work with puppet animation. After this film, the electronics giant Philips commissioned some animated works from him, happy to fill the void left by George Pal (a discussion of Pal appears later in this section). Geesink was thus able to hire a staff, which primarily consisted of former artists of the Eindhoven studio. In the 1950s and 1960s, his production company, which in 1947 had been called Dollywood, made numerous films taking advantage of the development of television. Productions included *Kermesse fantastique** (1951), a ten-minute promotion for Philips Electronics, which shows a bizarre amusement park; *Gala Concert* (1951); *Prins Electron* (1954); *Philips World Parade* (1954); the series Dutchy (1955); *Piccolo, Saxo and Co.* (1960); *The Travelling Tune* (1962); and *Philips Cavalcade, 75 Years of Music* (1966). Dollywood was terminated in 1971 when, to avoid bankruptcy, Joop Geesink sold it to the studio Cinecentrum. The company's misfortune was due mainly to poor performance of Geesink's other ventures, particularly the Holland Promenade-Projekt, which he had envisioned as a Disneyland of the Netherlands.

One of the very first associates of Geesink was Marten Toonder (Rotterdam, 2 May 1912–Laren, 27 July 2005), who worked in the field of comic strips. Famous for his character of the cat Tom Poes, Toonder is actually considered the father of Dutch comic strips and is sometimes called the 'European Walt Disney'. In 1943, Toonder left his partner and turned to animation. During the German occupation, he made a few films – among them, *Tom Poes en de laarzenreuzen* (Tom Poes and the Giants in Boots) – before going underground as a partisan. In 1945, he reopened the studio and initiated what became a prolific output, mainly in advertising and occasionally of short documentaries and instruction films. Among the studio's creative works are *De gouden vis* (The Golden Fish, 1951), a Chinese fairy tale about Prince Li Pai, who asks a golden fish how he has to live; *Moonglow* (1955); and *Suite tempirouette* (1956).

Germany in Nazi Time[49]

The 1932 elections established the Nazi Party as the largest among the ones represented in Germany's Parliament. Its Führer (= leader) Adolf Hitler was appointed as chancellor on 30 January 1933. It was the beginning of one of the strangest and bloodiest adventures of Western history.

Adolf Hitler was known for his enthusiasm about animated cartoons. On 20 December 1937, the Minister for Public Enlightenment and Propaganda, Joseph Goebbels, would annotate in his diary: 'I'll present to the Führer twelve Mickey Mouse movies for Christmas; he'll be very pleased and happy about this treasure'.

Both Hitler and Goebbels loved cinema in general and shared a unique passion for cartoons, which eventually led to the formation of the German Animation Company (Deutsche Zeichenfilm GmbH). Hitler continuously criticized the quality of German animation films. The film industry was apparently aware of the shortfall and had great expectations. In 1934, the *Kinematograph*, in an article entitled *Der deutsche Zeichentrickfilm muss wiederkommen* (German Animation Has to Come Back), announced:

> The global success of Mickey Mouse proved that there is an audience for these films in any country with a movie theatre. Every German theatre owner will confirm that their customers love to watch them; we simply have a lack of them. Why on Earth can't Germany make films like that?[50]

Walt Disney soon became the great rival for the animation production in Nazi Germany. At the same time, unlike the United States and the USSR, Goebbels and Hitler gave less thought to the use of cartoons for war propaganda.[51] In much the same way, cartoons didn't pay

---

[49] By Ulrich Wegenast.
[50] 'Kinematograph' No. 126, Berlin, 4 July 1934.
[51] The total number of animation films produced in Germany during World War II for propagandistic purposes alone was rather low compared to other countries like the United States or the USSR. Worth mentioning is *Der Störenfried* (The Troublemaker, 1940) by Hans Held. In the film, all the animals of the forest band together to get rid of a troublemaker: the fox. Militarization has progressed so far that even hedgehogs are wearing German army helmets and wasps are flying in combat formation (the original sounds of German dive bombers were added to the 'wasp squadron' scenes).

much attention to the anti-Semitic issue[52] and even less to the 'degenerate art' problem.[53]

Up to the late 1930s, most of the German animated productions were commercials. The focus varied considerably, from luxury goods to advertising more general items like the *Volksempfänger* (People's Receiver) and even behavioural standards. Examples are *Zwergenland in Not* (Dwarf Country in Danger, 1939), advertising potassic fertilizers, and *Die Schlacht um Miggershausen* (The Battle for Miggershausen, 1937), advertising modernization and automation in agriculture.

However, in Nazi Germany, animation filmmaking was officially ennobled as a profession and art. A 1943 memo on career choices reads: 'By creating the profession of the animation creator within the Film Council of the Reich Film Chamber as it was initiated by the Deutsche Zeichenfilm GmbH, the cultural degree of this newest form of art has been approved.'

The two major film companies, UFA and Tobis, planned to upgrade the quality of the product. UFA hired animated fairy tale specialist Kurt Stordel (1901–1973) as supervisor of the project *Quick macht Hochzeit* (Quick Gets Married, 1941), which remained unfinished. Tobis established a small animation unit in Berlin-Dahlem. Under its director Louis Seel, a veteran of American, German, and Brazilian cartoons, the unit intended to produce a film on the mountain spirit Rübezahl – which eventually was considered too dark and was shelved.

In 1941, Goebbels founded the Deutsche Zeichenfilm GmbH, its headquarters located in the Berolina House in Berlin. It was supposed to start production of feature-length animated films by 1947, with their first picture hitting the theatres by 1950.

While Zeichenfilm GmbH strictly produced what we now call family entertainment, Mars Film focused on war teaching and training films for the armed forces. The new CEO for the Deutsche Zeichenfilm GmbH was Oberregierungsrat (senior government official) Karl Neumann, the former CEO of the Kulturfilm Zentrale and a faithful cohort of Goebbels. Among others, theatre critic Friedrich Luft (1911–1990) and cartoonists Horst von Möllendorff (1906–1992), E. O. Plauen (1903–1944), and Manfred Schmidt (1913–1999) were hired. E. O. Plauen's legal name was Erich Ohser; he was responsible for the comedy newspaper strip *Vater und Sohn* (Father and Son). Manfred Schmidt would become famous in the 1950s with his comics based on the character of detective Nick Knatterton.

The production took off, in spite of the ongoing war and even though the production sites were moved from the capital to Munich and Vienna as a result of the bombings on Berlin. The last safe haven for animation film production, however, was Prague; its production facility was run by Horst von Möllendorff. Goebbels let Deutsche Zeichenfilm GmbH employees watch the newest Walt Disney releases while Disney movies were disappearing from the German theatres. Copies and documents found in the occupied territories – for instance, at Disney's Paris office – were seized for inspection, and the company was given copied Disney's multiplane camera.[54] Artistic directors of the Deutsche Zeichenfilm GmbH were Werner Kruse and, after him, Frank Leberecht, a dramaturge. In 1942, Deutsche Zeichenfilm GmbH had seventy-two employees; in 1943, the number was already at 263. Despite the enormous expenses (all in all, about RM 6 million, equal to about AM$ 230 million in 2015), the Deutsche Zeichenfilm GmbH only produced the 1-minute short *Armer Hansi* (Poor Hansi), directed by Gerhard Fieber. Goebbels liked it, in spite of the deficiencies he detected and criticized. Hansi is a canary who wants to fly out into the world. There, he experiences all kinds of mishaps and continuing danger. Eventually, he returns to the safety of the cage from which he escaped. One of the film's distinctions is the use of Oskar Sala's electronic music.[55]

---

[52] *Van den vos Reynaerde* (Reynard Cycle, 1943) is an example of anti-Semitic animation. The film was produced by Nederland Film and directed by Egbert van Putten. Another example was, according to film historian specialist Jeanpaul Goergen, a Jewish caricature of a thief in Heinz Tischmeyer's animated tale *Vom Bäumelein, das andere Blätter gewollt* (The Little Tree That Wanted Different Leaves, 1940), painted in a Stürmer style. The film portrays a conifer that prefers foliage to his conifer needles. When the conifer's wish comes true, a Jew steals the new leaves.

[53] Ulrich Kayser's film *Die Historie der deutschen Puppe* (The History of the German Puppets, 1940) illustrates the history of the puppet, from prehistoric times, to the Gothic and Renaissance, up to the 1930s; naturally Bauhaus puppets were considered to be abnormal. According to the narrator, it was not until the Nazis took over that 'the German ways of life and motherliness . . . found their way back to the soul of the child'.

[54] Ignoring cameraman Erwin Kramp's efforts to patent his own invention to produce the depth-of-field effect.

[55] Sala was a significant developer and virtuoso performer of engineer Friedrich Adolf Trautwein's Trautonium, an early electronic musical instrument played by pressing a resistance wire against a metal rail fitted with a chromatic scale, which sent electricity to a neon oscillator and amplifier to create musical pitches. Sala also later contributed to the creation of the score for Alfred Hitchcock's *The Birds* (1963).

Gerhard Fieber (Berlin, 1916–Berlin, 2013) had a passion for drawing that had already started in his school days when he caricatured his teachers. He studied art and printing in Berlin and worked as a draughtsman for advertising and humour for the press. In the 1930s, he worked for the publicity film department of the UFA and met the most important creators of promotional films.

Between 1942 and 1945, he was the art director for the Deutsche Zeichenfilm GmbH. He moved one unit of the studio to Dachau because of the bombardment of Berlin and settled next to the concentration camp. He would tell in a later interview:

> During the working hours you were busy with trickfilm figures, at the same time you could see prisoners on the street who were harnessed in front of wagons as a replacement for horses. Nevertheless you had to draw funny figures – it was horrible.

The Deutsche Zeichenfilm GmbH never created art, nor was it ever economically successful. However, Goebbels decided to make the first feature-length film and a series with the title Schnuff, der Niesser, with a staff of about 500 working on it. Hans Fischerkoesen was called in to carry out the project.[56] The business was officially closed in October 1944.

In early 1944, the Prag Film AG produced *Hochzeit im Korallenmeer* (Wedding in the Coral Sea) in Prague, nominally directed by Horst von Möllendorff.[57] Czech film artists rightfully claim to be the authors of the film: Jiří Brdečka, Eduard Hofman, and Stanislav Látal are confirmed to have been the main producers of ideas and work. Indirectly, the topic is war: Two fish want to get married in the Coral Sea, but the bride is kidnapped by an octopus. Together with an army of sea creatures, the groom manages to reunite the couple. In the end, the happily united couple hugs in their new home while everybody else is in ruins. The film doesn't refrain from political allusions like the Kozachok-dancing octopus.

Hans Fischerkoesen

Der Schneemann (The Snowman, 1944) is one of the best-known films of the Nazi era. Directed by Hans Fischerkoesen, it's the story of a snowman who desperately wants to see the summer but melts. Just like in Poor Hansi,

Figure 13.4 Hans Fischerkoesen, *The Silly Goose*, 1944.

---

[56] It was finished by East Germany DEFA after the war and released as *Purzelbaum ins Leben*.
[57] Horst von Möllendorff (Frankfurt-am-Oder, 26 April 1906–17 December 1992) was a cartoonist and humorist who was invited to Prag-Film, in Prague, as the artistic director of the animation department. Little information exists on *Wetterhäuschen* and *Klein, aber oho*, which are considered to be two other Prague films by Möllendorff. When the war ended, von Möllendorff returned to Berlin and resumed his work as a cartoonist.

the main character wants to leave his environment to enjoy new experiences and he fails. The snowman has a merry/melancholic undertone, which makes it hard to classify. During the war years and the Nazi regime, the message was certainly very much intended – according to the principle 'Cobbler, stick to your last!' Still, the snowman, like all of Fischerkoesen's movies before and after the Nazi regime, features a playful nature and an original visual comedy.

Fischerkoesen also made a name by using several inventions and innovations in animation technology and included, among others, three-dimensional elements in his animations.

In 1943, he produced *Verwitterte Melodie* (The Dilapidated Melody, based on a script by Horst von Möllendorf). He apparently used a multiplane camera, as we can tell from the movements of the characters within the space and the depth of perspective. This film, too, conveys a light-hearted and melancholic atmosphere at the same time. A bee finds an abandoned gramophone in the middle of a flower field. By use of his stinger, he manages to make the record on the turntable play *Wochenend und Sonnenschein* (Weekend and Sunshine) with its jazzy sounds.[58]

Fischerkoesen's third and last short from the war was *Das dumme Gänslein* (The Silly Goose). The film has an anti-Semitic colouring. The fox represents the 'malicious Jew'. The little undisciplined bird refuses to keep in single file with the other geese, and the fox ambushes it while the famous Yiddish hit *Bei Mir Bistu Shein* (To Me You're Beautiful) is playing in the background.

Hans Fischerkoesen was born Hans Fischer on 18 May 1896. The affix 'koesen' was taken from his hometown Bad Kösen on Saale in Saxony. He produced his first animation in 1919. *Das Loch im Westen* (The Hole in the West) was about racketeering in the years of crisis in post-war Germany and in the aftermath of the Weimar Republic.

The Brothers Diehl

In 1937, the brothers Ferdinand (1901–1992), Hermann (1906–1983), and Paul Diehl (1886–1976) produced the puppet film *Die Sieben Raben* (The Seven Ravens). It was clumsy and too lengthy, but it was the first German feature-length puppet film and treated the topic of forests as the archetypal German marvel (like so many films of that time did).[59]

In 1951, the brothers built a great reputation with the spiny character Mecki, who already had his film debut as early as 1938 in *Der Wettlauf zwischen dem Hasen und dem Igel* (The Race between the Tortoise and the Hare). He appeared in several commercials, political campaigns, and educational films during the 1950s Adenauer administration. For film journalist Thomas Basgier, he is the 'prototype of a bourgeois economic-miracle-Philistine'.

Heinz Tischmeyer

Heinz Wolfgang Tischmeyer (born in 1913) started his career at the age of sixteen as an apprentice with the Waechter Animation Studio in Berlin. Beginning in 1928, he made humorous animated commercials and technical animations for industrial productions. Between 1931 and 1933, Tischmeyer was animation artist at the George Pal animation studio in Berlin before the UFA animation studio recruited him. An anti-Nazi, in 1934 he left for Switzerland but was forced to return to Germany. Between 1936 and 1942, Tischmeyer owned an animation studio doing contract work. Among his clients were Naturfilm Hubert Schonger Berlin for youth and children's fairy tales, Kinomatfilm Wuppertal for commercials, and Bayer I.G. Farben Leverkusen for medical and technical animations and commercials. Among other films, Tischmeyer worked on the fairy tale *Die Bremer Stadtmusikanten* (The Town Musicians of Bremen) and the already-mentioned *The Little Tree That Wanted Different Leaves*.

Tischmeyer was then brought on board the Deutsche Zeichenfilm GmbH by Werner Kruse, where he supervised one of the five production teams of Poor Hansi.

Hans Held

After studying drama and scenography and, later, painting, design, and typography in Munich, Hans Held (1914–1995)

---

[58] The American scholar William Moritz even finds a subversive message in the film; maybe it's simply an attempt to escape the madness of the war and the Nazi regime. See William Moritz, 'Resistance and Subversion in Animated Films of the Nazi Era: The Case of Hans Fischerkoesen', *Animation Journal*, Vol. 1, No. 1, Fall 1992.

[59] Ferdinand Diehl began his apprenticeship in 1927 at Emelka Film. In 1929, he opened a production company with his brothers Paul and Hermann. Their first movie was *Kalif Storch* (Caliph Storck, 1929), based on a tale by Wilhelm Hauff and made with silhouettes. The company specialized in animated puppets: humanlike and quite realistic figures, such as those featured in *Die Erstürmung einer mittelalterlichen Stadt um das Jahr 1350* (The Storming of a Medieval City in the Year 1350). Of the brothers, the most involved in creative work were Ferdinand, who was responsible for direction, animation, and the characters' voices, and Hermann, who created the puppets.

owned an animation studio in Berlin-Babelsberg. Only a black-and-white fragment of his film *Das Gespenst* (The Ghost), based on an idea by Horst von Möllendorff, has survived until this day. The film was produced by Nederland Film in the Hague. In 1940, he directed the aforementioned *The Troublemaker*. Held's studio produced the animated sequences for the famous live-action film *Münchhausen* (directed by Josef von Báky, starring Hans Albers) in 1942, the UFA's 25-year anniversary film. Hans Held was appointed director of Bavaria's animation department but was fired in 1944. After the war, Held abandoned animation and created cartoons for newspapers and magazines like Mecki, the hedgehog character for the TV guide Hör Zu, among others.

Wolfgang Kaskeline

Wolfgang Kaskeline (1897–1973) exemplifies a certain continuity between the Weimar Republic and the post-war Republic of Germany. He worked mainly in the commercials sector. Among others, he produced the short films *Zwei Farben* (Two Colours, 1933) and *Der blaue Punkt* (The Blue Spot, 1936). Kaskeline was director of the UFA's animation department for a while. He started to produce animations in the early 1920s and made commercials for Sarotti-Mohr chocolate. In 1926, he founded Kaskelinefilm and produced commercials and documentaries even after the war. In 1949, he founded the first private film academy in Berlin (which was renamed to Kaskeline-Filmakademie in 1987 and state certified).

Avant-Garde

A few other abstract, avant-garde films existed outside the government-controlled production. They were created in a sort of inner emigration and regarded as 'ostracized art'. Still, they were partially presented in public. Hans Fischinger stands out among the representatives of a languishing avant-garde. The younger brother of the more famous Oskar (discussed later in this section), Hans was born in Gelnhausen in 1909. Having graduated in fine arts, he joined his brother in his Berlin studio in 1931. He collaborated on *Studien* (Studies) *No. 9* and *No. 10* before filming *Studie No. 12* (1932) on his own. While working on *Studie No. 14*, the filming of which was never completed, the two brothers were divided by arguments and artistic jealousy. Hans promptly moved to Alzenau, near Frankfurt. In 1937, he filmed *Tanz der Farben* (Colour Dance), a seven-minute abstract film funded by his family. Despite the ostracism of abstract art during the Nazi regime, the film premiered on 26 February 1939 at the Hamburg Waterloo Theatre, ran for two weeks, and was well received by audiences and reviewers. The filmmaker was working on a new project when the war began, and he had to enlist. The date of his death is uncertain; he probably died on the Rumanian front in 1944. Notwithstanding his adverse fortune, Hans Fischinger was an excellent artist. His style differed profoundly from Oskar's. As Fischinger expert William Moritz pointed out, Hans 'preferred slender, hard-edged, streamlined figures, with serpentine, elegant but somehow jazzy movements'. Oskar loved 'working with charcoal and delicately smudging the edges, while Hans preferred to work with ink and paint, mixing grey-shades and painting the forms with brushes'.[60] A very special film is *Strich-Punkt-Ballett* by Herbert Seggelke (Hannover, 13 June 1905–Düsseldorf, 10 July 1990). Produced in 1943 without a camera, it was directly painted on celluloid, entirely in the tradition of the experimental films of Len Lye or Norman McLaren.[61] Jazz was thought by the Nazis to be degenerate, and jazz music was added to *Strich-Punkt-Ballett*, announcing a new and free era. Young people who listened to American jazz in Nazi Germany were called 'Swingjugend' (swinging youth). They were hunted by the Gestapo.[62]

---

[60] William Moritz, 'The Films of Oskar Fischinger', *Film Culture*, Nos. 58, 59, 60, New York, 1974, p. 49.

[61] In 1955, Seggelke persuaded painters Jean Cocteau, Gino Severini, Ernst Wilhelm May, and Hans Erni to attempt to use the same technique with the musical accompaniment of a polonaise. The result was a documentary entitled *Eine Melodie – Vier Mahler* (One Melody, Four Painters) with commentary by Cocteau, in which live-action images of the artists at work mixed with their brief experiments. Curiously, the finest sequences are those by the less famous artists, May and Erni; Severini drew Veronesi-style vibrating rods, while Cocteau played with asterisks, points, and holes in the stock.

[62] More details in this era's production are worth mentioning. Kurt Stordel, for instance, concentrated on fairy tales: Between 1935 and 1938, he produced *The Town Musicians of Bremen*, *Sleeping Beauty*, and *Puss in Boots*, but Stordel became famous for his animated colour film *Purzel, Brumm und Quak*, also known as *Purzel, der Zwerg* (Purzel, the Dwarf). Stordel's drafts and techniques lean towards Walt Disney. In the late 1930s, Stordel already made use of pencil tests. He produced two more films: *Zirkus Humsti Bumsti* (Humsti Bumsti Circus) in 1944 and *Rotkäppchen* (Little Red Riding Hood) in 1945. After the war, Stordel produced contract works like *Eine Hochhausstadt* (A High-Rise City)

Oskar Fischinger[63]

Oskar Fischinger was born on 22 June 1900 in Gelnhausen, Hesse (Germany). Before finishing school (where musical education was taught), he studied violin and started an apprenticeship as an organ builder. Ingo Petzke praises: 'Although he would continue for his whole life to make films directly related to music, this was as much of a musical education he ever received',[64] In 1916, during the war, he moved to Ginnheim, a district of Frankfurt. Here he underwent an apprenticeship as a technical draughtsman followed by engineering studies, which, in 1922, he finished successfully as a certified engineer. In a Frankfurt literary circle he met Bernhard Diebold,[65] a critic open to novelty. Fischinger drew two rolls of paper illustrating the dynamics of Fritz von Unruh's drama, *Der Platz* (The Square)[66] and Shakespeare's *Twelfth Night*. When the members of the circle found the experiment hard to understand, Fischinger did not get discouraged but wondered what elements could have made his graphs clear to everybody. Following Diebold's suggestion, he found the answer in movement, and through cinema he studied the possibilities of moving paintings. Around 1920, he designed a machine that enabled him to conduct experiments with abstract films. He placed a parallel, pipe-shaped conglomerate of coloured waxes and clay on a sort of slicer with a rotating blade. He set the camera in front of the device so that the shutter was synchronized with the movement of the blade. Cut after cut, the camera filmed the changing features traced by the veins inside the wax.

In April 1921, Diebold introduced Fischinger to Walther Ruttmann, who was then leaving painting for cinema. In 1922, Fischinger moved to Munich and founded two companies: one, in partnership with Louis Seel, oriented towards the production of animated, conventional short films and the other, in partnership with a fellow named Güttler, for developing another of Fischinger's inventions, a motor which burned inert gases without pollution. Walther Ruttmann, who also lived in Munich, visited Fischinger a few times, and in November 1922 licenced one of his machines for filming the wax cuttings along with the rights to use it for commercial purposes.

After four years of work, Fischinger's two companies closed, submerged by debts, grudges, and lawsuits. Depressed, Fischinger also had to face the fact that Ruttmann had used his machine to film some scenic effects for some Lotte Reiniger's films, including *The Adventures of Prince Achmed*. 'Others are lapping up the cream that belongs to me', he wrote to Diebold – a strong expression, since Ruttmann was using a machine that had been legally licensed.

Albeit difficult, the four years Fischinger spent in Munich were not wasted. Demonstrating from the beginning an extraordinary prolificacy, the artist completed *Wachsexperimenten* (Wax Experiments), in which he explored the possibilities of the wax machine, some hand-coloured experiments and, finally, *Orgelstabe* (Organ Staffs), a work featuring several rolls

---

in 1958, a documentary of the Grindelberg Project in Hamburg, one of the first big urban residential developments in West Germany, completed in 1956. Johann Weichberger, whose career was divided between Germany and Austria, is mentioned later in this section. Finally, special effects should not be forgotten. A very remarkable (live-action) film is Anton Kutter's *Weltraumschiff-1 startet* (Spaceship-1 Launches). Produced by the Bavaria-Filmkunst GmbH in 1937, it tells a fictionalized story of the first manned space flight some fifty years after the first Zeppelin. The hero, Astronaut Commodore, leaves for his mission, watched by many journalists and the world public. Using model animation, the film depicts the spacecraft speeding up a giant ramp towards space and, eventually, returning safely to Earth. The most striking detail is that the spaceship has no Nazi symbols such as swastikas. It is not even explicitly a German enterprise but a mission of the International Space Flight Union. Several other films used model animation during the Nazi era – for example, the renowned architecture movie *Das Wort aus Stein* (The Stone Word, 1939) by Kurt Rupli.

[63] By Giannalberto Bendazzi.
[64] Ingo Petzke, *Oskar Fischinger* (from the lecture series 'The German Avant-Garde Film of the Twenties', University of Guadalajara, Mexico, 26–30 September 1988).
[65] Born Bernhard Dreyfuss in 1886 in Zurich, Switzerland, he officially took his mother's family name of Diebold in 1902, when his parents divorced. Primarily a theatre critic and playwright, he spent about twenty years in Germany before the Nazis banned him. He died in Zurich in 1945.
[66] Second part of the Das Geschlecht trilogy (The Generation Trilogy).

of abstract film composed of parallel bars moving with different rhythms. Fischinger also worked on six traditional animated shorts (the *Münchener Bilderbogen* [Picture Sheets from Munich], created for Seel); special effects for some unidentified full-length films; and a charming, original experiment entitled *Seelische Konstruktionen* (Spiritual Constructions).[67]

Fischinger's lifelong, Grail-like pursuit of colour music was triggered in the mid-twenties when he met the Hungarian/American composer and theoretician Alexander Laszlo.[68] The latter toured Germany in the mid-1920s, giving many performances of colour music, and utilized both material of his own and material he bought from Fischinger, with whom he gave some performances in 1926. Oskar also devoted himself to multiple-screen shows.

Vakuum (Emptiness) and *Fieber I, II, III* (Fever I, II, III), were the names for some of the cinema performances in the series called Raumlichtmusik, and then Raumlichtkunst, to be shown with up to five projectors working simultaneously.

In 1927, tired of Munich and broke, Fischinger decided to move to Berlin. During the trip (on foot!), he shot pictures of people and places he met. Later, he used these pictures for a film (released much later by Elfriede/Fischinger Archive), made of very quick flashes: *München-Berlin Wanderung* (Munich-Berlin Walking Tour). In 1928, he accepted a job with the UFA, where he created special effects for Fritz Lang's *Frau im Mond* (The Woman in the Moon), but an accident in which he broke an ankle convinced him, in 1929, to rescind his contract. While in the hospital, he worked intensively in charcoal and decided to devote himself to the creation of abstract films synchronized to music. From 1929 to 1930, he composed eight *Studien* (Studies), plus more in 1932, accompanying them with different kinds of music, from fandango to jazz to Brahms's *Hungarian Dance No. 5*.

In 1930, he gave a copy of his *Studie No. 6* to Paul Hindemith, who intended to use it as an exercise for the students in his conservatory. Starting from their impressions of the visual rhythm, the students composed several musical scores for the film.

The German public showed an appreciation for avant-garde production, and Fischinger was able to expand his staff. In 1931, he hired his cousin Elfriede Fischinger (1910–1999), an artist ten years his junior who would later become his wife. Shortly thereafter, his brother Hans joined him for a brief period. *Studie No. 8* remained unfinished due to lack of funds needed to purchase the rights to Dukas' *The Sorcerer's Apprentice* (it was completed later). Fischinger hired his brother as an assistant to help on later studies. Together they collaborated on *Studien 9 and 10*. Oskar made *11* and *13* (the latter unfinished), while Hans worked on *12* and prepared the drawings on paper for *14*, although he never made them into a film. Shortly afterward, in 1933, Hans left.

While working on the *Studien*, Oskar found time to research a purely visual rhythm without any musical support; the result was *Liebesspiel* (Loveplay, 1931). He also tried other experiments. With Béla Gaspar, he explored the problems of colour film. He worked to create synthetic sound – a field that was to be McLaren's glory. Fischinger designed a series of images that generated special sounds when they were transported to the optical sound track area of the film. Using a procedure he developed with Gaspar (Gasparcolor), he made *Kreise* (Circles, 1933–1934), his first important work in colour, featuring a play of circles in space. Also in 1934, he filmed a colourized version of *Studie No. 11*, with music by Mozart, and entitled it *Studie No. 11 A*. Then he made an advertising film for Muratti cigarettes. Ironically, of all his artistic creations, it was this work that made him famous. With the support of a good commercial distribution system, the short circulated in theatres for a long time. From 1934 to 1935, the artist worked on his most ambitious project: 'rhythmic' animation linked to the third dimension and colour. The film, entitled *Komposition in Blau* (Composition in Blue), with music from the overture to Otto Nicolai's *Merry Wives of Windsor*, was shot in Gasparcolor utilizing solid forms.

---

[67] This may be a pun in German on the name of the client for Münchener Bilderbogen.
[68] Born in Budapest in 1895 as László Sándor, he died in Los Angeles in 1970 after a remarkable career as a pianist, conductor, and composer.

Meanwhile, abstract art, which in Hitler's and Goebbels's dictionary meant degenerate, had been prohibited. For some time, Fischinger managed to continue his activity by defining his films as 'decorative' rather than abstract. Then he accepted an invitation by Paramount, a company that had followed the artist's European success, and decided to cross the ocean. On 11 February 1936, Fischinger left Germany.

Once in Hollywood, the artist was asked to set up a long abstract sequence for *The Big Broadcast of 1937* (1937), a typical Hollywood musical show featuring brief appearances by a large number of stars. Fischinger utilized a jazz score, entitled *Radio Dynamics*, by Ralph Rainger, one of Paramount's musicians.[69] Eventually, the producers decided to make *The Big Broadcast of 1937* in black and white and wanted to transform the abstract short accordingly. Fischinger, who had worked on the short with colour in mind, refused. The contract was broken in September. Following advice from his friends – among them painter Lyonel Feininger – Fischinger decided to simultaneously make his living by painting.

Fischinger's Hollywood career continued. In 1937, he made *An Optical Poem* for MGM based on Liszt's *Second Hungarian Rhapsody*; in 1942, he was approached by Orson Welles, who was planning a biographical film on Louis Armstrong, although this effort never reached fruition. Fischinger took also a trip to New York to seek financial support for his projects, which included an abstract feature film inspired by the *Symphony from the New World* by Dvořák. This idea failed, although personal exhibitions of Fischinger's work had already opened in two New York galleries in 1938.

Fischinger's brief stay at Disney was the result of his wish to make a concert feature, which he made public in the Berlin film trade paper. He also contacted star conductor Leopold Stokowski for some rights while both were in Berlin about the possibility of a film based on Bach's *Toccata and Fugue*. Stokowsky suggested the project to Disney, who started working on *Fantasia* and hired Fischinger. Disney basically utilized the work that Fischinger had generated for *Fantasia* as 'inspirational drawings'. The artwork was systematically manipulated by the crew (as ordered by Walt himself) and changed to a more figurative form, more easily accepted by audiences. Eventually, Fischinger left the production and in the film's credits there is no trace of his collaboration, by his request.

Throughout the years, Fischinger's house became a meeting place for intellectuals of various kind. The Whitney brothers, Maya Deren, and musician John Cage – creator of aleatory music – would visit there. Much of the conversation focused on Oriental philosophy, and Fischinger never stopped expounding on his theory of the correspondence between optical vibration and sound vibration.

Fischinger's exhibitions, however, increased, and so did his contacts with the Guggenheim Foundation. In 1940, the curator of the Solomon Guggenheim Foundation, baroness Hilla Rebay Von Ehrenwiesen, financed a new short film by Fischinger, *An American March*, with the music of *Stars and Stripes Forever*. She gave a grant to Oskar, who bought the film originally entitled *Radio Dynamics* from Paramount and remade it film with the new title, *Allegretto* (1936–1943). In 1946, the painter Jordan Belson, impressed by Fischinger's films, wanted to meet him. Fischinger himself introduced the young and promising artist to the Guggenheim Foundation for the purpose of obtaining financing.

Still in 1946, Fischinger began his last work, *Motion Painting No. 1*, with a musical score from Bach's *Third Brandenburg Concerto*. *Motion Painting No. 1* is based on the constant transformation of a painting on Plexiglas, a sort of return, twenty years later, to Eggeling's way of making cinema. The extraordinary power of this work, however, was not understood by the Guggenheim Foundation, which considered it disappointing and refused to grant the money necessary to make copies of the film. This episode ended the long period in which Fischinger had been encouraged, but also overwhelmed, by his patron.

In the following years, Fischinger did not have further opportunities to make auteur films. In the late 1940s, he returned to his inventions, patenting

---

[69] Rainger made another attempt at animation by preparing music for a very different project, the Fleischers' *Gulliver's Travels*.

his lumigraph, a living room instrument, large as a big piano. In 1953, due to financial problems, he abandoned his studies on stereoscopic film. Suffering from diabetes, he gradually reduced his volcanic pace of activity, limiting himself to painting. In 1961, he tried to begin *Motion Painting No. 2* but soon abandoned the project. Fischinger died on 31 January 1967 at the age of sixty-six.

The roots of Fischinger's interest in cinema can probably be found in Diebold's encouragement as well as in the artist's meeting with Walther Ruttmann (thirteen years older than Fischinger, Ruttmann was a prestigious painter and filmmaker who certainly influenced the young artist). It seems that Fischinger and Eggeling also became friends, or at least if they never met personally, Fischinger held Eggeling's work in great esteem. Fischinger also maintained a close relationship with Moholy-Nagy. Conversely, he did not appreciate Hans Richter.

Since his beginnings, Fischinger questioned himself about the meaning of his work. Until then, two opposite forces had propelled him: an emotional, spiritual, even esoteric irrationalism, and a mathematical, logical, mechanical engineer's mind. All music composers have experienced the same ambivalence, and he tried to reconcile his divided temperament in colour music, the most original and successful among his experiments. But as for music, his attitude fluctuated. Initially, he argued that music was only a means to attract audiences, who already knew certain tunes or who, in any case, found them pleasant. In short, music had merely an accessory-like function. Later on, he considered music as a teaser (and a very acceptable one from a linguistic standpoint), used to induce the public to concentrate on an abstract film. More than any other artist, he kept alive the search for a visual rhythm, meticulously linked to sound rhythm. He loved music and wanted to steal its secrets of harmony, melody, and counterpoint and translate them to the field of images. He praised the nineteenth-century composers because, in his opinion, they had created a new world, 'the abstract language of sound'.

Despite his many masterpieces, this writer's feeling is that Fischinger, like his colleagues and competitors, failed in his ideological purpose. The languages of sound and image cannot be translated one into the other, although they can be very well married (think of dance, for instance). Colour music, at its best, has always been a high form of choreography. The above sentence can't, however, be rewritten backwards without losing its truth.

According to his biographer William Moritz[70] in *Composition in Blue*, he had wanted to express joy. *An Optical Poem* was a digression on the relation between body and movement, between the parts of a whole and the whole itself. *Radio Dynamics* was based on the concept that colours are relative and that their value depends on the way they are perceived.

A person of multiple interests, Fischinger studied astronomy and atomic and molecular science, deepening his knowledge of physics and reading Einstein. Another of Fischinger's many facets was his love of Goethe, whose philosophy he found very close to his own (particularly the first part of *Faust*). Fischinger's conception of the world and life led him to practice Buddhist philosophy and yoga. He often drew human eyes, including the third eye of knowledge, always changing its colour. His interest in Buddhism increased in his last years and came to involve his lifestyle during a time when Buddhist theories, especially the Zen version, were very popular among American intellectuals.[71]

Fischinger's production includes at least five major works, the first of which is the group of *Studien*. Sharing the same stylistic and technical choices, the *Studien* can be considered chapters of one novel. They are composed of abstract elements (dots, geometrical forms), intertwining and moving in correspondence with sound, each of these elements playing an instrumental part in the creation of an optical symphony.

Composition in Blue has more historic than aesthetic importance. Although it is sometimes questionable and pompous, trying too hard to amaze, it is the first abstract film utilizing all three dimensions like a moving set design. Here, Fischinger uses

---

[70] Personal communication with the author, 1984.
[71] William Moritz, 'Oskar Fischinger' (unpublished manuscript, circa 1972).

not only forms and colours (with a primitive though fascinating Gasparcolor), but also space: abstract sculpture made real through rhythm.

An Optical Poem, the film Fischinger made for MGM, has been defined by some as the 'abstract rendition' of the cat-and-mouse chase that the production company was to release in a figurative edition later on. The film is a long-travelling pan shot in the horizontal direction, a long trip across an abstract space in which polychromatic geometric forms intertwine and 'chase' each other following the rhythm of Liszt's music. Colour is used with a freedom unknown to American animators. The basic tonality of the film is strident yellow ochre, with the appearance of unusual colours, such as saturated brown.

Radio Dynamics is perhaps the artist's masterpiece. The finesse and complexity of invention are balanced for the most part, and the novelty of visual elements is more advanced than in earlier works. William Moritz based his interpretation of this work on yoga spirituality.[72]

Finally, the most recent effort, *Motion Painting*, was no longer mechanically linked to music but became an interpretation of the music itself. Featuring two different movements and different rhythms interrelating, this is a painting in movement as well as an animated film. As never before, both film and fine art critics are summoned. It is yet another demonstration of the lack of precise boundaries in the visual arts.[73]

Austria

The early 1920s boom years didn't last, and soon the modest Austrian film industry collapsed, coinciding with the flow of the American product. In 1923, Astoria Film closed, and both live and animation Austrian cinema was at a virtual standstill for the remainder of the decade.

One hardworking animation artist who remained active during these lean years was the aforementioned Peter Eng, an employee in the animation department of Astoria who, after the studio's closing, doggedly continued to produce drawings, caricatures, and animation commercials until 1929 (in a text published in 1923, Eng described how difficult it had already become to land animation jobs, and how hiring a studio consumed a big part of the revenue). Eng produced the 1929 *Ja warum fahrn's denn ned?* (Why Don't You Drive [i.e. use public transportation]?), commissioned by the Vienna Public Transport Company, along with a series of humorous posters explaining how passengers should and should not behave.[74]

The leading Austrian animation studio during the 1930s was that of Bruno Wozak (25 September 1903–25 September 1944) and Karl Thomas (14 June 1903–?).[75] Stylistically inspired by Walt Disney's films and by art nouveau, both studied at the Academy of Fine Arts: Wozak studied sculpture and caricature; Thomas, graphics and painting. In July 1938, the review *Die Wiener Bühne* defined Bruno Wozak's advertising skills as a perfect mix of 'pencil and patience'. One of the most complex works made by the studio was *Das Hammerbrot Schlaraffenland* (The Bread-Factory Wonderland, 1936), produced by Rudi Maier, a live-action documentary with animated sections in the middle.

Wozak and Thomas were aided by a group of assistants, the best of which was Wilhelm Jaruska (born in 1919). In the same years, Wozak and Thomas directed the cigarette advertisement *Nur die Ruhe . . .* (Only the Peace. . ., 1937) and numerous other advertising films, some such as *Tiden Krever* (Time Requires, 1936), were even produced for other European countries.

Wozak/Thomas also made the public relations film *Reise durch Österreich* (Journey through Austria, 1937), about railway and road improvement in Austria. The film clearly shows Disney's influence in its characterization of inanimate things. When, at the Salzburg railway station, two locomotive cars switch places at the head of each other's trains, the animation technique characterizes the different type of machinery: The modern, electric locomotive

---

[72] William Moritz, 'The Films of Oskar Fischinger', *Film Culture*, Nos. 58, 59, and 60, 1974, pp. 156–157.
[73] We gratefully thank Barbara Fischinger and Cindy Keefer for correcting the factual mistakes of this paragraph.
[74] Eng's family, from the town of Olmütz (today the Czech city of Olomouc) was of Jewish origin, which, as a consequence of the Nazi occupation, caused them hardship and ultimately cost Peter his life. Peter's brother, the famous architect and philosopher Paul Engelmann (a friend of Ludwig Wittgenstein), left Europe early enough to emigrate to the United States. Peter and his wife Anna Pölz were not so fortunate and, around 1939, committed suicide together, seeing no chance to escape the Nazis.
[75] Thomas may have died during World War II; however, the date of his death is unavailable.

158 Chapter 13: Austria

Figure 13.5 Bruno Wozak and Karl Thomas, *Das Hammerbrot Schlaraffenland*, 1936.

moves in a linear way, with simple cut-out animation, whereas the steam locomotive, which blows smoke everywhere, changes form as it contracts into an 'anticipation' pose, then exits the station at full speed.

The colour films *Aida* and *Carmen* (both 1935) were sponsored by the industrialist Arthur Werther and planned to be part of a group of opera parodies.

Only *Carmen* survived: The film adapted many elements from Georges Bizet's opera, but the story was reduced to about ten minutes, with a different ending. Stefan Wessely and his wife directed the film; Wilhelm 'Bil' Spira (Vienna, 1913–?) was the main animator, assisted in animation and time-consuming ink-and-paint by artists Susi Weigel and Wilhelm Jaruska.[76]

In *Carmen*, the narration is introduced by a short presentation of the main characters: José, El Toro (the bull), Torero (the bullfighter) and, of course, Carmen. Remarkably, the bull is turned here into a minotaur-like figure, with surprisingly human behaviour. As the original opera, the film begins with a military parade nearby a factory, where female workers are doing their job. Carmen arrives and meets José the soldier. Carmen and José go together to the inn, where people are singing and drinking. The couple dance on the table and, immediately after, Torero the bullfighter enters and attracts the attention of Carmen. José, consumed with jealousy, jumps out of his skin and sprouts horns from his head, transforming into a sort of bull-man, and starts to duel with the bullfighter.[77] Finally, José and the bullfighter and Carmen arrive at the arena, where the bull has been waiting impatiently for his challenger. This sets off a battle among all three suitors and, when the bull wins the fight, Carmen chooses him over the two men; the story ends with Carmen and the bull leaving the arena arm in arm.

On 12 March 1938, Austria was annexed to Hitler's Germany.[78] Wozak no longer wished to continue an

---

[76] Weigel (1914–1990) and Jaruska (1916–2008) were both also skilled graphic artists and illustrators; they were art students with Spira at the Wiener Kunstgewerbeschule (later renamed the University of Applied Arts – and where Maria Lassnig would found her Studio for Experimental Animation). Bil Spira's ingenious animation apparently made the Wesselys quite jealous, as his work, in effect, superseded their role as 'directors'.

[77] The use of animation here to symbolize Jose's strong feelings is special. In German, when one is extremely angry, we say, 'aus der Haut fahren' – literally, 'jump out of your skin'. Likewise, Jose's becoming a bull-man is also a wordplay: when a woman leaves one man to go with another, we say she 'puts the horns on' (i.e. cuckolds) her first man. This wordplay is depicted literally in this quite short sequence.

[78] Austria annexation, also known as *Anschluss* (link, connection) was part of Hitler's process of unification of all German-speaking lands. Austria resumed status as an independent nation in 1945 but without immediately obtaining full sovereignty from the Allies; such full sovereignty was recognized in 1955.

animation career, and the Wozak-Thomas Studio closed in 1941.[79] There remained, however, some opportunity during the occupation for Austrian animators to work on German productions.

One of these animators was Johann Weichberger (Trieste,[80] 1910–Vienna, 1992), who started his art studies at the Wiener Kunstgewerbeschule, where he met his future wife Else Knoll. In 1933, he went to Bern to work for two years with advertising producer Julius Pinschewer. The years with Pinschewer provided him with the necessary knowledge and experience to work with animation. After a short period back in Vienna, in 1938, Weichberger went to Berlin, where he worked on films for DEGETO (Deutsche Gesellschaft für Tonfilm) and perhaps also Mars Film, which produced animation for military instruction films. During these years, he made the *Fritz und Fratz* serial of silent shorts, distributed by the Degeto-Kulturfilm GmbH for their 16mm 'Schmalfilmschrank' (Small-Film Cabinet) series aimed at the home market.

Fritz and Fratz are two twins who, together with their uncle, go on adventures, with extraordinary travels on the open seas and dangerous situations. These fanciful shorts, with titles like *Der Spuk an Bord* (Spook Onboard), *Die wilde Jagd* (The Wild Hunt), *Afrika* and *Der geheimnisvolle Tempel* (The Mysterious Temple) recall stylistic and technical features of Bruno Wozak and Karl Thomas's films, as well as the Disney school.

A total of twelve shorts were produced, with the ending of each story typically setting the situation for the following episode in the series. In 1941, together with Susi Weigel (who aided Johann also in the Fritz und Fratz series), Weichberger directed the four-part serial *Peterle's Abenteuer* (Peterle's Adventure).

If Weichberger's careful and precise drawing was less dynamic in style than typical American animation of the period, his are in any case among the best short films produced by Austrian filmmakers during the 1940s.

After surviving the bombing of Berlin on 21 November 1943, the Weichberger family returned to Vienna. In 1944, Weichberger moved briefly to Zlín (now in the German-occupied Protectorate of Bohemia and Moravia), where he worked on German-commissioned films, perhaps subcontracted via Deutsche Zeichenfilm AG.[81] He returned to Austria in 1945 and, with only a few collaborators, founded the Herold film company in 1948 which, whose productions included *Österreichs beste Mannschaft* (Austria's Best Team, 1949), an advertisement about national cigarette production, in opposition to the black market.

With the television boom, Weichberger found a new market but did not forget theatrical films: He made many animated title sequences and some special effects with object animation. He also designed a rotating globe for *Wochenschau* (a theatrical newsreel). Walt Disney's influence was very strong on the animators who worked after World War II with producer Franz Bresnikar (Vienna, 1908–Vienna, 1996). After mechanical engineering studies, and just before the war years, Bresnikar's interest in art and theatre introduced him in the acting world, although not professionally. After the war, he founded his own production company. During the period of the 'Besatzung' (the occupation of Austria by World War II allies Britain, France, Russia, and the United States) from 1945 to 1955, it was quite difficult to build substantial production in the region both because of the scarcity of equipment, materials and talent and the domination of US animation production which, economically and stylistically, largely overshadowed Austrian production.

Bresnikar's animation technique was similar in ways to the American one: Bresnikar himself acted out played the scenes in front of the animator Paul Obczovsky, who made some sketches from which he developed the animation sequences. One of his first productions, from 1953, was a series based on animals competing in Olympic events, inspired by the Olympic Games hosted in Helsinki the previous year.

Between 1955 and 1960, Bresnikar was one of the best specialists in cinema commercials and in the so-called 'sound slides' or 'speaking stripes', in which Franz was also the speaker. In the final part of his activity, Bresnikar increasingly focused his work on cinema and live action.

Switzerland[82]

The resurrection of Lortac and Cavé's film *M. Vieux-Bois* in the 1930s could not have been better timed, because it happened exactly when a new breed of production, of the kind

---

[79] Wozak and Thomas became soldiers; Wozak died in the war.
[80] This was called the Austro-Hungarian Empire; it is now Italy.
[81] Also in Zlín at the time, working in the animation section of the advertising film studio opened in the 1930s by the Bata Company, were Hermína Týrlová and Karel Zeman.
[82] By Rolf Bächler.

we commonly associate with Swiss independent animation at present, was just about to assert its existence, and little did it matter that it was welcomed by its adepts as a proof of a tradition that never was. Because although being its initial, it remained an unmatched effort in the history of Swiss animation, and the only product of Pencil-Film as well, which for reasons unknown did not follow up with more Töpffer adaptations as allegedly planned at the outset. This does not mean that there was no animation at all – quite the opposite. But the activity was clearly oriented to commercially viable fields of production; in other words, commissioned films of all kinds and for all purposes – except for the still exclusively cinema-based entertainment market that already did not seem to offer enough opportunities for profitable business ventures alongside (or against) the predominant foreign competition.

The most prosperous and long-lasting enterprise in the commercial field was again due to some kind of import or knowledge transfer from outside – a phenomenon not uncommon in animation in general; however, as for many artistic occupations, breaking new ground often finds its literal expression in having to leave one's own place of origin in order to find the appropriate circumstances in which to prosper. In this situation, it was the German dean of commercials, Julius Pinschewer, of Jewish origin, who decided to emigrate after the Nazi takeover. In the business from as early as 1910 and owning a thriving company in Berlin, he checked the options according to good client relations but picked Switzerland of all places when, in the midst of a world in turmoil, he witnessed how a farmer peacefully drove his cattle past the government building in the capital Bern without anybody showing signs of being alarmed or even paying attention. He settled there in 1934 and successfully resumed his activity, although never on the same level as before in terms of figures, up to his demise in 1961.

Film as a field for personal expression on the other hand, with no prospect of a revenue, let alone a market, was by and large considered the domain of amateurs, or non-professionals, which never lacked in number and produced a considerable output over the years, earning international recognition and awards in their well-organized circles while, due to its nature, their work largely remained private in its dissemination.

Out of the limited number of still existing bits and pieces of animation defying this framework but nonetheless produced with professional means and ambitions up to the 1950s, there is one that deserves being mentioned for its particularity: *Chromophony* (Chromophony, 1939) by Charles Blanc-Gatti (Lausanne, 26 January 1890–Riex, 8 April 1966). Seeking his fortune as a painter in Paris, Blanc-Gatti became preoccupied with the synaesthesia of sound (i.e. music) and light (colour), resulting in a concept of 'Chromophonic Art' and culminating in the manifesto of the 'Musicalist Artists' (1932). When his interest finally turned from paintings, luminous sceneries and a complex installation called 'Chromophonic Orchestra' to animated film, the professed 'painter of sounds' succeeded in convincing some business people back in Switzerland to set up an animation studio for commercials based on his creative theory, Montreux-Colorfilm, and become its director (1938). After a flamboyant self-promotional film and two rather scanty, traditional commercials, Blanc-Gatti focused all his interest on his own project, *Chromophony*. Alas, it did not turn into the technical and artistic achievement it was intended to be, and it was far from being the first attempt at combining images and music in film in a comparable way. Apparently ignorant of this fact and the much more advanced research of the likes of Oskar Fischinger, however, the frustrated artist abandoned filmmaking (as did Montreux-Colorfilm) and took on Walt Disney instead, at the discovery of *Fantasia* when it was finally released in France in 1946, accusing him of plagiarism.

Denmark[83]

Jørgen Myller (1910–1995) was the man who created the basis for professional animation in Denmark in the 1930s and early 1940s. Inspired by American organization and aesthetics, Myller trained the two talents Anker Roepstorff (1910–1982) and Henning Dahl Mikkelsen (1915–1982), who became the first generation of animators in Denmark. They were responsible for the first experiments with both colour and sound. After a period in Berlin and London, where he was taught commercial arts and animation, Myller returned to Copenhagen in 1931 and, by 1932, started his own studio, Animated Cartoon Company. The company produced primarily advertising films, in a systematic and professional way. The first Danish animated film with a soundtrack was one of his commercials, *Dansen går* (The Dance Goes On, 1932); the first puppet film with a soundtrack most

---

[83] By Annemette Karpen.

probably was *Store Claus og Lille Claus* (Big Claus and Little Claus), directed by Christian Maagaard Christensen in 1930.

In 1934, Myller produced *Carmen*, an opera parody in colour with an English soundtrack.

As the studio did not become an economical success in Copenhagen, Myller, Dahl Mikkelsen and Roepstorff brought this film with them to London, where they worked the next few years for Anson Dyer on the Sam Small series. In 1938, they returned to Copenhagen and established the studio Colour Cartoon Company, producing commercials again. They got a new apprentice, the young talented Børge Ring, as a fine addition to their staff.

In 1939, Myller also got involved in Vepro, another cartoon company. The artists put all their talent, creativity, and humour into their short commercials, lacking possibilities to make entertainment films. It was in these two companies that new young artists were trained, such as Bjørn Frank Jensen (1920–2001), Børge Hamberg (1920–1970), and Keld Simonsen (1920–1988). They became an important addition to the first generation of Danish animators. Vepro closed down in 1942, and Myller's status as the focal point of Danish animation was by this event concluded.

The production of *Fyrtøjet* (The Tinderbox, 1946) became a milestone in Danish animation, as it was both the first long animated film and the first long colour film in Denmark.

The idea of this rather free adaptation of Hans Christian Andersen's fairy tale originated at a meeting between clothing manufacturer Allan Johnsen (1908–1983) and graphic designer Finn Rosenberg Ammitsted. Johnsen was very fascinated by the thought of film production and decided to invest in cinema, like other industrialists whose business had been halted by the war. In the late summer of 1942, he hired a group of people to write a script, which he got in a couple of months. It was logical to hire Jørgen Myller and Henning Dahl Mikkelsen, the best and most experienced animators in town. However, they demanded as a condition that a storyboard be worked out. Johnsen, knowing nothing about animation production, thought this a total waste of time and money, so the collaboration did not materialize. This was, of course, a fatal mistake, but Johnsen was keen to get on with the process and made his own company, Dansk Farve og Tegnefilm A/S, on 5 December 1942.

He hired the young assistants trained by Myller and Dahl Mikkelsen, and later Børge Hamberg (1920–1970), who had recently returned from Germany. Hamberg was chief animator together with Bjørn Frank Jensen, while Finn Rosenberg Ammitsted was responsible for the backgrounds. Bjørn Frank Jensen tried to keep the style close to Disney.

The work went on quite well after the plan with a young talented and enthusiastic team of animators. However, the production got delayed in 1944 due to the German occupation of Denmark. The experienced Keld Simonsen (1920–1988) was asked to do the animation of the last scenes of the film: the dramatic scene at the gallows, the wedding of the princess and the soldier, and the wedding party. The staff by this time also included a lot of inbetweeners, among them Harry Rasmussen (1927–1987), Ib Steinaae (1927–1987), and Kaj Pindal (born in 1927). Later, Henning Dahl Mikkelsen was consulted. He made several suggestions and a very interesting layout for the introduction scene where the princess is carried to her tower. Long shadows are seen before the figures arrive in the picture, thus making a very dramatic effect and a fine example of how an experienced animator worked.

Johnsen had made another mistake: He had not made a prerecording of the sound. Obviously, he did not know the technique of measuring the sound on a dopesheet/X-sheet.[84] This mistake gave the animators a lot of trouble, and the consequence was that the original idea of an opening in December 1944 was postponed by one year.

Johnsen had to spend more money than expected as a result of the delay. The film company Palladium became a co-producer and obtained distribution rights. Palladium also made it a condition that a professional film director be hired. In the middle of 1944, Svend Methling (1891–1977), a stage and live-action film director, got the job. On 19 September 1944, the Danish police were arrested by the Gestapo and deported to German concentration camps. As a consequence, some people who had been politically active against the Germans got hired at the studio and went underground, and some Jews were hidden in the studio before being shipped safely to Sweden.

The film, shot in Agfacolor and developed in Berlin, became quite an adventurous experience. Allan Johnsen was very courageous as he several times went back and

---

[84] Synchronized dialogue for animation is in most cases recorded prior to the animation of the characters. The dialogue track is then analyzed frame by frame and transcribed onto a 'dope sheet' or 'X-sheet' (short for 'exposure sheet'), which gives the animator a precise reference to animate speech in perfect synchronization with the sound track.

forth with the film material in his luggage. In time, the work copy was finally edited. In January 1945, Johnsen and Henning Ørnback went again to war-torn Berlin, this time to have the negative developed. When this was done, the two men got out of the town by truck with the negatives and film materials in their backpacks.

Another delay of the opening of *The Tinderbox* was that the production of cels had stopped, so the animators had to wash and reuse the same cels over and over again – a time-consuming and difficult process. The 'colorines' (as the young ladies who did the painting were called) had difficulties making the colour stick to the glossy cels, as better-grade materials for producing paints were now devoted to weapon production. Johnsen had in 1944–1945 a staff of close to 200 people working on the film in various locations in Copenhagen. This, of course, slowed the work.

By 4 May 1945, Denmark was liberated from German occupation. With freedom, the commerce returned to normal, and the theatres could show old and new American and English films. This was good for the audience but serious competition to *The Tinderbox*. To make the situation even more complicated, Johnsen had to hire Éclair Laboratories in Paris to make the copies of *The Tinderbox*, as Agfacolor in Berlin had been destroyed.

By the fall of 1945, the film was ready for recording of the dialogue and music. The music had already been composed in 1944, but the actors had difficulties in making the dialogue correspond with the lip movements. The mistake was again Johnsen's, as he had thought it cheaper to make the sound track when the film was completed. By 16 May 1946, the film opened in the Palladium cinema. The reviews were tepid, especially by those critics who were now able to see Disney's productions and compared *The Tinderbox* with these.

Despite all this, *The Tinderbox* became a success in Denmark, several European countries, and the United States. Although it has some flaws in colour, figure animation, and lip-syncing, by and large it is a film with great humour, fantasy, and interesting music and is a good adaptation of Andersen's fairy tale.

In 1960 and again in 1980, *The Tinderbox* had a reopening in some Danish cinemas; in 1984, it was again screened in a new copy and, from 1990, it was sold in a home video version. The film was better received this time, as it had acquired historical and nostalgic value; it was called a 'surprising' film,[85] 'stupefying and very well animated'.[86] *The Tinderbox* was also of great importance for the animation milieu and the animators who worked on it many years later.

Sweden

From the 1920s on, Swedish animation grew in the field of advertising. Outside the commercial world, the filmmakers Emile Agren and M. R. Liljeqvist made similar efforts, but their attempts were not organized, remaining merely individual and spontaneous impulses. In 1934, another independent artist, painter Robert Högfeldt, released *Bam-Bam, eller så tuktas ett troll* (How We Tame a Troll), an entertaining ten-minute film. Born in the Netherlands in 1894 to Swedish parents and educated in Düsseldorf and Stockholm, Högfeldt won fame for his paintings of trolls, the magic wood-dwelling creatures of Nordic fairy tales. He also worked as a book illustrator. *How We Tame a Troll* was his only cinematographic work. In the 1940s, the only notable work was an unsuccessful attempt at a feature film: In 1941, Einar Norelius of ABC Film (1900–1985), who had collaborated with Robert Högfeldt, filmed some minutes of *Nils Holgerssons underbara resa* (Nils Holgersson's Wonderful Journey), on a popular subject by children's writer Selma Lagerlöf. The project failed due not to the lack of funding, which was quite abundant, but to a clause in the contract with Selma Lagerlöf, which stated that one single movie should contain her entire book, without cuts or revisions; this would have produced an exceedingly long movie.

Norway[87]

A vital production period of animated cinema commercials in the late 1920s ended with the coming of sound and the dominance of American cartoons. In the 1930s, the animated advertising films were back on the screens, but this time they were made outside Norway. The clients, again with the tobacco company J. L. Tiedemann in the lead, ordered them from the rest of Europe, particularly from Germany.

---

[85] 'Banc-Titre', *Scandinavie*, No. 25, Paris, November 1982, p. 22.
[86] Kaj Pindal, letter to the author, 27 January 1985.
[87] By Gunnar Strøm.

These short advertising films were of very high standard, often three to four minutes long, and many of them were made in Gasparcolor. The films were commissioned through the company Desider Gross in Prague. Desider Gross himself travelled several times to Norway to show examples of cinema commercials for Norwegian industry leaders. The Norwegian companies ordered their films through Gross, who made production contracts with distinguished filmmakers like Hans Fischerkoesen, George Pal, and Alexandre Alexeïeff. Even Oskar Fischinger's *Komposition in Blau* (1935) was made into the commercial *Fargesymfoni i blått* (Colour Symphony in Blue, 1936) for Tiedemann's cigarette brand Medina. The 1936 film *Tiden krever* (Time Requires) is probably the only surviving film by Austrian animator Bruno Wosak. Alexeïeff's *Opta Empfangt* (1936) was made into *Et mesterstykke av Tiedemann* (A Masterpiece by Tiedemann, 1938). Both films advertised the Medina cigarettes. *En Harmoni (Blue Master)* (Harmony, Blue Master, 1938) used the same soundtrack as Fischinger's *Komposition in Blau* and the visuals were also clearly inspired by Fischinger's film, but it was made well after the master left Germany. These films are among the best cinema commercials ever. Of course, this very fruitful collaboration between Norway and Germany ended with World War II.[88]

Snow White and the Seven Dwarfs made a huge impact when it premiered in the spring of 1938. The film was not dubbed but was released in the original American version with Norwegian subtitles.

There was no proper Norwegian animation studio operating in the 1930s; no animated short film is known from this time. But the success of *Snow White* inspired the engineer Harald B. Snilsberg to start working on a Norwegian animated feature based on the Norwegian folk tale *Gjete kongens harer* (Watching the King's Hares). Reportage of Snilsberg working on the film was released as part of the weekly cinema newsreel in 1943. A few drawings from the film are kept in the national library in Oslo, but it is no surprise that the film was never finished.

The only animations done by Norwegians in the 1930s were sequences in documentaries and educational films. Some of them may have been made by Sverre Halvorsen, Niels Sinding-Hansen, and the other animators who were working in the late 1920s. The cartoonist Wilfred Jensenius (1911–1999) made his first animation for a film made for the political party Høyre (the Conservatives) for the elections in 1936. During the war, Jensenius was in prison in Germany but, after the war, he opened a studio outside Oslo making animated films for the national agricultural ministry. The studio was partly financed by money from the Marshall aid.

In the second half of the 1940s, sequences for documentaries and educational films continued to be the only animation made in the country. The period ended with the debut of the most famous of all Norwegian animators, the puppet filmmaker Ivo Caprino (1920–2000), who made his first puppet film *Tim og Tøffe* (Tim and Tøffe) in 1948. The film was well received, and Caprino was awarded a travel grant that brought him to Czechoslovakia, where he visited the studios of Jiří Trnka and Karel Zeman. Ivo Caprino was born into a family that predisposed him towards the arts. His Italian father, Mario, was a craftsman known throughout Norway for his furniture (the street on which Ivo's animation studio opened was named after Mario). Ivo's mother, a caricaturist, was the niece of Romantic painter Hans Gude.

Poland

The most active Polish animator was Włodzimierz Kowanko, who worked in Krakow, Katowice, and Warsaw. His best films were *Mr. Twardowski* (1934), based on a popular tale, and *The Mice's Expedition for a Cake*. Kowanko's style shows traces of American influence. Jan Jarosz, from Lwów,[89] began his career in the mid-1920s. In 1931, he made the notable *Puk's Adventures*. Later, he experimented with a hand-drawn soundtrack in an advertising film. In the 1930s, Jaryczewski was active in Poznan; in 1924, he released *Female Stars and Male Stars*.

In the field of puppet animation, the finest artists include Karol Marczak (former assistant to Ladislas Starewich in Paris and director of *The Golden Pot*, 1935) and Maksymilian Emmer and Jerzy Maliniak (*Toy Soldiers*, 1938, partially animated). It was precisely a puppet animator, Zenon Wasilewski (1903–1966), who represented the only link between pre-war and post-war productions. A poet and a satirical cartoonist, Wasilewski learned the basics of animation in the mid-1930s while drawing for Kowanko. In 1938, he made some advertising films with

---

[88] For more information on these films, see Gunnar Strøm's articles on Desider Gross in *Animation Journal*, Spring 1998 and Spring 2000.
[89] Today, this is Lviv, Ukraine.

puppets. The following year, he used this same technique in a tale featuring the dragon of Wawel (*Krakow's Hill*); because of the German invasion in September 1939, the film was left unfinished, without a sound track. Wasilewski spent the war years in the Soviet Union as a representative of the Polish Resistance. Afterwards, he returned to his country, establishing his residence in Łódz, where he founded a production and distribution company (which would later become the important Se-Ma-For). In 1947, Wasilewski released a second version of his previously filmed tale, renamed *In King Krakus's Time*. In the following years until his death, he divided his time equally between painting and cinema. His releases include *The Two Little Dorothies* (1956) and *Dratewka the Shoemaker* (1958), for children, and *Caution! The Devil* (1958) and *The Crime on the Street of the Ventriloquist Cat* (1961), for adults.

Stefan and Franciszka Themerson

Writer Stefan Themerson (Płock, 25 January 1910–London, 6 September 1988) and painter Franciszka Weinles (Warsaw, 28 June 1907–London, 29 June 1988) married in 1931. They had already discovered their calling to experimental literature and art to which, from then on, they devoted their lives, both separately and often together.

In 1928, Stefan experimented with the manipulation of photographs; from 1930 to 1937, the couple produced the short films *Apteka* (Pharmacy, 1930); *Europa* (1932), *Drobiazg Melodyjny* (Melodic Trifle, 1933); *Zwarcie* (Short Circuit, 1935); and *Przygoda Człowieka Pocziwego* (Adventure of an Honest Man, 1937; this is the only surviving one among the films shot in Poland and is an allegoric, lyrical, satiric, but rather conventional narrative story). The Themersons moved from Warsaw to Paris in 1938 and, at the outbreak of the war in 1939, they enlisted in the Polish Army abroad. In 1940, Franciszka moved to London; Stefan joined her in 1942. Here they made two more films: the anti-war *Calling Mr Smith* (1943), and *The Eye and the Ear* (1945), an experiment in visualizing sound.

In the meantime, their activity in other areas was frantic. There were bread-and-butter jobs and mind-opening jobs. In 1948, they founded Gaberbocchus Press,[90] a small avant-garde publishing house. In their later life, they were both successful in their own chosen fields. Stefan, particularly, became one of the most praised experimental poets in the world, but also wrote novels, short stories, and essays, freely crossing the genres – and not disdaining comedy.

About the films, Marcin Gizycki wrote:

> Despite the fact that of these seven works only the last three have survived, and the rest are known from descriptions and single frames, there is no doubt that the Themersons were the most important Polish independent experimental filmmakers in the inter-war years and their films can easily be placed among the greatest achievements of European avant-garde film of the time.[91]

In an article of 1937, Stefan Themerson recounted the inspiration for his film work:

> One night long, long ago, three feet of scratched film-scrap tore across the screen in front of the author of this story. The screen glittered, blazed with its very own light and died. The slovenly projectionist must have joined two reels with a scratched bit of film. . . . Let me now praise slovenliness. The method was simple; in normal photograms, objects were placed on light-sensitive paper. We arranged them on semi-transparent paper, using a sheet of glass for support; the camera (an old-fashioned box with a crank) was placed underneath and pointed upwards with

---

[90] 'Gaberbocchus' is the Latin translation of 'Jabberwocky'; *Jabberwocky* is the nonsense title of a nonsense poem by Lewis Carroll, originally included in *Through the Looking Glass*.

[91] Marcin Gizycki, 'The Films of Stefan and Franciszka Themerson', in Jan Kubasiewicz, Monica J. Strauss, and Marcin Giżycki (eds.) *The Themersons and the Gaberbocchus Press: An Experiment in Publishing 1948–1979*, MJS Books and Graphics, New York, 1993 (on the occasion of an exhibition of the same name held at La Boetie, Inc., 9 East 82nd Street, New York, between October 1993 and January 1994); this first appeared in Polish in Polish Art Studies VIII (Warsaw, 1987).

the light source situated above the glass. Usually, but not always, by moving the lights (frame after frame) we obtained movement of the shadows and their deformations.[92]

Gizycki comments:

> The above quote assures us that *Pharmacy* was an interesting experiment with animation. The true subject of this kind of animation was not drawings or objects, but the elusive nature of pure light. The film also contained shots of pharmaceutical accessories and of a siphon, face, clock, and hand. The Themerson's [sic] own photograms from 1928–1929 were used as well. The images were given a sequence according to their poetical and visual value.[93]
>
> The couple's typical variety of styles, techniques, and passions allowed them to make films adopting and adapting the most common home objects and going from animation to live action and vice versa without apparent strain.

Czechoslovakia

The initiator of Czechoslovakian animation was Karel Dodal (Prague, 27 January 1900–Fort Lee, New Jersey, 6 July 1986), who gained experience in animation in the 1920s during his apprenticeship at the production company Elekta-Journal. In 1933, along with his partner and later wife Irena Rosnerová (Ledeč nad Sázavou, 29 November 1900–Buenos Aires, October 1989),[94] he established in Prague the IRE Film Studio, directing and producing several advertising films. Karel headed the visual side, while Irena was the scriptwriter and the director of the live-action scenes. Quite ambitious filmmakers, in their over thirty commercials they experimented with sound and colour, puppets, and animated objects and even made two successful abstract films: *Fantaisie érotique* (1937, original title in French)[95] and *Myšlenka hledající světlo* (Ideas Search for Light, 1938, produced partly abroad).

The first one was based on the movement of dots/bubbles and was a modernist experiment in animated colour graphics; the second one was basically a geometrical dance, with a predilection for ovoidal and round shapes and for stylized beams of light.

On 5 October 1938, Czechoslovakia capitulated to Nazi Germany; Karel Dodal moved to the small Paris branch of the IRE Film Studio but closed it almost immediately and then took refuge in New York. Irena stayed in Prague and worked as a stage director, but, on 20 June 1942, she was arrested and deported to the Theresienstadt concentration camp.[96] She was set free on 5 February 1945 and then was able to reach her husband in the United States.[97]

The Dodals incorporated Irena Film in New York to make commercials but, in 1948, moved again, this time to Argentina. In 1961, Karel came back to the United States, while his wife stayed in Buenos Aires, where she had become an outstanding figure in theatre and ballet. Her live-action film *Apollon Musagete* (1951) is still considered a classic of the video dance.

In 1941, in the midst of the war, Dodal's first wife and collaborator Hermína Týrlová (1900–1993) moved from Prague to Zlín and joined Bata's studio. In Zlín, she animated and directed the puppet film *Ferda Mravenec* (Ferda the Ant, 1943). Showing Ptushko's influences, this work marked the beginning of a long and fruitful career in the field of children's films.

Great Czechoslovakian animation, however, was rooted in Prague. In 1935, Atelier Filmovych Triku (AFIT) opened at 33 Stépánská Street. The small studio, which

---

[92] Marcin Gizycki, 'The Films of Stefan and Franciszka Themerson', in Jan Kubasiewicz, Monica J. Strauss, and Marcin Giżycki (eds.) *The Themersons and the Gaberbocchus Press: An Experiment in Publishing 1948–1979*, MJS Books and Graphics, New York, 1993.
[93] Marcin Gizycki, 'The Films of Stefan and Franciszka Themerson', in Jan Kubasiewicz, Monica J. Strauss, and Marcin Giżycki (eds.) *The Themersons and the Gaberbocchus Press: An Experiment in Publishing 1948–1979*, MJS Books and Graphics, New York, 1993.
[94] We acknowledge Eva Strusková for her decisive research on these two filmmakers.
[95] The Dodals also made it into an advertising film for a soap, with the title of *Hra bublinek* (Play of Bubbles, 1937).
[96] Theresienstadt (now Terezin, Czech Republic) was one of the most grotesque inventions of the SS: a mock-luxury camp, intended for the cream of middle European Jews, artists, writers, scientists, musicians, and scholars. Concerts, chamber and jazz music performances, and stage performances were also produced there. Irena was forced to write the script of a film and direct plays for the Yiddish theatre. This camp, created as a propaganda stunt to deceive the public about the ultimately deadly mission of Nazi concentration camps, hosted a total of about 145,000 inmates, of whom about 80,000 died.
[97] On 5 February 1945, Heinrich Himmler sold 1,210 Jews from Theresienstadt to Swiss Jewish organizations for $1.25 million.

employed about six people, produced tricks for live-action cinema, models, special effects, and animated titles. In 1941, during the German occupation, Nazi leader Joseph Pfister took over the studio and made out of it the animation department of the (German) Prag Film, one of the largest production companies of the Reich. The staff quickly expanded to include students from art schools. The artistic direction was entrusted to the inexperienced Austrian Richard Dillenz, who quit after the flop of an amateurish opera-like feature inspired by Orpheus and Eurydice. Before the arrival of Dillenz's replacement, Berlin's Horst von Möllendorff became the new artistic director. The animators at the studio produced the already mentioned Wedding in the Coral Sea. In September 1944, the studio closed and reopened only at the end of the war.

Hungary

In pre-war Hungary, Valker István[98] (Lugos, 1903–Budapest, 1982) was the first to combine live-action film with animation (*Polly Tricks* [1934–1938]). He animated the popular tale *The Miller, His Son and the Donkey* (1934) with Dávid Teréz (Tissa David) who emigrated from Hungary first to Paris and then to New York, where she would make a name for herself. Animation, as the overall Hungarian film industry, hence, suffered from a diaspora of talent. Next to Tissa, among the artists who left to work abroad were: George Pal, John Halas, Jean Image, Ferdinánd Huszti Horváth (who originally designed Walt Disney's *Snow White*), Etienne Raïk (a collaborator of Alexandre Alexeïeff's and a fine puppet animator who mainly made commercials), Wilma de Quiche (working with Paul Grimault in Paris), Jules Engel, Péter Földes, Kálmán Viktor Oszkár, and Géza von Cziffra.

George Pal

When Marczincsák Julius György (Cegléd, Hungary, 1 February 1908–Beverly Hills, 2 May 1980) was still a child, his stage entertainer parents divorced, and he was raised by his grandparents. In 1928, he graduated from the Budapest Academy of Arts with a degree in architecture and highly developed drawing skills. Then he got employment at Hunnia Films, where he drew lobby posters and titles for silent movies. He also quickly learned the craft of motion picture cartooning.

In 1931, he married Zsoka (Grandjean Erszbet Josefa, 1909–2002) and moved to Berlin, where he founded the Trickfilm Studio Pal und Wittke, with the immensely powerful UFA Studios as its main customer from 1931 to 1933.

During this time, he patented 'Pal-Dolls' (later known as 'Puppetoons'). They were made with wooden puppets, set against cardboard backgrounds. Both puppets and backgrounds were detailed and ornately decorated. Animation was achieved using the 'replacement technique', which involved a separate puppet (or puppet part) for each motion, rather than hinged parts. During the peak of production, an average short would use 9,000 puppets. The best-known *Puppetoon* creations (in the 1940s in the United States) were Jasper and his two friends, Professor Scarecrow and Blackbird.[99]

When the Nazis came to power in Germany, in 1933, the government placed the foreign born on watch lists. The two Hungarians left for Prague and then on to Paris, where they received an invitation from Philips Radio to move to Eindhoven, Netherlands. It was in Eindhoven that the first real *Puppetoon* was created: *Ship of Ether*. The ship was made of glass and was puppet animated on waves also made of glass.

Sometime around 1935, György started signing 'George Pal' in the Puppetoon screen credits for director and producer, and used Pal also, instead of Marczincsák, on legal documents.

Barney Baliban, the president of Paramount Pictures' New York office, contacted Pal and offered him a contract. The filmmaker moved to America, where he gladly accepted what Frank Freeman, the president of Paramount Studios in Hollywood, offered him: a studio of his own and a staff of twenty-five collaborators.

---

[98] Surname first, given name second, according to Hungarian customary usage.

[99] These stereotypes of African-Americans, which were very successful, received the first reprimand for racism in 1947 by the new, but already authoritative, monthly *Ebony*. They would later be shunned in the United States as examples of political incorrectness. This historian will not probe as boundless and burning a question as racism but recalls that George Pal was considered a courageous showman in Europe who had chosen a minority group representative as his leading character.

From 1941 to 1947, Pal created more than forty *Puppetoon* shorts. His studio staffers included people like the old Willis H. O'Brien and the young Ray Harryhausen. He was given an honorary Academy Award in 1944 for 'the development of novel methods and techniques in the production of short subjects known as Puppetoons'.

In 1949, he released a full-length film, *Destination Moon*, which combined live action with 'tricks'. The film was a success both with the public and critics (and won an Academy Award for special effects), and he was allowed to make another: *When Worlds Collide*. This film also did quite well, so he went on making such classics as *War of the Worlds*, *The Time Machine*, and *The Seven Faces of Dr. Lao*. His last two films, *The Power* (1968) and *Doc Savage* (1975), were flops.

George Pal belongs to the tradition of Georges Méliès, Emile Cohl, Aleksandr Ptushko, Karel Zeman, and Terry Gilliam: animators and 'magicians' who loved special effects and eventually combined them with fairy tale storytelling. His live-action films aren't actually great but are the delight of influential trash culture cognoscenti, so his popularity as a science fiction specialist usually overshadows his contributions to sheer animation. Pal's best works date from the 1940s, when working for Paramount. We should not forget such films as *Jasper and the Beanstalk* (1945) and *John Henry and the Inky-Poo* (1946).

Pal's contribution to puppet animation is fundamental and long lasting. He came after the 'realism' of Ladislas Starevitch and shared with Aleksandr Ptushko the taste for absolute perfection in lip-syncing and rich movements. (Ten years later, Jiří Trnka and the Czech school would contradict this recipe and promote stone-faced marionettes, whose attitude and expression were provided by position, lighting, and body movements.)

In the end, Pal was not so much a great artist, in command of his own poetic world, as an inimitable technician of movement and a showman of taste. His elegantly stylized puppets give excellent acting performances and his films display lively mass scenes, pathos, and the style of framing used in live-action cinema.

Yugoslavia

A Pole by birth, Sergij Tagatz spent many years in Russia and worked for the Ermolev Film Studio in Yalta, where he made his first experiments with animation. He went to Zagreb in 1922 and filmed a number of animated commercials. In 1923, he created animated trailers for films starring Jackie Coogan; but eventually he made a career as a live-action cinematographer.

In 1931 three brothers of Jewish ancestry (Modnschein Maar) arrived in Zagreb from Berlin, where they had had to sell their company of animated advertisements and flee from Hitler. Continuing their work in Zagreb, they remained in operation until 1936, when due to the risk of bankrupt they sold their firm and went to Belgrade, abandoning animation.

The Maar brothers created attractive and eye-catching advertising. They were the first real businessmen connected with animated film in Zagreb.

The war dispersed artists, equipment, and films, and, when the war ended, occupation troops prohibited filming.

Greece[100]

Chronologically, the first animated Greek film was *O Duce afighete* (The Duce Narrates) by Stamati Polenaki (1908–1997). The film was designed in 1942 on the island of Sifnos during the World War II Italian occupation and was actually shot in Athens, in 1945, by Papaduka and Merevidi. The Duce Narrates, a fresh anti-fascist satire, was rediscovered in 1980. *Siga tus keravnus* (Imagine! What Lightnings!) was made in 1946 by Yanni Russopulos and tells the wonderful adventures of the gods on Olympus.

After the Liberation, between 1946 and 1949, strategically located Greece faced a bloody civil war between the right, supported by Britain and the United States, and the left, supported by the USSR. Eventually the right won. But it was not the time for animation filmmaking.

Italy

Luigi Liberio Pensuti (1903–1945) was the only animator to work continuously in the country, first on his own and, since 1935, as head of the animation department of the Istituto Nazionale Luce (the state agency for cinematography). His production was basically educational, but he is remembered for some war propaganda films like *Il dottor*

---

[100] By Michela Morselli.

Churkill (Doctor Churkill, 1942), where Winston Churchill acts like Dr. Jekyll/Mr. Hyde and is much more a funny character than a political enemy.

The brothers Carlo (1907–1964) and Vittorio (1911–1984) Cossio made some shorts in the 1930s: *Zibillo e l'orso* (Zibillo and the Bear, 1932); *La secchia rapita* (The Stolen Bucket, 1937), based on the playful poem by Alessandro Tassoni (1565–1635); and *La macchina del tempo* (The Time Machine, 1937), based on H. G. Wells's (1866–1946) story. In both the latter movies, the artists experimented with colour and stereoscopy, using a procedure devised by Milan engineer Gultiero Gualtierotti. Due to technical reasons (the procedure required very expensive equipment), their work did not continue. In 1940, the Roman painter Luigi Giobbe (1907–1945) made his debut with *Il vecchio lupo di mare norvegese e il vecchio lupo di mare americano* (The Old Salt from Norway and the Old Salt from America). Soon afterwards, he invited the Cossio brothers to Rome, and together they made two short films inspired by the classical Neapolitan masque: *Pulcinella e i briganti* (Pulcinella and the Brigands), also known as *Pulcinella nel bosco* (Pulcinella in the Forest) and *Pulcinella e il temporale* (Pulcinella and the Storm). As far as puppet animation is concerned, Sicilian Ugo Saitta (1912–1982) is worth mentioning for his short comedy set in the Middle Ages, *Teste di legno* (Wooden Heads, 1939, also known as *Pisicchio e Melisenda* [Pisicchio and Melisenda]).

A case of a filmmaker who made animated films without calling them by that name was Luciano Emmer (1918–2009). An eclectic director whose fame especially lies in his documentaries on fine arts, he debuted in 1938 with *Racconto di un affresco* (A Tale of a Fresco). By editing details of Giotto's frescoes in the Padua Scrovegni chapel, he both told the story of the fourteenth-century masterpiece and a story of his own. He adopted the same approach as Beaton Angelico, Hieronymus Bosch, Piero della Francesca, and particularly Francisco Goya (*I disastri della guerra* [Disasters of War], 1950). Alexandre Alexeïeff writes:

> Goya had omitted any chronological tie between his engravings. Emmer assorted and juxtaposed them like ellipses in a conversation: if you say 'I'm sad, and you – happy', the omission of 'you are' adds dynamism to the sentence. The still frames are too long-lasting to be used for classical animation, so they create a feeling of abrupt and discontinuous movements, like in the Japanese fan dance.[101]

Outstanding comic strip artist and illustrator Antonio Rubino (San Remo, 1880–Baiardo, 1964), made *Nel paese dei ranocchi* (In the Country of the Frogs), giving an original interpretation of art nouveau. This film was variously butchered by the distributors. Nino Pagot made his debut in the 1940s. An artist characterized by an uncommon vigour, he later became the director of a quite influential team, the longest-lived Italian animation establishment. Born in Venice on 22 May 1908,[102] Pagot moved to Milan, where he began short experiments in animation. In 1938, he founded his own production company and invited his much younger brother Toni (Milan, 16 December, 1921-Roncello, Milan, 7 July 2001) to join him. During World War II, Pagot managed to keep working, employing his skills on a few war propaganda shorts. In 1946, he released a mid-length film, *Lalla, piccola Lalla* (Lalla, Little Lalla), which was his first critically acclaimed work.

The feature-length film *I fratelli Dinamite* (The Dynamite Brothers, 1949), resulted from the efforts of Nino Pagot and a few other animators, including Osvaldo Cavandoli, Osvaldo Piccardo, and Toni Pagot, who had just recently returned from a German prison camp. The episodes of *I fratelli Dinamite*, which are based on the mischievous doings of the brothers, are linked together by a tea party sequence in which the rascals' aunt informs her friends of the children's adventures. Episodes, just to mention a few, are set on a desert island, in hell, and at the Venice Carnival. The most amusing segments happen at a carnival, while the episode in hell should be noted for its bizarrely sinister originality and horror film atmosphere. It is a similar feeling to that which characterizes Nino Pagot's comic strips. The film didn't make money, and the production company soon turned to advertising.

The other post-war feature film was *La rosa di Bagdad* (The Rose of Baghdad). The movie was first shown in 1949, after seven years of troubled work. The producer and director, Anton Gino Domeneghini (Darfo, 1897–Milan, 1966), was a major advertising artist in pre-war Italy. Domeneghini resorted to cinema as a means

---

[101] Alexandre Alexeïeff, 'La synthèse cinématographique des mouvements artificiels' (lecture, IDHEC, Paris, 1966). Films created by using camera movements and editing to enhance still images comprise a small, but not negligible, section of animation. Polish specialists call them 'repolero'. The best example is probably *The Hangman* (1964) by the Americans Paul Julian and Les Goldman.
[102] He died in Milan on 22 May 1972.

Figure 13.6 Nino Pagot, *I fratelli Dinamite*, 1949.

of keeping his artistic team together during the war. Because of bombings, the group left Milan and moved to Bornato in the countryside of Brescia.

The film was completed, edited, and scored in the following years. Angelo Bioletto, well-known creator of the Perugina figurines, which a popular contest had promoted throughout Italy in the 1930s, designed the characters. Backgrounds were created by Libico Maraja and music was composed by Riccardo Pick Mangiagalli. Domeneghini himself was responsible for the subject of the film. The fable owed something to *Snow White*, and while it had an awkward narrative progression, it nevertheless boasted some beautiful sequences: Princess Zeila singing as the sun sets, the dance of the snakes, the final celebration with fireworks. Although this film did well at the box office, Domeneghini discontinued the film's production and turned again to advertising.[103]

An interesting attempt was made by Francesco Maurizio Guido, known as 'Gibba' (Alassio, 1924). Referring to the Oscar-winning live-action film *Sciuscià* (Shoeshine, 1946, directed by Vittorio De Sica), he filmed *L'ultimo sciuscià* (The Last Shoeshine, 1947). Gibba intended to break with the comic tradition; his desire was to bring animation into the highly emotional, neorealist movement (the little shoe shiner eventually goes to heaven). His film, however, was rather bad, and his project proved to be unfeasible.

Spain
Catalan Vibrancy

The 1920s and 1930s were politically unstable years for Spain, yet an unstable country ever since the French invasion (1795–1814). Under the reign of Adolfo XIII, General Miguel Primo de Rivera established a mild dictatorship (1923–30); then a fragile republic followed in 1931, with the king going to exile but not abdicating. From 1936–1939, the bloody Spanish Civil War was fought, and eventually General Francisco Franco gained power, without relinquishing it until his death in 1975.

The very scant animation production does not, however, reflect social instability so much as animation's being, more or less, a draughtsman and craftsman's hobby. We have already mentioned Joaquín Xaudaró (1872–1933) who, in 1917, had made *Jim Trot's Adventures*. A very well known, hence reasonably wealthy, illustrator, he loved animation so much as to create and fund in 1932 the SEDA (Sociedad

---

[103] Both films claim to have been the 'first' feature-length Italian animated film, since both were screened at the Venice Film Festival of 1949. With them, animation gave Italian cinema the gift of colour; the first live-action feature-length colour film, *Totó a colori* (Totó in Colours), arrived only in 1952.

Española de Dibujos Animados). More a collective of artists than a production company, it gave birth to four films.

Un drama en la costa (1933) was the posthumous work of Xaudaró. K-Hito (born Ricardo García Lopez, 1890–1984) shot *El rata primero* (The First Rat, 1933) and *Francisca la mujer fatal* (Francisca the Femme Fatale, 1934), while Francisco López Rubio made *Serenata* (Serenade, 1934). José Martinez Romano and the caricaturist Menda made their debut in 1935 with *Una de abono* (One for Safety) and the short western *Buffalo Full*.

Sculptor and live-action film director Adolfo Aznar (La Almunia de Doña Godina, 1900–Madrid, 1975) filmed *Pipo y Pipa en busca de Cocolín* (Pipo and Pipa in Search of Cocolín, 1936), a puppet film based on characters by illustrator and background artist Salvador Bartolozzi (1882–1950). In 1936, puppet animators Feliciano Pérez and Arturo Beringola filmed *El intrepido Raúl* (Ralph the Intrepid), whose plot was far from original: a princess kidnapped by a dragon and saved by a knight.[104]

In addition, there were some animated commercials; and it's actually rather correct to say that the best animated films made in the country during this era were just the commercials, blessed by richer budgets.

The Edad Dorada

On 1 April 1939, winning General Francisco Franco declared the end of the Spanish Civil War.

The country was in shambles, and yet its film cartoons suddenly flourished, to the point that the 1940s were nicknamed the *Edad Dorada* (golden age) of Spanish animation.

Franco was a right-wing despot, close to Hitler, who had helped him with German troops. He couldn't stand the English and the Americans, who heartily reciprocated his feelings. On the other hand, he was a pragmatist and understood that Spain could not embark in World War II, which started just a few months later. Spain chose neutrality and isolationism.

The population still needed some entertainment and, lacking American, French, and German films, the option was national production. Nationalism was the only ideal that really moved cool-headed Franco, so Spanish film production was promoted – even Spanish animated film production.

The *Edad Dorada* lasted about ten years, although, in 1942, the short films lost momentum and, in 1945, Washington and Madrid decided that an anti-communist, anti-Soviet alliance was highly advisable, with the consequence that Hollywood came back to the Spanish screens with a vengeance and chased the modest home production away.

Barcelona's Entrepreneurs

'For the first time', wrote Emilio de la Rosa, clear differences became visible between the animated films made in Barcelona and the ones made in Madrid and Valencia.

In the latter locations, productions remained isolated, with scattered, barely connected authors, continuing the momentum of earlier decades. Or (what is the same) with lack of infrastructures, self-taught artists/filmmakers, who had to exercise the tasks of producers and managers of their own works, resulting in fatigue and economic leverage. The animators from Madrid, some coming from the old SEDA, drew well and had learned to animate, but were never able to get control of their companies. In most cases they went bankrupt (taking with themselves work, enthusiasm and projects) because of bureaucratic or economic problems one could hardly imagine.

Emilio de la Rosa writes:

In Barcelona, instead, a clear division of labour was created, and an industrial infrastructure was built, for the first time in the country. Two key names, not always recognized, Jaume Baguñá and Alejandro Fernández de la Reguera, must be pointed out. . . . They knew how to find talented artists and recycle them as a staff of animators; second, they dealt with the authorities in order to fund a unique output of cartoons. This professional separation between producers and animators would allow them, for the first time in Spain, to develop their business and evolve their art, getting brilliant results and being competitive with the films coming from abroad.[105]

During the last months of the war, publisher Jaume Baguñá founded Hispano Gráfic Films along with cartoonist Salvador Mestres (Vilanova i La Geltrú, 3

---

[104] The film was reissued in 1947 under the new title *La princesa y el dragón*.
[105] Emilio de la Rosa, *Cine de animación en España*, in Giannalberto Bendazzi, *Cartoons – 110 años de cine de animación* (Ocho y medio, Madrid 2003); translation from Spanish by the author.

December 1910–Barcelona, 2 March 1975), who was the company's artistic director. The first output was the series Juanito Milhombres (seven episodes, 1940–1942), directed by Salvador Mestres, the screen adaptation of a successful comic strip character originally called by the Catalan name Joan Milhomes.

In 1940, publisher Alejandro Fernández de la Reguera founded Dibsono Films, which released *SOS Doctor Marabú* (1940), directed by Enric Ferrán de los Reyes, better known under the pen name of Dibán (Villa Libertad, Entre Ríos, Argentina, 1911–Barcelona, 1986). Carlos Fernández Cuenca praised it as 'one of the most remarkable, brilliant and fluid films of the time'.[106] More Dibsono short cartoons were directed by Francesc Tur (Barcelona, 1885–1960) in 1941: *El aprendiz de brujo* (The Sorcerer's Apprentice), *El viejo Don Sueño* (Old Mr. Sleep), and *Rapto de luz* (Light Rapture).

The Fernández la Reguera staff also began an interesting series based on Don Cleque, an antihero or, better, a Spanish antihero: sickly, ugly, bald, and altogether pathetic. This character appeared in 1941 in *Don Cleque va de pesca* (Don Cleque Goes Fishing, directed by Francesc Tur), in which the hungry guy has to look for food but ends up not eating.

In 1942, Hispano Gráfic Films and Dibsono Films merged into Dibujos Animados Chamartín. The new company, which employed the best Catalan artists, was located in the very central Paseo de Gracia, in Barcelona, in the prestigious Casa Batlló, designed by architect Gaudí.

Three series were successfully developed and lasted for some years. The first one was Don Cleque, entrusted to Tur and Guillem Fresquet (Barcelona, 1914–91). Don Cleque, over time, acquired a sworn enemy, Two Fingers, and his adventures became less realistic and more fanciful: He travelled to distant places such as the jungle in *Don Cleque de los monos* (Don Cleque of the Apes, 1943) or the American West in *Don Cleque en el Oeste* (Don Cleque in the West, 1944) and *Don Cleque y los Indios* (Don Cleque and the Indians, 1944).

The second series, probably more popular, was dedicated to the anthropomorphic bull Civilón; the director was the most talented of the team, Josep Escobar (Barcelona, 1908–94).

The third series was Garabatos (Scribbles), a sort of animated variety show which caricatured the stars of the entertainment world, both foreign (Greta Garbo, Mickey Rooney) and national. There were fourteen instalments of this bizarre combination between animated cartoons and comic books. The 'cover' of each episode featured the caricature of a star, made by Escobar; then four 'pages' of comics followed and, finally, a 'page' of jokes.

The good fortune of the Casa Batlló crew ended in 1945, when the company dissolved due to distribution problems and to the financiers' wish to move the studio and business to Madrid. Along with his brother Josep María, Jaume Baguñá founded Editorial Científico-Cinematográfica and produced educational movies for the next few years.

Among smaller-scale Barcelonese productions, a series deserves mention: Fáquir González (Fakir González, featuring a fakir struggling against his own magic), designed in the early 1940s by painter Joaquím Muntañola (Barcelona, 1914) for his own company CEIDA.

Barcelonese Feature-Length Films

One more historical oddity let Barcelona become the first place in Europe to host a continuative production of such a rare, daring, expensive enterprise as an animated feature film. In short: The state offered the possibility to produce a national film in exchange for the permission to dub and distribute an American one – which was the actual moneymaking business.

Arturo Moreno (Valencia, 1909–Barcelona, 25 June 1993) had worked in advertising in the 1930s and, in 1942, within his own small production company, Diarmo Films, Moreno made the short *El capitán Tormentoso* (The Boisterous Captain). Looking for a distributor, Moreno got in touch with the Balet y Blay company, who got carried away and invited him to make a feature film; the result was *Garbancito de la Mancha* (1945), the first Spanish animated feature film and the first in colour (Dufaycolor system) in Europe.

Figure 13.7 Arturo Moreno, *Garbancito de la Mancha*, 1945.

---

[106] Carlos Fernández Cuenca, 'El mundo del dibujo animado', in *Festival internacional del cine de San Sebastian*, festival catalogue, San Sebastian, 1962, p. 30.

Garbancito (in Castillian, 'small chickpea') was a Quixotesque child, fighting as defender of the weak against the child-eating giant Caramanca. Garbancito was helped by the goat Peregrina and by a good fairy, who gave him the power to become a chickpea. Developed from a subject by Julián Pemartín,[107] the story was published as a children's book simultaneously with the film's release.

It was a hit and, even many decades after its first release, the Fleischer-like animation and the good direction of Arturo Moreno can be appreciated. Balet y Blay entrusted Moreno with another project, *Alegres Vacaciones* (Happy Vacations, 1948), in which the characters of the previous film leave their studio in Barcelona and travel to Palma de Majorca, Valencia, Andalusia, Madrid, and Morocco (a boring film). The third, and last, feature film produced by Balet y Blay was *Los sueños de Tay-Pi* (The Visions of Tay-Pi, 1952), directed by Austrian screenwriter Franz Winterstein after Moreno had moved to Venezuela. This jungle-based story, featuring monkeys wearing tuxedoes and weeping crocodiles, went almost unnoticed and led the production company to bankruptcy.

Meanwhile, the former artists of Chamartín studio released *Erase una vez* (Once Upon a Time), based on Perrault's tale *Cinderella*.[108]

Art critic and historian Alexandre Cirici-Pellicer (Barcelona, 1914–1983) was artistic director and Josep Escobar director of animation. The film, the best ever made in Spain up to that time, received favourable reviews, was declared to be of 'national interest' by cinema authorities, and received praise at the Venice Festival. Giuseppe Flores D'Arcais remembers, 'A.C. Pellicer's film was much more convincing than Disney's *Cinderella*'.[109] The background design was particularly praised for its links to Catalan architectural and decorative tradition. However, the film was not successful at the box office.

Madrid

In Madrid, Salvador Gijón, who in 1936 had collaborated on Adolfo Aznar's *Pipo y Pipa en busca de Cocolín* (Pipo and Pipa in Search of Cocolín), produced and directed in 1943 *No la hagas y no la temas* (Do No One Wrong and Fear No Wrong) and, in 1944, the trilogy *Rapto en palacio* (Kidnapping in the Palace), *La venganza del brujo* (The Revenge of the Wizard) and *La reina vencida* (The Defeated Queen). They were the first titles of a modest but long filmography, which lasted until 1970 and included a series with two recurring characters, the detective Camelon and his faithful dog Tobalito, which continued, with starts and stops, until the late 1960s. Gijón was a better animator than screenwriter: His characters moved well, but his stories were weak and naïve.

Another puppet animator was Angel Echenique, whose major work was probably his collaboration with live-action film director José Maria Elorrieta on *La ciudad de los muñecos* (Puppet City, 1945), a feature film mixing live action and animation.

Manuel Alonso Añino, an animator in the old SEDA of Joaquín Xaudaró and K-Hito, produced *Josele en una noche de miedo* (Josele in a Thrilling Night, 1945) using a camera that gave the drawings shadows, producing an attractive sense of volume and depth. Josele was an uneven film, with characters close to those of Añino's peers of the 1930s, a little harsh, 'ugly', and angular.

Fernando Morales made a few films in the early 1940s, including *Un día de feria* (Market Day, 1941) and the colour film *Una extraña aventura de Jeromín* (The Strange Adventure of Jeromín, 1942).

Valencia

In the Mediterranean city of Valencia, José María Reyes and Carlos Rigalt made four films of which we only know the titles: *Tarde de toros* (Evening of Bulls, 1939); *Tempranillo hace tarde* (Tempranillo Is Late, 1940); *Riega que llueve* (Irrigate, While It Rains, 1941); and *La taberna y la caverna* (The Public House and the Cave, 1941). Joaquín Pérez Arroyo, with the help of his sons, was able to produce seven episodes based on his own character Quinito (1943–1947). Pérez Arroyo is also credited as director of the shorts *De la raza*

---

[107] Julián Pemartín Sanjuán was born in Jerez de la Frontera on 13 July 1901 and died in Madrid on 30 April 1966. Poet and scholar of Andalusian folklore, he was the theorist of the Falange, the fascist movement that supported Francisco Franco. José Antonio Primo de Rivera, the Falange founder and leader (1903–1936, son of former dictator Miguel Primo de Rivera) was his cousin. His collaboration on *Garbancito de la Mancha* is one of the rare explicit acquiescence of Spanish animation to political power.

[108] Initially, the film was announced as *La Cenicienta*, Spanish for *Cinderella*. Walt Disney Productions, however, claimed international rights over the title (Disney's *Cinderella* was released in 1950). It was thus necessary to adopt the new title, which means 'once upon a time' in Castilian.

[109] Giuseppe Flores D'Arcais, *Il film per ragazzi* (The Films for Younger People), in Flavia Paulon (ed.) *Il cinema dopo la guerra a Venezia* (The Films after the War in Venice), Ateneo, Rome, 1956, p. 79.

calé (Of Gipsy Race, 1942) and *Noche de circo* (Night at the Circus, 1943).

Portugal[110]

A Extraordinária Aventura do Zeca (Zeca's Extraordinary Adventure) an eight-minute short by Adolfo Coelho, Aquilino Mendes and Mário Costa, was made in 1938.

> Zeca sails to Madeira, where he finds the Queen of the Bananas. While she is sleeping a Giant Spider posts a message stating that the Queen is a fraud. When she wakes up and sees the message, she gets furious and organizes a tournament to prove that the fruit from Madeira is the best there is.[111]

Live action, still images, and puppet manipulation are mixed in the first manifestation of puppet animation in Portugal – as we know to date.

In 1943, after four years' work, eighteen-year-old Servais Tiago (born i 1925) completed *Automania*, a five-minute car race between Pim and Barnabé full of action and accidents. Tiago used a cut-out technique, putting his black-and-white drawings on a three-level multiplane board and filming it all with a Pathé-Baby, the popular 9.5-mm home camera.

Thanks to the Pathé-Baby circuit, *Automania* was screened and won prizes abroad. Tiago was 'pointed out as a phenomenon'[112] and got a job at Kapa Studios, where he created animated commercials (i.e. *Perfumes Kimono* and *Malhas Locitay*, both 1947) to be screened in the Lisbon theatres.

In October 1945, the magazine *Filmagem* reported the news of the then-credited-as first national experiments of puppet animation, by Francesco Neves from Oporto. By that time, this director had been animating a puppet for two years and was promising to finish his work 'as soon as I can get more film stock'.[113]

The taste for social satire was far from vanishing. In the early 1940s, in the weekly *O Papagaio*, Portuguese teenagers followed the adventures of *O Boneco Rebelde (*The Rebel Guy), a comic strip where the protagonist dealt with themes like 'respect for nature, love for animals, non-violence, scientific curiosity, ecological concerns, respect for other cultures'.[114] The author was a very young rising star, Sérgio Luiz (1921–1943), who decided he wanted motion for his *Boneco*. Unfortunately, he died at twenty-one of renal tuberculosis. The remaining fragments of the film he had commenced give evidence of his skill and of his quality ambitions.

---

[110] By Alberto Rigoni.
[111] Fernando Mateus and Paulo Cambraia, *80 anos do cinema de animação em Portugal* (Amadora: Centro Nacional de Banda desenhada e Imagem, 2003).
[112] Ilda Castro, 'Conversa com Servais Tiago' in *Animação Portuguesa – Conversas com. . .*, Camara Municipal, Lisbon, 2004.
[113] In *Filmagem*, October 1945, quoted in António Gaio, *History of Portuguese Animation Cinema* (Espinho, Portugal: Nascente-Cooperativa Acção Cultural/Ministerio da Cultura/Instituto do Cinema Audiovisual e Media, 2002). During World War II (which ended in Europe in May 1945), buying film stock wasn't easy, even in neutral Portugal. The country had been living under António Salazar's fascist dictatorship since 1932 (it would last until 1974).
[114] Carlos Bandeiras Pinheiro and João Paulo Paiva Boléo (eds.), *Aventuras do Boneco Rebelde*, Edição Baleiazul, Bedeteca, 1999.

14
SOVIET UNION

Russia

Towards the end of the 1920s, the Soviet production of animated films increased, but the innovative thrust lost momentum. In 1929, the non-Stalinist Anatoli Lunacharsky had to quit his position as People's Commissar (Minister) for Culture (officially, 'of Enlightenment').

In 1934, the important First Congress of Soviet Writers sanctioned a new current of creative effort, which was to be known as 'socialist realism'. Instead of exploring new territory in the avant-garde, as in the preceding decade, Soviet writers, painters, composers, and filmmakers set themselves to the service of the Communist Party, obeying these rules: that the protagonist be a positive hero (a supporter of the aims of the Party), that the style be comprehensible, and that current workers' lives be depicted.[1]

Animation filmmakers were not actually supposed to follow these very precepts, as by the mid-1930s their work had already been branded as 'children oriented'. They were then supposed to adjust themselves to the less political but sternly pedagogical ideas of the time (not only Russian, and not only communist): be obedient, don't waste, don't dirty, don't shout, don't move, don't breathe.[2] Animators turned to national cultures, adapting classical texts, producing fairy tales, and utilizing the figurative and plastic suggestions of popular traditions.[3]

In such a situation, between 1930 and 1935, the impetuous Merkulov, Komissarenko, and Khodataev abandoned animation and returned to painting and sculpture.

These were the last years of independent satire. Just two examples: In *Blek end uait* (Black and White, 1932), Leonid Amalrik (1905 [or 1919]–1997) and Ivan Ivanov-Vano illustrated a poem of Vladimir Mayakovsky, inspired by a poet's blitz visit to Cuba. Racism and capitalist oppression were the targets of the film. Nikolai Khodataev directed *Organchik* (A Little Music Box, 1933), based on a chapter of the nineteenth-century novel *Story of a Town* by Mikhail Saltikov-Shchedrin. The novel, about the inane bureaucracy of the Russian government under the czar during the mid-nineteenth century, was banned during Stalin's reign, as were all books by Saltikov-Shchedrin. The film was shelved in the same year it was made because it was considered a satire on current politics (in attacking the tsarist bureaucracy, it allegorically attacked the Stalinist ruling class and its policy of *dekulakization* – i.e. the fight against the richer peasants). It was a faux pas, as this ruling class considered itself the Camelot of the world's proletariat, and therefore infallible.

The director of *The Interplanetary Revolution* and *China in Flames* was so shocked that he made just one more film, *Karyera Fyalkina* (Fyalkin's Career, 1935). The original sound track was received in terrible condition and was restored as much as possible. Born in 1892, he died in 1979, completely forgotten.

Until the early 1930s, animators had little money and even scarcer facilities but independently chose their subjects and their styles, and the various studios that had

---

[1] What is really worth stressing here is the realist component ('depiction of life in the forms of life itself') as opposed to the modernist/stylized one. With the forceful advent of 'socialist realism', art and literature were thrown back in time, relegated to the pre-modernist age. In other words, the collision is broader than with avant-garde in a narrow sense.

[2] In 1939, the definitive standards regarding Soviet animation were issued by decree.

[3] In the beginning, with Russian nationalism reawakening under Stalin's rule, this was mainly Russian folklore, but gradually, with more animation studios being founded in other republics, other cultures would be featured, too – e.g. from the Caucasus or Central Asia.

animation departments were in competition. In September 1933, the national Principal Management of the Photo-Cinematographic Industry (GUKF) issued an order to provide animators with facilities and equipment and to look for writers specialized in scripts for animated cartoons. Critic G. K. Elizarov writes:

> If we consider the GUKF's inclination towards American animated cartoons, we understand that the decree was aimed at creating a Soviet strong animated character.[4] A competition was even organized among animators and scriptwriters in order to invent such a figure.[5]

In January 1934, a 'tentative' large animation studio was set up by the GUKF under the direction of Viktor Smirnov, a former executive of the New York Soviet film office.[6] On 10 June 1936, the state film studio Soyuzdetmultfilm was officially founded. Although on 20 August 1937, the name was changed to Soyuzmultfilm, dropping the particle 'det', meaning 'child', the target was crystal clear. No animated film aimed at adults was to be made in the USSR until the early 1960s.

Smirnov had had ample opportunity to study the Tayloristic methods adopted by North American studios, especially Walt Disney, and applied everything (style and taste included) directly to his work in Russia. According to Soyuzmultfilm director Fedor Khitruk, 'The rule was: do what Disney does. No drama, no feelings, just laughter. There was a clash between our Russian soul, emotional, sentimental, and this search for the funny things.'[7]

The birth of Soyuzmultfilm meant the death of the times of the pioneers and of the tiny enterprises based on artistic and/or political passion. Structure, machinery, and large crews were necessary, and training courses were organized for young newcomers. One consequence of this orientation was a propensity for round forms typical of American cartoons, which represented an involution from the creativity that had characterized Soviet animation in its early years.

The Soviet Mickey Mouse failed to emerge. Daniil Cherkes (1899–1971) had introduced in his *Sen'ka Afrikanets* (Sen'ka the African, 1927)[8] a curious boy with a large cap who young audiences had liked enough. Aleksandr Ptushko's Bratishkin looked like him, but children were bored by his propaganda. The same thing happened to the protagonist of *Tip-Top v Moskve* (Tip-Top in Moscow, 1928) by Aleksandr Ivanov to *Buzilka* (1928) by Leningrad-based Aleksandr Presnyakov and Igor Sorokhtin to *Klyaksa* (Ink Blot, 1934) by Lev Atamanov.

In Leningrad, the Mezhrabpom animators, anticipating the experiments of Fischinger and Norman McLaren, experimented with drawing the sound track itself. In the autumn of 1929, during the shooting of *Plan velikih rabot* (The Plan of the Large Works, a live-action film directed by Abram Rom), composer and musical theorist Arseny Avraamov, along with extremely brilliant experimenter Evgeny Sholpo and animator Mikhail Tsekhanovsky, understood that the projector's photo cell would detect the fluctuations in intensity and frequency of the patterns in the optical sound track and convert them to audible changes in the volume and pitch of sound, no matter whether such

---

[4] G. K. Elizarov, *Sovetskaia mul'tiplikatsiia: Spravochnik*, Komitet po kinematografii pri sovete ministrov SSSR Gosfilmofond, Moscow, 1966.

[5] This can be directly traced to Stalin's enjoyment of Disney animation. In 1935, Disney had sent a reel of Mickey Mouse shorts to the Moscow Film Festival, and when Stalin, who had his own private cinema in the Kremlin Hall, was shown the reel, he purportedly exclaimed: 'This is what Soviet animation should look like!' From then on, there was no question any more about experimentation, and Smirnov, who was at the right place at the right time, was promoted from second-tier bureaucrat at Sovexportfilm to director of Soyuzdetmultfilm.

[6] Viktor Fedorovich Smirnov (23 October 1896–20 October 1946) was director of the Soyuzkino studio in Moscow (1930–1931), then managing director of the New York–based Amkino Company (1931–1933), which distributed Soviet films in the United States. Smirnov then had the opportunity to study Disney's and the Fleischers' production methods. In 1934, he went back to Russia. By order of the General Management of Cinema and Photography, he organized and led an experimental studio of animated cartoons, where he worked as the only producer and director. Smirnov passionately promoted both cel technology, as opposed to the 'outdated' cut-out method, and the Tayloristic approach to animation filmmaking. In 1936, the Soyuzmultfilm Studio was founded, and he temporarily abandoned animation to return in 1943–1944 as the general manager of Soyuzmultfilm itself. In 1944, he left cinema forever. This bureaucrat without imagination (the films he directed are uninteresting) was not even the actual founder of the big Soyuzmultfilm Studio, as has often been stated; however, his example and his championing of the Disney style and the production methods of the American studio system decisively shaped two decades of Soviet animation.

[7] Fedor Khitruk, letter to author, circa 1988.

[8] Co-directed with Ivanov-Vano and Merkulov.

patterns literally represented a real, recorded sound or a sound that was hand-drawn by someone. Similar experiments were done by Boris Yankovsky (1905–1973) and Nikolay Voinov (1900–1958). While McLaren would actually use this approach in his finished films, the Russians rarely did. Only Voinov was able to use the painstaking technique for some regularly released films, such as *Vor* (The Thief, 1934, by Aleksandr Ivanov and Panteleymon Sazonov; script by Béla Balázs).[9]

In 1930, Mikhail Tsekhanovsky produced the post-synchronized version of his *Post*, then started working on the feature film *Skazka o pope i rabotnike ego Balde* (The Tale of the Priest and his Servant Balda, from Pushkin), but was stopped.[10] Tsekhanovsky's student Mstislav Pashchenko deserves recognition. His *Dzhyabzha* of 1938 was a film for children based on the folklore of the Nanaic people, one of the Soviet Union's ethnic minorities living in the far north of European Russia.

Aleksandr Ptushko (Lugansk, Ukraine, 19 April 1900–Moscow, 6 March 1973) was an actor, designer, and journalist. He had studied architecture in Kiev before devoting himself to mechanical engineering. Among other inventions, he created an adding machine that was widely used up until the collapse of the Soviet Union. Eventually, Ptushko was able to concentrate all his technical, pictorial, and theatrical interests on the field of animation. His first directing hit in animation was *Sluchai na stadione* (It Happened at the Stadium, 1928), where he introduced the character of Bratishkin, who would be the protagonist of a few more films from Ptushko himself and from Yuri Merkulov and Vladislav Tvardovsky.

A puppet specialist, Ptushko used these in his first important film and in the first full-length film of Soviet animation. *Novy Gulliver* (The New Gulliver, 1935, mixes marionettes, the Lilliputians, with live-action cinema, as Petya Gulliver was played by an actor). A boy, Petya, fascinated by his reading of *Gulliver's Travels*, falls asleep and dreams of himself as the protagonist. Noticing the corruption of Lilliput's aristocrats and the miners' oppression, Petya helps the miners in their armed revolution before waking up.

In contrast to Swift's book, Ptushko's Gulliver is a political polemicist and a supporter of the theories of the October Revolution. His didactic verbosity limits the film, which otherwise stands out for its excellent scenographic configurations as well as for the animators' skilled exchanges of facial elements on the wooden actors. The puppets are very expressive, and their lips are well synchronized with the dubbed sound. Some of the musical numbers would become popular long-lasting hits, especially the jazzy song *Moya lilliputochka, pridi ko mne* (My Lilliputian Girl, Come to Me).

In 1939, Ptushko showed his second feature film, *Zolotoy klyuchik* (The Little Golden Key), based on the fable by the same title written by Aleksey Tolstoy[11] in 1935. It was actually a variation of Carlo Collodi's *Pinocchio*: The characters are more or less the same, but the action is complicated by a magical key that opens the door to an extraordinary, underground world. In the happy ending, all the good-hearted people go into the world of joy, and all the bad ones are punished. The technique of the puppet animation here is even better than in *The New Gulliver*, and the combination of actors in the flesh and wooden actors is perfect.

His time had come, however, too. With the choice of Disney-style animation, there was no more room for his ingenious creations. Ptushko left animation to make

---

[9] Nikolay Voinov's invention took the name of 'Nivotone' (1931), and Boris Yankovsky's invention (1932) was called the 'Vibro-exponator'.
[10] The score was composed by Dmitri Shostakovich. While the film was still in production (1936), the official newspaper *Pravda* condemned his entire work in the article 'Khaos vmesto musiki' (Chaos instead of Music, *Pravda* 28, January 1936). Shostakovich was banned, and the film went under in the wake of these events (it didn't quite help that Tsekhanovsky made grandiose use of constructivist design vocabulary). Tsekhanovsky's entire artistic vision actually suffered immensely in the aftermath, as he turned to rotoscoping as his main technique until the end of his career. Ironically, when in the late 1950s the climate started to change, he was lambasted again for his film *Kashtanka* (1952), which couldn't stand up to the creative innovations that were finally taking place by then. Critic Mikhail Gurevich (letter to author, circa 2010) recalls:

> The only part left of the footage is an introductory sequence (fully edited with soundtrack), conditionally titled *Bazar* (Market). Marked with strokes of formal brilliance, it gives a revealing hint to the radical aesthetics of the unfinished project. This introduction is not based on Pushkin's verse; it uses texts of poet Aleksandr Vedensky instead, a member of avant-garde – or, rather, leftist-modernist – literary group OBERIU, perhaps the last manifestation of unofficial culture in Leningrad and in the country.

[11] Writer Aleksey Nikolayevich Tolstoy (1882–1945) should not be confused with his older colleague Aleksey Konstantinovich Tolstoy (1817–1885). Both were distant relations to Leo Tolstoy (1828–1910) of *War and Peace* fame.

live-action fables and legends,[12] special and full of magic – the Méliès way of filmmaking – such as *Kamenny tsvetok* (The Stone Flower, 1946); *Sadko* (Id, 1953); and *Alye parusa* (Scarlet Sails, 1961).

The Brumberg sisters were especially active in the field of children's cinema. Valentina (Moscow, 2 August 1899–28 November 1975) and Zinaida (Moscow, 2 August 1900–9 February 1983), who nearly always worked together, made *Ivashko i Baba Yaga* (Ivashko and the Baba Yaga, 1938) and *Skazka o zare Saltane* (The Tale of Tsar Saltan, 1943), a thirty-five-minute version of Pushkin's transcription of a popular fairy tale.

When the war approached, the satirical vein of the Russian animators was revived and directed towards governmental propaganda – e.g. *Ne toptat' fashistskomu sapogu nashei rodiny* (The Fascist Boot Won't Trample the Soil of Our Motherland, 1941) by Ivan Ivanov-Vano and Aleksandr Ivanov – and many more films have been made before and since. In October 1941, with the German troops a few kilometres from downtown Moscow, the Soyuzmultfilm studio was evacuated in its entirety to Samarkand, Uzbekistan, and production was maintained throughout the war years.[13] In June 1943, the workers and (most of) the equipment came back home.

Lithuania[14]

In 1918, Lithuania regained its independence, which had been lost piece by piece in the second half of the eighteenth century. It was a small country unfit for the cinema industry. Stasys Usinskas was a painter, puppeteer, set designer, and teacher who studied in Kaunas and later in Paris. He is the author of the first Lithuanian sound puppet film, *Storulio sapnas* (The Dream of a Fatty, 1938). It was not a typical animated film, but rather the film recording of a puppet performance in which some animation techniques were also used.[15] In 1939, Stasys Usinskas had his puppets patented in Washington and presented his film at the World Exhibition in New York.

Painter Petras Aleksandravičius, together with cameraman S. Vainalavičius (who had participated in *The Dream of a Fatty*) shot one of the first – maybe the first in Lithuania – promotional films, *Du litu – laimingas medžiotojas* (Two Litas – The Happy Hunter). It is dedicated to the lottery of the Jaunoji Lietuva, the Young Lithuania Union. This film was issued in 1937 upon an initiative of the union's administration and was aimed at attracting as many buyers as possible.

On 15 June 1940, the Red Army entered the country, and Lithuania was annexed by the Soviet Union.

Ukraine[16]

The founder of Ukrainian animation, Viacheslav Levandovsky, began working in 1932 on the first sound animation film *Tuk-Tuk i yego priyatel Zhuk* (Knok-Knok and His Friend Beatle), which was completed in 1935 by his colleagues Evgeny Gorbach (1901–?) and Semen Guyetsky (1902–1974). Since 1933, Levandovsky had worked in Moscow, where he developed and used the techniques of cut-out and puppet animation in an innovative manner.

In the mid-1930s, Gorbach and Guyetsky created *Murzilka v Afrike* (Murzilka in Africa, 1934) and *Zhuk v zooparke* (The Beatle in the Zoo, 1936). Ippolit Lazarchuk (13 August 1903–23 February 1979) produced *Lesnoy dogovor* (The Wood Deal, 1937) and *Zapreschenny popugay* (The Forbidden Parrot, 1938), an anti-fascist film that was not released. In the year preceding the war, the release of animated films ceased. Until 1959, there existed only educational and popular science (technical) animation at the Kievnauchfilm (Kiev popular science films) studio.

Georgia[17]

The first Georgian attempt at filmmaking with good animation was *Chemi bebia* (My Granma), directed in 1929 by Kote Mikaberidze (Temriuk, Krasnodar region, Russia, 31

---

[12] In fact, puppet animation went into hibernation as a whole until the late 1950s, when it was resurrected by Vladimir Degtyarev, best known for *Who Said Meow?* (1962).

[13] Production levels were somewhat lower than in the pre-war years, but Soyuzmultfilm did become part of the propaganda machine and produced a number of so-called film posters – i.e. political cartoons. The time in Samarkand was not entirely devoted to those kinds of films, however, and a number of fairy tales and children's films were produced, too.

[14] By Valentas Askinis and Cinzia Bottini.

[15] It is interesting to mention that Stasys Usinskas drew inspiration from Czech puppeteer Josef Škupa, Jiří Trnka's mentor and creator of the characters Špejbl and Hurvínek, who performed in Lithuania in 1934.

[16] By Elena Kasavina and Giannalberto Bendazzi.

[17] By Lali Gorgaslidze, Lia Beruashvili, and Giannalberto Bendazzi.

July 1896–Tbilisi, 9 January 1973). It was a film of combined techniques, live-action plus puppet and object animation, and cut-outs. During the same period, Vladimir (Lado) Mujiri (Zugdidi, Georgia, 10 October 1907–Tbilisi, Georgia, 11 July 1953) established an independent animation studio. Despite the fact that it was closed down seven times, the equipment crashed, and his colleagues were fired by the 'nomenklatura' several times, he managed to obtain some Western European filming equipment and learn how to use it. Nomenklatura was a word belonging to the Communist regime. This was the elitist group of Party appointees in the ganglions of the administrative, industrial, and military system.

Animated films were then produced at the Sakh.Kin.Mretsvi (Georgian State Film Industry [GSFI]), founded in 1923 on what was left of the Belgian private company Filmae, established in Tbilisi in 1918. On 15 September 1930, Mujiri was appointed producer-director there and created some shorts with political and satirical propaganda topics, including *Shors Akvani* (Cradle No Longer, 1930); *Gazapkhuli* (The Spring, 1930, on how successful collective farms were in the nation); *Industrializatsiis Dghe* (The Industrialization Day, 1931); *Radiomautsqhebloba* (Radio Broadcasting, 1931); and *Meotkhe Gadamtsqhveti Tseli* (The Fourth Crucial Year, 1932).

The first sound Georgian animation film was *Argonavtebi-Kolkhida* (The Argonauts, 1935), in which the Ancient Greek myth about the conquest of the Golden Fleece was used as a pretext to praise the Soviet reclamation of Kolchian marshes.[18] The film premiered on 7 November 1935 at the Rosa Luxemburg Movie Theatre in Tbilisi.

Mujiri produced two more films before the war: *Gaidzvera* (The Sly, 1936), about a clever and brave hare who rescues his naive wife and babies from the sly fox; *Chiora* (Birdy, 1939), the first Georgian colour cartoon, after a famous local fairy tale centred on a clever bird who deceives a fox and manages to rescue his chicks.

In 1938–1952, GSFI – Sakh.Kin.Mretsvi was renamed Tbilisi Cinema Studio and included an animation department with seventy workers, including painters, animators, inbetweeners, and clean-up and ink-and-paint specialists. At this stage, up to eighteen people would work in a small room: The staff's friendship became legendary.

In 1941, Georgia became involved in World War II. Anti-fascist and propaganda films were created, including *Gadaatcharba* (Surpassed, 1942) and Sergei Fedorchenko's *Rotsa Gebelsi Ar Stqhuis* (When Goebbels Does Not Lie, 1941).

The development of animation slowed down, and more than once the production of cartoons came to an abrupt stop. However, before his death at the age of 45, Lado Mujiri managed to produce six animated films: *Sami Megobari* (Three Friends, 1943); *Oqros Bibilo* (The Gold Crest, 1947); *Gazapkhulis Stumrebi* (The Spring Guests, 1948); *Ganatsqhenebuli Satamashoebi* (The Afflicted Toys, 1949); the tiny animation opera *Mamatsi Mtamsvlelebi* (The Courageous Cragsmen, 1950), co-directed by Arkadi (Kako) Khintibidze (Ozurgeti, Dzimiti, Georgia, 8 January 1898–Tbilisi, Georgia, 4 April 1963); *Prtosani Megobrebi* (The Winded Friends, 1950); and *Garibis Bedniereba* (The Pauper's Happiness, 1952), co-directed by Khintibidze, after Sulkhan Saba Orbeliani's short story 'Garibis Bedi'. In addition, some cartoons were filmed by Mujiri's production designer Konstantine Chankvetadze (1912–1983), such as *Rtsqhili Da Tchiantchvela* (The Flea and the Ant, 1938) and *Norci Msroleli* (The Young Rifleman, 1939).

Armenia

In 1937, Lev Konstantinovich Atamanov (Moscow, 1905–1981), who was of Armenian descent (Atamanyan was his original family name), joined the Armenian film studio established in 1924 in Yerevan and produced the black-and-white animated *Shunn u Katun* (Russian title: *Pes i kot* [The Dog and the Cat], 1938)[19] from Hovhannes Tumanyan's poem by the same title[20] and which is to date considered the first Armenian animated film. After that, Atamanov made *Tertern u Aytze* (Russian title: *Pop i koza* [The Priest and the Goat], 1939–1941), a funny tale, again in black-and-white drawings, about the pranks of a goat that drives a priest crazy. It was completed just before the Nazi assault on the Soviet Union and the consequent involvement of the country in World War II: The tragic

---

[18] Jokingly, colleagues called it 'the three Lados film', as it was made by director Lado Mujiri; production designer Lado Gudiashvili (Tbilisi, 18 March 1896–Tbilisi, 20 July 1980); and screenwriter Lado Gugushvili.

[19] Once upon a time, a dog asks a tailor cat to sew him a hat, but the dog got neither the hat nor the fur given to make it. From that time on, the cat and the dog were the bitterest of enemies.

[20] Hovhannes (or Ovanes) Tumanian (1869–1923) is the national poet of Armenia. He was also a novelist.

events of those years forced Atamanov to go back to Moscow. The final cut of his third film, *Kakhardakan Gorg* (Russian title: *Volshebnyj kover* [The Magic Carpet]),[21] the first in colour, was postponed, and the film was released in 1948.

Animation was held in great estimation. Its national ancestors were considered the authors of some prehistoric rock carvings and some medieval miniatures: In these, closer observers have found a regard for motion and attempts to make pictures seem animated. Despite such a venerable ancestry, the group of animators and artists collected in Yerevan disbanded, and Armenian animation would be frozen for almost two decades.

Azerbaijan

In 1933, the employees of Azerbaijanfilm Studio prepared to produce cartoons and purchased the necessary materials from Moscow. The same year, they used technical animation in the production of such documentaries as *Lokbatan* and *Oil Symphony* (directed by B. Pumpyansky). Animation was fully used in the educational film *Jat* (directed by Basov), which was shown all over the Union by 1938. Just after the release of this film, a group of enthusiasts at the studio decided to create an animation film for the first time. The theme was taken from Azeri folk stories. *Unhappiness of Abbas* (1939) was directed by young director E. Dikaryov and written by A. Papov. The art directors were G. Khalygov, J. Zeynalov, M. Magomayev, and A. Mirzayev; the director of photography was G. Yegiazarov.

The studio was going to make *Sindbad the Sea Traveller*, which was going to be a sound film, but the start of World War II left the work incomplete.

After the war, the studio used animation in science films and documentaries. Artists J. Zeynalov, M. Refiyev, Aga-Nagi Akhundov, Nazim Mammadov, and Boris Aliyev and director of trick photography A. Milov were involved in the production.

---

[21] A tale about the fight between good and evil: A monster deprives people of water; the heroes defeat him thanks to the help of a magic carpet.

15
ASIA

Japan[1]

In the 1930s, Japanese militarism grew so much as to dominate national politics;[2] the Fifteen Years' War began in September 1931 with the invasion of Manchuria by the Japanese Army and, the following year, the foundation of the puppet state of Manchukuo. In 1933, the League of Nations condemned the Japanese way of acting, leading Japan to resign its membership: The population gradually entered into a sort of contrived isolation brought about by the major powers, thereby widening the ideological expansionist culture. At the outbreak of the Sino-Japanese War in 1933, movie houses were forced to screen massive doses of pedagogical, documentary, and propagandist films. The Ministry of Army and especially the Ministry of Navy commissioned animated short films to be shown along with the newscasts to spread propagandist messages to younger people. With the invasion of China in July 1937, Japan started the Eastern Asian War and the 'total war', during which an economic restructuring to face the war effort was carried out, as well as an even stricter social authoritarianism and reorganization in policy and in political parties. People from every walk of life supported the imperialist war. As a matter of fact, since the Public Security Preservation Law had been issued and enforced in 1925, any display of class antagonism, or even non-alignment with the ideology of the ruling power coalition, was persecuted and suppressed.

Regarding control over film production, the government took a further step by approving the Film Law in 1939, which fully reshaped the relationship between the film industry and the state, compelling film companies to file requests for authorization and register all those working in the field and imposing restriction on screening foreign pictures along with hard and fast censorship. In 1941, the Propaganda Department (in agreement with the two major movie companies of that time, Toho and Shochiku) made several amendments to the law in order to 'rationalize' the film industry: Small animation companies were consolidated into larger corporations, which resulted in the coordination of production.[3]

The war period continued with the Japanese attack on Pearl Harbor – and the official beginning of World War II for the Asiatic nation. In the beginning, times were good for the Japanese, who occupied the Philippines, Malaysia, the Indonesian archipelago, New Guinea, Burma, and Singapore until, in 1942, the Americans started to prevail. Soon after China's invasion, starting in 1937, the Japanese submitted to the rationing of textile products and, by 1941, day-to-day necessities. With the worsening of the war situation, the civilian population endured air raids and bombings, which culminated in the dropping of the

---

[1] By Marco Pellitteri and Lisa Maya Quaianni Manuzzato.
[2] It is important to remember that Japanese expansionism has roots in the Meiji Period, so we can summarize the steps of the expansion: annexation of Ryūkyū Island in 1879; occupation of Taiwan, relinquished by the dying Chinese Empire with the Peace Treaty of Shimonoseki in 1895; sharing with Russia of hegemony over Manchuria and the acquisition of the South Manchuria Railway Company after the victory over the Tsarist Empire in 1905; imposition on Korea of protectorate status under Japan and final colonization of the peninsula in 1910; and recognition, at the Versailles Conference (1919), of the mandate over the Pacific islands (Caroline, Marianne, and Marshall) seized from defeated Germany in the First World War and of ex-German railway and mining rights in the Jiaochou peninsula.
[3] In this decade, the book *Manga eigaron* (On Animation), Daiichi Geibunsha, Tokyo, 1941, by Imamura Taihei (1911–1986), a Japanese pioneer in animation theory, was published. Imamura – who wrote from a leftist perspective – was particularly attracted to documentary and animation.

atomic bomb upon Hiroshima (6 August 1945) and Nagasaki (9 August 1945).

Ofuji Noburo

After the debut of the pioneers in the 1910s, two important names were at the forefront of the artistic field in Japan: Ofuji Noburo and Masaoka Kenzo.[4] The most famous artist was Ofuji Noburo (Tokyo, 1 June 1900–28 July 1961). When he was eighteen, he became the pupil and co-operator of Kouchi; in 1925, he founded Jiyu Eiga Kenkyujo. In *Bagudajo no tozoku* (Burglars of Baghdad Castle, 1926, a parody based upon the American film *The Thief of Baghdad*), he used *chiyogami* paper for the costumes of the characters and the backgrounds, a special ornamental paper that was at the time available only in Japan. In 1927, he changed the name of his company to Chiyogami Eigasha (Chiyogami Cinema Company). That same year, he made one of his masterpieces, *Kujira* (The Whale), a remarkable feat of action and suspense: After being shipwrecked and surviving in a whale, three men can only think to seize possession of a girl until the gods intervene, causing only the girl to survive. The movie was purchased by a French distribution company and circulated successfully in 1929 as an example of innovative animation. For that movie, Ofuji used a special technique, cutting off figures of *chiyogami* and setting them up on overlapped glass boards. Filmed in black and white, the movie offered an extremely charming world of transparencies and shadows. In *The Whale*, the audience can also admire the effort of perfectionist animation, pointing to 'total' fluid motion. Many years later, in 1952, Ofuji would remake the film in Konicolor: Inspired by the stained glass windows of churches, he used transparent, coloured cellophane as a new material, thus continuing with the same technique. That film, shown in 1953 in competition at the Cannes Film Festival in the short animation category, would win appreciation from Pablo Picasso.

Ofuji also experimented with film technology: His work *Kogane no hana* (The Golden Flower, 1929), drawn from a *rakugo* (comic monologue), was originally produced in Cinecolor (although it was released in black and white); with *Kuro nyago* (The Black Cat, 1929), he tried out the Tojo Eastphone sound recording system, even though the film was released as a silent movie. *Sekisho* (The Inspection Station), made in 1930, was his first actual talking picture, and *Katsura hime* (Princess Katsura, 1937) was his first colour film. Furthermore, the author also proved his versatility in comic animation movies, using traditional techniques such as drawn animation.[5] However, following the war, most of his works were silhouette animations, often about religious themes, like Buddha's mercy towards a man in the underworld in *Kumo no ito* (A Spider's Thread, 1946), the first-prize winner at the Venezuela International Film Festival. This period was also full of international acknowledgements: In addition to the already-mentioned remake of *The Whale*, *Yureisen* (The Ghost Ship) of 1956, made with Fujicolor, was awarded a special prize at the Venice Film Festival in the children's movies section. *The Ghost Ship* tells of a prince and his peaceful crew, killed by pirates, on whom the ghosts of the victims will take revenge.

A strict artist, Ofuji did not believe in animation as a comic art but fought for a dramatic cinema for adults that could comprise erotic themes; for a long time, he was the only producer of artistic films. His deeply personal style, great talent, and cultural background (as he proved in his later works) were partially overshadowed by the most superficial part of his work: his original technique based on *chiyogami* cuttings. After his death, his artistic prominence was acknowledged with the prestigious Ofuji Award – created by his older sister Yae – at the Mainichi Film Concours. Through the years, the Ofuji Award has been granted to such artists as Kuri Yoji and Tezuka Osamu, among others.

---

[4] Surname first, given name second, according to Japanese customary usage.
[5] He also made a curious propaganda movie: *Sora no arawashi* (Aerial Ace, 1938), where a Japanese Army airplane creates clouds that evoke the familiar figures of Popeye and Stalin.

Masaoka Kenzo

As previously discussed, small animation companies in Japan underwent a process of consolidation, which resulted in the coordination of production.

This also happened to the studio of Masaoka Kenzo (Osaka, 5 October 1898–23 November 1988), but he continued leading his group; in addition to propaganda movies imposed by the historical period, he managed to produce folk story–based short films.

Masaoka studied Japanese and Western music and painting. He started working in cinema as an assistant director, set designer, and actor; starting at the end of the 1920s, he worked in animation at the Nikkatsu Uzumasa Film Studio in Kyoto, starting off with the superb *Sarugashima* (The Monkeys' Island, 1930), which became so popular that a sequel was made. *Chikara to onna no yononaka* (The World of Power and Women, 1933) was the first animated talking picture made in Japan, for which some of the most fashionable actors provided the voices of the characters. The film, addressed to an adult audience, tells the funny story of an employee who falls in love with a secretary, despite his huge, jealous wife. Seo Mitsuyo also took part in the production as an assistant animator.

In 1933, Masaoka founded the Masaoka Eiga Kenkyujo at his house in Kitano, Kyoto; he contributed to the change from drawings on paper to celluloid sheets (very expensive in those days) and to the grand-scale development of the technique. *Chagama ondo* (A Dance Song with a Kettle, 1934), about forest creatures lured by the gramophone playing in a Buddhist monastery, and *Mori no yosei* (A Fairy in the Forest, 1935), were part of his new production studio. These films helped to increase his fame which, thanks also to the graphics and the attitude that characterized the *Silly Symphonies*, led him to be called the 'Japanese Disney'. He was also called the 'Japanese Méliès' for his skill in special effects, as shown in *Kaguya hime* (Princess Kaguya). But, due to the considerable expense, his company had to close down. He worked by contract at the J.O. Studio[6] until he set up another company, the Nippon Dogasha (Japanese Animation Company). *Benkei tai Ushikawa* (Benkei the Soldier Priest and Little Samurai Ushikawa, 1939), particularly commended for its expressive use of music, dates back to that period. Yet, the economic situation not being the most favourable, the company ended up being taken over. In 1941, Masaoka started working at Doga Kenkyujo, Shochiku's new animation department, where his masterpiece, *Kumo to churippu* (The Spider and the Tulip, 1943), was produced.

This poetic film was partly based on a country tale written by Yokoyama Michiko, a lady who won a literary competition published by the daily newspaper *Asahi Shinbun*. The story, which unfolds in a nature setting, depicts a ladybird that is chased by a villainous, Don Juan–like womanizing spider but manages to save herself, taking refuge in the tulip petals. The intervention of the Thunder God – who instigates a powerful storm – ultimately tears the spider away, letting the ladybird come out from her shelter and ushering in the return of harmony. The interesting direction – with such suggestive shots as the raindrops seen from below and the skilful usage of music, almost making it an operetta – incensed the military censorship, which disapproved of its non-propagandistic subject.[7]

Figure 15.1 Masaoka Kenzo, *Kumo to churippu* (The Spider and the Tulip), 1943.

---

[6] The J.O. Studio, established in 1933, was an important landmark in Japanese animation during the 1930s, especially for its modern equipment which, in the passage from silent film to talkies, contributed to establishing Kyoto as an animation production centre.

[7] The spider villain – whose features recall the blackface make-up used in American minstrel shows – is, in the context of the alliance period among axis power, sometimes interpreted as a racist characterization. However, it is improbable that the author's intentions included policy and ideological motives and in fact – as we have mentioned – this movie incurred the strict censorship of the time.

Masaoka also produced some films in the post-war period, such as *Sakura – Haru no genso* (Cherry Blossom – The Illusion of Spring, 1946), where he depicted the spring of Kyoto, and *Suteneko Torachan* (Tora-chan, an Orphan Kitty, 1947), a sugary story about a family of anthropomorphic cats that adopt a little orphan feline: These works express a personal and mature style that was clearly formed by watching, with admiration, productions from overseas. After *Torachan to hanayome* (Tora-chan and the Bride, 1948) and *Torachan no Kankan mushi* (Tora-chan's Ship Sweeper, 1950), Masaoka retired because of sight problems, continuing, however, to dedicate his life to animation by drawing storyboards, writing essays, and teaching. Seo Mitsuyo and Mori Yasuji were among his pupils.

Several animators continued to work in the difficult war environment, among them Seo Mitsuyo (26 September 1911–24 August 2010), who opened a studio under his name in 1933. Among his productions, a series about the fighting Osaru Sankichi (Sankichi the Monkey), which used to have a certain fame, *Osaru no Sankichi: Totsugeki-tai* (Sankichi the Monkey: The Storm Troopers, 1934), set during the Sino-Japanese War, is about the Imperial Army efficaciously attacking a fortress badly protected by Chinese pandas. But Seo Mitsuyo, too, suffered from the destiny of that period and, by 1940, his studio belonged to the bigger company Geijutsu Eigasha. During the war, he succeeded in producing the medium-length movie *Momotaro no umiwashi* (Momotaro's Sea Eagle, 1943) and, finally, *Momotaro, umi no shinpei* (Momotaro's Divine Sea Warriors, 1944), the first feature-length Japanese animation movie.

On a Pacific island, zoomorphic imperial sailors build a runway, do some training, and finally conquer an enemy base in New Guinea. Despite this being a propaganda film aimed at recruiting – as evident in the description of the joyful life of the natives under the Japanese soldiers – it is fascinating in its own way, particularly due to the realism of the action; of particular value is the sequence in silhouettes (likely realized by Masaoka), where the occupation of Indonesia by European men is narrated. It is a remarkable work considering the productive effort required during a difficult period – an effort that was unparalleled for many years during the post-war period. Momotaro, the man of one of the most famous Japanese legends (famous for having defeated fierce demons in Onigashima with the help of a dog, a monkey, and a pheasant), assumed a key role in the period of war propaganda. In the post-war period, Seo would achieve *Osama no shippo* (The King's Tail, 1949), an animated musical, which was never distributed. He would eventually give up animation to become a draughtsman with the nickname of Seo Taro.

An important figure of the post-war period, Yokoyama Ryuichi (Kochi, 17 May 1909–8 November 2001), had already begun to operate during the war. He joined the research staff at Photo Chemical Laboratory (PCL), the forerunner of Toho, where he started studying animation production. He viewed Disney's *Skeleton Dance*, and it was love at first sight. In 1936, he started to publish (in the *Asahi Shinbun* of Tokyo) *Eddoko Kenchan*, a series of comics later called Fukuchan[8]: In 1944, Yokoyama made this into a medium-length propaganda movie called *Fukuchan no sensuikan* (Fukuchan and the Submarine), though the film was attributed to Sekiya Isoji.[9]

Much as in the United States, some of the best-known characters proved to be ideal vehicles for propaganda: Even Norakuro, the black dog of the Imperial Army and the protagonist of the homonymous manga (published since 1931, with popularity and merchandizing success uncommon for the era) followed Fukuchan and Momotaro in that direction. Norakuro appeared in five animation shorts, starting in 1933 with *Norakuro nitohei – Kyoren no maki* (Private Second-Class Norakuro), filmed by the cut-out animation master Murata Yasuji. Seo later also worked with the character.

Arai Wagoro (Kojimachi, 11 December 1907), a dentist who was interested in animation as a hobby, was

---

It should also be noted that the cultural-political climate in the pre-war years had (through the trendy Japanese 'modern boys', who were strongly westernized) spread through Japan a passion for contemporary American music, particularly black music, which probably influenced Masaoka's operetta-like film. The stereotyped representation of the character can also be explained by both the cultural and geographical distance between Japan and United States at that time (thanks to Ilan Nguyen for the information).

[8] Yokoyama stopped the series of Fukuchan in 1971 with Episode 5534. He was awarded, for his importance in the cultural Japanese landscape, with the ministerial prize Person of Cultural Merit in 1994, the first cartoonist to receive that honour. He was also honoured, in 2000, with the dedication of the Ryuichi Yokoyama Memorial Manga Museum in his birthplace of Kochi.

[9] Sekiya was credited due to the missing qualification of Yokoyama as director, a qualification that had been made compulsory by the Film Law since 1939.

encouraged by continuous praise to become a professional. The first of his films was *Kogane no tsuribari* (The Golden Hook, 1939), made with silhouettes, which was soon followed by the well-received *Ocho fujin no genso* (Fantasy of Madame Butterfly, 1940), whose story – adapted from the famous Giacomo Puccini opera – was well suited for propaganda.

Oishi Ikuo is also well known for the funny *Ugoki ekori no takehiki* (The Fox versus the Raccoon, 1933): A fox disguised as a samurai spends the night in a desert temple, but a family of *tanuki* (Japanese raccoon dogs), thanks to their magic powers and ability to transform, throw the undesired creature out. Graphically, the characters have a style that is more caricatured and simple in comparison with other works of the same period, influenced by Felix the Cat and benefiting from very fluid movement.

Kimura Hakuzan

Another noteworthy artist is Kimura Hakuzan, a pupil of Seitaro. He made the first Japanese erotic animated film: *Suzumibune* (The Tourists' Boat, 1932). An individual work, it is a story outlined with a humorous touch, inspired by the erotic prints of the end of the eighteenth century. Censored by Japanese authorities, it was not distributed until 1945, when it was discovered by Americans and reproduced.

A Brave New World
The Changed Frame

Further to the defeat in World War II, Japan came under the control of the General Headquarters (GHQ) and of General Douglas MacArthur, Supreme Commander of the Allied Powers (SCAP) in particular. In September of the same year, the Civil Censorship Detachment (CCD) was created, controlled by the SCAP, which replaced military censorship and exerted strict control over all civil mass media. It was imposed to avoid issues involving Japanese imperialism, as well as any attempt to criticize the allied forces, or simply concerning topics such as A-bombs. Furthermore, the Civil Information and Education Section (CI&E) was supposed to try to infuse the occupants' way of life.

The country, which had just come out of the war, was exhausted both in spirit and in terms of infrastructure:

Nearly seventy percent of its merchant fleet, the Archipelago's main means of connection, had been torpedoed; bombings and colonies' abandonment led to the loss of over two-thirds of its industrial strength. Finally, air strikes over urban areas had caused eight million homeless; nearly five million were unemployed from the destruction of production plants all over the country and from the abandonment of those in occupied territories and in the former colonies – not counting the over six million soldiers also repatriated from the front.[10]

The emperor himself, in a famous radio message on 15 August 1945, asserted that the Japanese had to 'endure the unendurable, tolerate the intolerable'.

Mochinaga Tadahito and His Legacy

Puppet animation also began during those years, thanks to founder Mochinaga Tadahito (3 March 1919–1 April 1999). He was born in Tokyo but soon after moved to Manchuria[11] with his family and, in the following years, he often came back to Japan. During secondary school, he discovered an interest in animation: He was charmed by one of the *Silly Symphonies*, *Water Babies* (1935) and, thanks to *Magic Clock* (1928), produced in France by Ladislas Starewitch, he also started to become interested in puppet animation.

He was employed by the Animation Department of Geijutsu Eigasha (Art Film Company) in 1939; as the assistant of director Seo Mitsuyo, he worked on *Arichan* (Ant Boy, 1941), a poetic short film for the Ministry of Education in which an ant is charmed by some violin music played by a cricket. The importance of this film lies primarily in the use of the first four-level multiplane camera used in Japan, which Mochinaga himself built for this production. He subsequently created settings and dealt with the image composition for *Momotaro's Sea Eagle*.

Sick from too much work and the repeated air bombardments, he migrated with his wife Ayako to Manchuria's

---

[10] Francesco Gatti, *Storia del Giappone contemporaneo* (A History of Contemporary Japan), Mondadori, Milan, 2002, p .112.
[11] Mochinaga's father used to work for the South Manchuria Railway Company, which came under Japanese control in 1905.

capital city Changchun in 1945, where he had some relatives. Changchun was under Japanese control until the end of World War II. Mochinaga entered Man'ei (the Manchurian Film Association, one of the greatest Asian studios of that age) and decided to stay there even when, as soon as the war finished, the company was taken over by the Chinese and renamed the Tong Pei Film Studio (Northeast Film Studio). The civil war between the Nationalists, led by Chiang Kai-Shek, and the Communists of Mao Zedong forced the members of the studio to flee northward to the city of Hao Gang in 1946. There they founded the new Tong Pei Film Studio, where Mochinaga enthusiastically took part in the construction of new Chinese cinematography, helped by his wife.

He made the first puppet animation in China in 1947: a thirty-five-minute film entitled *The Emperor's Dream*, whose aim was to satirize an incapable Chiang Kai-Shek and denounce his control by Americans. Mochinaga also fulfilled several roles in the production of the Chinese cel animation *The Turtle Caught in the Jar* (also a caricature of Chiang) but was credited only as director under the Chinese name Tsuyon. In 1949, the group was able to go back to Changchun, working for the new animation division of the art department: Te Wei, an animator from Shanghai,[12] was the leader, and Mochinaga started a friendship with him. With the foundation of the Popular Republic of China, the Culture Division had a new policy for animated productions, now entirely addressed to a child audience. The animation division was moved to Shanghai – where Chinese animation was born and professional personnel were easily available – thus becoming a department of Shanghai Film Studios. Mochinaga directed *Thank You, Kitty* (1950), the story of a cat who watches a village during the night in order to protect its inhabitants. Thanks to the respect he had acquired over the years, Mochinaga was nicknamed Fan Ming ('bright direction').

Mochinaga and his wife Ayako returned to Japan in 1953 after years of cooperation that ended up professionally enriching both young Chinese animators and the Japanese artist. Throughout his career, Mochinaga personified a vital connection between the worlds of Chinese and Japanese animation.

In 1953, television started broadcasting in Japan; in 1955, Mochinaga founded Ningyo Eiga Seisakusho (the Puppet Animation Film Studio) in Tokyo, thus starting advertisement production for the new medium. Among his followers there were Kawamoto Kihachiro and Iizawa Tadasu. From 1956 to 1959, he directed nine short puppet films for children, often shown in primary schools, based mainly on Japanese traditional legends but also on foreign fairy and folk tales, such as *Chibikuro Sanbo no tora taiji* (Little Black Sambo and His Twin Brother, 1957). Thanks to the screening of *Little Black Sambo and His Twin Brother* at the Vancouver International Film Festival, Mochinaga was contacted by Arthur Rankin, Jr. (born in 1924) of the American production company Videocraft International and, in 1961 – together with the surviving personnel of Geijutsu Eigasha – founded MOM Film Studio to animate puppet films for Videocraft (later, Rankin/Bass Productions) to broadcast on American television. MOM started with 130 segments (five minutes each) of *The New Adventures of Pinocchio* (1961), followed by such works as *Willy McBean and His Magic Machine* (1963), *Rudolph the Red-Nosed Reindeer* (1964), *Ballad of Smokey the Bear* (1966), and *Mad Monster Party?* (1967). Videocraft directed all the productions, sending the script and pre-recorded voices and sounds to Mochinaga and the members of his team, who handled creation of the puppet models and the animation.[13] With such commissions, MOM represented an example of remarkable industrialization in animation, with a staff of 130 people (Okamoto Tadanari, Nakamura Takeo, and Oikawa Koichi among them). Mochinaga directed the studio until his departure in 1967.

In the following years, he continued to promote cooperation between artists in China and Japan, maintaining a relationship with Shanghai Film Production and teaching the technique of animation from 1985 to 1989 at Beijing Film Academy. He also organized original initiatives such as the Retrospective of the Shanghai Animated Film Studio in Tokyo and collaborated with the Hiroshima and Shanghai Festivals. He produced and directed his last short film in puppet animation in 1992: the melancholic *Shonen to kodanuki* (A Badger and a Boy), in which a badger is transformed into a baby girl to follow a boy riding her bike. He presented the work at both the Hiroshima and Shanghai Festivals,

---

[12] Te Wei had worked in animated productions for anti-Japanese propaganda; subsequently, he was well known as a director of films realized with the Chinese brush-and-ink technique.

[13] Mochinaga was credited as 'Tad Mochinaga'.

confirming himself as a Japanese animator who lived in two worlds.[14]

Ichikawa Kon

Born in Uji Yamada,[15] in the province of Mie, on 20 November 1915 (he died in the same town on 13 February 2008), Ichikawa Kon discovered his vocation while watching Walt Disney's movies. As he recalled later, in them he found everything that interested him: cinema, painting, and drawing. During 1936–1937, the J.O. Studio, which had a small animation department, opened in Kaiko No Yashiro, near Kyoto, and Ichikawa was hired. Animation, however, turned out to be an economic liability for the studio and was gradually eliminated: Production decreased and, eventually, the team dissolved. 'I was the only one left', Ichikawa recalled, 'and I did everything. I would draw, animate, film and write the scripts'.[16] In 1939, he directed a short, *Kachikachi yama* (The Hare Gets Revenge over the Raccoon, 1939); the film, which definitely derives its drawings and structure from the *Silly Symphonies*, makes remarkable use of music.[17]

When the animation department finally closed, Ichikawa was assigned to a group of assistant directors for live-action movies. In 1944, the studio (which, meanwhile, had been renamed Toho Eiga and had moved to Tokyo, following a merger with other companies) decided to produce an animated puppet film and promoted young Ichikawa, the only animation expert, to director. The movie, entitled *Musume Dojoji* (A Girl at Dôjô's Temple, 1947), was an adaptation from a Kabuki drama. Those who were able to view it proclaimed it excellent, but the American authorities commanding the occupation troops in defeated Japan prohibited the showing of the film. Late in his life, Ichikawa claimed that *A Girl at Dôjô's Temple* was his best work.[18]

In the 1950s, the director turned to live-action films. After some comedies, in 1953 he made his first masterpiece, the dramatic *Pusan* (Mr. Pu). In 1956, he attained well-deserved international fame with *Biruma no tategoto* (The Burmese Harp). In 1959, he directed his third masterpiece, *Nobi* (Fires on the Plains). Ichikawa can be considered one of the masters of Japanese cinema, along with Kurosawa Akira, Ozu Yasujiro, and Mizoguchi Kenji. His inspiration, however, waned with his documentary on the Tokyo Olympic Games of 1964, and among the many uninteresting dramas he was then appointed to direct, some films brought him back to his animator past (*Topo Jijio no botan senso* [Topo Gigio and the Missile War], 1967; *Hinotori* [The Phoenix], 1978).

---

[14] In October 1986, he was the only Japanese officially invited to witness the celebrations of the sixty years of Chinese animation at Shanghai Animation Film Studio. In the *China Cinema Encyclopedia* (Shanghai: Shanghai cishu chubanshe, 1996), Mochinaga is listed as 'Fan Ming: an animation director, Japanese'.

[15] This is currently Ise.

[16] Quoted in Angelo Solmi, *Kon Ichikawa*, La Nuova Italia, Florence, 1975, p. 75.

[17] More information about this period comes from an interview given by Ichikawa to Mori Yuki:

We made a series called *Hana yori Dangonosuke*. Dangonosuke, who is a sort of mixture between Mickey Mouse and Momotarô, is the protagonist, and he dispatches bad guys in each episode. It was a simple story. We began with a scenario. Music was composed next, and recorded with dialogue and sound effects, which were completed before we drew the pictures, basing the continuity on the soundtrack. . . . We were not able to draw pictures unless we could read music. So I took piano lessons, but I did not progress quickly because my fingers were already so stiff. I gave up at page sixty of the basic textbook. [Laughs]

(Ichikawa Kon and Mori Yuki, 'Beginnings', in James Quandt [ed.] *Kon Ichikawa*, Cinematheque, Toronto, 2010, p. 24)

[18] More information about this film comes from an interview given by Ichikawa to Mori Yuki:

The army was making consolation films for southern countries at that time. . . . First I tried to make Ryûnosuke Akutagawa's *Hana*, and I even started writing a scenario. I changed my mind and instead reinterpreted the classic *Dôjôji*, because I thought it would be better for foreign audience to see something Japanese and gorgeous. I wrote the script with my friend Keiji Asabe. . . . The film violated the censorship system of Ghq [General Headquarters of the American occupying forces]. Films whose scripts were not censored before shooting were not allowed to be public screened. We started making *A Girl at Dôjô Temple* before the war was over, and completed it in the fall of 1945. There was no such censor system when we started.

(Ichikawa Kon and Mori Yuki, 'Beginnings', in James Quandt [ed.] *Kon Ichikawa*, Cinematheque, Toronto, 2010, p. 32)

Although he quit animation except for a few sporadic productions, his precious compositions of images and pictorial shot balance illustrate his figurative achievements and his expertise in the field.

China

Historically, China has been one of the most restless countries of the twentieth century, troubled by civil war, foreign invasions, and internal upheavals. Chinese live-action cinema felt the influence of these events both in production and, more significantly, in content. The beginning dates back to 1923, when foreigners and Chinese entrepreneurs financed the construction of movie theatres in Shanghai, followed by developments in Hong Kong, Beijing, Nanking, and Chengchow.

For a long time, China was represented in the field of animation only by the four Wan brothers – the twins Wan Laiming (1900–1997[19]; his real name[20] was Wan Jiazong) and Wan Guchan (1900–1995; his real name was Wan Jiaqi), Wan Chaochen (1906–1992; his real name was Wan Jiajie), and Wan Dihuan (1907; his real name was Wan Jiakun). Having been attracted since childhood to figures in movement, the brothers made their first animated film, *Uproar in the Art Studio*, in 1926, followed by *The Revolt of the Paper Figures* in 1930. The Wans, who were set designers for live-action cinema, made these films in an amateurish fashion, repeating the Fleischers' formula of drawings that come to life independent of the will of a human protagonist.

In the early 1930s, their production increased and included two tales (*The Race of the Hare and the Tortoise* and *The Grasshopper and the Ant*) and patriotic films inspired by the Japanese attacks on Shanghai on 28 January 1932 and on Shenyang on 18 September 1931 (*Compatriot*, 1932; *Wake Up*, 1931; *The Price of Blood*, 1934).

In 1933, the Wans (now three, as the youngest, Dihuan, had left the group to devote himself to photography) found some stability within the production company Mingshin, which asked them to develop an animation department. For four years after 1933, they produced the *Cartoon Collection*, a series of six films. Some, such as *The Year of Chinese Goods* (the third of the series), encouraged audiences to buy national products.

The Painful History of the Nation (the fourth of the series) and *The New Wave* (the fifth of the series) denounced imperialist aggression. Another series was centred on Miss Lu's father (a little man with a square jaw who dressed in Western clothes). Another series mixed live-action shots (with child actress Zhang Minyu) with animated drawings.

In 1935, the Wans made the country's first animated sound film, *The Camel's Dance*.

The brothers were outspoken about their ideas and beliefs concerning art. In 1936, they wrote an article for a journal published by the production company for which they worked. In it, they praised American, Soviet, and German animation but also maintained the need to find an indigenous Chinese style and humour and stated their goal of teaching, not merely entertaining. All these themes would reappear later in the People's Republic of China.

When the Japanese invaded Shanghai (13 August 1937), the filmmakers escaped to the still-free city of Wuhan. The events inspired their new productions, including five films for the Manifestos of the War of Resistance series and seven for the series Songs of the War of Resistance (featuring the Fleischers' theme of the bouncing ball). Then Wuhan also fell into the hands of the Japanese army. Since it was not possible to work in Chungking, where the Wans' production company was based at the time, the brothers returned to Shanghai in 1940. There, Wan Laiming and Wan Guchan established another team of animators inside the unified Shinhwa Company and began their most daring venture – the first Chinese feature film.

Work began under shaky diplomatic protection, since the animators' atelier was located in the French concession (which the occupation troops respected, like other foreign concessions, until 1941). The film (shown to the public in 1941) was entitled *The Princess with the Iron Fan* and was based on a chapter from the traditional Chinese novel *Journey to the West*. In it, a monk, Shwangzang, crosses a mountain of flames in search of sacred Buddhist texts, accompanied by the pig Zhu Baizhe; the priest Shaseng; and Sun Wukong, the Monkey King. After many adventures, the film's true protagonist, Sun Wukong, manages to get a magic fan from the Buffalo King's wife and extinguishes the flames. Marie-Claire Quiquemelle wrote:

---

[19] Sources indicate that the twins were born in Nanking on 18 January 1900; however, according to Wan Laiming himself, the year was 1899.

[20] In China, many artists and writers become famous by their pen names instead of their real names given by their parents. For instance, Wan Laiming, Wan Guchan, and Wan Chaochen are all pen names.

Figure 15.2 Wan Laiming and Wan Guchan, *The Princess with the Iron Fan*, 1941. Credit: Cinema Epoch.

This production, on the 'orphan island' of the French Concession in the middle of the war, was a real feat not only on the artistic level but also on the technical level: seventy artists, in two teams, worked without a break for a year and four months, all in the same room, in limited space, in the cold of the winter, and in the atrocious heat of the summer.

To ensure the accuracy of the movement, certain scenes were filmed with actors to serve as a guide to the artists.[21]

The film was well received in China, Singapore, and Indonesia. Its success was probably helped by a veiled patriotism, particularly as Sun Wukong's victory over the Buffalo King was obtained with the alliance of the people. From an aesthetic viewpoint, the film made interesting contributions. Quiquemelle writes: 'This film, with its many inventions, sparkles with humour, fantasy and poetry. It is a delight to the spectator.'[22] While this statement is probably an exaggeration (the narration often drags, the drawings and the animation of the characters are flawed, and the fusion between American teaching and Chinese artistic tradition is not in sync), the originality and autochthonous strength of the film compensate for its defects.

As the war and the political situation grew worse, production on the following work, a feature film entitled *The World of Insects*, was stalled. In the meantime, other Chinese artists had turned to animation. In 1941, a group of young Hong Kong artists, founders of the Association of Chinese Animation, released *The Hunger of the Old Stupid Dog*. In Changqing, Qian Jajun (26 November 1916) produced some shorts. In 1946, in Manchuria, the Communist Party sponsored *The Emperor's Dream* (by Chen Bo'er, with animated puppets; screened in 1947) and the previously mentioned *The Turtle Caught in the Jar* (1948, by Fan Ming – i.e. Tadahito Mochinaga).

---

[21] Marie-Claire Quiquemelle, 'I fratelli Wan, sessant'anni di cinema d'animazione in Cina', in Marco Müller (ed.) *Ombre elettriche – Saggi e ricerche sul cinema cinese*, Electa, Milan, 1982; and *Les frères Wan et 60 ans de dessins animés chinois/ The Wan Brothers and 60 Years of Animated Films in China* festival booklet, Festival d'Annecy, Annecy, 1985.

[22] Marie-Claire Quiquemelle, 'I fratelli Wan, sessant'anni di cinema d'animazione in Cina', in Marco Müller (ed.) *Ombre elettriche – Saggi e ricerche sul cinema cinese*, Electa, Milan, 1982; and *Les frères Wan et 60 ans de dessins animés chinois/ The Wan Brothers and 60 Years of Animated Films in China* festival booklet, Festival d'Annecy, Annecy, 1985.

16
LATIN AMERICA

Mexico

New momentum was given to Mexican animation by Alfonso Vergara Andrade. In 1934, this otolaryngologist, enamoured of animated cartoons, founded AVA Studios in Mexico City along with two partners, Antonio Chavira and Francisco Gómez. The studio lasted three years and produced eight shorts.

Paco Perico en première (Paco Perico's Premiere, 1935) was basically a gag film according to the American model.[1] *Los cinco cabritos* (The Five Little Goats, 1936), directed by Bismarck Mier (the only old-timer who hadn't given up after the Pruneda studio had flopped), was the Mexican version of Disney's *Three Little Pigs* (1933). This is worth mentioning because it was the first Mexican colour animated film. The system used was the bichromic Cinecolor or bicolor, inferior to three-strip Technicolor. The next film was *Noche Mexicana* (Mexican Night, 1937), where the Holy Night party is unexpectedly ruined by obnoxious hosts.

In 1939, AVA (now Ava Color) went out of business. Doctor Vergara retired from cinema, and among the members of his group only Bismarck Mier and Carlos Sandoval (1917–2005) remained.

The 1940s and early 1950s were the Golden Age of Mexican live-action cinema, with such directors as Emilio Fernandez and Julio Bracho and such stars as Pedro Armendáriz, Jorge Negrete, Dolores del Río, and María Félix. Americanization was accentuated for both political (during World War II, even many communists accepted the United States, encouraged by the Stalin-Roosevelt alliance) and economic reasons (Hollywood producers started runaway production companies in cheaper countries).

In 1941, Walt Disney, his wife, and a group of fifteen top studio artists embarked on a famous goodwill tour in South America, visiting Mexico in 1942 and 1943. Two Mexican immigrants crossed the southern border along with the Disney 'grupo': Ernesto 'Ernie' Terrazas and Edmundo Santos.

This visit produced *The Three Caballeros* (which had its world premiere on 21 December 1944 at Cine Alameda in Mexico City). The film was praised and made money, but the Mexican animators who had worked on it received no screen credit and, furthermore, Mexican filmgoers were unhappy with the touristic and stereotyped image it depicted of their country. Story man 'Ernie' Terrazas invented the main Mexican character, the rooster Pancho Pistolas.[2]

Thereafter, most of Mexican animation history can be considered a continuation of the momentum given by the North American 'spiritual invasion' commenced by Disney. However, the rest of it can be considered the counterthrust given by some Mexican artists to this cultural colonization.[3]

Santiago Reachi – an advertising agent who, at the end of the 1930s, had founded the prosperous Publicidad Organizada S.A. and, above all, was the man who had brought Cantinflas[4] to work for the movies – founded the Caricolor studio, hiring four Californian animators:

---
[1] Manuel Rodríguez Bermúdez, *Animación: Una perspectiva desde México*, Centro Universitario de Estudios Cinematográficos, Mexico City, 2007, p. 126.
[2] Juan Manuel Aurrecoechea, *El episodio perdido: Historia del cine mexicano de animación*, Cineteca Nacional, Mexico City, 2004, pp. 31–39.
[3] The feelings that Mexicans harboured (and harbour) towards the United States are more contradictory and conflictual than those of any other people. It all goes back to the American-Mexican War of 1848, when the conquered Mexicans lost 52 per cent of their territory.
[4] Real name: Mario Moreno (1911–1993); he would become one of the greatest comic stars of world cinema.

Manuel Pérez, Rudy Zamora, Pete Burness, and Carl Urbano. The project was torpedoed by the war itself: The four Americans had to go back to serve their country, and only a short was completed – *Me voy de cacería* (I Go Hunting), a sort of homage to tequila.[5]

In 1947, Claudio Baña, Leobardo Galicia, and Jesús Sanchez Rolón established Caricaturas Animadas de México, but the peak of their production was just an animated sequence of a fly in *El diablo no es tan diablo* (The Devil Is Not So Devil, 1949), the first Mexican feature film that combined live-action and animation sequences.[6]

Colombia[7]

Around 1930, the Acevedo brothers from the city of Medellín gave birth to the first animation productions, but they never became famous. In their documentary *Colombia Victorious*, produced in 1933, we can see animated military ships sailing on the Putumayo River. The Acevedo brothers chose animation to show routes, tracks, or interesting spots on maps in various installments of their newsreel *Noticiero Nacional*, in which they showed the national aristocracy participating in everyday life during sports celebrations, bullfights, plays, ballets, processions, and even student demonstrations. Afterwards, there were some scarce attempts to build up a proper animation industry, but for about thirty years this was not possible.

Venezuela[8]

The first documented animation work realized in Venezuela, *La Danza de los Esqueletros* (The Skeleton Dance), dates back to 1934. It is a funny film in which some cannibals persecute three men, made by an (as of this writing) unidentified German technician at the request of then-President Juan Vicente Gómez. It lasts four minutes, eleven seconds and, though silent, it is likely that it was meant to be a musical, considering that the main characters dance and move as if following the rhythm of some music.

The next steps date back to the early 1940s, when the Department of Health backed a short film series to improve the Venezuelan people's health education, emphasizing, for instance, the use of the toothbrush for proper dental hygiene.

In 1942 and 1943, Fernando Álvarez and Luís Mejías produced *Tío Tigre y Tío Conejo* (Uncle Tiger and Uncle Rabbit), starring Potoco the monkey, created by the artist Carlos Cruz Diez; despite dire financial straits, it was fairly successful.

Álvarez and Mejías had gained the support of Rafael Rivero Oramas, founder of *Tricolor* magazine and considered to be the actual screenwriter of the film. Oramas offered them the opportunity to use Studios El Ávila, the property of his friend Rómulo Gallegos.

After achieving this goal, Álvarez travelled across Argentina with the purpose of improving his knowledge about local animation and the animation industry, while Luís Mejías went on working for ARS Publicidad and Bolívar Films. Three years later, Álvarez was back in Venezuela, and he and Mejías decided to open their own animation studio in El Conde.

They started a project oriented towards a Latin American audience called *El Arepón*. Its indisputable protagonist should have been the *arepa* (a dish made of ground corn dough or cooked flour, popular in Colombia, Venezuela, and other Spanish-speaking countries). Ultimately, the two partners stopped getting along, ending the company and the film.

Álvarez stopped working in this field, while Mejías became the leader of the animation department of Radio Caracas Televisión (currently known as TVes).

During the 1940s, the Department of Agriculture hired the Colombian Vargas Codazzi as a producer of short films promoting the Department's messages. Codazzi, to reduce expenses and working hours, chose to utilize the technique of cut-outs.

Codazzi paved the way for many foreign animators, who took their first steps in the country between 1945 and 1950, including the Ukrainian Halyna Mazepa de Koval; the Spaniards Juan Queralt and Arturo Moreno, director of *Garbancito de la Mancha* (Garbancito from La Mancha, 1945); and the Frenchman Georges (Jorge) Lebrel, among others.

---

[5] Juan Manuel Aurrecoechea, *El episodio perdido: Historia del cine mexicano de animación*, Cineteca Nacional, Mexico City, 2004, p. 41.
[6] Manuel Rodríguez Bermúdez, *Animación: Una perspectiva desde México*, Centro Universitario de Estudios Cinematográficos, Mexico City, 2007, p. 131.
[7] By Francesca Guatteri.
[8] By Francesca Guatteri.

Brazil

In 1933, João Stamato, a collaborator of Seth, co-directed *Macaco feio, macaco bônito* (Ugly Monkey, Pretty Monkey) with Luiz Seel.[9] In 1938, caricaturist Luiz Sá released the short *Avênturas de Virgolino* (The Adventures of Virgolino) and, a year later, *Virgolino apânha* (Virgolino's Troubles). In the 1940s, Humberto Mauro (1897–1983), one of the founding fathers of Brazilian cinema, worked briefly with animation. His eighteen-minute *O dragãozinho manso* (The Good Little Dragon) introduced the country to the use of animated puppets.

Argentina[10]

In 1928, after the six-year interval required by the Constitution, Yrigoyen ran again for president and was re-elected. When the president's senility and the dishonesty of his collaborators became objects of ridicule for the country, Cristiani could not resist the temptation to make fun of him once again. In 1929, he began filming *Peludópolis* from the newly founded Estudios Cristiani. (The title of the film, 'City of Peludo', referred to the radical president's nickname.)[11]

The film took two years to complete and was shown at Cine Renacimiento on 16 September 1931. The final edition, however, had undergone radical changes from the original project; history had forced Cristiani to re-edit. One year before the film was released, a coup by General José Félix Uriburu on 6 September overthrew the democracy. Cristiani hurried to modify the film in an attempt to save whatever sequences he could, but the result was not well received by the public.[12] More favourably disposed, critics encouragingly praised the artist. As the world's first *sound* animated feature film, *Peludópolis* was further proof of Cristiani's precociousness.

After suffering an economic loss from this project, Cristiani took a more careful approach to cinema, limiting his production to advertising. In 1938, he made a brief comeback to entertainment when writer and editor Constancio C. Vigil asked him to make a film from one of his short stories, 'El mono relojero' (The Monkey Watchmaker). For this short film, Cristiani used the North American

Figure 16.1 Quirino Cristiani making *Peludópolis*, 1931.

---

[9] This American producer was previously introduced at work in Germany and Austria.
[10] By Giannalberto Bendazzi and Francesca Guatteri.
[11] 'Peludo' in Argentinean-Castillian is the name of the little animal usually called an armadillo. The armadillo's behaviour is very shy and aloof – like the aloof president, who dominated through inscrutability.
[12] Very briefly, this is the plot: The state ship falls into the hands of the pirate El Peludo, who lands with his crew in the Quesolandina Republic. After several adventures, a boat appears on the horizon, carrying General Provisional (Uriburu) and Juan Pueblo (the people), who intend to remedy the troubles of Quesolandina. The name Quesolandina (Argentina) derives from the idiom 'le gusta el queso' (he likes cheese), referring to the greediness of corrupt officials.

technique of cel animation[13] and a style influenced by the cinema of the United States. The film was not successful with audiences. Of average quality, it suffered from the contrast between the filmmaker's comical, playful inspiration and the writer's strictly educational intent. A planned screen adaptation of Vigil's other stories did not take off, particularly because of the difficulty in finding a market. For this same reason, Cristiani gradually abandoned his advertising activity and focused on developing, printing, and sound recording in the new studio bearing his name. He returned twice to the creation of comic shorts, working on *Entre pitos y flautas* (Between the Pipes and Flutes, 1941) and *Carbonada* (1943); afterwards, he retired permanently from the field.

After Quirino Cristiani, animators in Argentina were not able to complete major projects. Juan Oliva, a painter and comic strip artist (Barcelona, August 1910–July 1975) emigrated to Argentina in 1930 and apprenticed with Cristiani for a few years. In 1937, he began animating his own productions. These were brief comic episodes about Julián Centella, a little gaucho, for insertion in the newsreel *Sucesos Argentinos* (Events in Argentina). In 1939, he founded the Compañía Argentina de Dibujos Animados (The Argentinean Company of Animated Drawings), with the intention of producing animated shorts that could compete with their American counterparts.

After his trial production *Desplumando avestruces* (Plucking Ostriches), Oliva released *La caza del puma* (Hunting the Puma, 1940). The movie features the child Rejucilo and his horse Ciclón. They succeed in their hunt for the puma by getting the animal drunk. Despite good-quality animation and drawings, at least for the standards of the time, the film didn't have much of an audience, and Oliva was forced to dissolve the company. He worked for a time in advertising before producing two shorts, *Filipito el pistolero* (Filipito the Gunslinger, 1942) and *Noche de sustos* (Night of Fright, 1942). Oliva then retired to drawing, painting, and teaching animation. Plagued by poor health (for many years, he was almost blind), he died on 3 July 1975.

Dante Quinterno (San Vicente, 26 October 1909– Buenos Aires, 14 May 2003) was a comic strip artist, publisher, and creator of the famous Indian Patoruzú, a sort of Argentinean Don Quixote. A man of vast financial means, in 1939, he planned a feature film based on his own comic strip character. After visiting the Fleischer and Disney studios in the United States, he assembled a good team, managed by his closest comic strip collaborators. For various reasons (such as the choice of the German colour film system Gasparcolor, which became unavailable after the outbreak of the war), the piece was reduced to eighteen minutes. It was released unsuccessfully in 1942 with the title *Upa en apuros* (Upa in Trouble). This was the first Argentinean colour animated film and for a long time was considered an example of good animation at the international level.

In the meantime, a new generation of animators was born, including Tulio Lobato and Oscar Blotta (assisted by Victor A. Iturralde Rúa), Alberto del Castillo, and Joseph Gallo. Veteran animator and writer Oscar Desplats explains: 'They were already very skilled artists, capable of tackling any kind of design.'[14]

José Maria Burone Bruché, Juan Oliva's follower, went through a couple of very different stages during two decades of work throughout Argentinean animation history to achieve, in his projects, the combination of the smooth and bohemian style of his previous independent works and the orderliness of professional television advertisement work. He began his activities in 1942, when he replaced Juan Oliva as director of the Emelco Animation Department for the production of commercial shorts. As Oscar Desplats recalled, 'Bruché stood out because his drawings, characters and creations reflected authentic national expression'. Precisely where his predecessor had found little opportunity to produce his art shorts, José Burone Bruché was able to film *Los consejos del viejo vizcacha* (The Old Vizcacha's Advice, 1945), a three-minute free adaptation of José Hernández's famous book of gaucho poems, *Martín Fierro*, written in 1872. *The Old Vizcacha's Advice* is about a miserable old gaucho who gives politically incorrect advice.

Bruché collaborated with Francisco Blanco for the creation of the backgrounds and Ubaldo Galuppo for the creation of the animation for the film, which was shot in Ferraniacolor.[15] Afterwards, with the same work team, Bruché involved himself in a very ambitious project: the modern rearrangement of *Fausto*, based on the text by Estanislao del Campo, and a series of one-minute films in black and white, for the producer Cinepa, entitled El

---

[13] For his previous film, Cristiani had used an original technique for animating cut-out figures, which he patented in 1917. *El Apóstol*, *Sin dejar rastros*, and *Peludópolis* were filmed with this method, which was used in other films as well until the early 1930s.

[14] Oscar Desplats, personal communication to Francesca Guatteri, October 2010.

[15] Ferraniacolor was a short-lived Italian colour stock system.

refrán animado or Refranes populares (Popular Sayings, 1947).

In 1950, he formed his own company, Burone Bruché Productions. He brought about a number of animated characters in many comedy shorts and custom advertising and educational films before devoting himself exclusively to commercials.

José Burone Bruché died at the early age of fifty-one while still hard at work, so his projects were carried out by the animators who had worked with him, Ubaldo Galuppo and Jorge Caro, who would later open their own studios.

In 1949, Enrique de Rosas founded Cinepa, a distributor and Argentina's first producer of short black-and-white 16-mm films intended for exhibition in homes and cinema clubs (he also manufactured 16-mm film projectors for his market under the brand name 'Hollywood'). Cinepa's animators were Galuppo, Jorge Caro, and Dante Pettenon.

In the years defined by Walt Disney's monopoly, Jorge Caro chose to draw inspiration instead from the style of Warner Bros. and MGM, two studios that, in the 1940s, maintained very high levels of creative standards and productivity.

At that time, amateur screenings were very fashionable, so selling material for such distribution turned out to be a big source of wealth. Even some of Oliva's old productions, such as *El refrán animado* or *La caza del puma*, began to be distributed in that form. The great success of this business led to the production of various short films in black and white.

Jorge Caro, a José Burone Bruché alumnus, started his profession right in his master's studio in 1950 with an animated series developed from an original character: a cheerful rabbit named Plácido that became very successful, particularly in *Puños de campeón* (Fists of Champion), which was released in cinemas in the early 1950s. Plácido is a humanized, two-legged rabbit, reminiscent of the American model of anthropomorphized animal characters. After several similar shorts, Caro moved to Peru, where he founded an animation studio.

17
AFRICA

Egypt

The small Egyptian animated production industry was mainly due to the Frenkel brothers. Born into a Jewish family in Jaffa, Palestine, Herschel, Salomon, and David Frenkel later established their lacquered wood furniture business in Cairo. Fascinated by animation after viewing the films of Felix the Cat, the three brothers began studying the frame-by-frame technique. In 1936, they released *Mafish Fayda* (Nothing to Do), featuring the character of Mish-Mish, an Egyptian youngster wearing a fez. Other productions based on the same character followed, including the good war propaganda film *Al difau'al watani* (National Defence, 1940) and *Enjoy Your Food* (1947). When the political environment in Egypt became too turbulent, the Frenkels left the country. The younger brother, David, moved to France, where he revived Mish-Mish by substituting his fez with a very French *casquette* and renaming him Mimiche. These films were not distributed in theatres but instead were sold for home use. In 1964, he made *Le rêve du beau Danube bleu* (The Dream of the Beautiful Blue Danube), the only major creation in his European production.

Another Egyptian pioneer was Antoine Selim Ibrahim (Cairo, 11 November 1911), whose *Aziza and Youness in El Sheik Barakat's Book* (1938) was the first animated film with an Arabic sound track. Ibrahim made more films in the 1940s (including *Dokdok*, 1940) and then made commercials and titles for live-action films. In 1972, he went to the United States and worked for Hanna-Barbera; then, from 1976 to 1980, he worked for DePatie-Freleng Enterprises. He later retired and devoted himself to painting.

Union of South Africa[1]

During the 1940s, the South African animation industry was divided in two directions: on the one hand, special effects animation from Killarney Film Studios (the new name for Schlesinger's previous company, African Film Productions), including optical effects and titling;[2] on the other hand, traditional hand-drawn cel animation from Alpha Film Studios.

Killarney Film Studios, which continued to be a major producer of local films and newsreels for the two decades to come,[3] created and maintained a separate animation and optical department, run by James Reindorp. The bulk of the department's work consisted of titles for film studios and live projects, as well as long-running weekly programming.

Partly due to the archaic facilities and technology available and largely due to the improvisatory methodology they employed while working, the staff at the Killarney studios gained ingenuity in the field of special effects. However,

---

[1] By Shanaz Shapurjee Hampson.

[2] According to Trevor Moses, senior industrial technician at the National Film, Video and Sound Archives in Pretoria, special effects animation was usually done for the opening titles or end credits sequences in live-action features or shorts. Some of these title sequences were complex, involved, and displayed a lot of sophistication.

[3] Newsreels and animation distribution were synonymous with theatre complexes, and these animated films and newsreels were used as fillers – precursors to the 'main attraction'. This phenomenon happened across the globe, with audiences being able to enjoy an entire evening's worth of entertainment (Leonard Maltin, *Of Mice and Magic: A History of American Animated Cartoons*, New American Library, New York, 1980, p. 2).

for economic reasons, innovation and experimentation were suppressed, and instead artists were encouraged to follow the client's brief in order to meet the high output demand.[4]

James Reindorp was a highly talented and competent cameraman. He had a fixed camera that was supported on four wooden poles (thereby allowing a tabletop to be winched up and down). In 1946, Reindorp left Killarney Film Studios to join the newly formed Alpha Film Studios as an animation cameraman, leaving Benny Mechanik, his assistant, to run the animation and optical department.

Mechanik continued to produce titles for the studio's live projects and long-running weekly news program *African Mirror*, as well as optical special effects and transitions. He created his own mattes for transitions by shooting them in black and white on high-contrast film stock. Vaseline was applied to the camera lens in patterns to create filters. Fades were created manually by dipping the actual film negative in a tray of ferrocyanide and counting off the exposure time of each frame, then fixing the film in sodium thiosulfate, a photographic fixing agent, and hanging it on wash lines to dry.[5] In 1955, 20th Century Fox bought the studio out; this year finally saw the arrival of a proper animation stand, with an adjustable camera for zooms and pans and portable lights.

It was Alpha Film Studios, Africa's largest studio, which produced traditional hand-drawn animation. When James Reindorp joined the newly established studio, Alpha Film Studios ultimately gained full momentum. In 1947, the owner, Bill Boxer, persuaded Denis Purchase, an English animator, to relocate to South Africa to produce animated commercials for the studio. American and European modes of animation production – and even socio-political ideologies – greatly influenced the manner in which South African artists approached their work during the 1940s and for decades to come, as the professionals training and advising South African animators were predominantly foreigners.

Because professional animation equipment was not available in South Africa, conditions at Alpha Film Studios were largely improvised: The animators used cellophane in place of traditional cels; a laborious spring system had to be created and set up to flatten the wrinkles out of each sheet before every frame was shot.

In addition to these challenges, the studio desperately needed to purchase both a new animation stand and a new optical printer; however, there was not enough money in the budget.

Reindorp then began a lengthy process of innovation, which would eventually culminate in a technological marvel. For two years, he was engaged in intense negotiations with Oxberry, the American manufacturer of the finest animation stands in the world, and initiated a design experiment process with the famous company to devise one stand that served both functions. Finally, after years of perseverance, Mr. Oxberry himself came out to South Africa in 1956 to install at Alpha Film Studios the first animation stand in the world with an aerial image feature for superimposition on live film. This dual-function animation stand allowed Reindorp and the staff at the studio to streamline their workflow and production pipeline, thereby increasing their output.

Alpha Film Studios specialized in animated commercials and the popular limited animation form known as the 'drawtoon', which echoed the work of the old lightning sketchers: The scene was first drawn in pencil and then erased so that only the animator could see the faint guidelines. The animator could then begin inking the sketch, once placed on the animation stand, a section at a time, pausing briefly for the cameraman to shoot the images in succession. Quite a few cartoonists passed through the studio's doors as 'drawtoonists', but it was Denis Purchase who created the bulk of the animation at the studio.[6]

During its prime, Alpha Film Studios was believed to have produced sixty seconds of cartoon animation per week, as well as a plethora of 'drawtoons', all of which were completed by a dedicated team of twelve skilled colourists. It is remarkable that such an understaffed studio was capable of such a feat.

During the first four decades of the twentieth century, South African animation was directed towards an adult, cinema-going audience as opposed to the later shift to children's programming in the television era. The affinity between animation and advertising emerged as early as 1916, and this economically driven partnership seems to have remained.

---

[4] As a result, South African animation slowly began to forge a niche for itself in the commercial market, culminating in the art form being very successful in the advertising industry after television was introduced to the country in 1976.

[5] Sarienne Kersh, 'History of South African Animation', *Screen Africa*, 20 November 1996, p. 22.

[6] Purchase was later joined by Stanley Pearsall, who had previously worked with David Hand (the director of Disney's *Snow White and the Seven Dwarfs* and *Bambi*) in England. Other notable, local 'drawtoons' artists from that time were Keith Stevens and John Garling.

Index

Abajo la careta or *La república de Jauja* (Down with the Mask or The Republic of Plenty; Ducaud) 87
A Ballada da Fonte (The Ballad of the Source; Carlos) 72
ABC Film 162
Åberg, Émile 68
Abreu, Vitorino 71
Abstraction and Empathy: Essays in the Psychology of Style (Worringer) 30
Acciaio (Steel; Ruttmann) 57
Acevedo brothers 190
Acosta (Alcorta), Miguel Angel 85
Acres, Birt 21, 22
Actualidades Valle (newsreel) 86
Adam Raises Cain (Sarg-Dawley) 49–50
Adam-Salomon, Antoine 16, 17
Admiral Palads (Admiral Palace; Klouman) 69
Adolfo XIII (Spain) 169
The Adventures of Ben Cockles (Lee) 88
The Adventures of Münchhausen (Cherkes) 80
Adventures of Prince Achmed (Reiniger) 90–1, 138, 153
The Adventures of Ranger Focus (Lee) 88
advertisements 23, 64n40, 157, 159, 167, 185, 192; *see also* commercials
Aelita (Protazanov) 76, 78
The Aerial Anarchists (Booth) 24
The Aerial Submarine (Booth) 24
Aesop's Fables 46–7, 114
Aesop's Fables Studios 44
A Extraordinária Aventura do Zeca (Zeca's Extraordinary Adventure; Coelho et al.) 173
Africa, animation in 88–9, 194–5
African Film Productions 88, 194
African Film Trust 88
Afrika (Weichberger) 159
Agfacolor 161, 162
Agren, Emile 162
Aida (Wozak/Thomas) 158
The Airship Destroyer (Booth) 23

Aito sunnuntaimetsästäjä (A True Sunday Hunter; Salén/Nyberg) 70
Akhundov, Aga-Nagi 179
Aladdin and His Wonderful Lamp (Fleischer) 117
Al difau'al watani (National Defence) 194
Alegres Vacaciones (Happy Vacations; Moreno) 172
Aleksandravičius, Petras 177
Aleksandrov, Grigory 96
A Lenda de Miragaia (The Legend of Miragaia; Faria de Fonseca/Cunhal) 72
Alesandri, Arturo 86
Alexeïeff, Alexandre 103, 130, 137, 140–7, 163, 166, 168
Alexeïeff, Claire Parker 141–7
Alexeïeff, Maria Polidorova 140
Alexeïeff, Nikolay 140
Alexeïeff, Vladimir 140
Algar, James 101
Alice in Wonderland (Disney) 101
Alice's Wonderland (series; Disney) 50
Alimenty (Nourishment; Sorokhtin) 81
Aliyev, Boris 179
Allegretto (O. Fischinger) 155
The All-Union Powerhouse (Cherkes) 80
Alpha Cinematograph Company 23
Alpha Film Studios 194, 195
Alpha Picture Palace 23
Alpha Trading Company 23
Als der Russe vor Przemysl stand (As the Russian Stood before Przemysl; Zasche) 63
Álvarez, Fernando 190
Alves, João Rodrigues 71
Alye parusa (Scarlet Sails) 177
Amalrik, Leonid 174
An American March (O. Fischinger) 155
American Vitagraph Company 25
Ammitsted, Finn Rosenberg 161
Amos 'n' Andy (radio) 114

Index

Anatole à la Tour de Nesle (Anatole at the Tour de Nesle; Dubout/Junca) 137
Anatole fait du camping (Anatole Goes Camping; Dubout/Junca) 137
Andersen, Hans Christian 161, 162
Anderson, Ken 102
Anderson, Sherwood 30
Andrade, Alfonso Vergara 189
Andy Panda 112
Anémic Cinéma (Duchamp) 55
Angelico, Beaton 168
Anger, Kenneth 128
Anglia Film 131
Animads 23
Animaland 131
Animat 137
Animated Cartoon Company (Copenhagen) 160
The Animated Grouch Chasers (Barré) 39
Animated Matches: Cricket: Vestas V. Pine 22
animation: abstract 56–8, 129, 132–5, 152, 155; addition of sound to 46, 47, 96–7; ancient examples 7–8; anti-Semitic 149n52, 151; *auteur* 2, 155; birth of the industry 38; coloring by assistants 42–3, 162; combined with live action 39, 41, 48, 54, 59, 64n40, 68, 74, 79, 85, 88, 136, 157, 165, 166–7, 172, 176, 187, 190; Disney's rules of 107–9; Disney's style of 109–10; drawing on cels 40, 42, 101, 110, 192; educational 45, 46, 84, 103, 104, 126, 138, 163, 167, 177, 179, 192; experimental 130; of illusory solids 142–3; influence of cinema on 12, 109; influence of science on 12–13; personality 37; propaganda 25, 32, 52, 53, 56, 62n31, 77, 83, 104, 111, 115, 121, 130, 131, 133, 148, 167, 168, 175, 177, 178, 180, 181n5, 182–4, 185n12, 194; rubber hose style 42, 45, 124; silent 30; underground movement 128; *see also* animation by country; animation techniques
animation by country: Africa 88–9, 194–5; Argentina 86–7, 191–3; Armenia 178–9; Australia 90–1; Austria 63–5, 157–9; Azerbaijan 179; Belgium 72, 147; Brazil 86, 191; Canada 129–30; Chile 86; Colombia 85, 190; Czechoslovakia 165–6; Denmark 65–7, 160–2; Egypt 194; Finland 70; France 54–5, 135–47; Germany 55–63, 148–57; Great Britain 52–3, 131–5; Greece 167; Hungary 70, 166–7; Ireland 53; Italy 72, 167–9; Japan 82–4; Latin America 85–7, 189–93; Lithuania 177; Mexico 85, 189–90; Norway 69–70, 162–3; Oceania 90–1; Poland 72, 163–5; Portugal 71–2, 173; Romania 72; Russia/Soviet Union 72–81, 174–7; South Africa 88, 194–5; Soviet Georgia 177–8; Spain 70–1, 169–73; Sweden 67–8, 162; Switzerland 65, 159–60; Netherlands 147–8; Ukraine 81, 177; Venezuela 190; Yugoslavia 167; *see also* United States
animation techniques: cel technique 40, 42, 101, 110, 192; clay techniques 42, 72, 136, 153; peg system 42; stop frame 53; 'totalization' technique 143; traveling shot 42; *see also* cut-outs; frame-by-frame technique; puppets; silhouettes
Añino, Manuel Alonso 182
Anitra's Dance (Grieg) 128
Ankeny, Jason 126
Anouilh, Jean 137
Anschütz, Ottomar 15
Anstey, Edgar 132
Antonovsky, Boris 81
Apollon Musagete (Irena Dodal) 165
Apteka (Pharmacy; Themersons) 164, 165
Aquino, Luís de 71
Aracuan Bird (Disney) 112
Arai Wagoro 183
Arcady (Brachlianoff) 136
Archer, Frederick Scott 14
Argentina, animation in 86–7, 191–3
Argonavtebi-Kolkhida (The Argonauts; Mujiri) 176
Arichan (Ant Boy; Mochinaga) 184
Armendáriz, Pedro 189
Armenia, animation in 178–9
Armer Hansi (Poor Hansi; Deutsche Zeichenfilm GmbH) 149
Armstrong, Charles 52
Armstrong, Louis 155
Armstrong's Trick Mar Incidents (Armstrong) 52
Arp, Jean 59
ARS Publicidad 190
art nouveau 168
Arthenack, Juan 85
Artistic Creation (Booth & Paul) 23
Artists and Models (Tashlin) 127
The Artist's Dream/The Artist's Inspiration (Shaw) 88
Artist's Dreams (or *The Dachshund and the Sausage*; Bray) 39
A Sátira (magazine) 71
Association of Chinese Animation 188
Astoria Film Company 63, 64, 157
Atamanov, Lev Konstantinovich 175, 178
Atelier Filmovych Triku (AFIT) 165–6
Aucassin et Nicolette (Reiniger) 63
Aurenche, Jean 137
Australia, animation in 90–1
Austria, animation in 63–5, 157–9
auteur animation 2, 155

Automania (Tiago) 173
Autour d'une cabine (Around a Bathing Hut) 17
AVA Studios (Ava Color) 189
Avênturas de Bille e Bolle (The Adventures of Bille and Bolle; Rossi) 86
Avênturas de Virgolino (The Adventures of Virgolino; Sá) 191
Avery, Frederick Bean 'Tex' 112, 119–23, 125, 127
Aviation Vacation (Avery) 120, 121
Avraamov, Arseny 175
Azerbaijan, animation in 179
Azerbaijan Film Studio 179
Aziza and Youness in El Sheik Barakat's Book (Ibrahim) 194
Aznar, Adolfo 170, 172

Babbitt, Art 101, 104
Baby . . . e la 'Lucrezia Borgia' (Baby . . . and the 'Lucrezia Borgia'; Zambonelli) 72
Bagudajo no tozoku (Burglars of Baghdad Castle; Ofuji) 181
Baguñá, Jaume 170, 181
Baguñá, Josep Maria 171
Bailey, Harry 114
Bairnsfather Cartoons (Dodsworth) 53
Balázs, Béla 176
Balet y Blay company 171, 172
Baliban, Barney 166
Balla 34
Ballad of Smokey the Bear (Mochinaga et al.) 185
Ballet mécanique (Mechanical Ballet; Léger) 54, 58
Bam-Bam, eller så tuktas ett troll (How We Tame a Troll; Högfelt) 162
Bambi (Disney) 102, 104, 131
Baña, Claudio 190
The Band Concert (Disney) 99, 101
Barbe-bleue (Bluebeard; Painlevé) 136
Barber of Seville (Lantz) 112
Barbera, Joseph 114, 120, 121, 127
Barcarole (Pfenninger) 56
Barks, Carl 99n10
Barney the Bear (Ising) 126
Barnum, P. T. 106
Barré, Raoul 38–9, 40, 42, 46, 47, 129
Barrymore, John 102
Bartolozzi, Salvador 170
Bartosch, Berthold 60, 61, 62, 130, 137, 138–40
Bartosch, Maria Ebel 138, 140
Bartram, Nikolai 80
Basgier, Thomas 151
Bastick, F. Harold 23
Batram, N. 79
Battleship Potemkin (Eisenstein) 30

Baudelaire, Charles 20
Bauhaus 30, 56
Bayeux Tapestry 8
The Bear That Couldn't Sleep (Ising) 126
The Bear's Tale (Avery) 120
Beaudet, Louise 47, 129
Beijing Film Academy 185
Being and Time (Heidegger) 30
Belgium, animation in 72, 147
Believe It or Else (Avery) 120
Belle Époque 29
Belson, Jordan 155
Belyaev, Ivan 75
Benkei tai Ushikawa (Benkei the Soldier Priest and Little Samurai Ushikawa; Masaoka) 182
Bennett, James Gordon 36
Benois, Alexandre 141
benshi 84
Benzin (ballet) 66
Bergdahl, Victor 67–70
Berge, Hans 69
Beringola, Arturo 170
Berlin—Die Sinfonie der Großstadt (Berlin—The Symphony of the Great City; Ruttmann) 57
Bermúdez, Manuel Rodríguez 85
Bertrand, René 136
The Best Cigarette Is a Jones (commercial; Armstrong) 52
Betty Boop (Fleischer) 109, 115, 116–17
bichromic Cinecolor 189
bicolor 189
Bierling, Lore 56
The Big Broadcast of 1937 (O. Fischinger) 155
Big Heel Watha (Avery) 122
Bimbo (Fleischer) 115, 116, 117
Bio Film 69
Bioletto, Angelo 169
Biophon 97n6
The Birth of a Nation (D.W. Griffith) 30
The Birth of the Robot (Lye) 133
Biruma no tategoto (The Burmese Harp; Ichikawa) 186
Bishop, Bainbridge 20
bitumen of Judea 13–14
Bizet, Georges 158
Blackbird (Puppetoon) 166
Blackton, James Stuart 25–6, 31, 67, 88
Blair, Lee 101
Blair, Mary Robinson 101
Blair, Preston 101, 110, 112, 114, 119, 121
Blanc, Mel 112n38, 120, 125
Blanc-Gatti, Charles 160

Index

Blanco, Francisco 192
Blek end uait (Black and White; Amalrik/ Ivanov-Vano) 174
Blitz Wolf (Avery) 121
Blotta, Oscar 192
Bluto (Fleischer) 117
Bobby Bumps 40, 48
Bolivar Films 190
Bonzo (Studdy) 53
Booth, Walter Robert 23–4
Borcosque, Carlos 86
Bosch, Hieronymus 168
Bosko (Harman/Ising) 118–19, 126
Bosko the Talk-Ink Kid (Harman/Ising) 118
Bouchéry, Wilfried 147
Boumans, Ivan 10
Bourdelle, Émile-Antoine 63
Bowers, Charles R. 39, 42, 47
Bowsky, Willard 117
Boxer, Bill 195
Brachlianoff, Arcady 136
Bracho, Julio 189
Bradley, Scott 120
Bragaglia 34
Brandenburg Concerto No. 3 (J. S. Bach) 155
Braque, Georges 30
Brasch, Sven 65
Bratishkin (Ptushko) 175, 176
Brave Little Tailor (Disney) 100
Bray, John Randolph 39–40, 41, 44, 48, 69, 129
Bray Studios 40–2
Brazil, animation in 86, 191
Brdečka, Jiří 150
Brecht, Berthold 138
Bresnikar, Franz 159
Bresson, Robert 136
Brewster, David 13
Brinck, Birger 58
Bringing up Father 40, 86n9
Brooks, Mel 122
Bruché, José María Burone 192
Brumberg, Valentina 79, 177
Brumberg, Zinaida 79, 177
Brunet, A. 147
Bruno (Harman/Ising) 118
Bubble and Squeak (Moreno) 132
Bucky's Burlesques (Buxton) 53
Budd, Leighton 41
Buddy (Harman/Ising) 119
Buffalo Full (Romano) 170
Bug Vaudeville (McCay) 37

Bugs Bunny 95, 109, 112, 119, 120, 121, 123–4
Bugs Bunny Nips the Nips (Freleng) 125
Bully Boy series (Speed) 52
Burness, Pete 114, 190
Burone Bruché Productions 193
Bushkin, Aleksandr 75, 76
Busoni, Ferruccio 59
Bute, Mary Ellen 128
Butting, Max 56
Buxton, Dudley 52
Buzilka (Presnyakov/Sorokhtin) 175

Cadet Rouselle (Dunning/Low) 130
Cage, John 155
Calder, Alexander 59
Calling Mr. Smith (Themersons) 164
Callisto, la petite nymphe de Diane (Callisto, the Little Nymph of Diana; Marty) 136
Calloway, Cab 117
A Call to Arms (Lu Hsun) 30
calotype 14
The Camel's Dance (Wan brothers) 187
cameras 15
Campo, Estanislao del 192
Canada, animation in 129–30
Canadian Broadcasting Company (CBC) 130
Canemaker, John 36
Caniff, Milton 38
Cannon, Bobe 120
Cantinflas 189
Capra, Frank 99
Caprino, Ivo 163
Caprino, Mario 163
Captain Easy 38
Cap'taine Sabord appareille (Captain Sabord Gets Underway; Rigal) 136
Cap'taine Sabord dans l'île mystérieuse (Captain Sabord in the Mysterious Island; Rigal) 136
Carbonada (Cristiani) 192
Caricaturas Animadas de México 190
caricature and caricaturists, 23, 25, 32, 39, 41, 51, 52, 56, 63, 64, 65, 69, 70, 75, 81, 82, 83, 86, 87, 100, 103, 108–9, 118, 125, 127, 130, 137, 149n52, 150, 157, 163, 170, 171, 184, 185, 190, 191
Caricolor studio 189
Carlos, João 72
Carlson, Wallace A. 41, 48
Carlson Studios 41
Carmen (Dyer) 131
Carmen (Myller) 161

Carmen (Wozak/Thomas) 158
Carmen criolla (Creole Carmen; Ducaud) 87
Carné, Marcel 95
Caro, Jorge 193
Cartoon Collection (Wan brothers) 187
Cartune Classics 111
Carvalho, Manuel Santos 71
The Case of the Lost Sheep (Lantz) 112
Castel, Louis-Bertrand 20
Castillo, Alberto del 192
Cauchemar (Nightmare; Bartosch) 140
Caution! The Devil (Wasilewski) 164
Cavalcanti, Alberto 133
Cavandoli, Osvaldo 168
Cavé 54, 65, 159
Cecil the Seasick Sea Serpent (Clampett) 124
CEIDA 171
cel technique 40, 42, 101, 110, 192
Centella, Julián 192
Chagama ondo (A Dance Song with a Kettle; Masaoka) 182
The Chairs' Flirtation (Kuczkowski) 72
chalk talks 25, 88; *see also* lightning sketches
Chamartín studio 172
Chankvetadze, Konstantine 178
Chansons de Charles Trenet (Songs of Charles Trenet; Philippart) 147
Chaplin, Charlie 30, 45, 46, 109, 122
Charbonnier, Pierre 136
Charles Mintz Screen Gems 113
Charles Urban Trading Company 23, 52
Charlot cubiste (Cubistic Charlie Chaplin; Murphy) 54
Chavira, Antonio 189
Chemi bebia (My Grandma; Mikaberidze) 177
Chen Bo'er 188
Cherkes, Daniil Yakovlevich 77, 79–80, 175
cheval 54
Chiba City Art Museum 8
Chibikuro Sanbo no tora taiji (Little Black Sambo and His Twin Brother; Mochinaga) 185
Chikara to onna no yononaka (The World of Power and Women; Masaoka) 182
Chile, animation in 86
Chilly Willy (Avery) 123
China in Flames (Khodataev) 174
Chinese Magic (Booth & Paul) 23
Chinese shadows 56, 60n25, 61
Chiora (Birdy; Mujiri) 178
Chiyogami Eigasha (Chiyogami Cinema Company) 181
chiyogami paper 181
Chomón, Segundo de 70, 71

Chongire hebi (The Cut-Up Serpent; Kouchi) 83
Choque de trenes (Train Collision; Chomón) 70
A Chord of Color (Ginna) 35
Chouinard Art School 101, 111
Christensen, Christian Maagaard 65, 161
chromatic motifs 34
Chromophonic Orchestra 160
Chromophony (Blanc-Gatti) 160
Chronophone system 97n6
chronophotography 10, 15
Chukovsky, Kornei 79
Churchill, Frank 98, 102
Ciclón (horse) 192
Cinderella (Disney) 101, 172
Cinderella (Perrault) 172
Cinderella Meets Fella (Avery) 120, 121
Cine Syndicate 22
Cinecentrum 148
Cinecolor 113, 181, 189
cinema: abstract 34; and the addition of sound 96–7; birth of 12, 21; classical 30; colour in 37; early 20th century 30; educational films 45, 46, 48, 53, 54, 56, 63, 83, 84, 87, 103, 104, 126, 129, 130, 131, 138, 151, 163, 167, 171, 177, 179, 192, 193; narrative vs. non-narrative 30–1; training films 40, 44, 104, 126, 149
cinema of attractions 21, 30
Cinepa 192, 193
Cinephonograph 97n6
Cirici-Pellicer, Alexandre 172
Citizen Kane 40
Civil Censorship Department (CCD) 184
Civil Information and Education Section (CI&E) 184
Clair, René 58, 61, 95
Clair-Picabia 34
Clampett, Bob 120, 123–4, 125
Clark, Les 101, 107
clay techniques 42, 72, 136, 153
Clouzot, Henri-Georges 34
The Clown and His Donkey (Armstrong) 52
Coal Black and de Sebben Dwarfs (Clampett) 123, 125
Codazzi, Vargas 190
Code of Motion Picture Production 116
Coelho, Adolfo 173
Cohl, Émile (Émile Courtet) 2, 5, 26, 30, 31, 32–3, 37, 54, 73, 86, 167
Colbrandt, Marc 147
Collard, Robert *see* Lortac
Collodi, Carlo 176
collodion process 14

Colombia Victorious (Acevedo brothers) 190
Colombia, animation in 85, 190
Colonel Heeza Liar (Bray) 48, 69
Colonel Heeza Liar in Africa 40
Color Classics (Fleischer) 117
Color Cry (Lye) 134
Color Rhapsodies (Lantz) 114
colour: Agfacolor 161, 162; bicolor 189; chromatic motifs 34; Cinecolor 113, 181, 189; color drama 35; Disney's use of 99, 101, 102; Dufaycolor 171; in early cartoons 42–3, 62–3, 75, 109, 110, 115, 117, 124, 133–5, 154, 156–7; experiments with 25, 134–5, 153–4; Ferraniacolor 192; Fujicolor 181; Gasparcolor 154, 157, 163, 192; Konicolor 181; Montreux-Colorfilm 160; and music 19–20, 34–5, 78, 154, 156; in silent cinema 37; Technicolor 99n9, 111, 122, 138, 181; three-color process 140
A Colour Box (Lye) 133, 134
Colour Cartoon Company (Copenhagen) 161
Colour-Music (Jameson) 20
Colour-Music—The Art of Mobile Colour (Rimington) 20
colour organ 20
Columbia Distribution Company 113–14, 118
Colvig, Pinto 102
Come Take a Trip in My Airship (Fleischer) 45
ComiColor Cartoons 113
comic strips 32, 38, 46, 99, 104n27, 109, 114, 115, 127, 131, 147, 148, 168, 171, 173, 192
commercials 23, 52, 54, 55, 63, 65, 66, 68, 69–70, 71, 79, 83, 123, 137, 149, 151, 152, 157, 159, 160–3, 165–7, 170, 173, 192–5; *see also* advertisements
Communism and Humanity (Bartosch) 138
Compagnie Belge d'Animation (CBA) 147
Compañia Argentina de Dibujos Animados (The Argintinean Company of Animated Drawings) 192
Compatriot (Wan brothers) 187
Composing Pictures, Still and Moving (Graham) 111
Compositions (Grant) 129
Confidence (Lantz) 111
Coogan, Jackie 167
Cooper, Merian C. 42
Cornelius, Ola 69
A Corny Concerto (Clampett) 123
Corra, Bruno 34
Cossio, Carlo 168
Cossio, Vittorio 168
Costa, Mário 173
Cottrell, William 101
Couchés dans le foin (Asleep in the Hay; Delaurier) 136

Couchés dans le foin (Asleep in the Hay; Vanpeperstraetes) 147
The Country Cousin (Disney) 103
Course in General Linguistics (Saussure) 30
Crafton, Donald 26
Crane, Roy 38
Cri-Cri, Ludo et l'orage (Cri-Cri, Ludo, and the Storm; Payen) 137
Cri-Cri, Ludo et le soleil (Cri-Cri, Ludo, and the Sun; Payen) 137
The Crime on the Street of the Ventriloquist Cat (Wasilewski) 164
Cristiani, Quirino 86–7, 191
Crockwell, Douglass 128–9
Crocodile (Chukovsky) 79
Crooks and Christmas (Lee) 88
Crosland, Alan 97
Cross-Country Detours (Avery) 120
The Crowd (Vidor) 30
cubism 30, 35, 59
Cuenca, Carlos Fernández 171
Culhane, James 'Shamus' 101, 112, 114, 115, 117
Cunhal, António 72
A Cure for Cross Words (Booth) 24
Cürlis, Hans 60
cut-outs 33, 53, 54, 59, 60, 61, 66, 68, 70, 76, 78, 81, 83, 85, 90, 128, 130, 138, 158, 173, 175n6, 177–8, 183, 190, 192n13; *see also* silhouettes
Czechoslovakia, animation in 165–6
Czerkas, Stephen 42

Dadaism 30, 34, 55, 56, 57, 59
daedaleum 13
The Daffy Doc 124
Daffy Duck 112, 119, 120, 124
Daffy Duck and Egghead 121
Daffy the Commando (Freleng) 125
Da Gradi, Don 101
Daguerre, Louis-Jacques-Mandé 14
daguerreotype 14
Daix, Didier 54
Dal'zovyot (Distance Calls; Sorokhtin) 81
Dance of the Hours (Fantasia) 101
Dansen går (The Dance Goes On; Myller) 160
Dansk Farve og Tegnefilm A/S 161
The Daring Young Man on the Flying Trapeze (Munro) 130
Darwin, Erasmus 20
Das dumme Gänslein (The Silly Goose; Fischerkoesen) 150
Das Gepenst (The Ghost; Held) 152
Das Hammerbrot Schlaraffenland (The Bread-Factory Wonderland; Maier) 157, 158

Das Loch im Westen (The Hole in the West; Fischerkoesen) 151
Das Neue Dreigestirn (The Three New Stars; Zasche) 63
Das Ornament des verliebten Herzens (The Ornament of the Enamoured Heart; Reiniger) 60–1
Daumenkino 15n17
Davies, Marion 40
Davies, Roland 131
Davis, Marc 107
Dawley, Herbert M. 42, 49–50
Dawns (Verkharna) 79
Dean Film 56
de Forest, Lee 45, 97
De gouden vis (The Golden Fish; Toonder) 148
dekulakization 174
De la raza calé (Of Gipsy Race; Pérez Arroyo) 172–3
de la Rosa, Emilio 170
Delaurier, Jean 136
della Francesca, Piero 168
del Río, Dolores 189
Dely, Otto 63
Demeny, Georges 15
De moord van Raamsdonk (Raamsdonk's Assassination; Van Neijenhoff) 147
Denis, Maurice 63
Denis, Maurice 63
Denmark, animation in 65–7, 160–2
Den skønne Irmelin (The Beautiful Irmelin) 65
DePatie-Freleng Enterprises 194
Deren, Maya 128, 155
Der Fuehrer's Face (Disney) 104
Der geheimnisvolle Tempel (The Mysterious Temple; Weichberger) 159
Der Platz (von Unruh) 153
Der Rattenfänger von Hameln (The Pied Piper of Hamelin; Reinhardt) 60
Der Schneemann (The Snowman; Fischerkoesen) 150
Der Sieger (The Victor; Ruttmann) 55
Der Spuk an Bord (Spook on Board; Weichberger) 159
Der Tschechoslowakische Staat (The Czechoslovakian State; Masaryk) 138
Der Wettlauf zwischen dem Hasen und dem Igel (The Race between the Tortoise and the Hare; Diehl brothers) 151
Der Zar und seine lieben Juden (The Tsar and His Dear Jews; Zasche) 63
De Sica, Vittorio 95
Desider Gross company 163
Desplats, Oscar 192
Desplumando avestruces (Plucking Ostriches; Oliva) 192

Dessins Animés Européens (DAE) 135–6
De Stijl 30, 56
Destination Moon (Pal) 167
Det nye aar? (The New Year? Halvorsen) 69
De Tre Små Mend (The Three Little Men; Petersen) 66
Detouring America (Avery) 120
Deutsche Gesellschaft für Tonfilm (DEGETO) 159
Deutsches Filmmuseum 62
The Devil in the Studio (Booth & Paul) 23
de Vries, Tjitte 22
Diaghilev Ballet 141
Diarmo Films 171
Dibsono Films 171
Dibujos Animados Chamartín 171
Dick Tracy 123, 124
Dickinson, Thorold 140
Dictionnaire Universel (Furetière) 19
Die Abenteuer des berühmten Detektivs Harry Packs (The Adventures of the Famous Detective Harry Packs; Tuszynski/Eng) 63
Die Abenteuer des braven Soldaten Schweijk (The Adventures of the Good Soldier Schweik; Grosz) 56
Die Abenteuer des Prinzen Achmed (The Adventures of Prince Achmed; Reiniger) 61
Diebold, Bernhard 153, 156
Die Bremer Stadtmusikanten (The Town Musicians of Bremen; Tischmeyer) 151
Die Brücke 30
Die Dame mit der Maske (The Lady with the Mask) 59
Die goldene Gans (The Golden Goose; Reiniger) 63
Diehl, Hermann 56, 151
Diehl, Paul 56, 151
Die Niebelungen (Lang) 56
Die Schlacht um Miggershausen (The Battle for Miggershausen) 149
Die Sieben Raben (The Seven Ravens; Diehl brothers) 151
Die Suppe (The Soup; Pinschewer) 55
Dietrich, Jimmy 111
Die wilde Jagd (The Wild Hunt; Weichberger) 159
Diez, Carlos Cruz 190
Dillenz, Richard 166
Dinky Doodle 48
Dinner Time (Terry) 47, 96
The Dinosaur and the Missing Link (O'Brien) 42
Disney, Elias 50
Disney, Flora Call 50
Disney, Roy Edward 104
Disney, Roy Oliver 46, 50, 102, 103–4
Disney, Walter Elias 2, 38, 40, 98–103, 105–7, 125, 148; early career 50–1; influences on 47, 81; as Mickey's

voice 100; rules of animation 107–9; Stalin's appreciation of 175; trip to South America 104, 189; *see also* Mickey Mouse; *Steamboat Willie*
Disney Animation: The Illusion of Life (Thomas/Johnston) 107
Disney Design: 1928–1979 (Canemaker) 100
Disneyland 101, 102, 105
Disney's Nine Old Men 106, 107–9
Disney studios 46, 85, 149; animation philosophy 100–1; contribution to the war effort 104; diversification after the war 105; influence of 159, 175; lack of credits in 110; merchandising of characters 103; production process 101; television shows 105; *see also* Walt Disney Productions
Dobrzynski, Stanislaw 72
Doc Savage (Pal) 167
Dodal, Karel 165
Dodsworth, Jack 52–3
Dog on a Leash (Balla) 34
Doga Kenkyujo 182
Dokdok (Ibrahim) 194
Dollywood 148
Domeneghini, Anton Gino 168–9
Donald Duck (Disney) 38, 95, 99, 102, 103, 109, 112
Don Catarino y su apreciable familia (Pruneda) 85
Don Cleque series (Tur/Fresquet) 171
Don Cleque de los monos (Don Cleque of the Apes; Tur/Fresquet) 171
Don Cleque en el Oeste (Don Cleque in the West; Tur/Fresquet) 171
Don Cleque va de pesca (Don Cleque Goes Fishing; Tur) 171
Don Cleque y los Indios (Don Cleque and the Indians; Tur/Fresquet) 171
Don Prudencio y su familia (Arthenack) 85
Don't You Believe (Lee) 88
Dorothée chez les fantômes (Dorothy and the Phantoms; DAE) 136
d'Orsi, Ugo 102
Dovzhenko 75, 139
Drame chez les fantoches (Drama amongst the Puppets; Cohl) 33
Dratewka the Shoemaker (Wasilewski) 164
drawtoons 88, 195; *see also* lightning sketches
Dream Factory 95
Dream of Toyland (Cooper) 22
Dreamland 63
Dreams of a Rarebit Fiend (McCay) 37
Dreams That Money Can Buy 59
Dreamy Dud 41, 48
Dreyer, Carl Th. 30
Drobiazg Melodyjny (Melodic Trifle; Themersons) 164

Droopy (Avery) 120
Dubout, Albert 137
Ducaud, Andrés 87
Duchamp, Marcel 34, 55, 59
Dufaycolor system 171
Dukkemagerens Drøm (The Puppet Maker's Dream) 65
Du litu—laimingas medžiotojas (Two Litas—The Happy Hunter; Aleksandravičius/ Vainalavičius) 177
Dumb-Hounded (Avery) 122
Dumbo (Disney) 101–4
Du musst zur Kipho (Seeber) 56
Dunning, George 129, 130
Dutchy series (Geesink) 148
Dyer, Anson 53, 131, 161
Dzhyabahz (Pashchenko) 176

earthen goblet of Burnt City 7
Eastman, George 15
Echenique, Angel 172
Éclair Laboratories 162
Eddoko Kenchan (Yokoyama) 183
Edison, Thomas A. 19, 21n30, 24, 25, 39, 42, 97n6, 106
Editorial Cientifico-Cinematográfica 171
Educated Fish (Fleischer) 117
Education for Death (Disney) 104
Educational Films 46
Eggeling, Viking 57–8, 59, 138, 146, 156
Egghead 119
Egypt, animation in 194
Einstein, Albert 30
The Einstein Theory of Relativity (Fleischer) 45
Eisenstein, Sergei M. 30, 75, 96, 139, 146
Ekster, Alexandra 76
El Apóstol (Cristiani) 87
El aprendiz de brujo (The Sorcerer's Apprentice; Tur) 171
El Arepón (Álvarez/Mejías) 190
El capitán tormentoso (The Boisterous Captain; Moreno) 171
El diablo no es tan diablo (The Devil Is Not So Devil) 190
Elekta-Journal 165
El hotel eléctrico (The Electric Hotel; Chomón) 70, 71
El intrepido Raúl (Ralph the Intrepid; Peréz/Beringola) 170
Eliot, Thomas S. 30
Elizarov, G.K. 175
Ellington, Duke 30
Ellitt, Jack 133
Elmer Fudd 119, 120
'El mono relojero' ('The Monkey Watchmaker'; Vigil) 191
Elorrieta, José Maria 172
El rata primero (The First Rat; K-Hito) 170

El refrán animado or Refranes populares (Popular Songs; Bruché) 193
El rompecabezas de Juanillo (Arthenack) 85
Elton, G.R. 2
El toro fenómeno (The Phenomenal Bull; Marco) 70
El viejo Don Sueño (Old Mr. Sleep; Tur) 171
Emak-Bakia (Leave Me Alone; Man Ray) 55
emaki (picture scrolls) 8
Emelco Animation Department 192
Emmer, Luciano 168
Emmer, Maksymilian 163
Emperor's Dream (Chen Bo'er) 188
Emperor's Dream (Mochinaga) 184
The Enchanted Drawing (Blackton) 25
Eng, Peter (Engelmann) 63, 64–5, 157
Engel, Jules 101, 166
engraving 142
En Harmoni (Blue Master) 163
Enjoy Your Food 194
En passant (Passing by; Alexeïeff) 142, 143, 146
En roulant ma boule (McKay) 130
Entr'acte (Clair) 58
Entre pitos y flautas (Between the Pipes and Flutes; Christiani) 192
Erase una vez (Once upon a Time [Cinderella]; Chamartín studio) 172
Ermolev Film Studio 167
Ernst, Max 59
Escape (Bute) 128
Escobar, Josep 171, 172
Escudero, Jaime 86
Essanay 41
Estudios Cristiani 191
Et mesterstykke av Tiedemann (A Masterpiece by Tiedemann) 163
Etting, Emler 128
Eugster, Al 46, 101, 114, 117
Europa (Themersons) 164
Ever Been Had? (Buxton) 52
Evolution (Fleischer) 45
Experimental Animation Workshop 76, 79
expressionism 56
The Eye and the Ear (Themersons) 164
eye harpsichord (clavecin oculaire) 20

Fables (Barré) 39
Fables Studio 46
Falling Hare (Clampett) 124
The Fall of the House of Usher (Webber-Watson) 128
Famous studio 118

Fanden i nøtten (The Devil in the Nut; Cornelius) 69
Fantaisie érotique (Dodals) 165
Fantasia (Disney) 48, 99, 101–4, 121, 123, 155, 160
Fantasmagoria I, II, and III (Crockwell) 128
Fantasmagorie (Cohl) 2, 5, 30, 31
Fantoche cherche un logement (The Puppet Looks for Lodging; Cohl) 33
Fáquir González (Fakir González; Muntañola) 171
Fargesymfoni i blått (Colour Symphony in Blue) 163
Faria de Fonseca, Raul 72
Farmer Al Falfa (Terry) 41, 47
Fastekuren (The Fasting Cure; Petersen) 66
Faure, Élie 144
Fausto (Blanco/Galuppo) 192
Fauvism 30
Fedorchenko, Sergei 178
Feininger, Lyonel 155
Félix, María 189
Felix the Cat (Messmer/Sullivan) 39, 41, 44, 45, 46, 53, 101, 114, 184, 194
Female Stars and Male Stars (Jaryczewski) 163
Ferda Mravenec (Ferda the Ant; Týrlová) 165
Ferguson, Norman 110
Fernandez, Emilio 189
Fernández de la Reguera, Alejandro 170–1
Ferrán de los Reyes, Enric (Dibán) 171
Ferraniacolor 192
A Feud There Was 121
Fialkin's Career (Khodataev) 77
Fieber, Gerhard 149–50
Fieber I, II, III (Fever I, II, III; O. Fischinger) 154
15.000 Dibujos (15,000 Drawings; Escudero/Trupp) 86
Fifth Period, "The Three Markets (1920–1991)" 2
Filho, Eugênia Fonsêca 86
Filipito el pistolero (Filipito the Gunslinger; Oliva) 192
Filmae 178
Filmag 64
Filmagem (magazine) 173
Film Law (Japan) 180
Filmstudie (Richter) 59
Finist (Alexeïeff) 144
Finland, animation in 70
fireworks 20n28
Firpo, Angel Luis 87
Fir-pobre-nan (Cristiani) 87
Firpo-Dempsey (Cristiani) 87
The First Circus (Sarg-Dawley) 49
First Period, "Before Phantasmagorie (0–1908)" 2, 5
Fischerkoesen, Hans 55, 56, 150–1, 163
Fischinger, Elfriede 154

Fischinger, Hans 152, 154
Fischinger, Oskar 20, 55, 56, 128, 152–7, 163, 175
Fisher, Bud 39, 47
Fitzgerald, Francis Scott 30
Flaherty, Robert J. 30, 95
Flash Gordon 38, 109
Flashing Film Ads 24
Fleischer, Charles 45
Fleischer, Dave 44–5, 80, 85, 109, 111, 115, 118
Fleischer, Ethel 45
Fleischer, Joe 44
Fleischer, Lou 45
Fleischer, Max 44–5, 48, 80, 85, 109, 111, 115, 116, 118
Fleischer Group 44, 109
Fleischer Studios 45, 115–18, 127
Flip the Frog (Iwerks) 113
flipbooks 15, 78
Flores D'Arcais, Giuseppe 172
Florey, Robert 128
Flowers (Ginna) 35
Flowers and Trees (Disney) 99
The Flying House (McCay) 37
Fogelberg, Ola 70
Földes, Péter 166
Follet, F.M. 41
Fono (Filho) 86
Ford, Greg 121
Ford, Henry 106
Forton, Louis 32–3
Foster, Harold 38
Foster, John 114
Fourth Period, "The Birth of a Style (1951–1960)" 2
Fox, William 37
The Fox Hunt (Hoppin/Gross) 137
Fram Film 69
frame-by-frame technique 21–2, 24, 26, 31, 42, 47, 53, 70, 73, 85, 119, 147, 194
France: animation in 54–5, 135–47; Golden Age cinema in 95
France bonne humeur (France in a Good Mood; Rigal) 136
Francisca la mujer fatal (Francisca the Femme Fatale; K-Hito) 170
Franco, Francisco 169, 170
Frantzisson, Boris 79
Franz Ferdinand (Archduke) 29
Frascari, Carlo Amedeo (Zambonelli) 72
Frau im Mond (The Woman in the Moon; Lang) 154
Free Radicals (Lye) 133, 134
Freeman, Frank 166
Freleng, Isadore 'Friz' 50, 119, 120, 124–5

Frenkel, David 194
Frenkel, Herschel 194
Frenkel, Salomon 194
Fresquet, Guillem 171
Freud, Sigmund 29
Fritz und Fratz (Weichberger) 159
Fromenteau, Albert 147
Fryer, Bryant 129
Fujicolor 181
Fukuchan no sensuikan (Fukuchan and the Submarine; Yokoyama) 183
Fumées (Vapours; Alexeïeff) 143
Funny Little Bunnies (Disney) 105
Furetière, Antoine 19
Furniss, Harry 52
futurism 30n2, 34
'Futurist Manifesto' (Marinetti) 30
Fyrtøjet (The Tinderbox) 161–2

Gaasetyven eller Et Ande-Eventyr (The Goose Thief or a Duck Story; Petersen) 66
Gabby (Fleischer) 118
Gaberbocchus Press 164
Gadaatcharba (Surpassed) 178
Gaidzvera (The Sly; Mujiri) 178
Gala Concert (Geesink) 148
Galicia, Leobardo 190
Galipaux 18
The Gallant Little Tailor (Reiniger) 63
Gallegos, Rómulo 190
Gallo, Joseph 192
The Gallopin' Gaucho (Disney) 98
Galuppo, Ubaldo 192, 193
Galway Film Fleadh 53
Ganatsqhenebuli Satamashoebi (The Afflicted Toys; Mujiri) 178
Gandy Goose (Terry) 115
Gang Busters (radio serial) 49
Gang War 96
Garabatos 171
Garbancito (Moreno) 171–2
Garbancito de la Mancha (Garbancito from La Mancha; Moreno) 171, 190 Garbo, Greta 171
Garden Gopher (Avery) 122
'Garibis Bedi' (Orbeliani) 178
Garibis Bedniereba (The Pauper's Happiness; Muriji) 178
Garras de Oro (Dawn of Justice) 85
Gaspar, Béla 154
Gasparcolor 154, 157, 163, 192
Gastrotomía (Surgery of the Stomach; Cristiani) 87

Gaudreault, André 21
Gaumont, Léon 32
Gaumont America 41
Gazapkhuli (The Spring; Mujiri) 178
Gazapkhulis Stumrebi (The Spring Guests; Mujiri) 178
G. B. Animation 131
Geesink, Johan Louis 'Joop' 148
Geijutsu Eigasha (Art Film Company) 183, 184, 185
General Post Office Film Unit 133
The General (Keaton) 30
Genval, Ernest 147
George Pal animation studio 151
Georgia (Soviet), animation in 177–8
Georgian State Film Industry (GSFI) 178
Gerald McBoing Boing 2
German Animation Company (Deutsche Zeichenfilm GmbH) 148, 149–51
German Expressionist Cinema 55n10
Germany: animation in 148–57; avant-garde 152; Weimar Republic 55–63
Geronimi, Clyde 'Gerry' 101
Gershefsky, Edwin 128
Gershwin, George 30
Gertie the Dinosaur (McCay) 36–7
Gesamtkunstwerk (Total Work of Art) 20
Gethmann, Daniel 15n16
Ghibli 8
The Ghost of Slumber Mountain (O'Brien) 42
Gianini, Giulio 34
Gifford, Denis 23
Gijón, Salvador 172
Gill, André 32
Gillett, Burt 40, 46, 112, 114
Gilliam, Terry 167
Gilpin, Denis 131
Ginger Nutt the squirrel 131
Ginna, Arnaldo 34–5
Giobbe, Luigi 168
Giotto 168
Gizycki, Marcin 73, 164–5
Gjete kongens harer (Watching the King's Hares; Snilsberg) 163
Glackens, Louis 41
Gladtvet, Ottar 69–70
Glens Falls Sequence (Crockwell) 128
Goddard, Morrel 48
Goebbels, Josef 148, 149, 150, 155
Gogol, Nikolay 144, 146
Gold Diggers of '49 (Warner Bros.) 125
Golden Age 2, 95–7

The Golden Pot 163
The Gold Rush (Chaplin) 30
Goldwyn, Samuel 48
Golem (Wegener) 60, 61
Gómez, Francisco 189
Gómez, Juan Vicente 190
Gone with the Wind 95
Goodwin, Hannibal W. 14
Goofy (Disney) 99, 100, 102, 103
Gorbach, Evgeny 177
Gordon, Dan 118
Gottfredson, Floyd 99
Gould, Emanuel 'Manny' 48
Goya, Francisco 168
Graham, Donald Wilkinson 38, 99, 100, 101, 111, 131
Grant, Dwinell 129
Grant, Joe 101
Graphic Associates 130
The Grasshopper and the Ant (Starewitch) 73
The Grasshopper and the Ant (Wan brothers) 187
Great Britain, animation in 131–5
Great Depression 95, 96
The Great Piggy Bank Robbery (Clampett) 123, 124
The Great Train Robbery (Porter) 24
Greece, animation in 167
Grierson, John 62, 129, 133
Griffith, David W. 30, 43
Griffiths, Sid 53
Grimault, Paul 130, 137, 166
Grimault-Prévert 54
Grim Pastures (Dunning) 130
Grinevsky, Alexandra de 142
Gropius, Walter 30
Gross, Anthony 131, 137–8
Gross, Desider 163
Grosz, George 56
Group IVVOS 79
Gualtierotti, Gualtiero 168
Gude, Hans 163
Guerreiro, Joaquim 71
Guggenheim Foundation 155
Guido, Francesco Maurizio 'Gibba' 169
Gulliver chez les Lilliputiens (Gulliver and the Lilliputians; Mourlan) 54
Gulliver's Travels (Fleischer) 112, 115, 117–18
Gulliver's Travels (Swift) 176
The Gumps 41
Gunning, Tom 21
Guyetsky, Semen 177

Index

Hagen, Louis 61
Halas, John 131, 166
Halas and Batchelor studio 131
Hal Roach Studios 126
Halvorsen, Sverre 69, 163
Hamberg, Børge 161
Hamilton, Rollin 50
Hanawa Hekonai Meito 'shinto' no maki (Hanawa Hekonai, the New Sword; Kouchi) 83
Hand, David 131–2
The Hand of the Artist (Paul-Urban) 23
Handy, Henry Jamison 3
Hanfstaengl, Franz 16
Hanna, William 120, 121, 127
Hanna-Barbera Productions 123, 194
Hannah, Jack 103, 112
Hansen, Niels Sinding 69
Hanslick, Erwin 60, 138
Haplea (Iorda) 72
Happy Harmonies 126
Happy Hooligan 40
Happy New Year (Seeber) 55
Hardaway, Ben 'Bugs' 112
Harding, LaVerne 112–13
Hare Ribbin' (Clampett) 123
Harline, Leigh 102
Harman, Hugh 50, 118–19, 124, 126, 127
Harrington, Curtis 128
Harris, John P. 21
Harrison, Ben 48
Harryhausen, Ray 167
Hartman, Karel 147
The Haunted Hotel (Blackton) 26, 32
Hays Code 116n45
Hazel the squirrel 131
Hearst, William Randolph 40–1, 48, 106
Hedin rider kjephesten (Hedin Rides the Wooden Horse; Klouman) 69
Hee, T. 101
Heidegger, Martin 30
Heimebrennerens mareritt—Drikkens følger (The Moonshiner's Nightmare—The Results of Drinking; Fram Film) 69
Heisenberg, Werner 30
Heksen og Cyklisten (The Witch and the Biker) 65
Held, Hans 151–2
Hemingway, Ernest 30
Hennesy, Hugh 101
Hepworth, Cecil 53
Hergé 147
Herold film company 159

Heron, Andrew 23
Heron Films Ltd. 23
Herr Meets Hare (Freleng) 125
Herschel, John 14nn10–11
Hilberman, Dave 104, 114
Hilltop House (radio serial) 49
Hindemith, Paul 59, 154
Hindoo Jugglers (Booth & Paul) 23
Hinotori (The Phoenix; Ichikawa) 186
Hirschfeld-Mack 58
Hispano Gráfic Films 170, 171
His Story of Time (Holdsworth) 132
Histoire de Monsieur Vieux-Bois (The Story of Mr. Vieux-Bois; Töpffer) 65
Histoire sans paroles (Story without Words; Zoubowitch) 136
Hitler, Adolf 57, 121, 133, 148, 155, 158, 167, 170
Hochzeit im Korallenmeer (Wedding in the Coral Sea; Prag Film AG) 150, 166
Hofman, Eduard 150
Högfelt, Robert 162
Holdsworth, Gerard 132
Holloway, Stanley 131
Holmes, Oliver Wendell, Sr. 14
Honegger, Arthur 140
Honey (Harman/Ising) 118
Hope, Bob 127
Hoppin, Hector 131, 137
Horgan, James 53
Horizontal-Vertikal Orchestra (Eggeling) 58
Horner, William 13
Horváth, Ferdinánd Huszti 166
Houssiaus (father-son advertising team) 72
Hoyt, Larry O. 42
H_2O (Steiner) 128
Hubley, John 104, 114
Huemer, Dick 39, 114
Humbertito de garufa (Cristiani) 87
Humorous Phases of Funny Faces (Blackton) 26
humour, Jewish 45, 102, 119
The Humpty-Dumpty Circus 25n42
Hungarian Dance No. 5 (Brahms) 154
Hungarian Rhapsody No. 2 (Liszt) 155, 157
Hungary, animation in 70, 166–7
The Hunger of the Old Stupid Dog (Association of Chinese Animation) 188
Hunky and Spunky (Fleischer) 117
Hunnia Films 166
Hurd, Earl 40, 48, 101
Hurter, Albert 101
Huysmans, Joris-Karl 20

Ibrahim, Antoine Selim 194
Ichikawa Kon 186–7
I disastri della guerra (Disasters of War; Emmer) 168
Idyll (Lee) 129
I fratelli Dinamite (The Dynamite Brothers; Pagot et al.) 168, 169
Iizawa Tadasu 185
Il dottor Churkill (Doctor Churkill; Pensuti) 167–8
I Love to Singa (Avery) 120
Il vecchio lupo di mare norvegese e il vecchio lupo di mare americano (The Old Salt from Norway and the Old Salt from America; Giobbe) 168
Image, Jean (Hajdú Imre) 137, 166
Images mouvantes (Moving Images; Philippart) 147
Imokawa Mukuzo genkanban no maki (Imokawa Mukuzo the Concierge; Shimokawa) 82
Ince, T.H. 43
Indelli, Leontina 'Mimma' 135, 136
Indian Fantasy (Hoppin/Gross) 138
Industrializatsiis Dghe (The Industrialization Day; Mujiri) 178
Inflation (Richter) 59
In King Krakus's Time (Wasilewski) 164
Inkwell Studios 45
Institute for Cultural Discovery 60
International Film Service (IFS) 39, 40–1, 48
The Interplanetary Revolution (Khodataev) 174
The Interpretation of Dreams (Freud) 30
iodide of silver 14
Iorda, Marin 72
IRE Film Studio 165
Ireland, animation in 53
Isao, Takahata 8
Ising, Rudolf 50, 118–19, 124, 126, 127
The Isle of Pingo Pongo (Avery) 120
Isn't It Wonderful? (Armstrong) 52
Issunboshi (The Tiny One Makes It Big; Yamamoto) 83
Istituto Nazionale Luce 167
István, Valker 166
It's a Grand Old Nag (Clampett) 124
Itala Film Studios 70
Italy: animation in 72, 167–9; Golden Age cinema in 95
Ivanov, Aleksandr 75, 79, 175, 176, 177
Ivanov-Vano, Ivan 76, 77, 80, 81, 174, 177
Ivashko i Baba Yaga (Ivashko and the Baba Yaga; Brumberg sisters) 177
Iwerks, Ub (Ubbe Eert Iwwerks) 50, 98, 99, 113, 126, 127

Jack and the Beanstalk (Porter) 24
Jack and the Beanstalk (Reiniger) 63

Jackson, Wilfred 98
Jacobs, Lewis 128
Jaeger, Harry 56
Jameson, D.D. 20
Jam Handy Organization 3
János vitéz (János the Knight; Kató-Kiszly) 70
Janssen, Pierre Jules César 15
Japan, animation in 82–4, 184
Jarosz, Jan 163
Jaruska, Wilhelm 157, 158
Jaryczewski 163
Jasper (Puppetoon) 166
Jasper and the Beanstalk (Pal) 167
Jat (Basov) 179
Ja warum fahrn's denn ned? (Why Don't You Drive; Eng) 157
Jazz Age 29
The Jazz Singer (Crosland) 97, 98
Jeannot l'Intrépide (Image) 137
Jennings, Humphrey 133
Jensen, Bjørn Frank 161
Jensenius, Wilfred 163
Jernmixturen (The Iron Elixir; Petersen) 66
Jerry the Tyke (Griffiths) 53
Jewish comedy *see* humour, Jewish
Jim Trot's Adventures (Xaudaró) 169
Jiyu Eiga Kenkyujo 181
Jodoin, René 129
Johann the Coffin Maker (Florey) 128
John Bull's Animated Sketchbook (Buxton/Dyer) 53
John Henry and the Inky-Poo (Pal) 167
Johnsen, Allan 161
Johnston, Ollie 107, 108
Jolson, Al 97, 98
Jones, Chuck 112, 120, 123, 124, 125–6
Josele en una noche de miedo (Josele in a Thrilling Night; Añino) 172
J.O. Studio 182, 182n6, 186
Jour en Afrique (A Day in Africa; Animat) 137
Journey to the West 187
Jouvanceau, Pierre 90
Joyce, James 30, 128
Juanito Milhombres series (Mestres) 170
Julius, Harry 90
Junca, Jean 137
The Jungle Book (Disney) 105
Just Mickey (Disney) 99
Justice, Bill 102
J. Walter Thompson (advertising agency) 132

Index

Kachikachi yama (The Hare Gets Revenge over the Raccoon; Ichikawa) 186
Kaeru wa kaeru (A Frog Is a Frog; Murata) 83
Kafka, Franz 30, 143
Kaguya hime (Priincess Kaguya; Masaoka) 182
Kahl, Milton 107
Kakhardakan Gorg/Volshebnyj koveri (The Magic Carpet; Atamanov) 179
Kaleidoscope (Lye) 133
kaleidoscope 13
Kameny tsvetok (The Stone Flower; Ptushko) 177
Kanai Kiichiro 82, 83
Kane, Helen 117
Kapa Studios 173
Kapten Grogg (Bergdahl) 69
Kapten Grogg bland andra konstiga kroppar (Captain Grogg among Other Strange Bodies; Bergdahl) 68
Kapten Grogg bland vilda djur (Captain Grogg among Wild Animals; Bergdahl) 67, 68
Kapten Grogg gifter sig (Captain Grogg Gets Married; Bergdahl) 67
Kapten Grogg har blivit fet (Captain Grogg Has Become Fat; Bergdahl) 68
Kapten Grogg och Kalle på negerbal (Captain Grogg and Kalle at the Darkies' Ball; Bergdahl) 67
Kapten Grogg på Stora Oceanen (Captain Grogg on the Big Ocean; Bergdahl) 67
Kapten Groggs underbara resa (Captain Grogg's Wonderful Journey; Bergdahl) 67–8
Kardan, Alexander 61
Karera Makdonalda (McDonald's Career; Bushkin) 76
Karyera Fyalkina (Fyalkin's Career; Khodataev) 174
Kaskeline, Wolfgang 152
Kastner, Frédéric 20
Katok (The Skating Rink; Zhelyabuzhsky) 79, 80
Kató-Kiszly István 70
Katsura hime (Princess Katsura; Ofuji) 181
The Katzenjammer Kids 40
Kawamoto Kihachiro 185
Kaye, Danny 127
Keaton, Buster 30, 45, 109, 122, 127
Keeping Up with the Joneses (Palmer) 41
Keith-Albee Theatre Company 44, 47
Kelly, Walt 104
Kermabon, Jacques 136
Kermesse fantastique (Geesink) 148
Kersh, Sarienne 88
Khalygov, G. 179
Khanzhonkov, Aleksandr 73
Khintibidze, Arkadi (Kako) 178

K-Hito (Ricardo García Lopez) 170, 172
Khitruk, Fedor 175
Khodataev, Nikolai Petrovich 76–8, 79, 80, 174
Khodataeva, Olga 77, 79
The Kid (Chaplin) 30
Kiddigraphs 53
Kiesslich, Kurt Wolfram 56
Kievnauchfilm (Kiev popular science films) studio 177
Kiko (Terry) 115
Killarney Film Studios 89n5, 194–5
Kimball, Ward 107
Kimura Hakuzan 184
Kinema Industries Ltd. 23
Kinematograph 148
kinetic art 34
Kinetograph 97n6
kinetoscopcs 21n30
King, Jack 40, 103, 119
King Kong (O'Brien) 42
The King of Jazz (Lantz) 111
King Size Canary (Avery) 122
The King with the Terrible Temper (Dyer) 131
Kinney, Jack 103
Kinomatfilm Wuppertal 151
Kipho (Seeber) 56
Kirs Filme 86
Kitaj v ogne (China in Flames; Komissarenko/Merkulov) 76, 77, 78
Kitayama Eiga Seisakusho 82–3
Kitayama Seitaro 82–3
Kitty Kornered (Clampett) 123
Klein, Isidore 102
Klouman, Thoralf 69
Klyaksa (Ink Blot; Atamanov) 175
K narodnoy vlasti (People's Power; Starewitch) 74
Kneitel, Seymour 45, 118
Knock Knock (Lantz studio) 112
Kobayashi Shokai 83
Kobierski, Lucjan 72
Koch, Carl 60–2
Kodak 15
Kogane no hana (The Golden Flower; Ofuji) 181
Kogane no tsuribari (The Golden Hook; Arai) 184
Ko-Ko (Koko) the Clown (Fleischer) 45, 116
Kollege Pal (series) 56
Komarov, Sergei 78
Komissarenko, Zenon Petrovich 76–9, 174
Komposition in Blau (Composition in Blue; O. Fischinger) 154, 156, 163
Konchalovsky, Petr 79

Konicolor 181
Korda, Alexander 137
Korin, Pavel 79
Kosmatov, Leonid 79
Kouchi Sumikazu 82, 83, 181
Koval, Halyna Mazepa de 190
Kowanko, Wlodzimierz 163
Krakow's Hill (Wasilewski) 164
Krazy Kat 40, 48, 113
'Krazy's Shoe Shop' (Mintz) 113
Kreise (Circles; O. Fischinger) 154
Kricfalusi, John 124
Kruse, Werner 149, 151
Kuczkowski, Feliks 72
Kujira (The Whale; Ofuji) 181
Kumo no ito (A Spider's Thread; Ofuji) 181
Kumo to churippu (The Spider and the Tulip; Masaoka) 182
Kuri Yoji 181
Kuro nyago (The Black Cat; Ofuji) 181
Kurosawa Akira 186

La belle au bois dormant (Sleeping Beauty; Alexeïeff) 142
La bergère et le ramoneur (Mr. Wonderbird; Grimault-Prévert) 54
La captive de Frok Manoir (The Captive of Frok Manor; Fromenteau) 147
La Cava, Gregory 39, 40, 48
La caza del puma (Hunting the Puma; Oliva) 192, 193
La ciudad de los muñecos (Puppet City; Echenique) 172
La condition humaine (Malraux) 140
La conquête de l'Angleterre (The Conquest of England; DAE) 136
La crabe aux pinces d'or (The Crab with Golden Claws; Misonne) 147
La Danza de los Esqueletros (The Skeleton Dance) 190
La découverte de l'Amérique (The Discovery of America; Indelli) 136
Ladouceur, Jean-Paul 129, 130
Laemmle, Carl 50, 111
Laferrère, Alfonso de 87
La Fortune enchantée (The Enchanted Fortune; Zoubowitch) 136
Lagerlöf, Selma 162
Lah, Michael 121
Lahyn Film 70
La intervención a la provincia de Buenos Aires (Intervention in the Province of Buenos Aires; Cristiani) 86
La joie de vivre (The Joy of Living; Animat) 137
Lalla, piccola Lalla (Lalla, Little Lalla; Pagot) 168

La macchina del tempo (The Time Machine; Cossio brothers) 168
La Marseillaise (Renoir) 62
Lambart, Evelyn 129
Lambeth Walk, Nazi Style 133
The Land of the Midnight Fun (Avery) 120
La naissance de Pim (Pim's Birth; Bouchéry) 147
Lang, Fritz 55, 56, 154
Langer, Mark 117, 118
Langford Advertising Agency 23
lantern slides 19
Lantz, Walter 40, 47–8, 50, 111–13, 119, 123
Lantz studio 111–13
La reina vencida (The Defeated Queen; Gijón) 172
Largo (Pfenninger) 56
Larkins, Bill 131
Larkins studio 131
La rosa di Bagdad (The Rose of Baghdad; Domeneghini) 168
Larson, Eric 107
La secchia rapita (The Stolen Bucket; Cossio brothers) 168
The Last Laugh (Murnau) 30
Laszlo, Alexander 154
La taberna y la caverna (The Public House and the Cave; Reyes/Rigalt) 172
Látal, Stanislav 150
Latin America, animation in 85–7
La Transmisión del Mando Presidencial (The Transfer of the President's Power; Serey) 86
Laugh-O-Gram Films 50
Laurel and Hardy 122
La venganza del brujo (The Revenge of the Wizard; Gijón) 172
La Voix du rossignol (The Voice of the Nightingale; Starewitch) 74, 75
Lawless Decade 29
Lazarchuk, Ippolit 177
Lazarev, Leonid Nikolayevich 80
Leah, Frank 53
Lebende Buddhas (Living Buddha; Ruttmann) 57
Leberecht, Frank 149
Le bijou (The Jewel; Lee) 129
Lebrel, Georges (Jorge) 190
'Le canard en ciné' (Lortac) 54
Le carillon du vieux manoir (The Bells of the Old Manor; Arcady) 136
Le cauchemar du fantoche (The Nightmare of the Puppet; Cohl) 33
Le chat de la mère Michel (Mother Michael's Cat; CBA) 147
Le clown et ses chiens (The Clown and His Dogs) 17

Le coche et la mouche (The Stage Coach and the Fly; Indelli) 136
Lee, Francis 129
Lee, Norman H. 88
Le forgeron Smee (Blacksmith Smee; Bouchéry) 147
Léger, Fernand 34, 54–5, 58, 59
Leite, Rui Correia 71
Le jour et la nuit (Day and Night; Hoppin/Gross) 137
L'elisir d'amore (The Elixir of Love; Reiniger) 62
Le loup et l'agneau (The Wolf and the Lamb; Image) 137
Le mystère Picasso (Clouzot) 34
Leni, Paul 55
Le Nez (The Nose; Alexeïeff/Parker) 144, 146
Le petit navire (The Little Boat; CBA) 147
Le premier cigare (The First Cigar) 18
Le procès (The Trial; Alexeïeff) 143–4, 147
Le rêve du beau Danube bleu (The Dream of the Beautiful Blue Danube; Frenkel brothers) 194
Les allumettes animées (Cohl) 73
Les aventures de Kapok l'esquimau (The Adventures of Kapok the Eskimo; Arcady) 136
Les Aventures des Pieds Nickelés (Lacking Agreement; Cohl) 32
Les demoiselles d'Avignon (Picasso) 30
Les fiançailles de Flambeau (Flambeau's Engagement; Rabier) 54
Les Films Jean Image 137
Les funérailles (Funeral Ceremonies; Animat) 137
Les Gémeaux 137
Les Grenouilles qui demandent un roi (The Frogs Who Wanted a King; Starewitch) 74
Les hommes d'aujourd'hui (magazine) 32
Lesnoy dogovor (The Wood Deal; Lazarchuk) 177
Les joies de l'eau (The Pleasures of the Water; Régnier) 136
Les passagers de la Grande Ourse (The Passengers of the Great Bear; Grimault) 137
Letmatrosen (The Ordinary Seaman) 65
L'etoile de mer (The Star of the Sea; Man Ray) 55
Le tour du monde en 80 jours (Around the World in 80 Days; Hoppin/Gross) 137–8
Levandovsky, Viacheslav 81, 177
L'éventail animé (The Animated Fan; Cohl) 33
Le voyage imprévu (The Unexpected Voyage; Fromenteau) 147
Lewis, Jerry 127, 128
L'Horloge magique (The Magic Clock; Starewitch) 74
Lichtspiel Opus I (Ruttmann) 56–7
L'Idée (The Idea; Bartosch) 139, 140
Liebesspiel (Love Play; O. Fischinger) 154
Life and Death of 9413 (Florey) 128
Life Begins for Andy Panda (Lantz studio) 112

Life of an American Fireman (Porter) 24
lightning sketches 23, 25–6, 31, 41, 52, 66, 68, 69, 88, 90, 195
Liljeqvist, M.R. 162
Liljeqvist, Rudolf Mauritz 68
Lille Kalle dröm sin snögubbe (Little Kalle Dreams His Snowman; Åberg) 68
Lippert, Aage 65
Listo 63
Lithuania, animation in 177
Little Herman (Terry) 41
Little King (Soglow) 114
Little Nemo in Slumberland (McCay) 35–6
The Little Prince (Saint-Exupéry, animated by Holdsworth) 132
Little Red Walking Hood (Avery) 120
Little Rural Riding Hood (Avery) 121
The Little Tree That Wanted Different Leaves (Tischmeyer) 149n52, 151
Littlejohn, Bill 114
live-action cinema: with animation 39, 41, 48, 54, 59, 64n40, 68, 74, 79, 85, 88, 136, 157, 165, 166–7, 172, 176, 187, 190; Arabian 31n4; in Austria 64; by Barré 39; by Blackton 26; by Booth 24; by Bowers 47; by Bray 48; British 53, 131, 134; in China 187; by Cohl 32; in Czechoslovakia 165–6; by Dawley 42, 49; in Denmark 161; by Disney 51, 100, 102, 105, 122; in Egypt 194; by M. Fleischer 44–5; in France 139; in Germany 55, 59, 62, 152; in Georgia (Soviet) 178; in Hungary 70n53, 166–167; in Italy 169; in Japan 83, 186; by La Cava 40; by Lantz 48, 111; by Léger 54; by Mayer 41; by Melbourne-Cooper 23; by McCay, 36–7; by Méliès 33; in Mexico 85, 189–90; by Murnau 37; photography as forerunner of 12; relationship with animation 21; replacing vaudeville 43; in Russia/Soviet Union 73, 74, 79, 175–7; in South Africa 88; in Spain 170; in Sweden 68; Tashlin's work with 127–8; in the U.S. 128; in Yugoslavia 167
Lloyd, Harold 45
Lobato, Tulio 192
Lo Duca 135
Löfving, Hjalmar 70
Lokbatan (documentary; Pumpyansky) 179
London Film Society 132
The Long Bodies (Crockwell) 128
Look Up (Cherkes) 80
Looney Tunes 118–19, 123
Loring, James M. 20

Lortac (Robert Collard) 54, 65, 159
Los cinco cabritos (The Five Little Goats; Mier) 189
Los consejos del viejo vizcacha (The Old Vizcacha's Advice; Bruché) 192
Los sueños de Tay-Pi (The Visions of Tay-Pi; Moreno) 172
The Lost Shadow (Wegener) 61
The Lost World (O'Brien) 42
Lot in Sodom (Webber-Watson) 128
Loucks 129
Lounsbery, John 107
The Loves of Zero (Florey) 128
Lovy, Alex 112
Low, Colin 130
Lucanus Cervus (Starewitch) 73
Lucky Ducky (Avery) 122
Luft, Friedrich 149
Lu Hsun 30
Luiz, Sérgio 173
L'ultimo sciuscià (The Last Shoeshine; Gibba) 169
Lumière, Auguste 19, 21
Lumière, Louis 19, 21
lumigraph 156
Lunacharsky, Anatoli 174
Lundy, Dick 102, 112
Luske, Hamilton 101
Lye, Len 34, 131, 132–5, 152

Maar brothers 167
Macaco feio, macaco bônito (Ugly Monkey, Pretty Monkey; Stamato) 191
MacArthur, Douglas 184
MacKay, Jim 129
Madame Butterfly (Puccini) 184
Mad Monster Party? (Mochinaga et al.) 185
Mafish Fayda (Nothing to Do; Frenkel brothers) 194
Magalhães, Xavier 71
Magical Maestro 121
Magic Clock (Starewitch) 184
magic lantern 19
magic pen drawings 70; *see also* lightning sketches
Magomayev, M. 179
Maier, Rudi 157
Malhas Locitay 173
Maliniak, Jerzy 163
Mallarmé, Stéphane 135
Malraux, André 144
Maltin, Leonard 112, 123
Malyutin 79
Mamatsi Mtamsvlelebi (The Courageous Cragsmen; Mujiri) 178

Mammadov, Nazim 179
The Man from the Diner's Club (Tashlin) 127
mangas 84, 183
Mangiagalli, Riccardo Pick 169
Mani'ei (Manchurian Film Association) 185
Man of Aran (Flaherty) 95
Man Ray 34, 55, 59
Manriquez, Carlos 85
Ma petite brosse à rimmel (My Little Mascara Brush; CBA) 147
Maraja, Libico 169
Marcadé, Jacques 78
Marco, Fernando 70
Marczak, Karol 163
Marey, Étienne Jules 15
Margolina, Irina 76, 78, 79
Marinetti, Filippo Tommaso 30, 35
Marins, Álvaro (Seth) 86, 191
Markopoulos, Gregory 128
Mars Film 149, 159
Marshak, Samuil 81
Martin, André 140
Marty, André 136
Marx Brothers 122
Masaoka Eiga Kenkyujo 181
Masaoka Kenzo 181–3
Masaryk, Tomas 138
Masereel, Frans 139
Matches' Appeal (Melbourne-Cooper) 22
Matches' Handball (Animated Matches: Playing Volleyball) 22
Mauro, Humberto 191
Max und Moritz (series) 56
May, Mabel 88
Mayakovsky, Vladimir 30, 174
Mayer, Henry 'Hy' 41, 46
McCay, Robert 37
McCay, Winsor Zenis 35–7, 39, 42, 44, 67, 68, 88
McCrea, Joel 95
McCutcheon, Wallace 24
McKay, Jim 130
McKimson, Bob 123, 124
McLaren, Norman 17, 34, 128, 129, 130, 131, 152, 175, 176
McManus, George 32
Mechanik, Benny 195
Mecki (Diehl brothers) 151
Mejías, Luis 190
Melbourne-Cooper, Arthur 22–3
Méliès, Georges 33–34, 167
Melodie der Welt (Melody of the World; Ruttmann) 57

Index

Memoirs of Miffy (Buxton) 53
Menda 170
Mendes, Aquilino 173
Meotkhe Gadamtsqhveti Tseli (The Fourth Crucial Year; Mujiri) 178
Mercer, Jack 115, 117
Merkulov, Yuri 76–7, 79, 174, 176
Merrie Melodies 119
Merry Mannequins (Iwerks) 113
Merry Wives of Windsor (Nikolai) 154
Messmer, Otto 41, 45–6, 101
Mestres, Salvador 170–1
Mesty kinematographicheskogo operatora (The Cameraman's Revenge; Starewitch) 74, 75
Methling, Svend 161
Metro-Goldwyn-Mayer (MGM) studio 85, 109, 120, 121, 123, 124, 126–7; Avery at 121–2; influence of 193
Meunier tu dors (Miller, You Are Sleeping; Delaurier/ Varé) 136
Me voy de cacería (I Go Hunting) 190
Mexico, animation in 85, 189–90
Meyerhold, Vsevolod Emilyevich 79
Mezhplanetnaya Revolyuciya (Interplanetary Revolution; Komissarenko/Merkulov) 76, 77, 78
Mezhrabpom animators 175
Mezhrabpomruss 76
MGM *see* Metro-Goldwyn-Mayer (MGM) studio
Miami Art School 117
The Mice's Expedition for a Cake (Kowanko) 163
Mickey Mouse (Disney) 38, 47, 50, 95, 96, 98–101, 103, 109; see also *Steamboat Willie*
Mier, Bismarck 85, 189
Mighty Mouse (Terry) 115
Mikaberidze, Kote 177
Mikkelsen, Henning Dahl 160, 161
Milhaud, Darius 59
The Milky Way (Ising) 126
The Miller, His Son and the Donkey (István/Teréz) 166
Milov, A. 179
Mimiche (Frenkel brothers character) 194
Minah Bird (Chuck Jones) 112
Mingshin 187
Minnie Mouse (Disney) 98
Minnie the Moocher (Fleischer) 115, 117
Mintz, Charles 48, 50, 109, 111, 113–14
Mirzayev, A. 179
The Miser's Doom (Booth & Paul) 23
Mish-Mish (Frenkel brothers character) 194
Misonne, Claude 147
Mi sueño 85

Mizoguchi Kenji 186
M-M! Come Again (Armstrong) 52
Mochinaga Ayako 184, 185
Mochinaga Tadahito "Fan Ming" 184
modernity, Western 95
Modnschein Maar 167
Moholy-Nagy 156
MOM Film Studio 185
Momotaro (Momotaro, the Peach Boy; Kitayama) 82
Momotaro no umiwashi (Momotaro's Sea Eagle; Seo) 183, 184
Momotaro, umi no shinpei (Momotaro's Divine Sea Warriors; Seo) 183
Mondrian, Piet 30
Monsieur Pipe 137
Monsieur Vieux-Bois (Lortac) 54
Montreux-Colorfilm 160
Moonglow (Toonder) 148
Moore, Fred 99
Morales, Fernando 172
Moreno, Arturo 171, 172, 190
Moreno, George 132
Morgan, J. P. 106
Mori no yosei (A Fairy in the Forest; Masaoka) 182
Mori Yasuji 183
Moritz, William 35, 152, 156
Moser, Frank 39, 40, 114
Moss, Howard S. 41
motion/movement 34, 153; analysis 9; importance of 12
Motion Painting No. 1 (O. Fischinger) 155, 157
Motion Painting No. 2 (O. Fischinger) 156, 157
Motoy Films (Moss) 41
Mourlan, Albert 54
Movietone system 97
Moya lilliputochka, pridi ko mne (My Little Lilliputian Girl, Come to Me) 176
Mozart, Wolfgang Amadeus 154
Mozzhukhin, Ivan 73
Mr. Asquith and the Clown (Armstrong) 52
Mr. Bug Goes to Town (Hoppity Goes to Town; Fleischer) 118
Mr. Smith Goes to Washington 95
Mr. Twardowski (Kowanko) 163
Mucha, Alfons 63
Mujiri, Vladimir (Lado) 178
Mul, Ati 22
multiplane technique 138n29
München-Berlin Wanderung (Munich-Berlin Walking Tour; O. Fischinger) 154
Münchener Bilderbogen (Picture Sheets from Munich; O. Fischinger) 153

Münchener Bilderbogen (Seel) 56
Munro, Grant 129, 130
Muntañola, Joaquím 171
Murata Yasuji 83, 183
Murnau, Friedrich Wilhelm 30, 55
Murphy, Dudley 54
Murzilka v Afrike (Murzilka in Africa; Gorbach/ Guyetsky) 177
Mushroom Dance (*Fantasia*) 101
The Music Box (Khodataev) 77, 80
music: in abstract animation 155, 156; aleatory 155; and ancient animation 9–10; atonal 30; by Bach 128, 155; and color 19–20, 34–5, 78, 154, 156; counterpoint 10, 59; *Dance of the Hours* (*Fantasia*) 101; dodecaphony 30; electronic 149; in *Fantasia* 103; by Grieg 128; in Japanese animation 84; in Masaoka's animation 182; in Merrie Melodies 119; by Mozart 154; *Musique concrète* 126; by Mussorgsky 103, 142, 144–5, 147; original compositions 154, 169, 175; polyphonic composition 10; Raumlichtmusik 153; by Saint-Saëns 128; by Shostakovich 176n10; by Sousa 155; in *Steamboat Willie* 96; by Stravinsky 30, 103; synchronization of 97, 98; *see also* Stalling, Carl
musical motifs 34
Musical Poster (Lye) 133
Musicalist Artists 160
Musique concrète 126
Mussorgsky, Modeste 103, 142, 144–5, 147
Musume Dojoji (A Girl at Dôjô's Temple; Ichikawa) 186
mutoscope 15n18
Mutt & Jeff Cartoons 39, 47, 48, 86
Muybridge, Eadweard (Edward Muggeridge) 15
M. Vieux-Bois 159
Myller, Jørgen 160, 161
My Man Godfrey (La Cava) 40
Myren, Paul 68
Myšlenka hledající světlo (Ideas Search For Light; Dodals) 165
Mystères du Château de Dès (Mysteries of the Castle of the Dice; Man Ray) 55

Nagant, Paul 147
Nakaura Takeo 185
Nanook of the North (Flaherty) 30
När Kapten Grogg skulle porträtteras (When Captain Grogg Was to Have His Portrait Done; Bergdahl) 68
narrator, in Japanese animation 84
Nash, Clarence 102
National Film Board of Canada 129, 130, 142
Naturfilm Hubert Schonger Berlin 151
Natwick, Myron 'Grim' 40, 101, 115, 117

Nederland Film 152
Negern och hunden (The Black Man and the Dog; Liljeqvist) 68
Negrete, Jorge 189
Neighbours (McLaren) 130
Nel paese dei ranocchi (In The Country of the Frogs; Rubino) 168
Nemeth, Ted 128
neorealism, Italian 95
Netherlands, animation in 147–8
Ne toptat' fashistskou sapogu nashei rodiny (The Fascist Boot Won't Trample the Soil of Our Motherland) 177
Netto, Fred 71
Neumann, Karl 149
Neurasthenia (Ginna) 34
Neves, Francesco 173
The New Adventures of Pinocchio (Mochinaga et al.) 185
The New Wave (Wan brothers) 187
The Newlyweds (comic strip; Cohl) 32
Newton, Isaac 20
Nichols, Charles A. 102
nickelodeons 21, 24
Nielsen, Asta 56
Niemeyer, Erna 58
Niépce Nicéphore 14
Night of St. John (Gogol) 144
Night on Bald Mountain (Moussorgsky) 103, 142, 144–5
Nikkatsu Uzumasa Film Studio 182
Nikolai, Otto 154
Nils Holgerssons underbara resa (Nils Holgerson's Wonderful Journey) 162
1905–1925 (Komissarenko/Merkulov) 76
1941 (Lee) 129
Ningyo Eiga Seisakusho (The Puppet Animation Film Studio) 183
Ninotchka 95
Nippon Dogasha (Japanese Animation Company) 182
Nobi (Fires on the Plains; Ichikawa) 186
Noble, Joe 53
Noche de circo (Night at the Circus; Pérez Arroyo) 173
Noche de sustos (Night of Fright; Oliva) 192
Noche Mexicana (Mexican Night) 189
No la hagas y no la temas (Do No One Wrong and Fear No Wrong; Gijón) 172
Nohain, Jean 136
Nohain, Mireille 136
Nolan, William C. 'Bill' 38, 40, 42, 46, 48, 111, 117
Norakuro 183
Norakuro nitohei—Kyoren no maki (Private Second-Class Norakuro; Murata) 183

Norci Msroleli (The Young Rifleman; Chankvetadze) 178
Nordisk Films Kompagni 65, 66
Norelius, Einar 162
Norling 129
Norstein, Yuri 81
Northwest Hounded Police (Avery) 122
Norway, animation in 69–70, 162–3
Nosferatu (Murnau) 30, 37
Noticiero Nacional (Acevedo brothers) 190
Novy Gulliver (New Gulliver; Ptushko) 176
Noxon, Gerald 133
Nude Descending a Staircase (Duchamp) 34
Nunes, Luís 71
Nur die Ruhe . . . (Only the Peace . . . ; Wozak/Thomas) 157
Nyberg, Yrjö (Norta) 70

Obasute yama (The Mountain Where Old Women are Abandoned; Yamamoto) 83
Obczovsky, Paul 159
O Boneco Rebelde (The Rebel Guy; Luiz) 173
O'Brien, Willis H. 41–2, 167
The Ocean Hop (Disney) 98
Oceania, animation in 90–1
Ocho fujin no genso (Fantasy of Madame Butterfly; Arai) 184
October (Eisenstein) 146
Odna iz mnogih (One among the Others; Khodataeva/Brumberg/Brumberg) 79
O dragãozinho manso (The Good Little Dragon; Mauro) 191
O Duce afighete (The Duce Narrates; Polenaki) 167
Øen (The Island; Petersen) 66
Ofuji Noburo 181
Ofuji Award 181
O'Galop (Marius Rossillon) 54
Ohser, Erich 149
Oikawa Koichi 185
Oil Symphony (documentary; Pumpyansky) 179
Oira no yakyu (The Baseball Match; Murata) 83
Oishi Ikuo 184
O Kaiser (Seth) 86
Okamoto Tadanari 185
Oklahoma! (Rogers & Hammerstein) 102
Old Doc Yak 41
Old Pop Perkins 46
Oliva, Juan 192, 193
Olive Oyl (Fleischer) 117
Olson, Arid 68
One Hundred and One Dalmatians (Disney) 102
O'Neill, Eugene 30
One of Many (Khodataev) 77
O Papagaio (weekly) 173

O pesadelo de António Maria (António Maria's Nightmare; Guerreiro) 71
Opta Empfangt (Alexeïeff) 163
An Optical Poem (O. Fischinger) 155, 157
optical sound 97
Opus films (Ruttmann) 56–7, 58
Oqros Biblio (The Gold Crest; Mujiri) 178
Oramunde (Etting) 128
Orbeliani, Sulkhan Saba 178
The Orchestra Conductor (Kuczkowski) 72
Organchik (A Little Music Box; Khodataev) 174
Orgelstabe (Organ Staffs; O. Fischinger) 153
Ørnback, Henning 162
Osama no shippo (The King's Tail; Seo) 183
Osaru no Sankichi: Totsugekitai (Sankichi the Monkey, The Storm Troopers) 183
Osaru Sankichi (Sankichi the Monkey; Seo) 183
Os Camelos (Camels; Alves) 71
Österreichische Kriegskaricaturen 63
Österreichs beste Mannschaft (Austria's Best Team; Weichberger) 159
Oswald the Lucky Rabbit 50, 98, 111, 112, 113, 120
Oszkár, Kálmán Viktor 166
Out of the Inkwell (Fleischer) 44
Ovrum, Eivin 69
Oxberry 195
Ozu Yasujiro 95, 186

Pabst, Georg Wilhelm 55, 56
Pacala in Love (Petrescu) 72
Pacala in the Moon (Petrescu) 72
Pacific Art and Title 118
Paco Perico en première (Paco Perico's Premiere; Chavira/Gómez) 189
Pagot, Nino 168, 169
Pagot, Toni 168
The Painful History of the Nation (Wan brothers) 187
Painlevé, Jean 136
Pal, George (Marczincsák Julius György) 55, 132, 147–8, 151 163, 166–7
Pal, Zsoka (Grandjean Erszbet Josefa) 166
Pal-Dolls 166
Palladium 161
Palmer, Harry S. 41
Palmer, Tom 119
Pancho Pistolas (in *The Three Caballeros*) 189
pantomimes lumineuses (Lit Pantomimes) 17
Papageno (Reiniger) 62
Paramount Pictures 41, 45, 117, 118, 120, 155, 166
Paris, John A. 13

Parker, Claire (Alexeïeff) 141–7
Parthenon frieze: implicit movement in 11; motion analysis 8–9; music in 10–11; as an object of philosophy 11–12
Particles in Space (Lye) 133, 134
Pashchenko, Mstislav 176
Passages from Finnegan's Wake (Bute) 128
The Passion of Joan of Arc (Dreyer) 30
Pathé, Charles 32, 39, 41, 54, 70
Pathé-Baby 173
Patiño, Salvador 85
Patoruzú (Indian character) 192
Paul, Robert William 23
Paulin, Gaston 18
Pauvre Pierrot (Poor Pierrot) 17
Pavlov, Ivan P. 30
Payen, Antoine 137
Peace and War Pencillings (Furniss) 52
Peace on Earth (Harman) 126
Pearce, Perce 101–2
Peberdy, Harold 129
peep-show machines 114
Peet, Bill 102
Péguy, Robert 32
Pekka Puupää (Peter Woodenhead) 70
Peludópolis (City of Peludo) 191
Pemartín, Julián 172
Pen and Ink Vaudeville Sketches 48; *see also* chalk talks; lightning sketches
Pencil-Film 65, 160
Pensuti, Luigi Liberio 167–8
Pérez Arroyo, Joaquín 172
Pérez, Feliciano 170
Pérez, Manuel 190
Perfumes Kimono 173
Persistence of Vision with Regard to Moving Objects (Roget) 12
Perugina figurines 169
Pesmen-Rubin Commercial Art Studio 50, 113
The Pet (McCay) 37
Peter Pan (Disney) 101
Peterle's Abenteuer (Peterle's Adventure; Weichberger) 159
Petersen, Ellen Margrethe Jakobsen 66
Petersen, Robert Storm (Storm P.) 65–7, 70
Petőfi Sándor 70
Petrescu, Aurel 72
Pettenon, Dante 193
Petzke, Ingo 153
Pfenninger, Emil 56
Pfenninger, Rudolf 56
Pfister, Joseph 166

phenakistiscope/phenatisticope 13
Phidias 8–9, 10
Philippart, Edmond 147
Philippi, Charles 102
Philips Cavalcade, 75 Years of Music (Geesink) 148
Philips World Parade (Geesink) 148
Phonofilm process 45, 97, 115n43
phonoscope 15
Photo Chemical Laboratory (PCL) 183
photodynamics 34
photogenic drawing 14
photography 14–15, 32
Photophone (RCA) 97
Picabia, Francis 58
Picasso, Pablo 30, 34, 135, 181
Piccardo, Osvaldo 168
Piccolo, Saxo and Co. (Geesink) 148
Pictures at an Exhibition (Moussorgsky, Alexeïeff/Parker) 144–7
Pierce, Tedd 117
Pierce-Arrow Company 49
Pierus (Geesink) 148
Pindal, Kaj 161
Pinocchio (Collodi) 176
Pinocchio (Disney) 101, 102, 103, 104, 121
Pinschewer, Julius 55, 70, 159, 160
pinscreens 141–2, 144
Pip, Squeak and Wilfred (Speed) 53
Pipo y Pipa en bisca de Cocolín (Pipo and Pipa in Search of Cocolin; Aznar) 170, 172
Pirandello, Luigi 30, 57
Piscator, Erwin 56
Pisicchio e Melisenda (Pisicchio and Melisenda; Saitta) 168
Pitoeff 141
Pitsch und Patsch (Pfenninger) 56
pixilation 68
Plan velikih rabot (The Plan of the Large Works; Rom) 175
Planck, Max 30
Plane Crazy (Disney) 98
Plane Daffy (Tashlin) 125
Plateau, Joseph 13
Plauen, E.O. 149
The Plow Boy (Disney) 100
Plucki en Egypte (Genval) 147
Pluto (Disney) 99, 102
Pochta (Mail; Tsekhanovsky) 81
Poem 8 (Etting) 128
The Pointer (Disney) 100
pointillism 35
Poland, animation in 72, 163–5

Polenaki, Stamati 167
Polidorov, Anatoly 140
Political Favourites (Booth & Paul) 23
Politsatira 79
Polly Tricks (István) 166
Poncet, Marie-Thérèse 7
Popeye (Fleischer) 38, 109, 115, 118
Popeye the Sailor (Fleischer) 117
Popeye the Sailor Man Meets Sinbad the Sailor (Fleischer) 117
Popeye the Sailor Meets Ali Baba's Forty Thieves (Fleischer) 117
Porky in Wacky-land (Clampett) 123
Porky Pig (Warner Bros.) 109, 119, 120, 123
Porky's Bedtime Story (Clampett) 123
Porky's Duck Hunt 124
Porky's Tire Trouble 124
Porter, Edwin Stanton 24–5
Portugal, animation in 71–2, 173
Potamkin, Harry Alan 81
Potoco the monkey 190
The Power (Pal) 167
Powers, Pat 98, 113
Powers, T. E. 39
Prag Film AG 150, 166
praxinoscope 16
Prekrasnaya Lukanida (The Beautiful Leukanida; Starewitch) 73
Presnyakov, Aleksandr 81, 175
Prévert, Jacques 137
Prévert, Pierre 137
The Price of Blood (Wan brothers) 187
Principal Management of the Photo-Cinematographic Industry (GUKF) 175
Primo de Rivera, Miguel 169
Primrose Production Company 63
Prince Achmed (Reiniger/Bartosch) 13, 153; review by Jouvanceau 90–1
Prince Valiant 38
The Princess with the Iron Fan (Wan brothers) 187–8
Prinčip, Gavrilo 29
Prins Electron (Geesink) 148
Private Snafu (Warner Bros.) 125
Prof. Small and Mr. Tall 114
Professor Mécanicas 54
Professor Scarecrow (Puppetoon) 166
Professor Steinacks Metode eller Foryngelseskuren (Professor Steinack's Method or The Rejuvenation Cure; Petersen) 66
Promenade-Projekt (Holland) 148

propaganda 25, 32, 52, 53, 56, 62n31, 77, 83, 104, 111, 115, 121, 130, 131, 133, 148, 167, 168, 175, 177, 178, 180, 181n5, 182–4, 185n12, 194
Propavshaja gramota (The Lost Diploma; Merkulov) 79
Protazanov, Yakov 76, 78
Proust, Marcel 30
Prtosani Megobrebi (The Winded Friends; Mujiri) 178
Pruneda, Salvador 85
Przygoda Czlowieka Pocziwego (Adventure of an Honest Man; Themersons) 164
Ptushko, Aleksandr 79, 165, 167, 175, 176, 177
Publicidad Organizada S.A. 189
Publi-Ciné 54
Puccini, Giacomo 184
Pudovkin, Vsevolod 75, 96, 139
Puk's Adventures (Jarosz) 163
Pulcinella e i briganti (Pulcinella and the Brigands; Giobbe and the Cossio brothers) 168
Pulcinella e il temporale (Pulcinella and the Storm; Giobbe and the Cossio brothers) 168
Pulcinella nel bosco (Pulcinella in the Forest; Giobbe and the Cossio brothers) 168
Puños de campeón (Fists of Champions; Caro) 193
Puppetoons 166–7
puppets 2, 7, 16, 22, 24, 33, 41–2, 47–9, 65, 70n53, 73, 75, 87, 123, 124, 132, 133, 136, 147–8, 149n53, 151, 160, 163–4, 165, 166–7, 168, 170, 172, 173, 176, 177–8, 184, 185, 186, 188, 191
Purchase, Denis 195
Pure Film Movement 84
Pusan (Mr. Pu; Ichikawa) 186
Pushkin 144, 176
Pushkin's New Home (Khodataev) 77
Puss Gets the Boot (MGM) 127
Pym dans la ville (Pym in the City; Arcady) 136
pyrophone 20
Pythagoras 20

Qian Jajun 188
quantum theory 30
Queralt, Juan 190
Questel, Mae 116, 117
Quiche, Wilma de 166
Quick macht Hochzeit (Quick Gets Married; Stordel) 149
Quimby, Fred 121, 126
Quinterno, Dante 192
Quinto (Pérez Arroyo) 172
Quiquemelle, Marie-Claire 187–8

Rabier, Benjamin 32, 54
Rabold, Toni 56
Racconto di un affresco (Tale of a Fresco; Emmer) 168
Race of the Hare and the Tortoise (Wan brothers) 187
Radio Caracas Televisión (TVes) 190
Radio Dynamics (O. Fischinger) 155, 156, 157
Radio Dynamics (Rainger) 155
Radiomautsqhebloba (Radio Broadcasting; Mujiri) 178
Raemakers Cartoons (Dodsworth) 53
Raïk, Etienne 166
Rainbow Dance (Lye) 133, 134
Rainbow Parade 114
Rainger, Ralph 155
rakugo 181
Rank, J. Arthur 131
Rankin, Arthur, Jr. 185
Rankin/Bass Productions 185
Rapto de luz (Light Rapture; Tur) 171
Rapto en palacio (Kidnapping in the Palace; Gijón) 172
Rasmussen, Harry 161
Raumlichtkunst 153
Raumlichtmusik 153
Raymond, Alex 38, 109
Reachi, Santiago 189
Reason and Emotion (Disney) 104
Red Hot Riding Hood (Avery) 121
Red Seal Distribution Company 45
Refiyev, M. 179
Régnier, Jean 136
Reichenbach, Harry 95
Reindorp, James 194–5
Reinhardt, Max 60
Reiniger, Lotte 55, 57, 59–63, 129, 131, 138
Reise durch Österreich (Journey through Austria; Wozak/Thomas) 157
Reitherman, Wolfgang 62, 105, 107
Rejucilo 192
Rennsymphonie (Richter) 59
Renoir, Jean 61, 62, 95, 138
Republic Pictures 124
Revista Musical (Pruneda) 85
The Revolt of the Paper Figurines (Wan brothers) 187
Reyes, José Maria 172
Reynaud, Émile 15–18
R.F.D. 10,000 B.C. (O'Brien) 42
Rhapsody in Blue (Gershwin) 30
Rhythm in Light (Bute) 128
Rhythmus (Richter) 58
Rhythmus 21 (Richter) 59
Rhythmus 23 (Richter) 59
Rhythmus 25 (Richter) 59
Richter, Hans 55, 56, 58–9, 138, 156
Riefenstahl, Leni 57
Riega que llueve (Irrigate, While It Rains; Reyes/Rigalt) 172
Rigal, André 54, 136
Rigalt, Carlos 172
Rimbaud, Arthur 20
Rimington, Alexander Wallace 20
Ring, Børge 161
Rinoplastía (Surgery of the Nose; Cristiani) 87
The Rite of Spring (Stravinsky) 30, 103
Rivero Oramas, Rafael 190
RKO Distribution Company 114
Roach, Hal 111
Roald Amundsen paa Sydpolen (Roald Amundsen on the South Pole; Halvorsen) 69
Roaring 1920s 29
Robert-Houdin Theatre 33
Rockefeller, Nelson 104
Rodrigues, Laurenço 71
Roepstorff, Anker 160, 161
Roget, Peter Mark 12
Rom, Abraham 175
Romania, animation in 72
Romano, José Martinez 170
Rómeó és Júlia (Romeo and Juliet; Kató-Kiszly) 70
Rooney, Mickey 111, 171
Rosas, Enrique de 193
Rosnerová, Irena 165
Rossellini, Roberto 95
rotoscope 44, 118
Rotsa Gebelsi Ar Stqhuis (When Goebbels Does Not Lie; Fedorchenko) 178
Roubaix, Paul de 136
Rough Sea at Dover (Birt Acres) 21
Rtsqhili Da Tchiantchvela (The Flea and the Ant; Chankvetadze) 178
Rúa, Victor A. Iturralde 192
Rubber Head (Clampett) 124
rubber hose animation 42, 45, 124
Rubino, Antonio 168
Rubio, Francisco López 170
Rudolph the Red-Nosed Reindeer (Mochinaga et al.) 185
Rufle, George 114
Russia/Soviet Union, animation in 72–81, 174–7
Russopulos, Yanni 167
Ruttmann, Walther 20, 55, 56–7, 58, 61, 62, 63, 138, 146, 153, 156

Sá, Luiz 191
Sachs, Peter 131
Sadko (Ptushko) 177
Saint François (Bartosch) 140
Saint-Ogan, Alain de 136
Saint-Saëns, Camille 128
Saitta, Ugo 168
Sakh.Kin.Mretsvi (Georgian State Film Industry, GSFI) 178
Sakura—Haru no genso (Cherry Blossom—The Illusion of Spring; Masaoka) 183
Sala, Oskar 149
Salén, Karl 70
Salkin, Leo 147
Saltikov-Shchedrin, Mikhail 174
Saludos Amigos (Disney) 104
Sam and his Musket (Dyer) 131
Sami Megobari (Three Friends; Mujiri) 178
Sammy and Sausage (Noble) 53
The Samoyed Boy (Khodataev) 77, 79
Sam Small (Dyer) 131, 161
Sanchez Rolón, Jesús 190
Sandoval, Carlos 85, 189
Santos, Edmundo 189
Sarg, Anthony Frederick 'Tony' 48–50
Sarg, Bertha Eleanor McGowan 48
Sarg-Dawley Co. 49–50
Sarrut, André 137
Saru kani kassen (Crab Takes Revenge on the Monkey; Kitayama) 82
Sarugashima (The Monkeys' Island; Masaoka) 182
Sascha 63, 64
satire 24, 39, 52, 71, 75, 76, 77, 79, 80, 81, 86, 87, 109, 167, 173, 174
Saussure, Ferdinand de 30
Savignac, Raymond 54
Savoia, Umberto di 87

Sazonov, Panteleymon 79, 176
Schaeffer, Pierre 126
Scheib, Ronnie 122
Schillinger, Joseph 128
Schlesinger, Isidore W. 88
Schlesinger, Leon 109, 118–19, 120, 124, 125, 127, 194
Schmidt, Manfred 149
Schnuff, Der Niesser (Deutsche Zeichenfilm GmbH) 150
Schoedsack, Ernest B. 42
Schönberg, Arnold 30
Schönbrunn 63
Schulberg, Budd 24

Schulz, Christoph 15n16
Schwartz, Ths. W. 69
Schwartz, Zack 102, 114
science, influence on animation 12–13
Sciuscià (Shoeshine; De Sica) 169
Scrappy 114
Screen Gems 127
Screen Magazine 46
Screwy Squirrel (Avery) 120
The Screwy Truant (Avery) 122
Scribner, Rod 124
Sea Dreams (Speed) 52
Searl, Leon A. 40
Sears, Ted 99, 115
Second Period, "The Silent Pioneers (1908–1928)" 2, 27
SEDA *see* Sociedad Española de Dibujos Animados
Seeber, Guido 55–6
Seel, Louis 56, 64, 65, 149, 153, 191
Seelische konstruktionen (Spiritual Constructions; O. Fischinger) 153
Segar, Elzie Crisler 117
Seggelke, Herbert 152
Segodnya (Today; Vertov) 75
Seitaro 184
Sekisho (The Inspection Station; Ofuji) 181
Sekiya Isoji 183
Selig Polyscope 41
Selznick, David O. 106
Se-Ma-For 164
Semi-Fusas (Seravat) 72
Sem' let Oktjabrja—Sem'let pobed (Seven Years from October—Seven Years of Victories; Presnyakov/Sorokhtin) 81
senga eiga 82
Sen'ka Afrikanets (Sen'ka the African; Cherkes) 79–80, 81, 175
Sennett, Mack 111
Sentry, Dennis 88
Seo Mitsuyo 182, 183, 184
Seo Taro 183
Seravat, Hernani Tavares 72
Serenade (Pfenninger) 56
Serenata (Serenade; Rubio) 170
Serenata nocturna (Evening Serenade; Geesink) 148
Serey, Alfredo 86
Seth (Álvaro Marins) 86, 191
The Seven Faces of Dr. Lau (Pal) 167
Seversky, Alexander de 104
The Shadow-Laughs (Fryer) 129
Shanghai Film Studios 184

Sharpsteen, Ben 101
Shaw, Harold 88
Shazka o zare Saltane (The Tale of Tsar Saltane; Brumberg sisters) 177
Sherlock Jr. 122
Shields, Hugh M. 41
Shimokawa Hekoten 82
Shinhwa Company 187
Ship of Ether (Pal) 166
Shitakiri susume (The Sparrows with the Forked Tongue; Yamamoto) 83
Shochiku 180
Sholpo, Evgeny 175
Shonen to kodanuki (A Badger and a Boy; Mochinaga) 185
Shooting of Dan McGoo (Avery) 121
Shors Akvani (Cradle no Longer; Mujiri) 178
Shostakovich, Dmitri 176n10
Shunn u Katun/Pes i kot (The Dog and the Cat; Atamanov) 178
Sifianos, Georges 10
Siga tus keravnus (Imagine! What Lightnings!; Russopulos) 167
silhouettes 49, 60n25, 61, 62–3; *see also* cut-outs
Silliettes (Sarg-Dawley) 49
Silly Symphonies 98–9, 103, 105, 111, 117, 125; influence of 182, 184, 186
Simonsen, Keld 161
The Simple Things (Disney) 99
Sindbad the Sea Traveller (Azerbaijanfilm Studio) 179
Sin dejar rastros (Without Leaving a Trace; Cristiani) 87
Sinding-Hansen, Niels 163
sing-along formula 45
The Sinking of the Lusitania (McCay) 37
Sixth Period, "Contemporary Times (1991–2015)" 2
Skärgården i Robinson (A Modern Robinson) 68
Skazka o belke khoziaushke I myshke zlodeike (The Tale about the Squirrel Hostess and the Mouse Villain; Levandovsky) 81
Skazka o pope i rabotnike ego Balde (The Tale of the Priest and his Servant Balda; Voinov) 176
Skazka o solomennom bychke (The Fairy Tale about the Straw Bull; Levandovsky) 81
Skeleton Dance (Disney Silly Symphonies) 98, 125, 127, 183
The Sketch (magazine) 53
Skibstrup, Alfred 65
Skippy Studio 111
Skobelev Committee 74
Skriabin, Aleksandr 20
slash system 39
Sluchai na stadione (It Happened at the Stadium) 176

Smirnov, Viktor 175
Smith, Albert E. 25
Smith, Paul J. 102, 112
Smith, Sidney 41
Snilsberg, Harald B. 163
Snow White and the Seven Dwarfs (Disney) 48, 68, 101, 102–3, 109, 111, 112, 117, 131, 163, 166
socialist realism 174
Sociedad Española de Dibujos Animados (SEDA) 169–70, 172
Sociéte Hoppin et Gross 137
Socrates 11
Soglow, Otto 114
Som det er—Som det foles (A Rather Good Intention; Petersen) 65
Some Day My Prince Will Come (Churchill) 102
Song Car-Tunes 45
Song of Spring (Ginna) 35
Sonnenersatz (Pfenninger) 56
The Son of Kong (O'Brien) 42
Son of Paleface (Tashlin) 127
The Sorcerer's Apprentice (Disney) 99, 101
The Sorcerer's Apprentice (Dukas) 154
Sørensen, Lydia 66
Sorokhtin, Igor 81, 175
SOS Doctor Marabú (Dibsono Films) 171
Sotre Claus of Lille Claus (Big Claus and Little Claus; Christensen) 161
sound, addition of 46, 47, 96–7
Soupault 144
South Africa, animation in 88, 194–5
Sovetskie igrushki (Soviet Toys; Vertov) 75
Soyuzdetmultfilm (Soyuzmultfilm) studio 175, 177
Spain: animation in Madrid 172; animation in Valencia 172–3; Barcelona's entrepreneurs 170–1; Barcelonese feature-length films 171–2; Catalan vibrancy 169–70; the *Edad Dorada* 170; silent animation in 70–1
Sparber, Izzy 118
Speed, Lancelot 52–3
Spira, Wilhelm 'Bil' 158
Spook Sport (Bute) 128
The Sporting Mice (Armstrong) 52
Squirrel War (Dyer) 131
Stagecoach 95
Stalin, Josef 175
Stalling, Carl W. 98, 120, 125–6
Stallings, Vernon George 39, 42, 46, 114
Stamato, João 191
The Star of Bethlehem (Reiniger) 63

Star, Nina (Janina/Jeanne Starewitch) 74
Starewitch, Ladislas (Wladyslaw Maryan Aleksandrowidz Starewitch) 72–5, 136, 163, 167, 184
Stars and Stripes Forever (Sousa) 155
Statement on Sound (Eisenstein/Pudovkin/Aleksandrov) 96
Steamboat Willie (Disney) 1, 2, 47, 95–7, 125
Stein, Gertrude 30
Steinaae, Ib 161
Steiner, Rolf 128
Stella Maris (Starewitch) 74
stereoptical process 115, 156, 168
Stokowski, Leopold 155
stop frame technique 53; *see also* frame-by-frame technique
Stordel, Kurt 149
Storm P. *see* Petersen, Robert Storm
Storm P. Museet 67
Storm P. tegner de tre små mend (Storm P. Draws the Three Little Men; Petersen) 66
Storulio sapnas (The Dream of a Fatty; Usinskas) 177
The Story of a Mosquito (or, *How a Mosquito Operates*; McCay) 36
Story of a Town (Saltikov-Shchedrin) 174
The Story of the Flag (Dyer) 53
The Story of the Kelly Gang (Tait) 90
Stravinsky, Igor 30
Strekoza i Muraveyi (The Dragonfly and the Ant; Starewitch)
Strempler, Luis 85
Strich-Punkt-Ballet (Seggelke) 152
stroboscope (stroboscopic disc) 13, 14
Studdy, George Ernest 'Studdy Dog' 52, 53
Student of Prague (Wegener) 60
Student von Prag (The Student of Prague; Seeber) 56
Studie No. 6 (H. Fischinger) 154
Studie No. 8 (H. Fischinger) 154
Studien (O. Fischinger) 156
Studien No. 9, No. 10, No. 11, No. 12, No. 13, and *No. 14* (H. Fischinger) 152
Studios El Ávila 190
Study of the Effects of Four Colors (Ginna) 35
Sturges, Preston 95
Style imagé (Philippart) 147
Such is Life at the Zoo (Mayer) 41
Such is Life in Italy (Mayer) 41
Sudekin, Serge 141
Suite tempirouette (Toonder) 148
Sullivan, Patrick Peter 39, 44, 45, 46
Sullivan Studio 45
Sullivan's Travels (Sturges) 95
Sumi-e (Lee) 129
Sumikazu Eiga Sosakusha 83

Sunrise (Murnau) 30
Superman (Fleischer brothers) 109, 118
suprematism 56
Supreme Commander of the Allied Powers (SCAP) 184
surrealism 30, 33, 34, 55, 56, 146
Survage, Léopold 35
Suteneko Torachan (Tora-chan, an Orphan Kitty) 183
Suzumibune (The Tourists' Boat; Kimura) 184
Swaffield, Walter 129
Swann's Way (Proust) 30
Sweden, animation in 67–8, 162
Swift, Jonathan 176
Swing Shift Cinderella (Avery) 121
Swinging the Lambeth Walk (Lye) 133
Switzerland, animation in 65, 159–60
The Sword in the Stone (Disney) 62
Sylvester the Cat 95
symbolism 20
Symphonie Diagonale (Eggeling) 58
Symphony from the New World (Dvořák) 155
Symphony in Slang (Avery) 122
synaesthesia 19–20
Synchronization or *Synchrony* (Bute) 128
Synchrony No. 2 (Bute) 128

Tableaux d'une exposition (Pictures at an Exhibition; Moussorgsky, Alexeïeff/Parker) 144–7
Taborda, Diógenes 'El Mono' 87
Tagatz, Sergij 167
Tagore, Rabindranath 30
Tait, Charles 90
Takamitsu Kogyo 83
Tako no hone (The Octopus Bone; Murata) 83
Talbot, William Henry Fox 14
The Tale of Genji 8
Tal Farlow (Lye) 134
Tanz der Farben (Colour Dance; H. Fischinger) 152
Tapia, Luís 70
Tarakanishe (The Big Beetle; Ivanov) 79
Tarantella (Bute) 128
Tarde de toros (Evening of the Bulls; Reyes/Rigalt) 172
Tashlin, Frank 109, 114, 119, 125, 127–8
Tassoni, Alessandro 168
Tbilisi Cinema Studio 178
Technicolor 99n9, 111, 122, 138, 181, 189
The Teddy Bears (Porter/McCutcheon) 24
Tegnerforbundet (Cartoonist Society) 69
The Telescope Has Two Ends (Kuczkowski) 72
television: American 185; animated series on 2, 127; in Argentina 192; in Belgium 147; Disney shows 105;

effect on movie studios 123; in Germany 128; in Japan 185; puppet shows on 124; in South Africa 195; in Switzerland 159; in Venezuela 190
Tempest, Dudley 52
Tempranillo hace tarde (Tempranillo Is Late; Reyes/Rigalt) 172
Ten Days Leave (Leah) 53
Tendlar, Dave 117
Tenkatsu Production Company 82
Teréz, Dávid (Tissa David) 166
Terrazas, Ernesto 'Ernie' 189
Terrible Vavila and Auntie Arina (Khodataev) 77
The Terrible Vengeance (Starewitch) 73
Terry, John 40, 41
Terry, Paul 41, 44, 46–7, 48, 96, 109, 114–15
Terry and the Pirates 38
Terrytoons 114–15
Terrytoons Studio 47
Tertern u Aytze/Pop i koza (The Priest and the Goat; Atamanov) 178
Teste di legno (Wooden Heads; Saitta) 168
Te Wei 184
Tezuka Osamu 181
Thalberg, Irving 106
Thank You, Kitty (Mochinaga) 184
thaumatrope 13
Théâtre Optique 16–19
Themerson, Franciszka 164–5
Themerson, Stefan 164–5
Thief of Baghdad, The 181
Third Period, "The Golden Age (1928–1950)" 2, 93
Thomas, Bob 103
Thomas, Frank 107, 108
Thomas, Karl 157–9
The Thousand and One Nights (Reiniger) 62
Three Blind Mice (Dunning) 130
The Three Caballeros (Disney) 104, 189
Three Little Pigs (Disney) 98, 103, 111, 114, 189
Thugs with Dirty Mugs (Avery) 120
Tiago, Servais 173
Tiden krever (Time Requires; Wosak) 163
Tiedemann, J.L. 162
Time for Beany (Clampett) 124
The Time Machine (Pal) 167
Tim og Tøffe (Caprino) 163
The Tinderbox (Fyrtøjet) 161–2
Tin Pan Alley Cats (Clampett) 123
Tintin 147
Tío Tigre y Tío Conejo (Uncle Tiger and Uncle Monkey) 190
Tip-Top (Netto) 71

Tip-Top v Moskve (Tip-Top in Moscow; Ivanov) 175
Tiro ao Alvo (Shoot the Pigeon; revue) 71
Tischmeyer, Heinz 151
Tishy the X-Legged Horse (Webster) 53
Tiziano Film 72
Tobis 149
Toccata and Fugue (J.S. Bach) 128, 155
Toepffer, Rodolphe 54
Toho Eiga 180, 183, 186
Tojo Eastphone sound recording system 181
Tokyo Puck (satirical paper) 82, 83
Tolstoy, Aleksey 176
Tom and Jerry (MGM) 95, 127
Tom and Jerry (Van Beuren studio) 114
Tom Poes (Toonder) 148
Tom Poes en de laarzenreuzen (Tom Poes and the Giants in Boots; Toonder) 148
Tönende Handschrift (sound writing) 56
Tong Pei Film Studio 185
Tony Sarg's Almanac 49
Toonder, Marten 148
Toot, Whistle, Plunk and Boom (Disney) 102
The Tooth Carpenter (or *The First Dentist*; Sarg-Dawley) 49
Topical War Cartoons (Mayer) 41
Topo Jijio o botan senso (Topo Gigio and the Missile War; Ichikawa) 186
Torachan no Kankan mushi (Tora-chan's Ship Sweeper; Masaoka) 183
Torachan to hanayome (Tora-chan and the Bride; Masaoka) 183
The Tortoise and the Hare (Disney) 103
Tosca (film) 62
Tout va très bien, madame la marquise (Everything Is Well, Madame la Marquise; Vanpeperstraetes) 147
Toy Soldiers (Maliniak) 163
Tractatus logico-filosoficus (Wittgenstein) 30
Trade Tattoo (Lye) 133, 134
Trajan's Column 7
Traquinices de Chiquinho e seu inseparável amigo Jagûnço (The Escapades of Chiquinho and His Inseparable Friend Jagûnço) 86
The Travelling Tune (Geesink) 148
Treasure Island (Disney) 102
Trenet, Charles 136
Trickfilm Studio Pal und Wittke 166
Tricolor magazine 190
Tripping the Rhine (Mayer) 41
Triumph des Willens (Triumph of the Will; Riefenstahl) 57
Trnka, Jiři 163, 167
Trois thèmes (Three themes; Alexeïeff/Parker) 144, 145, 147

Trolldrycken (The Magic Brew; Bergdahl) 67
The Troublemaker (Held) 148n51, 152
True-Life Adventures (Disney) 101
Trupp, Carlos 86
Tryllesekken (The Magic Sack) 65
Tryuki i multiplikatsya (Tricks and Animation; Bushkin) 76
Tsekhanovsky, Mikhail 81, 175, 176
Tsubo (Yamamoto) 83
Tsukinomiya no ojosama (Princess of the Moon Palace; Murata) 83
Tsuyon *see* Mochinaga Tadahito 184
Tuk-Tuk i yego priyatel Zhuk (Knok-Knok and his Friend Beatle; Levandovsky) 177
Tumanyan, Hovhannes 178
Tur, Francesc 171
Türck, Walter 61
Turner, Bill 115
Turtle Caught in a Jar (Mochinaga) 184, 188
Tusalava (Lye) 133, 134
Tuszynski, Ladislaus 63
Tvardovsky, Vladislav 81, 176
Tweety Bird (Clampett) 123
Twelfth Night (Shakespeare) 153
Two Little Dorothies (Wasilewski) 164
Týrlová, Hermína 165
Tytla, Vladimir William 104
Tzara 59

UFA (Universum Film Aktiengesellschaft) production company studios 55, 57–9, 151, 154, 166
Ugarte, Marcelino 86
Ugoki ekori no takehiki (The Fox versus the Raccoon; Oishi) 184
Ukraine, animation in 81, 177
Uma história de Camelos (A Camels Tale; Alves) 71
Una de abono (One for Safety; Romano) 170
Una extraña aventura de Jeromín (The Strange Adventure of Jeromín; Morales) 172
Una noche de gala en el Colón (Gala Night at the Colón Theatre; Ducaud) 87
Una signora dell'Ovest (The Girl of the Golden West; film) 63
Un bon bock (A Good Beer) 16, 17
Un chien andalou (An Andalusian Dog; Buñuel-Dali) 34
Uncle Tom's Cabaña (Avery) 121
Un concours de beauté (A Beauty Contest; Saint-Ogan) 136
Un día de feria (Market Day; Morales) 172
Un drama en la costa (Xaudaró) 170
Une nuit sur le mont chauve (A Night on Bald Mountain; Alexeïeff) 142, 144–6
Unhappiness of Abbas (Dikaryov/Papov) 179

United Artists 111
United States: American avant-garde 128–9; and the Disney domination 98–109; early animation in 24–6, 35–7, 110; Lantz studio 111–13; Metro-Goldwyn-Mayer studio 126–7; other animators 111–18, 127–9; silent animation in 38–52; the Warner Bros. studio 118–25; and the westward shift 109–11
Universal Pictures 50, 111, 113
Unnatural History series 48
Upa en apuros (Upa in Trouble) 192
Uproar in the Art Studio (Wan brothers) 187
Upside Down; or, the Human Flies (Booth & Paul) 23
Urban, Charles 23
Urbao, Carl 190
Uriburu, José Félix 191
Usagi to kame (The Rabbit and the Tortoise) 83
Ushiwakamuru (Ushiwakamuru, the Little Samurai; Yamamoto) 83
Usinskas, Stasys 177
The U Tube (Speed) 52

Vainalavičius, S. 177
Vakuum (Emptiness; O. Fischinger) 154
Valle, Federico 86–7
Valle, Marie 69
Van Beuren, Amadée J. 46–7, 114, 119, 127
'Van Boring' (Tashlin) 127
Van Doesburg, Theo 30
Van Hecke, M. 147
Van Hovenbergh, Henry 15n16
Van Neijenhoff, Otto 147
Vanpeperstraete, Norbert 147
Vanpeperstraete, Roger 147
Varé, Jean (Maurice Hayward) 136
Vater und Sohn (Ohser) 149
vaudeville 21, 25, 36, 41, 43
Venezuela, animation in 190
Vepro 161
Vertov, Dziga 75, 79
Verwitterte Melodie (The Dilapidated Melody; Fischerkoesen) 151
Victory through Air Power (Disney) 104
Vida y Milagros de Don Fausto (Life and Miracles of Don Fausto; Borcosque) 86
Videocraft 185
Vidor, King 30
Vieira, Manuel Luís 71
Vigil, Constancio C. 191, 192
Vigo, Jean 95
Viñas, Moisés 85

The Violinist's Hands (Balla) 34
Virgolino apânha (Virgolino's Troubles; Sá) 191
Visconti, Luchino 95
visual filming 72
visual music 57
Vita futurista (Futuristic Life; Ginna) 34
Vita-Film 63
Vitaphone system 97
Vivaphone 97n6
V'la le beau temps (Here Is the Good Weather; Rigal) 136
V mordu Vtoromu Internacionalu (In the Face of the Second International; Bushkin) 76
Voinov, Nikolay/Nicolai 79, 176
von Cziffra, Géza 166
Von Ehrenwiesen, Hilda Rebay 155
von Möllendorff, Horst 149, 150, 151, 152, 166
von Stampfer, Simon 13, 14
von Sternberg, Josef 55
von Unruh, Fritz 153
Vor (The Thief; Ivanov/Sazonov) 176
Vormittagsspuk (Ghosts before Breakfast; Richter) 59
Votes for Women: A Caricature (Armstrong) 52

Wachsexperimenten (Wax Experiments; O. Fischinger) 153
Waechter Animation Studio 151
Wagner, Richard 20
Wake Up (Wan brothers) 187
Waldman, Myron 117
Wallace, Oliver 102
Walt Disney Productions *see* Walt Disney studios
Walt Disney World 105
Walter Lantz productions 111–12
Wan brothers 187–8
Wan Chaochen (Wan Jiajie) 187
Wan Dihuan (Wan Jiakun) 187
Wan Guchan (Wan Jiaqi) 187
Wan Laiming (Wan Jiazong) 187
War Cartoons (Buxton) 52
War Cartoons (Tempest) 52
War of the Worlds (Pal) 167
War of the Worlds (Welles) 123
War Studies series (Studdy) 52
Warner Bros. studio: 118–25; Avery at 121–1; Clampett at 123; Freleng at 124–5; influence of 193; Stalling at 125–6; Tashlin at 127
Warren, Jack 53
Wasilewski, Zenon 163
Wasström, Erik 70
The Waste Land (Eliot) 30
Water Babies 184

Webber, Melville 128
Webber-Watson duo 128
Webster, Tom 53
Wedding in the Coral Sea (*Hochzeit im Korallenmeer*) 150, 166
Wegener, Paul 57, 60
Weichberger, Else Knoll 159
Weichberger, Johann 159
Weigel, Susi 158, 159
Weiss, Alfred 45
Welles, Orson 40, 123, 143, 155
Wells, H.G. 168
We Must Be Vigilant (Khodataev) 77
Werther, Arthur 158
Werth-Regendanz, Alexander 138
Wessely, Stefan 158
What Price Porky (Clampett) 123
What's Buzzin' Buzzard? (Avery) 122
What's Cookin' Doc? (Clampett) 123
Wheatstone, Charles 15n15
When Worlds Collide (Pal) 167
When You Wish upon a Star (Harline) 102
Whistle While You Work (Churchill) 102
Whitaker, Judge 102
Whiteman, Paul 111
Whitney, James 129, 155
Whitney, John 129, 155
Whitten, Norman 53
Who's Afraid of the Big Bad Wolf? (Churchill) 98, 102
Why They Love Cavemen (Sarg-Dawley) 49
Wieghorst, Karl 66
Wiene, Robert 55
Wiener Bilderbogen Nr. 1 (Viennese Picture Book No. 1; Seel) 64–5
Wild and Woolfy (Avery) 121
Wild Hare, A (Warner Bros.) 120, 125
Williams, Richard 107
Willie Whopper (Iwerks) 113
Willing Waldo 46
Willy McBean and His Magic Machine (Mochinaga et al.) 185
Wimpy (Fleischer) 117
Winchelsea and Its Environs (Furniss) 52
Winkeler, Henry 147
Winkler, George 48
Winkler, Margaret J. 50
Winkler Pictures 48
Winterstein, Franz 172
Wittgenstein, Ludwig 30
Wizard of Oz 95
Wochenende (Weekend; Ruttmann) 57

Woody Woodpecker 95, 109, 112
The World of Insects (Wan brothers) 188
World War I 29
Worringer, Wilhelm 30
Wosak, Bruno 163
Wot a Night (Foster/Stallings) 114
Wozak, Bruno 157–9
Wright, Frank Lloyd 81, 105
Wrill écoute la BBC (Wrill Listens to the BBC; Fromenteau) 147

Xaudarò, Joaquín 169, 170, 172
Ximémez, Alfredo 85

Yacheistov, Georgi 80
Yamamoto 'Sanae' Zenjiro 82, 83
Yamamoto Manga Seisakujo 83
Yankovsky, Boris 176
The Year of Chinese Goods (Wan brothers) 187
Yegiazarov, G. 179
Yokoyama Michiko 182
Yokoyama Ryuichi 183
Youghal Clock Tower (Horgan) 53
Young, Cy 102
Yrigoyen, Hipólito 87, 191
Yugoslavia, animation in 167
Yureisen (The Ghost Ship; Ofuji) 181

Zambonelli (Carlo Amedeo Frascari) 72
Zamora, Rudy 190
Zander, Jack 114
Zapreschenny popugay (The Forbidden Parrot; Lazarchuk) 177
Zasche, Theo 63
Zazou chez les nègres (Zazou with the Black People; CBA) 147
Zeller, Wolfgang 61, 62
Zeman, Karel 163, 167
Zeynalov, J. 179
Zhang Minyu 187
Zhelyabuzhsky, Yuri 79, 80
Zhuk v zooparke (The Beatle in the Zoo; Gorbach/Guyetsky) 177
Zibillo e l'orso (Zibillo and the Bear; Cossio brothers) 168
Ziegfeld, Florenz 106
zoetrope 13
Zolotay klyuchik (The Little Golden Key; Ptushko) 176
Zorn, John 126
Zoubowitch, Bogan 136
Zri v koren/Krestovy pokhod (Go to the Roots of Things or The Crusade; Antonovsky) 81
Zsirb Ödön (Kató-Kiszly) 70
Zut, Flûte et Trotte (Daix) 54
Zwarcie (Short Circuit; Themersons) 164
Zwergenland in Not (Dwarf Country in Danger) 149